DATA MODELING
FUNDAMENTALS

THE WILEY BICENTENNIAL—KNOWLEDGE FOR GENERATIONS

*E*ach generation has its unique needs and aspirations. When Charles Wiley first opened his small printing shop in lower Manhattan in 1807, it was a generation of boundless potential searching for an identity. And we were there, helping to define a new American literary tradition. Over half a century later, in the midst of the Second Industrial Revolution, it was a generation focused on building the future. Once again, we were there, supplying the critical scientific, technical, and engineering knowledge that helped frame the world. Throughout the 20th Century, and into the new millennium, nations began to reach out beyond their own borders and a new international community was born. Wiley was there, expanding its operations around the world to enable a global exchange of ideas, opinions, and know-how.

For 200 years, Wiley has been an integral part of each generation's journey, enabling the flow of information and understanding necessary to meet their needs and fulfill their aspirations. Today, bold new technologies are changing the way we live and learn. Wiley will be there, providing you the must-have knowledge you need to imagine new worlds, new possibilities, and new opportunities.

Generations come and go, but you can always count on Wiley to provide you the knowledge you need, when and where you need it!

WILLIAM J. PESCE
PRESIDENT AND CHIEF EXECUTIVE OFFICER

PETER BOOTH WILEY
CHAIRMAN OF THE BOARD

DATA MODELING FUNDAMENTALS

A Practical Guide for IT Professionals

Paulraj Ponniah

WILEY-INTERSCIENCE
A JOHN WILEY & SONS, INC., PUBLICATION

Published by John Wiley & Sons, Inc., Hoboken, New Jersey
Published simultaneously in Canada.

For general information on our other products and services or for technical support, please
contact our Customer Care Department within the United States at (800) 762-2974,
outside the United States at (317) 572-3993 or fax (317) 572-4002.

Wiley also publishes its books in a variety of electronic formats. Some content that appears in print
may not be available in electronic formats. For more information about Wiley products, visit
our web site at www.wiley.com.

Library of Congress Cataloging-in-Publication Data

Ponniah, Paulraj.
    Data modeling fundamentals: a practical guide for IT professionals / by Paulraj Ponniah.
        p. cm.
      ISBN-13: 978-0-471-79049-5 (cloth)
      ISBN-10: 0-471-79049-4 (cloth)
     1. Database design.   2. Data structures (Computer science)   I. Title.
      QA76.9.D26P574 2007
      005.74--dc22
                                                    2006038737

Printed in the United States of America

10   9   8   7   6   5   4   3   2   1

To
Daniel Arjun, my dear son-in-law
and to
Reisha and Shoba, my dear daughters-in-law

CONTENTS

III DATA MODEL IMPLEMENTATION   227

7 Data Modeling to Database Design   229

8 Data Normalization

9 Modeling for Decision-Support Systems

IV PRACTICAL APPROACH TO DATA MODELING

10 Ensuring Quality in the Data Model

PREFACE

Do you want to build a hybrid automobile? First, you need to create a model of the car. Do you want to build a mansion? First, you need to have blueprints and create a model of the dwelling. Do you want to build a spaceship? First, you need to design a miniature model of the vehicle. Do you want to implement a database for your organization? First, you need to create a data model of the information requirements.

Without a proper data model of the information requirements of an enterprise, an adequate database system cannot be correctly designed and implemented for the organization. A good data model of high quality forms an essential prerequisite for any successful database system. Unless the data modelers represent the information requirements of the organization in a proper data model, the database design will be totally ineffective.

The theme of this book is to present the fundamentals and ideas and practices about creating good and useful data models—data models that can function effectively as tools of communication with the user community and as database blueprints for database practitioners.

THE NEED

In every industry across the board, from retail chain stores to financial institutions, from manufacturing enterprises to government agencies, and from airline companies to utility businesses, database systems have become the norm for information storage and retrieval. Whether it is a Web-based application driving electronic commerce or an inventory control application managing just-in-time inventory or a data warehouse system supporting strategic decision making, you need an effective technology to store, retrieve, and use data in order to make the application successful. It is no wonder that institutions have adopted database technology without any reservations.

In this scenario, the information technology (IT) department of every organization has a primary responsibility to design and implement database systems and keep them running. One set of special skills for accomplishing this relates to data modeling. Information technology professionals with data modeling skills constitute a significant group. Information technology professionals specializing in data modeling must be experts with a thorough knowledge of data modeling fundamentals. They must be well versed in the methodologies, techniques, and practices of data modeling.

xvii

ADDRESSING THE NEED

How can IT professionals desirous of acquiring data modeling skills learn the required techniques and gain proficiency in data modeling? Many seminar companies, colleges, and other teaching institutions offer courses in database design and development. However, such courses do not have data modeling as a primary focus. Very few courses, if any, concentrate just on data modeling. So, eager IT professionals are left with the choice of learning data modeling and gaining expert knowledge from books exclusively on this subject. How many such books should they read to learn the principles and concepts?

This book intends to be the one definitive publication to fulfill the needs of aspiring data modelers, of those experienced data modelers desiring to have a refresher, and even of expert data modelers wishing to review additional concepts. In this volume, I have attempted to present my knowledge and insights acquired through three decades of IT consulting, through many years of teaching data-related subjects in seminar and college environments, and through graduate and postgraduate levels of studies. I do hope this experience will be of use to you.

WHAT THIS BOOK CAN DO FOR YOU

Are you a novice data modeler? Are you fairly new to data modeling but aspire to pick up the necessary skills? Alternatively, are you a practicing data modeler with experience in the discipline? Are you a generalizing specialist, meaning that you want to add data modeling as another skill to your arsenal of IT proficiency? Irrespective of the level of your interest in data modeling, this is the one book that is specially designed to cover all the essentials of data modeling in a manner exactly suitable for IT professionals. The book takes a practical approach in presenting the underlying principles and fundamentals, augmenting the presentation with numerous examples from the real world.

The book begins in Part I with a broad overview of data modeling. In Chapter 1, you are introduced to all the essential concepts. Before proceeding into further details, you need to familiarize yourself with the data modeling techniques. Chapter 2 explores the leading techniques—the approaches, the symbols, the syntax, the semantics, and so on.

Part II of the book presents the fundamentals in great detail. It does not matter what your knowledge level of data modeling is. You will find this part interesting and useful. You are presented with a real-world case study with a completed data model. You are asked to study the anatomy of the data model and understand how the actual design and creation of the data model works. Part II also digs deeper into individual components of a data model with several real-world examples.

In Part III, you will learn the transition from data model to database design. In recent times, decision-support systems have come to the forefront of computing. Part III describes decision-support systems such as data warehousing and data mining and guides you through data modeling methods for these systems. This is essential knowledge for modern data modelers.

In Part IV of the book, you will find a chapter exclusively devoted to quality in the data model. Every data modeler aspires to create a model of the highest quality. This chapter is required reading. A new wave known as agile software development is on the rise producing great benefits. You will learn about this movement and gain insights into agile data modeling—its principles and practices.

Finally, are you looking for practical suggestions on data modeling distilled from years of experience of many practitioners? If so, the final chapter is for you. The book aptly concludes with such a chapter filled with numerous practical tips and suggestions.

PAULRAJ PONNIAH

Milltown, New Jersey
April 2007

ACKNOWLEDGMENTS

The authors listed in the bibliography at the end of the book greatly expanded and enhanced my understanding and appreciation for data modeling. I am deeply indebted to the authors, individually and collectively, for their insights and presentations. A great part of this book is a reinterpretation of their concepts and observations. I wish to express my special thanks to these authors.

I must also record my gratitude to the several professional colleagues who had worked with me on various data modeling and database projects during my long IT consulting career. Also, thanks are due to the many students in my data modeling and database classes over the years. Interactions with my colleagues and students have shaped this book in a format especially suitable for the needs of IT professionals.

INTRODUCTION TO
DATA MODELING

DATA MODELING: AN OVERVIEW

CHAPTER OBJECTIVES

- Introduce the process of data modeling
- Present why data modeling is important
- Explain how a data model represents information requirements
- Describe conceptual, logical, and physical data models
- Briefly discuss the steps for building a data model
- Show the role of data modeling in system development
- Provide an initial glimpse of data modeling history and trends

James Watson and Francis Crick, working at Cambridge University, deduced the three-dimensional structure of DNA (deoxyribonucleic acid). In 1953, they published a brief paper describing their now-famous double helix model of DNA. This important milestone of creating a true model of DNA gave a tremendous boost to biology and genetics. For the discovery and creation of the double helix model, Watson and Crick shared the Nobel Prize for Physiology and Medicine in 1962.

Well, what does Watson and Crick's achievement have to do with our current study? Essentially, they built a model. The model is a true representation of the structure of DNA—something we find in the real world. Models are replicas or representations of particular aspects and segments of the real world. Building of models is quite common in many disciplines. When you think about it, the representation "$5 + 4 = 9$" is a mathematical model using symbols and logic. This model represents the fact that if you put five things together with four things of the same kind, you get nine things of the same kind. In physics, we create models to represent physical properties of the world. In economics, we create models of economic trends and forecast economic outcomes.

Let us get a more vivid picture of what we mean by a model. Let us say that you are interested in buying a new home in one of the upcoming posh developments. You go to the sales office of the real estate developer. They point to a large open site where they plan to build the houses and to complete the development in 3 years. Right now, you cannot see any houses; you cannot observe the layout of roads and houses; all you can notice is a lot of vacant space and numerous trees. How can you get a picture of how the development will look in the future? How can you imagine how the house you want to buy will be structured? While you appear puzzled, the sales staff leads you into a large room. On a big table, in the middle of the room, sits a scale model of the development. They had created the model based on the requirements of the future homeowners in the community. You see roads, houses, swimming pools, tennis courts, and other amenities in the future development. These are not the real roads and houses. These are just components in the model. The model is a true representation of the real estate development. The sales people are able to point to different components in the model and communicate with you clearly and vividly. Now, you are able to understand, and you are happy.

A model serves two primary purposes:

- As a true representation of some aspects of the real world, a model enables clearer communication about those aspects of the real world.
- A model serves as a blueprint to shape and construct the proposed structures in the real world.

DATA MODEL DEFINED

Data modeling is an integral part of the process of designing and developing a data system. While designing and developing a data system for an organization, you take into account all the information that would be needed to support the various business processes of the organization. If you are designing a data system for a banking institution, you have to provide data for the business processes of checking, savings, and loan account operations. If you are creating a data system for a medical center, you have to provide data for inpatient and outpatient services. You start with the analysis and gathering of details about which data elements would be needed for the business. You need to ensure that the results of *requirements definition* are completely implemented as the data content of the database that would support the organization.

You start with planning and requirements definition. Based on these, you have to come up with the proper database system. During this process, you have to keep on communicating with the business stakeholders about the data elements, their structures, relationships among the structures, and the rules governing the structures and relationships. You have to make sure that these data elements are exactly the ones that are needed to support the business. The users must be able to understand clearly what you are designing and give their affirmation.

Making the users understand the information content of the database system being built is one crucial aspect of the development process. The other significant aspect of the development process is your ability to create a database system that meets the information requirements exactly and conforms to what you have presented and described to your users. As database practitioners, what technique can we adopt to achieve these dual goals? How can we communicate with the users and keep them informed? How can we do what we promise to deliver and meet the information requirements exactly?

What Is a Data Model?

Data modeling provides a method and means for describing the real-world information requirements in a manner understandable to the stakeholders in an organization. In addition, data modeling enables the database practitioners to take these information requirements and implement these as a computer database system to support the business of the organization.

So, what is a data model? A data model is a device that

- helps the users or stakeholders understand clearly the database system that is being implemented based on the information requirements of an organization, and
- enables the database practitioners to implement the database system exactly conforming to the information requirements.

A data model, therefore, serves as a critical tool for communication with the users; it also serves as a blueprint of the database system for the developers. Figure 1-1 illustrates these two significant aspects of a data model. Notice how the data model serves the needs of the two groups: users and developers. Also notice the place of the data model between requirements definition and database system implementation.

Data modeling is a technique for exploring the data structures needed to support an organization. A data model must record and indicate the content, shape, size, and rules of the data elements used throughout the scope of the various business processes of the organization. It would be a conceptual representation or replica of the data structures required in the database system. A data model focuses on what data is required and

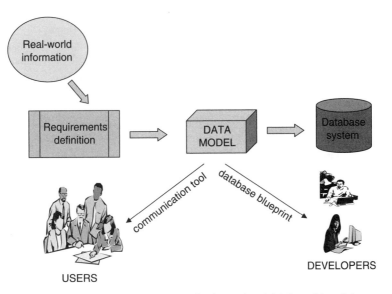

FIGURE 1-1 Data model: communication tool and database blueprint.

how the data should be organized. It does not necessarily reflect the operations expected to be performed on the data.

Data modeling can be applied to representation of the information requirements at various levels. At the highest conceptual level, the data model is independent of any hardware or software constraints. At this level, the data model is generic; it does not vary whether you want to implement an object-relational database, a relational database, a hierarchical database, or a network database. At the next level down, a data model is a logical model relating to the particular type of database—relational, hierarchical, network, and so on. This is because in each of these types, data structures are perceived differently. If you proceed further down, a data model is a physical model relating to the particular database management system (DBMS) you may use to implement the database. We will discuss these levels further.

Why Data Modeling?

You have understood that a data model is created as a representation of the information requirements of an organization. You have also noted that a data model functions as an effective communication tool for discussions with the users; it also serves as a blueprint for the database system. A data model, therefore, acts as a bridge from real-world information to database storing relevant data content.

But, why this bridge? Why not go from real-world information to the database itself? Let us take a simple example. A business sells products to customers. We want to create a database just to support such sale transactions, nothing more. In our database, we need to keep data to support the business. In the real world of this business, data exists about customers, products, and sales of products to customers. Now, look at Figure 1-2, which shows these data elements for the business.

The method for showing the information requirements as indicated in the figure is haphazard and arbitrary. If you are asked to depict the information requirements, you might do

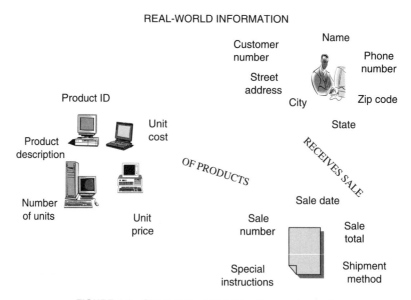

FIGURE 1-2   Sales: real-world information requirements.

TOWARD A DATA MODEL

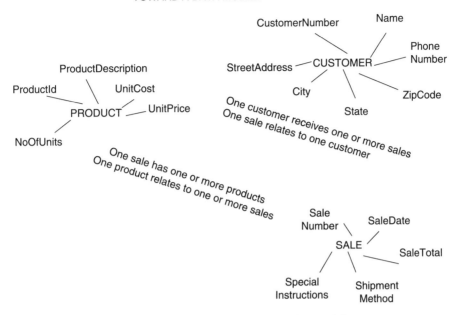

FIGURE 1-3   Sales: a step toward a data model.

it in a different way. If someone else does it, that person might do it in yet a different way. Now consider the database to be built to contain these data elements. Two overall actions need to be performed. First, you have to describe the database system to the users and obtain their confirmation. Then you have to create the database system to provide the necessary information. The depiction of information requirements as shown in the figure falls short of these expectations.

Let us try to improve the situation a bit. Let us try to depict the information requirements in slightly better and more standard manner. See Figure 1-3, where the depiction is somewhat clearer.

This figure presents a picture that could better help us to communicate with the users with a little more clarity and also enable us to proceed with the implementation of the database system. Now you can show the users the business objects of CUSTOMER, PRODUCT, and SALE about which the database system will contain data. You can also point to the various pieces of data about these objects. Further, you can also explain how these objects are related.

Still, this depiction falls somewhat short of the expectations. This figure is an attempt toward a good data model. When we take the depiction a few steps further and create a satisfactory data model—a true representation of the information requirements—we can achieve our goals of user communication and database blueprint. But that is not all. A data model serves useful purposes in the various stages of the data life cycle in an organization. Let us see how.

Data Life Cycle. Follow the stages that data goes through in an organization. First, a need for data arises to perform the various business processes of an organization. Then a determination is made about exactly what data is needed. Gathering of the data takes place. Then the data gets stored in the database system. In the next stage, data is manipulated by reading it from storage, combining it in various desired ways, and changing it. After a while some of the data gets archived and stored elsewhere. After some of the data completes its usefulness, the corresponding data elements get deleted from the database system. Figure 1-4 presents the stages in the data life cycle of an organization and also the interaction with the data model at the different stages.

Now let us walk through the various stages of the data life cycle. At each stage, we will note how a data model is helpful and serves useful purposes.

Needing Data. In this earliest stage, an organization recognizes the need for data for performing the various business processes. For example, to perform the process of taking orders, you need data about products and inventory. For producing invoices, you need data about orders and shipments. Thus, this stage in the data life cycle recognizes the need for data in the organization. At this stage, a high-level conceptual data model is useful to point to the various business processes and the data created or used in these processes.

Determining Needed Data. Once you recognize the need for data, you have to determine which data elements are needed for performing business processes. At this stage, you will come up with the various types of data, which data is really needed and which data would be superfluous, and how much of each type of data is needed. At this stage,

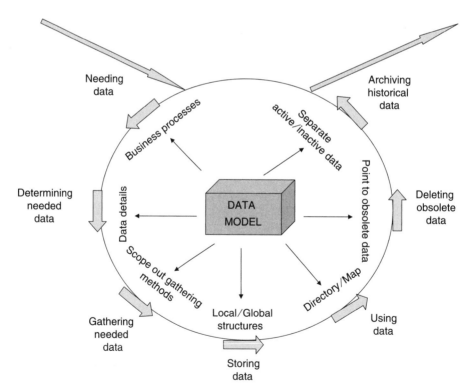

FIGURE 1-4   Organization's data life cycle.

all the required details of the needed data elements are discovered and documented in the data model.

Gathering Needed Data. After the determination of which data is needed, collection of data takes place. Here you apply a sort of filter to gather only the data that is needed and ignore the irrelevant data that is not necessary for any of your business processes. You will apply different methods of data creation and data gathering in this stage. The data gathering trials and methodologies are scoped out with the aid of the data model.

Storing Data. The collected data must be stored in the database using appropriate methods of storage. You will decide on the storage medium and consider the optimal storage method to suit the needs of users for accessing and using data. The data model in this stage enables you to assemble the components of the global data repository. Each part of the data model determines a specific local data structure, and the conglomeration of all the parts produces the global structure for data storage.

Using Data. Data, collected and stored, is meant for usage. That is the ultimate goal in the data life cycle. At this stage, you will combine various data elements, retrieve data elements for usage, modify and store modified data, and add new data created during the business processes. At this stage, the data model acts as a directory and map to direct the ways of combining and using data.

Deleting Obsolete Data. After a while, a particular data element in storage may become stale and obsolete. After a period of time, the data element may no longer be useful and, therefore, not accessed in any transactions at all. For example, orders that have been fulfilled and invoiced need not remain in the database indefinitely beyond the statutory time of legal and tax reporting purposes. An organization may decide that such orders may be deleted from the database after a period of 10 years. Deleting obsolete data becomes an ongoing operation. A particular data element may fall into the category qualifying for deletion. At this stage, the data model is used to examine the various data elements that can be safely deleted after specified periods.

Archiving Historical Data. However, some data elements may still be useful even long after any activity on those data elements had ceased. Data relating to customer purchases can be useful to forecast future trends. Historical data is useful in the organization's data warehouse. Any such useful data elements are removed from the current database and archived into a separate historical repository. The data model in this stage provides the ability to point to the original and final spots of data storage and trace the movement from active to archived repositories.

Who Performs Data Modeling?

In a database project, depending on the size and complexity of the database system, one or more persons are entrusted with the responsibility of creating the data models. Data models at various levels call for different skills and training. Creating a conceptual data model involves capturing the overall information requirements at a high level. A logical data model is different and is meant for different purposes. A physical data model, on the other hand, pictures the information at the lowest level of hardware and physical storage. So, who performs data modeling? Data modeling specialists with appropriate training, knowledge, and skills do the work of data modeling.

However, the recent trend is not to employ persons having data modeling skills alone. This is an age of generalizing specialists. Data modeling is usually an additional set of skills acquired by certain persons on the database project. These generalists are trained in the principles and practice of data modeling and assigned the responsibility of creating the data models.

Who Are the Data Modelers? This is another way of asking the same question. In an organization, who are these folks? What functions do they perform? How can we think of the various tasks performed by the data modelers? Are they like architects? Are they like librarians? Are they like document specialists?

The primary responsibility of data modelers is to model and describe that part of the real world that is of interest to the organization to achieve its goals and purposes. In doing so, a data modeler may be thought of performing the following functions.

Scanning Current Details. The data modeler scans and captures details of the current state of the data system of the enterprise. New models are built by looking at the current data structures.

Designing the Architecture. The data modeler is an architect designing the new data model. He or she puts together all the pieces of the architecture.

Documenting and Maintaining Meta-Data. The data modeler is like a librarian and custodian of the data about the data of the organization. The data modeler is also a tremendous source of information about the data structures and elements, current and proposed.

Providing Advice and Consultation. With in-depth knowledge about the composition of the data system of an organization, the data modeler is the expert for consultation.

INFORMATION LEVELS

By now, it is clear to you that a data model is a representation of the information requirements of an organization. A data model must truly reflect the data requirements of an enterprise. Every aspect of the data for the company's business operations must be indicated clearly and precisely in the data model. As we defined a data model, we also considered the two major purposes of a data model. A data model serves as a means for communication with the users or domain experts. It is also a blueprint for the proposed database system for the organization.

Let us examine the first purpose. A data model is a tool for communication with the users. You will use the data model, review its components, describe the various parts, explain the different connections, and make the users understand the ultimate data system that is being built for them. The data model, therefore, must be at a level that can be easily understood by the users. For this purpose, the data model must be devoid of any complexities. Any complexity in terms of the data structures must be hidden from the users. In the data model, there can be no indication of any physical storage considerations. Any reference to how data structures are laid out or perceived by analysts and programmers must be absent from the model. The data model must just be a conceptual portrayal of the information requirements in human terms. The data model must be a representation using a high level of ideas. The primary purpose here is clear communication with the domain experts.

Now let us go to the second major purpose of a data model. The data model has to serve as a blueprint for building the database system. In this case, the database practitioners must be able take the data model, step through the components, one by one, and use the model to design and create the database system. If so, a data model as a representation at a high level of ideas is not good enough as a blueprint. To serve as a blueprint, the data model must include details of the data structures. It should indicate the relationships. It should represent how data is viewed by analysts and programmers. It should bear connections to how database vendors view data and design their database products.

In order to build the database system and determine how data will be stored on physical storage and how data will be accessed and used, more intricate and complex details must be present in the data model. This is even more detailed than how data is viewed by programmers and analysts.

So, we see that a data model must be at a high and general level that can be easily understood by the users. This will help the communication with the users. At the same time, we understand that the data model must also be detailed enough to serve as a blueprint. How can the data model serve these two purposes? At one level, the data model needs to be general; at another level, it has to be detailed. What this means is that representation of information must be done at different levels. The data model must fit into different information levels. In practice, data models are created at different information levels to represent information requirements.

Classification of Information Levels

Essentially, four information levels exist, and data models are created at each of these four levels. Let us briefly examine and describe these levels. Figure 1-5 indicates the information levels and their characteristics.

Conceptual Level. This is the highest level consisting of general ideas about the information content. At this level, you have the description of application domain in terms of human concepts. This is the level at which the users are able to understand the data system. This is a stable information level.

At this level, the data model portrays the base type business objects, constraints on the objects, their characteristics, and any derivation rules. The data model is independent of all physical considerations. The model hides all complexities about the data structures from the users through levels of abstraction. At this level, the data model serves as an excellent tool for communication with the domain experts or users.

External Level. At the conceptual level, the data model represents the information requirements for the entire set of user groups in the organization. The data model is comprehensive and complete. Every piece of information required for every department and every user group is depicted by the comprehensive conceptual model. However, when you consider a particular user group, that group is not likely to be interested in the entire conceptual model. For example, the accounting user group may be interested in just customer information, order information, and information about invoices and

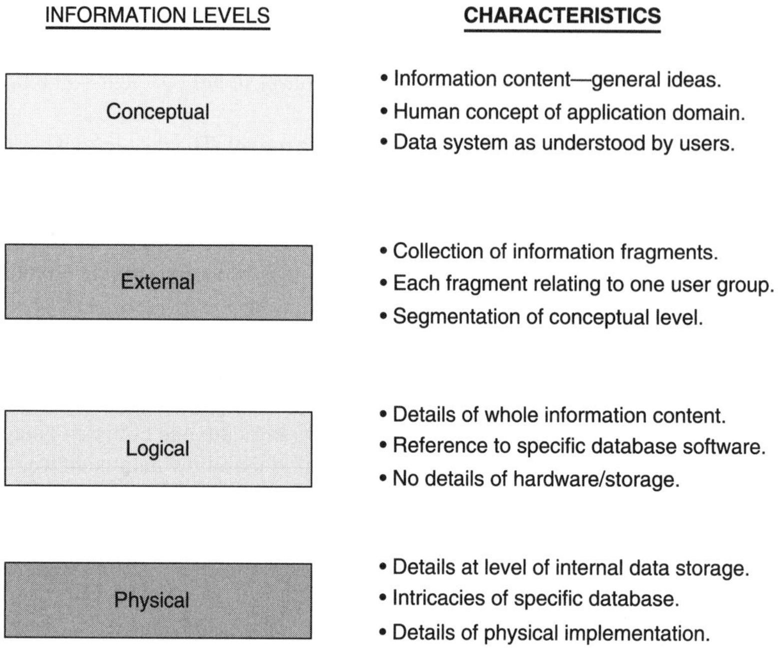

INFORMATION LEVELS   CHARACTERISTICS

Conceptual

- Information content—general ideas.
- Human concept of application domain.
- Data system as understood by users.

External

- Collection of information fragments.
- Each fragment relating to one user group.
- Segmentation of conceptual level.

Logical

- Details of whole information content.
- Reference to specific database software.
- No details of hardware/storage.

Physical

- Details at level of internal data storage.
- Intricacies of specific database.
- Details of physical implementation.

FIGURE 1-5   Information levels for data modeling.

payments. On the other hand, the inventory user group may be interested in only the product and stock information. For each user group, looking at the conceptual model from an external viewpoint, only a portion of the entire conceptual model is relevant. This is the external level of information—external to the data system. At the external level, portions of the entire conceptual model are relevant. Each user group relates to a portion of the conceptual model.

A data model at the external level consists of fragments of the entire conceptual model. In a way, each fragment is a miniconceptual model. If you consider an external data model, it contains representation of a particular segment of information requirements applicable to only one user group. Thus, if you create all the external data models for all the user groups and aggregate all the external data models, then you will arrive at the comprehensive conceptual model for the entire organization. External data model enables the database practitioners to separate out the conceptual data model by individual user groups and thus allocate data access authorizations appropriately.

Logical Level. At this level, the domain concepts and their relationships are explored further. This level accommodates more details about the information content. Still, storage and physical considerations are not part of this level. Not even considerations of a specific DBMS find a place at this level. However, representation is made based on the type of database implementation—relational, hierarchical, network, and so on.

If you are designing and implementing a relational database, the data model at this level will depict the information content in terms of how data is perceived in a relational model. In the relational model, data is perceived to be in the form of two-dimensional tables. So, a logical data model for a relational database will consist of tables and their relationships.

Data in the tables will be represented as rows and columns. The data model at the logical level will be used in the ultimate construction of the database system.

Internal or Physical Level. This information level deals with the implementation of the database on secondary storage. Considerations of storage management, access management, and database performance apply at this level. Here intricate and complex details of the particular database are relevant. The intricacies of the particular DBMS are taken into account at the physical level.

The physical data model represents the details of implementation. The data model at this level is primarily intended as a blueprint for implementation. It cannot be used as a means for communication with the users. The data model represents the information requirements in terms of files, data blocks, data records, index records, file organizations, and so on.

Data Models at Information Levels

When we began our discussion on data models, it appeared as if a data model is a single type of representation of information requirements for an organization. When we analyzed the purposes of a data model, it became clear that a single type of representation is not sufficient to satisfy the two major purposes. The type of representation that is conducive for communication with users does not have the lower level details needed for the model to serve as a blueprint. On the other hand, the type of representation with details about the data structure is necessary in a construction blueprint; but such a representation is not easy to be used as a communication tool with the users.

This has led to the need to create data models at different information models. We have understood the necessity for different types of representations for the different purposes. These are the data models at the various levels of information—conceptual data model, external data model, logical data model, and physical data model. Figure 1-6 shows the data models at the different information levels. Note the nature of the data model at each level and also notice the transition from one level to the next. The figure also indicates the purpose of the data model at each level.

Earlier we had developed an initial data model consisting of three business objects, namely, CUSTOMER, PRODUCT, and SALES. Let us use these three objects to illustrate data models at different levels. In the section of our real world, all the information we need is only about these three objects. For the purpose of illustrating the different data models, let us make this restrictive assumption and proceed. Also, we will assume that our ultimate database will be a relational database.

External Data Model. The external data model is a depiction of the database system from the viewpoints of individual user groups. This model may be used for communication with individual groups of users. Each individual user group is interested in a set of data items for performing its specific business functions. The set of data items relevant for a specific user group forms part of the external data model for this particular user group.

For the purpose of our example, let us consider three user groups: accounting, marketing, and inventory control. Try to figure out the data items each user group would be interested in. For the sake of simplicity, let us consider a minimum set of data items.

Figure 1-7 shows the set of data items each of these groups is interested in. This figure illustrates the formation of an external data model.

INFORMATION LEVELS   **DATA MODELS**

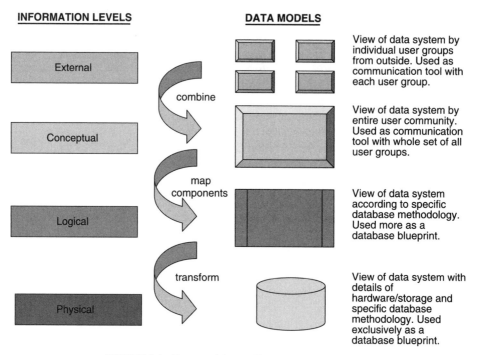

FIGURE 1-6   Data models at different information levels.

Conceptual Data Model. The conceptual data model is at a high and general level, intended mainly as a communication tool with the user community. In the model, there is no room for details of data structure or for any considerations of hardware and database software. This model does not even address whether the final database system is going to be implemented as a relational database system or any other type of database system. However, the model should be complete and include sufficient components so that it would be a true representation of the information requirements of the organization.

Figure 1-8 illustrates the idea of a conceptual data model. The information requirements we are considering relate to the data items for the user groups of accounting, marketing, and inventory control. That was the external data model shown in Figure 1-7. You see that the conceptual data model has representations for the three business objects of CUSTOMER, PRODUCT, and SALES. You can easily see the connection between the external data model and the conceptual data model. The figure also shows the intrinsic characteristics of these business objects—the data about these objects. Further, the conceptual model also indicates the relationships among the business objects. In the real world, business objects in an organization do not exist as separate entities; they are related with one another and interact with one another. For example, customer orders product, and products are sold to customers.

By looking at the figure, you would have noticed that for the conceptual data model to serve as a communication tool with the users, there must be some easily understood notations or symbols to represent components of the model. Some accepted symbol must indicate a business object; some notation must indicate the characteristics or attributes of a

USER GROUPS   EXTERNAL DATA MODEL

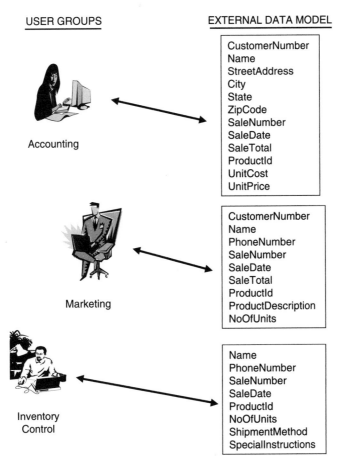

FIGURE 1-7   External data model.

business object; some representation must be made to show the relationship between any two objects. Over time, several useful techniques have evolved to make these representations. We will introduce some of the techniques at the end of this chapter. Further, Chapter 2 is totally dedicated to a discussion of data modeling methods, techniques, and symbols.

Logical Data Model. In a sense, the logical data model for an organization is the aggregation of all the parts of the external data model. In the above external data model, three user groups are shown. We assume that there are only three user groups in the organization. Therefore, the complete logical model must represent all the combined information requirements of these three user groups.

For the relational type of database system, the logical model represents the information requirements in the form of two-dimensional tables with rows and columns. Refer to Figure 1-9 for an example of the logical data model. At this stage, the figure just gives you an indication of the logical data model. We will discuss this concept a lot more elaborately in subsequent chapters.

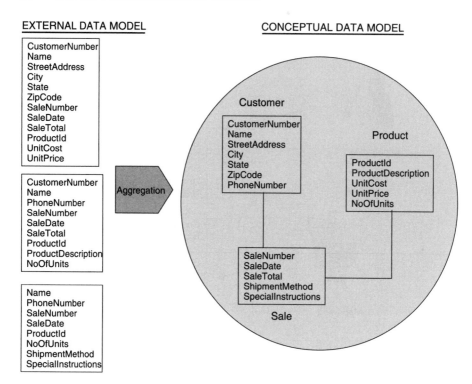

FIGURE 1-8 Conceptual data model.

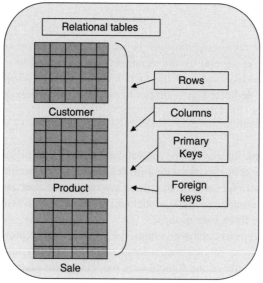

FIGURE 1-9 Logical data model.

LOGICAL DATA MODEL   **PHYSICAL DATA MODEL**

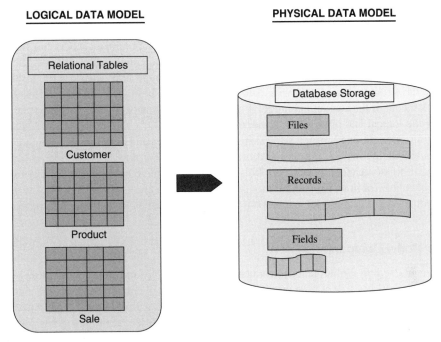

FIGURE 1-10   Physical data model.

As can be seen from the figure, the logical data model may serve both purposes—communication tool and database blueprint. In this case, it will serve as a blueprint for a relational database system along with the physical data model.

Physical Data Model. A physical data model has little use as a means of communication with the users. Its primary purpose is to act as a blueprint for the implementation of the database system. The details contained in a physical data model are beyond the normal comprehension of the users. The model expresses too many intricate details. It includes considerations of the particular DBMS and the hardware environment in which the database system gets implemented.

See Figure 1-10 for an example of the physical data model. Notice how the model represents the information requirements in terms of files, data blocks, records, fields, and so on. The model is a representation at the lowest level of abstraction with a lot of complex details.

CONCEPTUAL DATA MODELING

Having considered the different types of data models and their purposes, we are now ready to ponder the question how exactly is a data model created. What are the major steps? What are the various components that make up a data model? Let us get an initial introduction to the terminology, components, and the steps for creating a data model. Here we want to be brief and just introduce the topics. Part II covers the topics in elaborate detail with a comprehensive case study. So, let us now confine ourselves to getting a quick glimpse of the components and the steps.

For our purposes here, let us take a simple example to identify the components and the steps. We will deal with the conceptual data model because that is generic and is usually the first data model that is created. As you know, the conceptual data model has no considerations about the type of database system being implemented, no reference to the particular DBMS, and absolutely no concern about the storage and hardware environment where the ultimate data system will reside and perform. These are details that are deliberately kept out of the conceptual model. Later on in the following chapters, discussions will cover the logical and physical data models.

Again, as mentioned earlier, several standard techniques and notations exist for creating a data model. We will be discussing those in Chapter 2. For now, we will not get bogged down with specific techniques or symbols. We can use some meaningful and easily understood symbols for now. Remember the main goals at this stage: identification of the major components of a data model and overview of the major steps in the modeling process.

Data Model Components

Before proceeding further, let us introduce some terminology and identify the primary data model components. Our simple introductory data model will contain these components. At this early stage, we will not represent the components using any standard technique. That will come later. Let us just use very basic symbols to represent the components for now.

For the purpose of our simple data model, we will consider four basic components and define them. Most of the conceptual data models we come across in practice consist of these basic components. Remember, the data model reflects and represents the information requirements of an organization. What are the pieces of information a company or business is interested in? What are the parts of the information a company requires to run its business? Data model components are derived from such business considerations. Let us move on to identify the components.

Objects or Entities. When you analyze the information requirements of a company, you will notice that the company needs information about the business objects that are of interest to it. The company needs data about business objects. The organization needs to know how these business objects are related and the implications of such relationships.

What are such business objects? For example, a bank is interested in data about its customers and about checking, savings, and loan accounts. So, for a bank, CUSTOMER, CHECKING-ACCOUNT, SAVINGS-ACCOUNT, and LOAN-ACCOUNT would be examples of business objects. Similarly, for a hospital, PATIENT, PHYSICIAN, PROCEDURE, and HOSPITAL-VISIT would be examples of business objects. Each organization has its own set of business objects. A particular institution needs data about its own set of business objects. Data about the business objects or entities must be present in the data system for the organization to function.

Attributes or Characteristics. Consider a specific business object. Let us take the business object called CUSTOMER. What would this business object represent in a data model? The object will represent the set of all the customers of the organization. How can all the customers be grouped and represented by a single object called CUSTOMER? This is because all these customers mostly possess the same characteristics.

Each customer has an intrinsic characteristic known as *Customer Name*. Every customer has a specific name. Every customer has other inherent of intrinsic characteristics such as *Customer Address, Customer Phone Number, Customer Balance*, and so on. These intrinsic characteristics are known as attributes. The business object CUSTOMER has attributes of CustomerName, CustomerAddress, CustomerPhoneNumber, Customer Balance, and so on. Each individual customer will have distinct values for these attributes. Thus, attributes of an object or entity are representations of its inherent or intrinsic characteristics.

Identifiers. Let us get back to the definition of an object or entity. The object CUSTOMER represents all the customers of the organization. Each customer has a distinct set of values for the attributes of the object CUSTOMER. If the CUSTOMER object represents all and every customer, then how can we distinguish one customer from another represented through the object called CUSTOMER? Why do we need to make this distinction? Frequently in business situations, we need to find information about a single customer. Where does the customer live so that we may send invoices to the customer? What are the recent orders placed by that customer?

How can we distinguish one customer from another and indicate this distinction in the data model? We can use values of a particular attribute to make the distinction. You can say that you need information about that particular customer for whom the value of the CustomerNumber is 1234. In this case, CustomerNumber would be an attribute that can be used to distinguish one customer from another. Provided values of customer numbers are not duplicated in the data system, values of the attribute CustomerNumber can be used to make the distinction between customers. In such a case, the attribute CustomerNumber is an identifying attribute or an identifier for the object CUSTOMER. In practice, one or more attributes whose values would uniquely determine specific instances of an object are chosen as the identifier for that object.

Relationships. Let us get back to the example of business objects for a bank. Consider the objects CUSTOMER and CHECKING-ACCOUNT. These are two separate objects with their own attributes. For the purpose of running the banking business, the users in the bank need data about customers and checking accounts. They need the data about these two objects separately, but even more so about the relationship between customers and their checking accounts. For a particular customer, what is the status of the customer's checking account?

In a company's environment, business objects do not exist in isolation. They are related to one another. What is the relationship between CUSTOMER and CHECKING-ACCOUNT? Customers operate checking accounts. That is the relationship. For a data model to be a true representation of the real-world situation for a bank, the model must reflect the relationships among the business objects.

Simple Symbols. We have identified the primary components of a data model. We have introduced business objects, attributes, identifiers, and relationships. Let us assign some simple symbols to these components. Make a square box to represent a business object. Small circles connected to a square box may represent attributes. Two concentric circles may be used to represent identifiers. When two objects are directly related, let us indicate the relationship by joining the two square boxes by a straight line. For our initial discussion of the data modeling steps, these simple symbols are sufficient.

Figure 1-11 shows examples of these data model components.

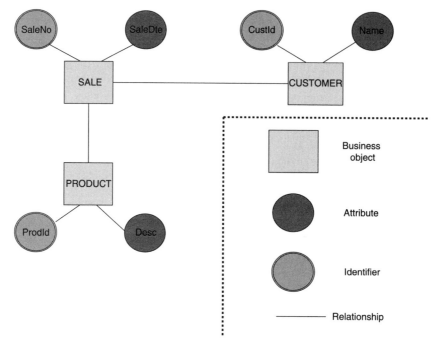

FIGURE 1-11 Data model components: simple representation.

Data Modeling Steps

Armed with the definition and description of the major data model components, let us quickly walk through the process of creating a conceptual data model using these components. A simple business example will illustrate the steps. Let us consider a rather easy and uncomplicated business.

The company is called Raritan Catering started by two sisters, Mary and Jane. They offer catering projects for birthday parties, anniversaries, student reunions, small business luncheons, and so on. They have four permanent employees and also use temporary help whenever necessary. For each project, the clients specify the type of food to be served and also the number of people to be served. Raritan Catering charges the client on a per-plate basis. Permanent and temporary employees working on a project are compensated based on the proceeds from the project. Twenty-five percent of the revenues from each project is shared among the employees working on that project.

In order to run the catering business, the two sisters perform various business processes. For the purpose of illustrating the data modeling steps, let us concentrate on the following major business processes:

- Plan for projects
- Assign employees to projects
- Bill clients
- Receive payments
- Compensate employees

With this information about the business processes and operations, let us walk through the process of creating a data model.

Identify Business Objects. In this step, the data modeler identifies those business objects about which data would be needed. How does he or she do this? The data modeler examines and studies the business processes that are necessary to run the business. In the case of Raritan Catering, we have noted the major business processes to run the business. The business needs information to perform these business processes.

Examining each of these processes closely, we can come up with the follow data elements that are necessary for each process. The data elements noted below comprise the basic information requirements for the processes.

Plan for Projects. For performing this business process, the business needs data about clients, their scheduled projects, and the type of food items to be served at the projects. Let us list these data items.

ClientName
ClientPhone

DateOfProject
NumberOfGuests
EstimatedCost
TypeOfFood

Assign Employees to Projects. For doing this function and assigning a particular employee to a specific project, the business requires some data about client, project, and employee. The following date elements are needed.

ClientName

DateOfProject

EmployeeName

Bill Clients. For performing this business process, the business needs to send invoices to the clients for the projects served. The following data items are required.

ClientName
ClientAddress
ClientCity
ClientState
ClientZip

DateOfProject
NumberOfGuests
AmoutCharged

Receive Payments. For this business process, the organization needs data about the payment received and from whom it is received. The following data items are essential.

ClientName

DateOfProject

PaymentDate
TypeOfPayment
AmountPaid

Compensate Employees. For this business process, the company must have information about each project and the employees who worked on the project. Here is the list of data items.

DateOfProject
AmountCharged

EmployeeName
EmployeeSSNo

After collecting the list of data items that would be required for all the business processes, the data modeler examines the list and groups together data items that are about the same thing. This process of aggregation results in the ability to identify the business objects. Let us aggregate the data items listed above for the five business processes. When you look at the data items and group similar data items together, it becomes clear to you that the data items relate to the following business objects:

CLIENT
PROJECT
EMPLOYEE
FOOD TYPE
PAYMENT

Identify Direct Relationships. In an organization, the business objects are interrelated. For Raritan Catering, clients order projects. So the business objects CLIENT and PROJECT are connected through this relationship. Similarly, other pairs of objects are likely to be connected by such direct relationships.

Let us examine each pair of potentially related objects. We are looking for potential relationships. The following direct relationships become apparent:

Employees are assigned to projects.
Projects use food types.
Clients order projects.
Client makes payments for projects.

Thus we can identify the following direct relationships between the pairs of business objects noted below:

EMPLOYEE —— assigned to —— PROJECT
PROJECT —— uses —— FOOD TYPE
CLIENT —— orders —— PROJECT
CLIENT —— makes —— PAYMENT

We have identified the direct relationships among the business objects. Well and good. But what about some compelling questions about each of these relationships? Let us take the relationship between EMPLOYEE and PROJECT. We see that information in our data system must tell us which employees were assigned to which projects. Right away, we observe that in our data system, the following restrictions would apply:

One employee may be assigned to one or more projects.

One project can have one or more employees.

That means the two objects EMPLOYEE and PROJECT are in a many-to-many relationship. See Figure 1-12, which illustrates the many-to-many relationship. Note also how the many-to-many relationship is indicated with asterisks (*).

Let us examine one more relationship. Take the relationship between CLIENT and PROJECT. We see that we need information in our data system about which clients ordered which projects. In this case, we note the following restrictions that apply to the relationship:

One client can order one or more projects.

However, one project can have only one client.

This is a one-to-one relationship. Relationships between business objects can be one-to-one or one-to-many or many-to-many. This aspect of a relationship is known as the cardinality of the relationship. The cardinality indicator such as "*" or "1" indicates how many instances of one object may be related to how many instances of the other object. Our data model must not only represent the relationships but their cardinalities as well.

Let us pause at this point and summarize what we have done so far. We have identified the business objects. We have noted the relationships among the objects and recorded the cardinalities of each relationship. Let us draw an initial data model diagram to represent the steps up to now. Figure 1-13 shows the initial data model diagram for Raritan Catering.

One employee may be assigned to one or more projects.
One project can have one or more employees.

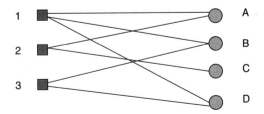

FIGURE 1-12   Many-to-many relationship.

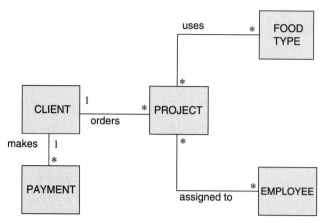

FIGURE 1-13 Raritan Catering: initial data model diagram.

Add Attributes. Attributes describe the business objects. Therefore, attributes are necessary components in a data model. After identifying the business objects and determining the relationships among the objects, the next step is to include the attributes and make the data model diagram even more complete.

Initially, when we examined the business processes and noted the data elements needed for each business process, we had made a list. This list of data elements will form the set of attributes to be included now. Let us collect the data items and form the set of attributes as follows:

CLIENT
  Name
  Address
  City
  State
  Zip
  Phone

PROJECT
  Date
  NoOfGuests
  EstCost
  AmtCharged

EMPLOYEE
  SSNumber
  EmpName

FOOD TYPE
  FoodName

PAYMENT
  Date

PymntType

Amount

Assign Identifiers. An identifier for a business object is one or more attributes whose values uniquely identify individual instances of the object. In this step, we examine the set of attributes for each object and determine which ones are candidates to be the identifier. If none of the known attributes of an object qualifies to be an identifier, then we have to introduce one or more new attributes to form the identifier. Let us examine the list of attributes.

For the object EMPLOYEE, one of its attributes, namely, SSNumber qualifies to be the identifier. The values of Social Security number are not duplicated. Therefore, the values of this attribute can be used to identify individual employees.

Scrutinizing the attributes of the other objects, we note that in each case there are no candidates for identifiers. So, for these objects, we have to add new attributes to serve as identifiers. After doing that, we come up with the following list of identifiers:

CLIENT

    ClientNo

PROJECT

    ProjectNo

EMPLOYEE

    SSNumber

FOOD TYPE

    TypeId

PAYMENT

    PymntSeq

Let us return to the data model diagram and add the attributes and identifiers. Figure 1-14 shows the revised and more complete data model diagram.

At this point, the data model diagram is generally complete.

Incorporate Business Rules. Already when we marked the cardinality indicators for the relationships, we have indicated some business rules in the data model. For example, a rule guiding this business is that a particular food type can relate to several projects and that many different food types may be served at a single project. We have incorporated this business rule by marking the relationship between PROJECT and FOOD TYPE as many-to-many.

For a different business, there could business rules governing how invoices may be paid. Partial payments may be allowed against a single invoice; on the other hand, one payment may cover several invoices. This is a business rule, and the data model must reflect this rule. Business rules govern objects, relationships, and even attributes. Business rules must be incorporated into the data model so that the model could truly represent the real-world business situation. We will elaborate on business rules later in Part II.

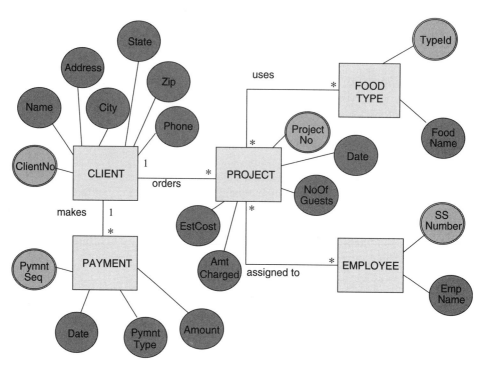

FIGURE 1-14   Raritan Catering: revised data model diagram.

Validate the Data Model. This step is really a review and validation step. We want to make sure the conceptual data model we have created satisfies two criteria. Does the data model truly reflect and represent the information requirements of the organization? Is the data model complete and simple enough to be used as a communication tool with the users? If so, we have succeeded in creating an effective conceptual data model.

In this step, you will review the models for completeness of the number of business objects. Have you missed any object that must be in the data model? Then you will review the relationships and ensure that the cardinalities are correctly specified. Again, you will go over the list of attributes and make sure no attributes are missing. Finally, you will verify the appropriateness of the identifiers. After this validation process, the data modeling steps are completed and the diagram represents the information requirements of the organization.

In real life, data modeling is not as simple as this example tends to make us believe. However, the overall steps for creating a conceptual data model are more or less the same for all situations. Part II pursues the topics in great depth. Using a comprehensive case study, you will go through the data modeling process in elaborate detail. What we have done in this section now is just a preliminary introduction to the modeling process.

DATA MODEL QUALITY

When we walked through the steps for creating a conceptual data model, we validated the model in the final step. We indicated a few of the tasks for validating the model. These tasks ensure that the model is of high quality. But ensuring data quality involves a lot more than indicated in that final step. The importance of high quality in a data model cannot be overemphasized. Further phases follow the data modeling phase for implementing a data system for an organization. If the model is inadequate and of poor quality, then the inadequacy will be propagated to all the phases that follow data modeling.

Chapter 10 is dedicated completely to data model quality. There we will discuss the topic in elaborate detail. We will examine the reasons for the need for high quality. We will explore quality dimensions as they relate to data models. We will study how to recognize a high-quality data model. Also, we will review the methods for ensuring high quality in a data model. In this section, we just want to introduce the concept of quality in a data model and catch a glimpse of the relevant topics.

Significance of Data Model Quality

Two basic concepts of quality are completeness and correctness. For a data model to be of high quality, it must be both complete and correct. Let us briefly examine these two concepts and see how they relate to the significance of data model quality.

Data Model Completeness. When you scrutinize a data model for completeness, let us suppose you find that representations of some of the business objects are missing in the model. Consequently, you will also find that any direct relationships among these objects will also be missing. What is the result of lack of completeness?

To that extent, the data model will not truly represent the information requirements of the organization. Therefore, the final data system implemented based on the defective data model will not be able support the business of the company. Business processes that depend on the data about the missing objects and relationships cannot be performed.

Data Model Correctness. Similarly, let us suppose that the attributes of an object shown in the data model are wrong. Also, assume that two of the relationships are shown in the data model with erroneous cardinality indicators.

To that extent, the data model represents the information requirements incorrectly. These errors will filter through to the final data system and will affect the corresponding business processes.

Data Model Characteristics

What makes a data model to be of high quality? When can we say that a data model is good and adequate? Can we specify any general characteristics for a high-quality data model? Let us explore some of these features.

Involves Users. Unless the relevant users are completely involved during the process of data modeling, the resulting model cannot be good and valuable. The domain experts need to provide continuous input. While reviewing business operations for the purpose of identifying the right business objects, the involvement of the users with appropriate expertise in the particular business domain is absolutely necessary. Also, the right stakeholders must participate in the process.

At every iteration in the modeling process, the data model will be used as a means of communication with the domain experts and stakeholders. The input from these users will enable the data modeler to refine the model as it is being created. With this kind of close participation, the data model is expected to be of high data quality.

Covers the Proper Enterprise Segments. If the goal is to represent the information requirements of the entire enterprise, then your data model must be comprehensive to include all the business processes of the whole enterprise. In this case, the final data system built based on the comprehensive model will be of use for all the users.

In practice, however, unless the enterprise is of small to medium size, all information requirements will not come within the scope of the data model. The data model will be created to cover only those enterprise segments of immediate interest. In a large company, it is possible to start with a data system to support the functions of only a few divisions such as marketing and finance. Then the data model will represent the information requirements to support only the business processes of marketing and finance. Here, the emphasis is on knowing what to include and what not to include so that the data model will be correct as well as complete.

Uses Accepted Standard Rules and Conventions. In the previous section when we reviewed the components of a data model and walked through the steps for creating a conceptual data model, we improvised and used our own simple set of symbols. For the purpose of introducing the data modeling process, these symbols and conventions were sufficient. However, if you showed the data model diagram to someone else, that person may not understand the representations. This is because the symbols and conventions are not an accepted standard. To this extent, our data model is not of high quality.

A good data model must be governed by standard rules and diagramming conventions. Only if you use industry-accepted standards can your data model be good and universal. We will introduce some modeling techniques toward the end of this chapter. Chapter 2 is completely dedicated to accepted standard modeling techniques.

Produces High-Quality Design. One of the primary goals of data modeling is to produce a good blueprint for the final database system of the organization. The completeness and correctness of the blueprint are essential for a successful implementation. A poor data model cannot serve as an effective blueprint.

For a data model to be considered a high-quality model, you must be able to complete the design phase effectively and produce an excellent end product. Otherwise, the model lacks quality.

Ensuring Data Model Quality

The importance of data model quality necessitates measures to ensure the quality. A poor-quality data model results in a poor-quality data system. Quality control must be given a high priority in the whole modeling process. Let us just mention how quality considerations must be approached and also a few quality control methods.

Approach to Data Model Quality. At every step of the data modeling process, you must review and ensure that the completed data model will truly serve each of its two major purposes. Is the data model clear, complete, and accurate to serve as an effective communication tool? Can the data model be used as a good working blueprint for the data system? The data model must be reviewed for clarity, completeness, and accuracy at every stage of its creation.

Quality control comprises three distinct tasks: review, detection, and fixing. Every step of the way, the model must be reviewed for quality control. There must be techniques and tools for detecting problems with quality. Once quality problems are detected, they must be fixed forthwith. The data modeling team must develop and use proper methods to fix the quality problems.

Quality Control Methods. Quality control methods include the three tasks of review, detection, and repair. Usually, these tasks are performed in two ways. First, the tasks are performed continuously at every modeling step. In this way, less problems are likely to surface at the end of the modeling process. Second, when the modeling is complete, the overall model is again reviewed for any residual quality problems. When any residual problems are detected at this stage, they are fixed to assure high quality for the complete data model.

Who performs the quality control functions? A good approach is to share these functions. In the review and detection tasks, the data modeling team and the users must work cooperatively. Fixing of quality problems is generally the responsibility of the data modelers.

DATA SYSTEM DEVELOPMENT

As an IT professional, you are familiar with how a database system for an organization is developed and implemented. You have fairly good ideas of the various phases and tasks of the development process. Perhaps you are also knowledgeable of who does what in the process. In this section, we want to consolidate your ideas with particular emphasis on data modeling. Where does data modeling fit in the whole process? What purposes does it serve and what is its significance?

Data modeling forms an integral part of the design phase. It plays the role of the link between the requirements definition phase and the actual implementation of the data system. We have already reviewed data models at the different information levels. We have discussed the external, conceptual, logical, and physical data models that, in their specific ways, represent the information requirements. Where do these types of data models fit in the development process? How are they used?

Data System Development Life Cycle

Modern organizations depend upon the effectiveness of their data systems for their success. The information content of the data system of an organization is a key asset for the enterprise. The data system provides information critical for achieving the organizational goals. The data system enables the fulfillment of the organization's core business and drives the various business processes. The importance of the data system cannot be overstated.

Because the data system is a precious asset, each organization develops the data system with utmost care utilizing the best available resources. The design and development of the data system must be substantially significant. If so, how should an organization go about establishing its data system? The organization needs to do sufficient planning for the data system project. The development of a data system calls for a coordinated systematic approach with distinct and purposeful phases. Organizations adopt a systematic life cycle approach. A life cycle approach addresses all the phases from beginning to end in an organized and methodical manner. Let us discuss a few major aspects of the data system development life cycle (DDLC).

Starting the Process. After all the preliminary administrative functions are performed, the following are a few major factors in starting the project.

Data-Oriented Approach. At the outset, you must realize that this project requires a data-oriented approach instead of a function-oriented approach. This means emphasis on the data remains throughout the development and implementation phases.

Development Framework. Create and work with a structured framework for the development of the data system. The following components of a framework may be adapted to suit your individual organization: scope of the data system, goals and objectives, expectations, justification, current and future requirements, implementation strategy, time constraints, and development tools and techniques.

Initiation Report. Initiate the project with a report whose standard contents would include the following: scope, goals and values, key business objects, core and primary business processes, tentative schedule, project authorization.

Planning. Do sufficient initial planning to get the project started. The planning for the data system should include the interpretation of the organization's long-term plan and application to the data system.

Feasibility Study. This is assessment of the organization's readiness for the implementation. Assess the resource requirements, estimate costs, and determine tangible and intangible benefits.

Requirements Definition. Business analysts and data analysts review the various business processes and study the information requirements to support the processes. The study would include one-on-one and group interviews with the users. Existing documentation must be reviewed. The analysts would watch and analyze how each business process is performed and what data is generated or used in each process.

Requirement definition comprises the following major tasks:

- Study overall business operations
- Observe business processes
- Understand business needs
- Interview users
- Determine information requirements
- Identify data to be collected and stored
- Establish data access patterns
- Estimate data volumes

When the requirements definition gets completed, an appropriate definition document will be issued. This document will be reviewed with the users and confirmed for correctness and completeness.

Design. Data modeling forms an integral part of the design effort. You design the data system based on the data models created at the different information levels. Conceptual design is based on the conceptual data model; logical design results from the logical model. The physical implementation works on the basis of the physical data model.

Figure 1-15 illustrates the design process. Note the different types of data models and how they are related. Also, notice how each part of the design effort rests on the particular data model.

Implementation. When the design phase is completed, the data system is ready for implementation. Completion of the physical data model and using it for implementation are responsibilities of the database administrator. He or she defines the data structures, relationships, business rule constraints, storage areas, performance improvement techniques, and completes the physical data model. This is at the physical level of hardware and storage.

Using the facilities of the selected DBMS, the database administrator establishes the data system. Once the structures and relationships are defined, the database is ready for initial data. Typically, organizations make the transition from earlier file systems to the database environment. Programmers extract data from the earlier systems and use the data to populate the new database. Special utility programs that are usually part of the DBMS enable the data loading with considerable ease.

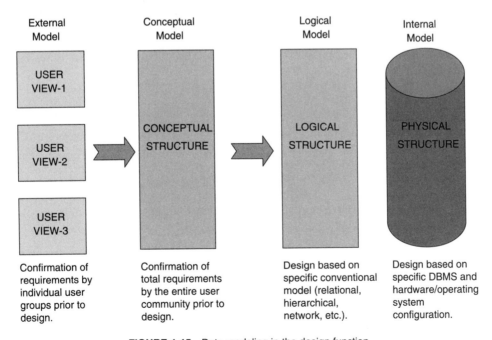

FIGURE 1-15 Data modeling in the design function.

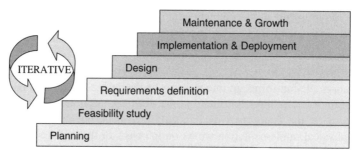

FIGURE 1-16 DDLC: major phases.

Phases and Tasks. The life cycle approach comprises systematic and well-defined phases or steps to complete the design and development of a data system. Each phase consists of specific major activities; each activity contains individual tasks. Although the project progresses from phase to phase, the people working on the project do not necessarily complete one phase and then move on to the next. Parts of the phases may be performed in parallel. Sometimes it becomes essential to repeat and refine some of the phases in an iterative manner.

Figure 1-16 shows the major phases of the DDLC. Note the sequence of the phases from bottom to top. Notice how the figure illustrates that the phases may be performed in an iterative fashion. Although some aspects of requirements definition remain to be completed, the design phase may commence. When you bring the design phase to partial completion, you may go back to the requirements phase and fine-tune some aspects there.

The scope of our discussion here does not call for detailed description of each phase. Nevertheless, let us highlight the objectives in each phase.

Planning. Review the organization's long-term business plan; plan specifically for the data system.

Feasibility Study. Study the state of readiness: estimate costs and explore benefits.

Requirements Definition. Define the business objects and relationships; document data requirements.

Design. Complete data modeling; design at conceptual, logical, and physical levels.

Implementation and Deployment. Complete physical design and define data structures and relationships using DBMS; populate data system; get data system ready for applications.

Maintenance and Growth. Perform ongoing maintenance; plan and manage growth of data system.

Roles and Responsibilities

Although we are mainly interested in data modeling within the DDLC, we here just want to identify who plays which roles in the entire process. Here is an indication of the participation by users and practitioners.

Planning: Senior management

Feasibility study: Business analysts

Requirements definition: Systems analysts, data analysts, user representatives

Design: Data modelers, database designers

Implementation and deployment: Systems analysts, programmers, database administrators

Maintenance and growth: database administrators

Modeling the Information Requirements

Let us now turn our attention to data modeling within the design phase. Let us discuss how data models are created to represent the information requirements. We will take a simple specific example. Let us consider the information requirements for an insurance company. Each of the user groups performs specific business processes. While performing business processes, each user group either uses relevant stored data or creates and stores data for later use. In either case, each user group is interested in a set of data elements.

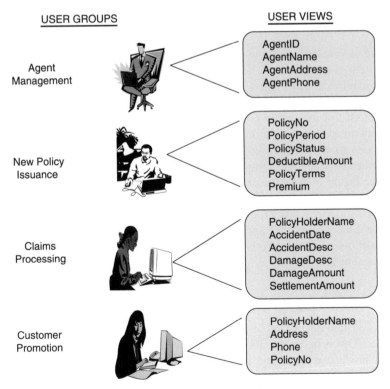

FIGURE 1-17   User groups and user views of data system.

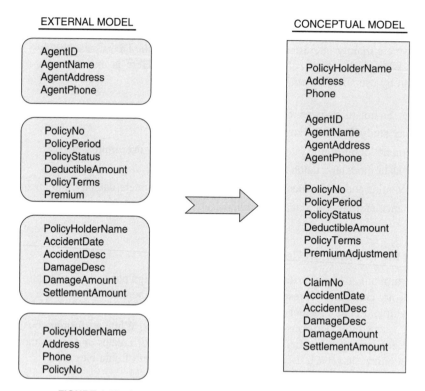

FIGURE 1-18   Insurance company: external and conceptual data models.

For the sake of simplicity, assume four user groups for the insurance company: agent management, new policy issuance, claims processing, and customer promotion. Each user group uses or requires a set of data elements. These sets of data elements form the user views of the data system. Figure 1-17 indicates the user views for these four user groups.

The complete list of user views comprises the external data model. The external data model is simply the various sets of data elements the different user groups are interested in. If you take into account all the user groups in the organization for which the data system is being implemented, then the aggregation of all the user views produces the conceptual data model. See Figure 1-18 for the external and conceptual data models for the insurance company.

The next data modeling task produces the physical data model from the conceptual. Every business object, attribute, and relationship represented in the conceptual data model gets transformed in the physical data model. Figure 1-19 gives an indication of the physical data model.

Applying Agile Modeling Principles

In recent years, system developers and data modelers have been adopting agile development principles. This is because agile development principles enable professionals to be proactive and produce results. The literature on agile system development and agile project management continues to grow. See the bibliography at the end of the book for some leading authors on these subjects. Throughout the subsequent chapters, we will be

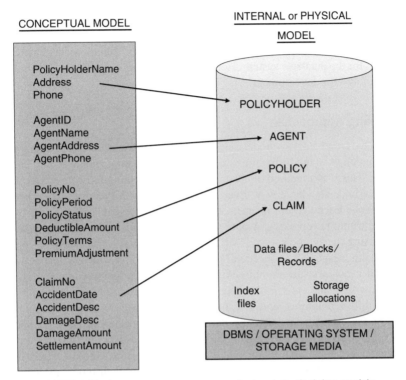

FIGURE 1-19 Insurance company: conceptual and physical data models.

mentioning agile modeling principles as they are applicable to our study. Chapter 11 is totally dedicated to agile modeling as it is practiced.

Agile modeling is not a complete software development process. It is more a set of valuable principles than a methodology for data modeling. The principles act as catalysts to any chosen modeling technique. Agile modeling enables putting values and principles into practice for effective, easy modeling.

DATA MODELING APPROACHES AND TRENDS

Thus far we have reviewed the basic concepts of data modeling. We discussed how and why information perceived at various information levels in an organization must be modeled. At each level, the data model serves specific purposes. We concentrated more on the conceptual data model at this stage and reviewed its components. We walked through the phases of the data system development life cycle. More explicitly, we covered the steps that are taken to create a data model—particularly, conceptual data model. We also touched upon the importance of data model quality.

Let us now conclude this introductory chapter with a historical note and review the evolution of data modeling over time. The need for data modeling was realized from the earliest times when database systems began to appear on the scene. Joint participation of users and information technology (IT) professionals in system development ensued. As organizations expanded in size and complexity, translating information requirements directly into database systems became almost impossible. Users had to understand and confirm the understanding of IT professionals. Information technology professionals also needed an intermediary representation of information requirements that could act as a blueprint for the database system. Hence, data modeling evolved as a distinct effort in the process of system development.

Data Modeling Approaches

Earlier when we created a data model diagram, remember we used a set of symbols. A few basic rules guided us in the formation of a data model. We used square boxes, circles, and straight lines. This was a method of abstraction for representing information requirements in a somewhat understandable way. Every modeling method, therefore, has a set of notations or symbols. Each symbol means something and represents some aspect of the real world we are trying to represent. A data modeling method also has a set of rules or procedures for using the symbols.

Data modeling, especially conceptual modeling, is a collaborative effort between data modelers and users who are domain experts. The real-world information requirements must somehow be made clear in the data model through natural language, easily understood and intuitive diagrams, and also through data examples. These examples are the examples of the type of data that the data model is expected to portray. Sometimes, these are referred to as data use cases because they are the data used by the system.

Data modelers adopt three major data modeling approaches: entity-relationship data modeling, fact-oriented data modeling, and object-oriented data modeling. Chapter 2 is fully dedicated to the discussion of data modeling methods. Therefore, in this section, we will just introduce these approaches and consider some major points.

Entity-Relationship Modeling. This approach, introduced by Peter Chen in 1976, is still the most popular and widely used technique. Vendors have produced several computer-aided software engineering (CASE) tools to support this method. This method perceives and portrays the information requirements of an organization as a set of entities with attributes participating in relationships. Based on earlier discussions and examples, we are already somewhat familiar with this method. Over the years, newer versions of entity-relationship modeling came on the scene. The newer versions included improvements and enhancements. Symbols used in entity-relationship modeling are not fully standardized although if you know one convention, it would be easy to guess the meaning of similar symbols in another convention.

Entity-relationship modeling portrays the information domain of an organization in a way that is free from any considerations of database software or hardware. Because of this independence, this method is well suited for conceptual data modeling. It does not burden the domain experts with unnecessary details. However, an entity-relationship (E-R) data model diagram has its shortcomings. The diagram does not clearly indicate constraints in the relationships. Does every instance of one entity always relate to instances of the related entity? How are constraints on mandatory and optional relationships indicated? Those practitioners who tried to remove the defects have attempted some enhancements to E-R modeling. But these attempts are not fully satisfactory.

Domain experts want to relate data use cases to the model diagram. They want to know how each use of a set of data is specified in the model. This link of data use case to the model is not obvious. Not all domain experts are comfortable with the notations in the

E-R model and find some of the notations, especially those for relationships, incomplete and imprecise. The fact-oriented data modeling approach attempts to overcome some of the deficiencies of the E-R approach.

Fact-Oriented Modeling. In the 1970s, an approach to data modeling arose by viewing the information domain in terms of objects playing roles. What are roles? A role is the part played by one object in a relationship. Object-role modeling (ORM) is such a fact-oriented modeling approach. This is perhaps the only major fact-oriented modeling technique with fairly wide industry support.

Let us try to understand ORM with an example. Consider the data use case for scheduling the time of doctors for patient visits. The domain expert who is familiar with this simple use case is able to verbalize the information content of this use case. The data modeler must be able to transform this verbalization into a data model to discuss easily and to validate the model. In this data modeling technique, the data modeler verbalizes sample data as instances of facts and then abstracts them into fact types. Constraints and rules of relationships and derivation get added to the model to make it complete.

Figure 1-20 shows an ORM diagram for doctor scheduling. Named ellipses indicate entity types and have a method for referencing them. The reference (last name) shown in parentheses within the ellipse for Doctor means that doctors are referred to by last names. The sample data form the fact instances, and these get abstracted into the fact types. The ORM diagram indicates the structure consisting of the fact types of Doctor, Time, Patient, and PatientName. A named sequence of one or more role boxes depicts a relationship. In this case, we have a three-role or ternary relationship: Doctor at Time is scheduled for Patient. We also have a binary or two-role association between Patient and PatientName. The model diagram also includes some counterdata to indicate appropriate constraints.

An ORM diagram presents all facts in terms of entities or values. Unlike as in E-R, attributes are not specified in the base ORM models. Object-role modeling allows for relationships with multiple roles. Object-role modeling diagrams tend to be large; nevertheless, an attribute-free model is simpler, more stable, and easier for validation. The arrow-tipped lines indicate uniqueness constraints showing which roles or combination of roles must

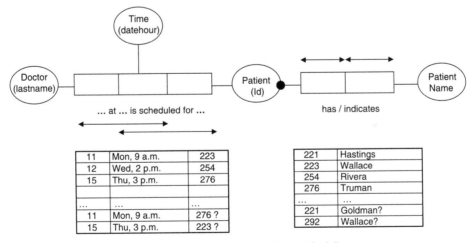

FIGURE 1-20 ORM diagram: doctor scheduling.

have unique entries. A black dot on Patient refers to a mandatory role constraint. The counterexamples of data with question marks (?) provide means to test such constraints while validating the model with a domain expert.

Compared with ORM, E-R has the following shortcomings:

- It is not closer to natural language for validation with domain experts.
- E-R techniques generally support only two-way relationships. Although *n*-way relationships in E-R are broken down into two-way relationships by introducing intersection identities, these intersection identifies seem arbitrary and not understood by domain experts.

Object-Oriented Modeling. In this approach, both data and behavior are encapsulated within objects. Thus, object-oriented modeling was primarily devised for designing code of object-oriented programs. However, this modeling approach can be adapted for conceptual modeling and eventually for database design.

By far, the most popular and widely used object-oriented approach is the Unified Modeling Language (UML). The Unified Modeling Language has an array of diagram types, and class diagrams form one important type. Class diagrams can represent data structures and may be considered as extensions of the E-R technique. Apart from this brief mention of UML here, we will postpone our detailed discussion of UML until the end of Chapter 2.

Modeling for Data Warehouse

As an IT professional, one must have worked on computer applications as an analyst, programmer, designer, or project manager. One must have been involved in the design, implementation, or maintenance of systems that support the day-to-day business operations of an organization. Examples of such systems are order processing, inventory control, human resources, payroll, insurance claims, and so on. These applications that support the running of the business operations are sometimes known as OLTP (online teleprocessing) systems. Although OLTP systems provide information and support for running the day-to-day business, they are not designed for analysis and spotting trends.

In the 1990s, as businesses grew more complex, corporations spread globally, and competition became fiercer, business executives became desperate for information to stay competitive and improve the bottom line. They wanted to know which product lines to expand, which markets to strengthen, which new stores and industrial warehouses would be worthwhile. They became hungry for information to make strategic decisions. Although companies had accumulated vast quantities of data in their OLTP systems, these systems themselves could not support intricate queries and analysis for providing strategic information.

Data warehousing is a recent paradigm specifically intended to provide vital strategic information. It is a decision-support system. In a data warehouse, data has to be viewed and represented differently. Data modeling appropriate for building OLTP database systems becomes ineffective for data warehouse systems. Techniques such as entity-relationship data modeling do not meet the requirements. Let us consider a simple example to illustrate why a different modeling technique becomes desirable.

Suppose we take all the sales data accumulated in the OLTP systems and want to use it for analysis. We want to ask a question such as: What are the sales of Product A for the current year, broken down by regions, compared with prior year and targets, sorting the sales in ascending sequence by region? After viewing the sales data, suppose we want to zero in on the region with the lowest performance. We would then want to ask a follow-up question such as: For the region with the lowest performance, what is the breakdown by sales representatives, districts, and shipment methods. This approach of querying and analysis is likely to lead us to the reasons for the low performance so that we can make strategic decisions to rectify the situation. Therefore, a data warehouse must contain data extracted from OLTP systems—data that can be viewed and modeled for querying and analysis.

In this example, we want a data model that enables analysis of sales by year, region, sales representative, and shipment method. We need a model that supports analysis of sales data or facts about sales by combinations of the business dimensions of year, region, sales representative, and shipment method. The model should depict the information content in a data warehouse using dimensional modeling. We will discuss dimensional modeling technique in great detail in Chapter 9. That chapter describes data modeling for decision-support systems extensively.

Other Modeling Trends

Some recent data modeling and related trends include very-high-level languages for querying information systems, enhanced schema or model abstraction methods, newer techniques for creating external models, and extended modeling languages such as extensible markup language (XML). In the remaining chapters, we will include discussions on these as and when necessary.

Let us now conclude with brief discussions on a few other trends.

Postrelational Databases. In our earlier discussions, we have noted that a relational data model views data in the form of two-dimensional tables. We have also seen that a conceptual model may be mapped to a relational model. Prior to the advent of the relational model on the database scene, other models such as the hierarchical and network models preceded the relational model. In these models, data is viewed differently. The hierarchical model presents data as hierarchical segments in parent–child relationships. On the other hand, the network model consists of data nodes arranged as a network. Still, a conceptual model while being transformed into a logical model may take any one of these forms.

The relational model is still the most popular and widely used model; most data system implementations are relational databases. However, the recent uses of data and the generation of newer types of data pose problems for the relational model. Now we have to deal with data in the form of images, sounds, and spatial elements. More complex data objects have become common in industry. A relational model does not seem to be adequate for representing recent trends in data usage. Organizations adopt postrelational models to address the recent requirements. Data modelers need to adapt their modeling techniques to accommodate postrelational models.

Let us briefly highlight a few of these postrelational approaches.

Object-Oriented Databases. In addition to features of relational databases, these databases possess additional features such as support for complex objects, encapsulation involving bundling of operations and data together, and user-defined data types.

Deductive Databases. These databases offer powerful and elegant methods for declaring and managing complex data. For data that has to be derived by the use of a series of recursions, this approach proves very effective.

Spatial Databases. These databases provide support for spatial data types (points, lines, multisided figures, etc.) and spatial operators (intersect, overlap, contain, etc.). Because of these facilities, spatial databases efficiently manage spatial data such as maps (land, counties, states or provinces, etc.) and two- and three-dimensional designs such town plans, flight paths, and so on.

Process Modeling. Data modeling primarily confines itself to creating conceptual, external, logical, and physical models. If you examine each of these models, they represent the data content, perhaps, in a static manner. However, other aspects of working with the data exist in an organization. Somehow these other aspects such as business processes that use the data content must also be modeled. Many types of model diagrams depict these other aspects. The Unified Modeling Language includes such diagrams: use-case diagrams, sequential diagrams, collaboration diagrams, state charts, and activity diagrams. Other modeling techniques include data flow diagrams, process flow charts, and function trees.

As our primary emphasis rests on data modeling, we do not intend to discuss the process modeling techniques in detail. However, we will list the functions of the important ones.

Use Case Diagrams. These provide comprehensive overviews of the processes in a system.

Activity Diagrams. These show activities of each process. Activity diagrams at successive levels refine the activities as you proceed to the lower levels. Domain experts understand activity diagrams intuitively and find them very valuable.

Function Trees. These decompose major functions into subfunctions at several levels.

Data Flow Diagrams. These display flow of information between processes.

Meta-Meodeling. Data modeling creates models of data content in a database system. Process modeling deals with modeling the activities and functions surrounding the data system. Modeling involves creating models of the application domain. Meta-modeling involves creating models of the models themselves. A meta-model represents the contents of the model itself.

You can create meta-models for data models at various levels. A meta-model at a particular level describes the data model at that level. Thus, a conceptual meta-model contains the representation of the components of a conceptual data model. A conceptual data model describes business objects and their relationships. A conceptual meta-model expresses the components of a conceptual model, that is, the representations themselves as meta-objects and meta-relationships. A meta-model may be used to verify and validate the corresponding data model.

CHAPTER SUMMARY

- A data model is a representation of the information content in the real world.
- Essentially, a data model serves two purposes: as a communication tool and as a blueprint for constructing the database.
- A data model plays a significant role in the data life cycle of an organization.
- In an organization, four information levels are discerned; data models are created at these levels.
- A conceptual data model depicts the information requirements of an organization at the highest general level. Logical and physical data models are representations at the next two lower levels with more intricate details.
- A conceptual data model has the following major components or building blocks: objects, attributes, identifiers, and relationships.
- The process of data modeling consists of specific modeling steps or activities.
- Quality of a data model is of paramount importance.
- Data system development life cycle (DDLC) phases: planning, feasibility study, requirements definition, design, implementation and deployment.
- Data modeling techniques have evolved and been refined during the past decade.

REVIEW QUESTIONS

1. Match the column entries:

1. Data model	A. Closest to the users
2. Storing data	B. Intrinsic characteristic
3. External model	C. Popular modeling technique
4. Attribute	D. Representation of real world
5. Patient	E. Completeness and correctness
6. Conceptual model	F. Data life cycle stage
7. Model quality parameters	G. Blueprint for database
8. Feasibility study	H. Fragment of logical model
9. Physical model	I. Determine state of readiness
10. Entity-relationship modeling	J. Business object for a hospital

2. Describe the two primary purposes served by a data model.
3. What are the various stages of the data life cycle in an organization? How can a data model be useful in these stages?
4. Name some major functions performed by a data modeler. What types of skills are needed to perform these functions?
5. Describe the notion of information levels in an organization. What are the typical levels and why are they important?
6. Name the different types of data models and relate them to the information levels. What are the essential purposes of these types of data models at these levels?

7. Name and briefly describe the components of a conceptual data model. Give examples.

8. Briefly describe the general data modeling steps. Indicate the activities at each step.

9. List the major phases of DDLC. What are the objectives of each phase?

10. Name any three data modeling approaches. Describe one of the approaches.

2

METHODS, TECHNIQUES, AND SYMBOLS

CHAPTER OBJECTIVES

- As preparation for in-depth study of data modeling, get to know the leading modeling approaches
- Review the main aspects of data modeling
- Provide an overview of common techniques
- Present the notations, symbols, and semantics of these techniques
- Specifically introduce Unified Modeling Language in some depth

Through our discussion of the basics of data modeling, you have understood that the modeling process attempts to depict the real world of an organization. You expect to create a model that truly represents the data requirements of the organization. Recall that the data model must serve not only as a tool for communication with the domain experts by representing their requirements but must also act as a blueprint for the data system to be implemented on computers. The kinds of models must be able to be encoded and manipulated by computers. For this reason, we presented data models at different levels of abstraction— conceptual, logical, and physical.

At this time, we will continue our discussions mainly pertaining to the conceptual data model. Once you have created the conceptual data model, you may then proceed to transform it into a logical model and, thereafter, into a physical model taking into consideration the hardware and software environment.

A data model refers to objects, their properties, and the relationships among one another. We can think of four aspects of an object: object name, object property, property value, and time. The time element relates to the time of capture of the data about the object. Many models drop the notion of time and replace it with methods of ordering of

Data Modeling Fundamentals. By Paulraj Ponniah
Copyright © 2007 John Wiley & Sons, Inc.

data or other explicit properties. Thus, an elementary idea of an object consists of object name, property, and property value.

An example of a specific object is *John Smith*; a value for a particular property for this object is *30 Main Street*. *John Smith* is a specific instance of the category EMPLOYEE; *30 Main Street* is a specific value for the category StreetAddress. This is an example of strictly typed data. Most common data models deal with strictly typed data. These models make clear distinction between data and categories of data. In strictly typed data models, properties of data can be abstracted and explored in terms of their categories. Usually each piece of data fits into some category and makes it easy for abstraction.

A data model defines the rules for the data structures and relationships. Generic rules for defining categories determine allowable objects and relationships. Disallowed objects, their properties, and relationships are excluded by the use of constraints. Different modeling techniques work with variable structuring rules and constraints. In the first part of this chapter, we will briefly discuss four common data modeling approaches. We will consider how data structures are perceived and defined. We will also review the basic notations and the diagramming techniques. After that, we will proceed to study six popular data modeling methods. We will conclude with a presentation of Unified Modeling Language (UML).

DATA MODELING APPROACHES

Of the four modeling approaches discussed here, we have already mentioned two of these briefly, namely, entity-relationship and relational. However, we will review these and the others on the basis of a limited collection of concepts through which the models can be expressed. These concepts may be summarized by the semantic concepts of type and aggregation.

Let us review how these concepts are applied in the four approaches. We will also briefly look at the data structures and relationships. This discussion of the four modeling approaches serves as a prelude to the study of the common modeling techniques that follows.

We will use a specific simple example to illustrate the four approaches. Let us say we want to model the real-world situation of students registering for courses at a university. The data model must represent the registration of students in courses. From these information requirements we can derive the objects, properties, and relationships utilizing the concepts of type and aggregation.

Semantic Modeling

In this approach, the concept of type plays a prominent role. A type is defined as the aggregation or collection of a certain number of properties into a unit or component. Further, the properties themselves are also considered as types. The student registration example cited above is specified as shown as follows:

> *type* registration = student, course
>
> *type* student   = name, student id, street address, city, state, zip code
>
> *type* course   = course name, course number, day-of-week, time

Figure 2-1 shows the abstraction hierarchy in semantic modeling.

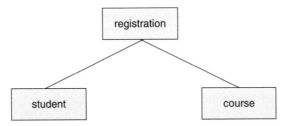

FIGURE 2-1 Semantic modeling: abstraction hierarchy.

Aggregation is represented in the model diagram by placing it above the properties. Base types such as name, student id, address, and so on are not represented in the graphical notation.

Relational Modeling

The concept of mathematical relation forms the basis for the data structure in the relational data model. A relation is visualized as a two-dimensional table with rows and columns containing only atomic values. Our example of student registration is defined as follows in the relational model:

registration (**student id**, **course number**)

student (name, **student id**, street address, city, state, zip code)

course (course name, **course number**, day-of-week, time)

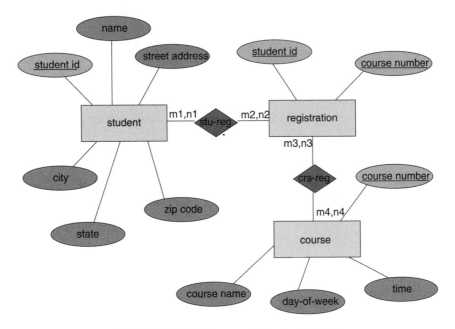

FIGURE 2-2 E-R diagram: student registration.

Relation registration has two attributes forming two table columns. The number of rows in each table depends on the actual data stored. Each row is uniquely identified by values of the columns shown in bold type. The relationships and reference between student and registration is expressed by the column *student id* in the registration table.

Entity-Relationship Modeling

The concepts of entity type, attribute type, and relationship type form the basis for the entity-relationship (E-R) model. The structuring concept is the entity type consisting of basic attribute types. A complete E-R model shows the attributes for each entity type (Fig. 2-2).

The parameters (m1,n1) and (m2,n2) denote maximum and minimum cardinalities of the relationships. Cardinalities specify how many instances of one entity type may be associated with how many instances of the other entity type. Cardinality parameters take the value of 0, 1, or * (indicating "many").

Binary Modeling

The binary model rests on many concepts. Central to this approach is the binary separation of object types into lexical and nonlexical object types. Lexical object types are those that can be used as names for other object types or for references to other object types. Nonlexical object types are named object types or those referred by other object types.

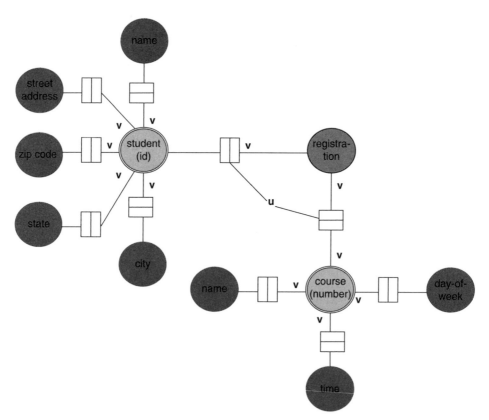

FIGURE 2-3 Binary model: information structure diagram.

A bridge type is a relationship between a lexical and a nonlexical object type. A relationship between two nonlexical object types is known as an idea type. Graphical constraints may be imposed on an information structure diagram of the binary model. Uniqueness constraint and totality constraint are among the imposable constraints. In a binary model, it must always be possible to refer uniquely to a nonlexical object type, that is, each binary model must be referable.

The information structure diagram for the student registration example becomes more complex than those using the other modeling approaches. Figure 2-3 shows this model diagram.

Note the dotted circles denoting lexical object types and closed circles representing nonlexical object types. Note the bridge type indicating the relationship between student and course. Uniqueness constraints are indicated by "u" and totality constraints by "v."

METHODS AND TECHNIQUES

In the 1970s, Peter Chen invented and introduced the entity-relationship modeling technique revolutionizing the way data is represented. Over time, many data modelers and others have refined and enhanced Chen's original version. A host of modeling techniques arose based on the concepts of entities and relationships.

As data and process requirements became more complex in the 1980s, object modeling techniques began to be applied to representing information requirements of an organization. Unified Modeling Language, introduced in the mid-1990s, was expected to overcome the shortcomings of earlier object modeling methods and become one definitive object modeling method. Unified Modeling Language is not quite up to this task yet. Although UML is the premier object modeling technique, it has done little to replace entity-relationship techniques.

Whether it is data modeling or object modeling, the primary purpose of a modeling technique is to describe the data elements of an organization. Because of this underlying purpose, you will be able to convert the notations of one method into those of another method. Syntactic aspects of a data model refer to the symbols used. How clearly the symbols are laid out and connected in a data model diagram helps in the readability of the model. The meanings conveyed by the symbols and their arrangement refer to the semantic viability of the model.

A good model must be technically complete and be clearly readable. Readability serves the first audience for a data model—the domain experts. Technical completeness provides a foundation for the data model to act as a blueprint for the data system. Technical completeness comprises proper and complete representations of entities, attributes, relationships, unique identifiers, subtypes and supertypes, and constraints on the structure and relationships.

We will now present a few leading data modeling techniques. After the presentation of the models, we will conclude with a comparison and evaluation of them. Mainly our evaluation will be based on readability and technical completeness. In order to facilitate the comparison and evaluation, we will use the same example to create data models using each of these different techniques.

The example relates to customer purchases. Customers place orders on the company to buy products or services. A customer order contains line items that may cover product items or service items or both. We will construct data models for the information requirements for the buying and selling activities of the company. For the sake of simplicity, we will restrict the model to a few important business objects.

Peter Chen (E-R) Modeling

Even after about three decades, this method is still widely used. This is because of its unique ability to represent attributes and relationships. Instead of inclusion as annotations on a diagram consisting of entities only, attributes are clearly denoted separately. This model also shows relationships intuitively and clearly with lines and diamonds mentioning the name of the relationships.

Figure 2-4 contains the E-R model diagram for the example described above. The model diagram shows the entities, their attributes, and the relationships among the entities. It also has an example of supertype and subtype. The cardinality parameters indicate the relationship constraints.

Entities and Attributes. Square-cornered boxes represent entities. Attributes, represented by ellipses, are attached to the corresponding entities. Entity names and attribute names appear inside these notations. Hyphens separate multiword names. Entity and attribute names are in the singular.

The diagram gives no indication of any constraints on the values of the attributes. It does not tell you whether values for a particular attribute are mandatory or optional for individual instances of the entity type. Also, the model does not denote if an attribute participates in being an identifier for the entity type.

Relationships. Among the various modeling techniques, the Chen model represents a relationship in a unique manner. A relationship type has its own symbol: a diamond or rhombus on a line between entities denotes a relationship. The Chen model allows

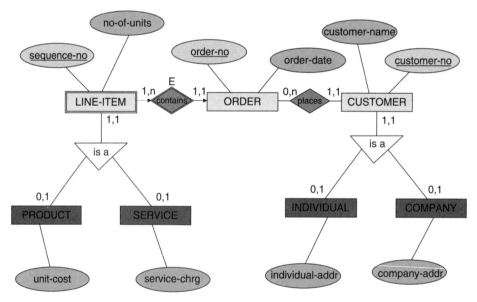

FIGURE 2-4 Chen model: customer purchases.

one-to-one, one-to-many, and many-to-many relationship types. Cardinality indicators at either end of the relationship line show the number of instances of the entities participating in the relationship. Relationships need not just be binary; several entities may participate in a single relationship and be linked through a single relationship rhombus.

Names. The Chen model definitely considers relationships as data objects in their own right; it therefore usually identifies them with names that are nouns. Sometimes the name of a relationship is the concatenation of the names of the two participating entities. However, later enhancements to this model attempt to indicate the action by means of a verb such as "places" between CUSTOMER and ORDER.

Cardinality/Optionality. The original version of the Chen model provided for showing only the maximum cardinality indicator at each end of the relationship line. A "1" as the cardinality indicator shows that one instance of an entity associates with one or more instances of the other entity. An "n" as the cardinality indicator denotes that more than one instance of an entity associates with one instance of the other entity. However, a single number does not provide for the fact that relationships could be mandatory or optional. In mandatory relationships, every instance must participate in the relationship associating with one or more of the other entity. In optional relationships, not every instance needs to participate; for example, in our sample, those CUSTOMER instances that have not placed any orders yet need not participate in the relationship. Later enhancements to the Chen model included maximum and minimum cardinalities to address the mandatory and optional conditions. For now, just note the two numbers shown as cardinality indicators for the relationships. We will cover this in more detail in later chapters because we will be using the E-R modeling technique for most of the examples later on.

Constraints. Quite often we need to indicate that each instance of a base entity must be related to instances of one other entity, but not more. This common case of constraints is the "exclusive OR" constraint. The Chen model does not deal with constraints in a direct manner. Other methods had to be adopted to include this and enhance the model.

Unique Identifiers. A combination of attributes and relationships that uniquely identify an instance of an entity forms a unique identifier for the entity. The Chen model has no provision to show combination of attributes as identifiers. However, if the unique identifier of an entity includes a relationship to another entity, the model indicates this by expressing the relationship name as "E" and connecting with an arrow the dependent entity represented by a double box (see ORDER and LINE-ITEM relationship in Fig. 2-4).

Supertypes and Subtypes. A subtype entity is a specialization of a supertype entity; a supertype entity is a generalization of a subtype entity. An instance of the subtype entity is also an instance of the supertype entity. Similarly, an instance of the supertype entity must be an instance of just one or another subtype entity.

The original version of the Chen model has no provision to indicate supertype and subtype entities. But later enhancements to the model included supertype and subtype entities. Separate boxes represent subtype entities. Each subtype entity is moved out of the supertype representation and indicated by a separate box. An "*isa*" linkage connects a subtype entity with its supertype entity meaning that each instance of the subtype *is an* instance of the supertype. Pay special attention in Figure 2-4 to the relationships

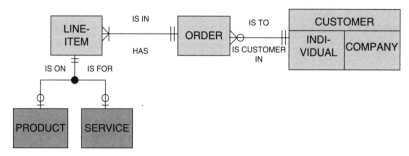

FIGURE 2-5   IE model: customer purchases.

between the supertype entity CUSTOMER and its subtype entities INDIVIDUAL and COMPANY. Also note the cardinality parameters for these relationships.

Information Engineering

In the late 1970s, Clive Finkelstein in Australia developed this data modeling technique. Later, he worked with James Martin to make it popular in the United States and Europe. Afterward, James Martin became the significant proponent of this method with his own revisions. Later on, Finkelstein publicized his own version of the revisions. You will notice traces of the dual origin of the technique in the information engineering (IE) data model.

Let us express our customer purchases example using IE notations and conventions. Figure 2-5 shows the information engineering model.

Entities and Attributes. Definitions of entities by Finkelstein and Martin varied slightly. Finkelstein defined entity as representing data to be stored for later reference; Martin reckoned entity as something, real or abstract, about which we store data.

As in the Chen model, square-cornered boxes represent entities. Entity names appear inside the boxes. Hyphens separate multiword names. Entity names are in the singular. But unlike the Chen model, the IE model does not show attributes at all. In the Finkelstein version, a separate document lists the attributes. Martin has another modeling method called bubble charts specifically for including attributes and keys.

Relationships. Relationships are simply indicated with solid lines connecting pairs of entities. There is no separate notation for the relationship type object. Symbols at each end indicate cardinality and optionality.

Names. Finkelstein's version does not name the relationships at all. However, Martin's version names relationships with verbs, mostly only in one direction.

Cardinality/Optionality. The IE model depicts each relationship as having two halves with one or more symbols describing each half. Optionality and mandatory conditions are expressed by placing a small open circle near the entity on the relationship line. For expressing an optional condition, if an instance of the first entity may or may not be related to instances of the second, a small open circle appears near the second entity. If the relationship is to be mandatory, that is, if an instance of the first entity must be related to at least one instance of the second entity, a short line crosses the relationship line. Further, if an instance of the first entity can be associated with one and only one of the second entity, another short line crosses the relationship. If it can be related to more than one instance of the second entity, a crow's-foot is placed at the intersection of the relationship line and the second entity box. Examine the placements of these symbols on the relationship lines in Figure 2-5.

Constraints. Relationship lines of three or more entities meeting at a small circle expresses a constraint between the relationships. A solid circle represents an "exclusive OR" condition; that is, each instance of the base entity must be related to instances of one other entity, but not more than one entity. In the figure, this is illustrated where each line item *is for* either one product or *is for* one service, but not both. Quite often we need to indicate that each instance of a base entity must be related to instances of one other entity, but not more. On the other hand, an open circle represents an "inclusive OR" condition; that is, an instance of the base entity may be related to instances of one, some, or all of the other related entities.

Unique Identifiers. The IE model does not include representations for unique identifiers. However, Martin's revised version shows unique identifiers in separate bubble charts.

Supertypes and Subtypes. Martin's version of the IE model denotes subtypes as separate entity boxes connected to the supertype entity by an "*isa*" relationship. Each instance of a subtype is an instance of the supertype. Refer to Figure 2-5 and see how this may be done.

Integration Definition for Information Modeling

Many agencies of the United States government use the IDEF1X (integration definition for information modeling) technique. This methodology has been adopted as a Federal Information Processing Standard.

Figure 2-6 shows the IDEF1X version for our customer purchases sample. We will go through the components illustrated in the figure and discuss them.

Entities and Attributes. Either square-cornered or round-cornered rectangular boxes represent entities. Round-cornered boxes denote dependent entities, that is, entities whose identifier is a concatenation of its identifier with that of the related entity. Refer to the LINE-ITEM entity in the figure. Square-cornered boxes show independent entities whose identifiers are not derived for others. Entity names appear outside, usually above the boxes. Hyphens, underscores, or blanks separate multiword names. Entity names are in the singular.

The IDEF1X model displays the attributes and identifiers within the entity box, the two sets separated by a dividing line. The identifiers (primary key) appear above the dividing line and all the other attributes below the line.

Relationships. Representation of relationships is not symmetrical; different symbols indicate optionality, depending on the cardinality of the relationship. You cannot examine and parse the symbols independently for cardinality and optionality. In effect, each set of symbols denotes a combination of optionality and cardinality of the entity next to it.

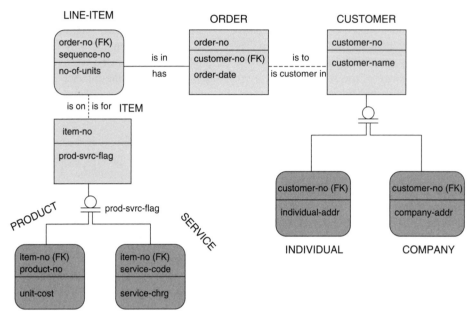

FIGURE 2-6 IDEF1X model: customer purchases.

Solid lines and broken lines connect the entity boxes to represent relationships. A solid line expresses a relationship if the relationship is between independent and dependent entities. However, this differentiation using solid and broken lines is not present in all implementations of IDEF1X. In addition to the relationship line, foreign keys are shown as attributes for implementation as a relational model. We will discuss foreign keys in great length in later chapters.

Names. IDEF1X names relationships with verbs or verb phrases in both directions. Note the verbs expressing the actions as shown in Figure 2-6.

Cardinality/Optionality. Expression of cardinality and optionality has many variations in this model. Although at the conceptual modeling level, so many subtle variations may not be considered necessary, IDEF1X enables good and detailed transformation when the conceptual is transformed into the logical and then into the physical model. Note the various symbols shown for the relationships in Figure 2-6. Usually, solid dot on the relationship line next to an identity box stands for zero, one, or more instances of that entity. The letter P indicates a mandatory relationship. A solid dot may mean "must be" or "may be" and "one or more" or "one and only one," depending on the other symbols around it. Let us summarize the notations with a figure: see Figure 2-7 showing IDEF1X components.

Constraints. IDEF1X has no explicit method for representing constraints between relationships. If entity A is related to entity B or entity C, this has to be represented by defining an intermediary entity D and use of subtype notation. This would show that entity A is related to entity D, which must be either B or entity C.

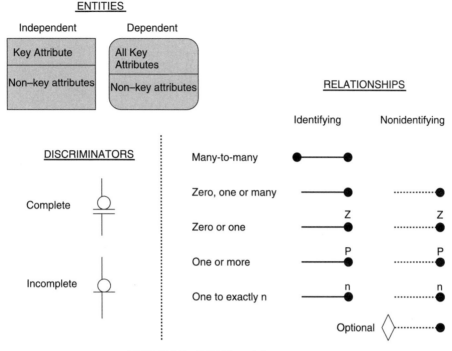

FIGURE 2-7   IDEF1X modeling components.

Unique Identifiers. The primary key is indicated as the unique identifier and shown inside the entity box. The primary key may consist of foreign key and non-foreign-key attributes because all relationships are indicated with foreign keys.

Supertypes and Subtypes. The IDEF1X model denotes subtypes as separate entity boxes connected to the supertype entity by a distinct symbol. Each instance of a subtype is an instance of the supertype. Refer to Figure 2-6 and examine how this is represented.

This model indicates two kinds of subtypes: complete subtyping denoted by a circle with two horizontal lines under it; incomplete subtyping with only one horizontal under the circle. In complete subtyping, all instances of the supertype must be occurrences of one or the other subtype. Incomplete subtyping does not include all possible instances of the supertype in the subtypes.

The model expresses mutually exclusive subtype by extending the subtypes from a single subtype symbol. Subtypes descending from different subtype symbols attached to the same supertype are not mutually exclusive.

Richard Barker's Model

Initially developed by a British company, this model was promoted by Richard Barker in the late 1980s. Oracle adopted this technique for its CASE method. Oracle later renamed the technique "Custom Development Method" and incorporated it in its database software suite.

Our product distribution example using Barker notations is illustrated in Figure 2-8. Note the various components and diagramming conventions.

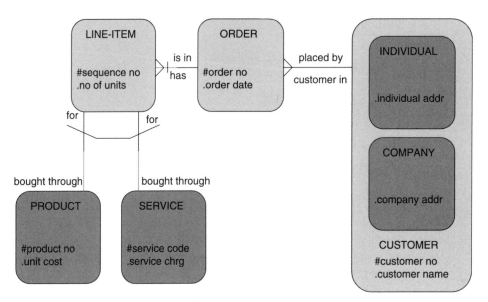

FIGURE 2-8   Barker model: customer purchases.

Entities and Attributes. Round-cornered rectangular boxes represent entities. Entity names appear inside the boxes at the top. Hyphens or spaces separate multiword names. Entity names are in the singular. Attribute names appear inside the entity boxes.

Sometimes Barker notation differentiates the kinds of attributes by marking them. A small open circle in front of an attribute name denotes an optional attribute; a small solid circle in front of the name marks a required attribute; a hash mark (#) in front of the name represents an attribute that participates in a unique identifier. However, Barker notation also accommodates all types of attributes by being marked with dots in front of them.

Relationships. Relationships are indicated with lines connecting pairs of entities. Each half of a relationship line may be solid or broken (dashed), with the solid half representing the mandatory nature of the relationship at that end and the dashed half indicating the optional nature of the relationship at the other end.

Many instances of an entity participating in the relationship is indicated by a crow's-foot on the relationship line at that end. The absence of a crow's-foot at an end indicates no more than one instance of that entity participating in the relationship.

Names. Naming conventions and symbols of relationships express relationships in a precise and understandable manner at each end. The Barker method has a unique way of expressing relationship names. Prepositions or prepositional phrases are used to name relationships; from such phrases you can make meaningful plain English sentences to describe the relationships. Note these phrases in Figure 2-8. For example, from the figure you can derive the relationships as follows:

Each customer may place one or more orders.
Each order must be placed by one and only one customer.

Cardinality/Optionality. As mentioned earlier, the bifurcation of a relationship gets expressed clearly, the two parts going in opposite directions. In a relationship half, the upper and lower boundaries of the maximum cardinalities are expressed by the presence or absence of the crow's-feet. A dashed line near an entity box denotes that the relationship is optional, meaning zero or more instances ("may be") participating in the relationship. On the other hand, a solid line near an entity box indicates that the relationship is mandatory, meaning at least one instance ("must be") participating in the relationship.

Constraints. The Barker method represents the "exclusive OR" with an arc across the corresponding two relationship lines. An arc indicates that each instance of one entity must or may be related to instances in one or more other entities, but not more than one. Refer to the arc in Figure 2-8 expressing the constraint that each line item must be for either one product or one service, but not both. Expressions for other types of relationship constraints do not exist in the Barker model.

Unique Identifiers. As you know, one or more attributes together make up the unique identifier for an entity. As mentioned earlier, hash marks (#) indicate attributes that are part of the unique identifier.

See Figure 2-8 and note the relationship between ORDER and LINE-ITEM. The unique identifier of LINE-ITEM is the combination of "sequence no" and the relationship "is in" one and only one ORDER. Note how this is indicated with a short line across the relationship line.

Supertypes and Subtypes. The Barker model represents subtypes as entity boxes within the supertype entity box. This elegant representation reinforces the concept that an instance of a subtype is an instance of the supertype and that subtypes and supertypes are not merely related entities. Also, this representation takes up less space on model diagrams.

This method represents only mutually exclusive subtypes. It does not allow overlapping subtypes. Also, subtypes are expected to be complete, that is, instances of the subtypes must account for all the instances of the supertype. In practice, however, this restriction gets overcome by adding an "OTHER" subtype entity to catch any remaining instances of the supertype.

Object-Role Modeling

G.M. Nijssen originally initiated this method that data modeling practitioners called NIAM (Nijssen's information analysis methodology). However, because many others got involved in its development and enhancement, the methodology became known with the more generalized name of natural language information analysis method. Many data modelers still use this method, now commonly known as object-role modeling (ORM).

In contrast with the methods explored until now, ORM takes a different approach for representing information. In ORM, the relationship or role is the primary modeling concept. You cannot depict entities independently apart from relationships. This method stands upon the notion that a model describes facts that includes entities, attributes, domains, and relationship—all together in combination.

Object-role modeling makes use of natural language extensively to render it more accessible to the domain experts and the user community in general. Nevertheless, it also has a great capacity to describe constraints and business rules.

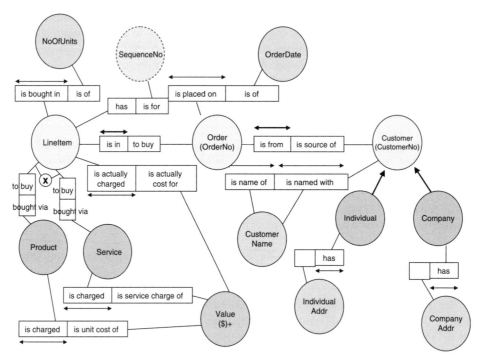

FIGURE 2-9 ORM model: customer purchases.

Figure 2-9 shows the model for our customer purchases example using the ORM technique. You will notice that this diagram is much more elaborate and detailed than diagrams using other modeling techniques. Study this figure more closely to follow the discussions about the components. Although the ORM model bases its portrayal mainly on the roles or relationships, for the sake of uniformity, we will discuss the components in the same order we adopted until now in discussing the other modeling techniques.

Entities and Attributes. An ellipse or a circle represents an entity. Our figure portrays entities with circles. Entity names appear inside the circles. Multiword names are shown without spaces. Entity names are in the singular. All names begin with a capital letter.

Circles also indicate attributes with the names of the attributes shown inside. Each attribute circle gets connected to the corresponding entity circle that it describes. Connection or relationship lines not only link entities to each other but also attach attributes to entities. Thus, in ORM you can ask the question: What is the kind of relationship an attribute has with an entity it describes?

The model records value domains explicitly as attribute definitions within separate circles, even for those attributes that are merely terms of reference. Attributes that have the same domains may be tied together with a common domain definition. Note the common definition of value (money) connected to the attributes representing unit cost of product, service charge for service, and actual cost for line item.

Relationships. Without specifying relationships per se, ORM presents the roles that are played by entities, attributes, and domains in the organization's data structure.

Nevertheless, these roles signify the relationships between entities. A set of adjacent boxes represents roles. In a two-way relationship, two adjacent boxes indicate the role, each box with a relationship name inside and connected to the appropriate entity using a solid line. Relationships need not just be binary; ORM permits tertiary and higher order relationships.

A quick note about the transformation of any model into a relational model for implementation: whereas other techniques allow entity representations to be directly transformed into relational tables, for ORM the portrayal of roles or relationships must be transformed into relational tables. The two or more parts of a relationship become columns in a relational table, each part serving as a foreign key.

Names. Verb phrases, usually containing "is" or "has," describe relationships. Sometimes a clever distinction gets established by using the past and present tenses for the verb phrases. Past tense signifies temporal relationships that happened at certain points of time; present term designates permanent relationships.

Cardinality/Optionality. In ORM, cardinality is meshed up with the unique existence of instances of a fact, relationship being a fact. Each instance of a fact comprises a single occurrence of each entity participating in the relationship. For example, each customer may be the source of one or more orders, each instance of a customer, being the source of an order, by definition, applies to one customer and one order. A double arrow indicates an entity's uniqueness for the relationship. In a one-to-many relationship, the arrowhead appears on the side closest to the "many" side; a bar appears over each half for a one-to-one relationship; the arrow crosses both halves of the relationship for many-to-many relationships. For a mandatory relationship, a solid circle next to the entity that is the subject of the fact designates the mandatory nature of the relationship.

Constraints. Circles linking relationships express constraints between relationships. An exclusion constraint, represented by an "x" in the circle, means that one or the other relationship may apply, but not both. Note this representation between the two roles of LineItem to Product and LineItem to Service. For an inclusion constraint, a dot replaces the "x" in the circle representing the constraint.

Unique Identifiers. Ellipses or circles using dashed or broken lines stand for unique identifiers or entity labels. Alternatively, identifiers may also be shown in parenthesis within the entity circle just below the entity name.

If two or more attributes are required to establish a unique identifier, a special symbol is used. Representation with a special symbol also applies to the need for relationships to establish uniqueness for an identity.

Supertypes and Subtypes. Apart from circles that signify a supertype, separate circles indicate the subtypes. A thick arrow points to the supertype from a subtype. For example, in the figure, note the representation of individual and company as subtypes for the supertype customer.

eXtensible Markup Language

This technique is not a data modeling method as such. Why then do we want to include this in our discussions at all? This is a method of representing data structures in text format by using specific tags or labels. Even though the method does not deal with data modeling in the strictest sense, it is a way of representing data structures. A data model describes data structures; XML provides a way of looking at data structures. Just this similarity alone warrants some discussion of XML in the context of data structures.

You must have heard of Hypertext Markup Language (HTML), which is used to describe pages to the World Wide Web. XML is similar to HTML. Both are subsets of the more generic language known as Standard Generalized Markup Language (SGML). While using these languages, a set of tags are inserted in the body of the text. When you go on the Internet, your browser software interprets the various HTML tags and displays the page properly on your computer screen. Hypertext Markup Language uses standard tags that can be correctly interpreted by any standard browser software.

On the other hand, XML allows users to define their own tags and allow the tags to be interpreted by specially written software. Because of this generality, XML and its tag system may be used to define data structures. Any group of XML users may define special tags to describe their own data structures.

Therefore, as part of the discussion here, we can use XML to describe the data structures for our customer purchases example. Figure 2-10 shows the XML representation for a customer purchase record with data.

You will notice that in the XML document, each tag is surrounded by the less-than and greater-than signs ($<$ and $>$). You will also note a number of different types of tags used. What do these tags mean and how are they to be interpreted? A document type declaration (DTD) defines the meaning of each tag. DTD defines tags using a set of elements. Thus, DTD code enables you to specify a data structure. An XML document contains the data; the DTD represents the data as a model. So, in a way, a DTD may be compared with

```
<?XML version="2.0"?>
<! --- **** Customer Purchases **** --- >
<ORDER>
        <PLACED-BY-CUSTOMER>
                <customer-no>123456</customer-no>
                <customer-name>ABC Electronics</customer-no>
        </PLACED-BY-CUSTOMER>
        <order-no>1122</order-no>
        <order-date>15 DEC 2006</order-date>
        <LINE-ITEM>
                <sequence-no>01</sequence-no>
                <no-of-units>80</no-of-units>
                <PRODUCT>
                        <unit-cost>995.00</unit-cost>
                </PRODUCT>
        </LINE-ITEM>
        <LINE-ITEM>
                <sequence-no>02</sequence-no>
                <no-of-units>1</no-of-units>
                <SERVICE>
                        <service-chrg>49.95</service-chrg>
                </SERVICE>
        </LINE-ITEM>
</ORDER>
```

FIGURE 2-10   XML representation: customer purchases.

```
<!DOCTYPE CUSTOMER-PURCHASES
[
<!ELEMENT ORDER (PLACED-BY-CUSTOMER, order-no, order-date,
LINE-ITEM*)>
        <!ELEMENT PLACED-BY-CUSTOMER (customer-no, customer-name)>
                <!ELEMENT customer-no (#PCDATA)>
                <!ELEMENT customer-name (#PCDATA)>
        <!ELEMENT order-no (#PCDATA)>
        <!ELEMENT order-date (#PCDATA)>
                <!ELEMENT LINE-ITEM (sequence-no, no-of-units)>
                        <!ELEMENT sequence-no (#PCDATA)>
                        <!ELEMENT no-of-units (#PCDATA)>
                        <!ELEMENT PRODUCT (unit-cost)>
                                <!ELEMENT unit-cost (#PCDATA)>
                        <!ELEMENT SERVICE (service-chrg)>
                        <!ELEMENT service-chrg (#PCDATA)>
]>
```

FIGURE 2-11   XML DTD: customer purchases.

any of the earlier data modeling techniques. Figure 2-11 displays the DTD for customer purchases. We will use this figure for our data model discussion.

Entities and Attributes. Notice all the elements defined in the DTD. Each element in the DTD refers to a piece of the whole structure. XML does not distinguish between entities and attributes while defining them as elements. All are defined as elements.

However, in some cases additional information about an element is given through one or more predicates. A predicate may add to the representation of either an entity or an attribute. Note the predicate PLACED_BY_CUSTOMER that amplifies the element CUSTOMER.

Relationships. Predicates attached to elements represent relationships. There is no other special way for denoting relationships.

Names. The same naming convention applies to all elements and predicates whether they represent entities, attributes, or relationships. XML does not allow spaces in names and it is case-sensitive. The case of a tag name in an element definition must be the same as used if the element had appeared as a predicate; the case of an element used in the XML document must be the same as it is in the DTD. All XML keywords must be in uppercase.

Cardinality/Optionality. The absence of any special characters following a predicate signifies that there must be exactly one instance of each of the predicate for each instance of the parent element. A question mark (?) following a predicate implies that it is not required. If it is followed by an asterisk (*), then the predicate is not required, however, if it occurs, it may have more than one instance. If it is followed by a plus sign (+), at least one instance is required, but it may have more than one.

Constraints. XML has no method for describing constraints between relationships.

Unique Identifiers. XML does not recognize and express any unique identifiers.

Supertypes and Subtypes. XML has no facility to identify subtypes. Special software would be needed to enforce supertype and subtype relationships.

Summary and Comments

In the foregoing discussions, we have reviewed six modeling techniques. Before we move to discuss another technique that is object-oriented, let us summarize what we have covered so far.

Chen Model. Being one of the earliest modeling techniques, the first version of the Chen model lacked some components to portray the various nuances of an organization's information requirements. However, later enhancements rectified these deficiencies.

Here are some comments on this model:

- It allows displaying of multiple inheritance and multiple type hierarchies; however, this multibox approach results in undue increase in the size of the model diagram.
- Separate symbols to each attribute and each relationship seem to produce clutter.
- The model does not clearly get across the fact that an instance of subtype is an instance of a supertype.

IE Model. Because two prominent authorities, Clive Finkelstein and James Martin, promulgated this method, it is still widely used. The two proponents complemented each other to produce a good technique.

The following are a few remarks about the IE model:

- It is reasonably concise and free from clutter.
- Notations for important components of attributes and unique identifiers are lacking.
- It has a compact approach to subtypes, easily understood by the nontechnical users.

IDEF1X Model. The symbols in this model do not clearly match and portray the necessary modeling concepts. Sometimes several symbols are needed to indicate a single concept. Particular situations need more than one set of symbols; the same set of symbols may have a different meaning depending on the context. For example, the symbol for optionality depends on the cardinality of the relationship. The solid circle symbol can mean different things depending on its setting.

With this background, here are a few comments:

- It is difficult to review an IDEF1X model with a nontechnical domain expert.
- It may be a good design tool for data modelers but is unduly hard for analysis with users.
- Making corrections and refining the model is not easy; one simple correction may involve changing many symbols.
- The multibox approach to subtypes and separate notation for each attribute and relationship use up extra room on the model diagram.

Barker Model. This modeling technique is ideally suited for requirement analysis with the domain experts. Several aspects distinguish this methodology making it more desirable than other techniques as a good communication tool with the users.

Here are a few remarks:

- Attributes are portrayed with indicators of their optionality.
- Subtypes are shown as entities inside other entities as opposed to the way of representing them as separate entities in other models.
- It permits "exclusive OR" constraints and expresses them better than other techniques.
- It has a unique and rigorous naming convention for relationships—relationship names are prepositions, not verbs.

ORM Model. Being perhaps the most versatile and most descriptive of the modeling techniques, ORM has extensive capabilities to describe objects and their roles. The model is not simply oriented toward entities and relationships. An object may be an entity, attribute, or a domain.

A few remarks:

- Ordinality and cardinality of attributes are treated in exactly the same way.
- It makes domains explicit, unlike flavors of entity/relationship modeling.
- It is much more detailed than most techniques resulting in model diagram becoming less aesthetic.
- The multibox approach for representing subtypes takes more room in the diagram.

XML Representation. As noted earlier, XML is not really a data modeling technique. Therefore, it lacks the ability to represent all the finer points of data structures and relationships. However, XML is a robust method for describing the essence of data structures and to serve as a template for data transmission.

The proper use of tags provides an excellent method to describe, organize, and communicate data structures. Although tags form the most apt tools, the responsibility and skill of database administrators are what make the tools work.

UNIFIED MODELING LANGUAGE

Unified Modeling Language is more an object modeling technique than a data modeling technique. As you have seen, most of the data modeling techniques deal with entities; UML, on the other hand, models object classes. However, modeling object classes resembles entity modeling. To this extent, UML may be adopted for modeling data.

Data Modeling Using UML

Classes or entity objects in UML compare well with entities as noted in all the modeling techniques discussed earlier. Similarly, associations in UML are equivalent to relationships. In addition to the ability to represent entities in class diagrams, UML can also

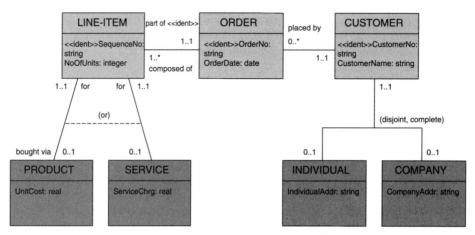

FIGURE 2-12 UML class diagram: customer purchases.

describe the behavior of each object. We will briefly review some of the other abilities in later sections. First, let us consider UML as a data modeling technique.

Class Diagram. Figure 2-12 shows the class diagram for the customer purchases example. This diagram looks similar to the model diagrams in the techniques discussed earlier. Note the rectangular boxes and lines joining them.

Entities and Attributes. Object classes in UML denote entities. A square-cornered rectangular box represents an object class. Usually, the box has three divisions: the top part contains the class name, the middle section has a list of attributes, and the bottom part, if present, shows descriptions of its behavior. Behavior descriptions are generally in pseudocode or some object-oriented language. Multiword names are shown without spaces. Entity names are in the singular. All names usually begin with a capital letter.

One or more of the following parameters qualify the attributes:

Stereotype: provides annotation such as ≪ident≫ indicating attributes that are part of a unique identifiers.

Visibility: shows to which classes the attribute must be visible while being implemented, (+) indicating that attribute must be visible to all, and (#) denoting that the attribute must be visible only to the subtypes of this class.

Type: indicates the data type (character, string, number, etc.).

Initial value: specifies a default value.

Multiplicity: defines the number of different values the attribute may have.

Relationships. In the object-oriented realm, associations denote relationships. Textual phrases convey information about relationships.

Names. A simple verb phrase can name a relationship completely. A triangle next to the name indicates how you read the name. Also, roles defined at each end may be used to describe the part played by the class in the association.

Cardinality/Optionality. Lower and upper limit symbols represent optionality and cardinality. Lower limits of 0 or 1 indicate optionality; 0 for optional and 1 for mandatory condition. The upper limit, indicating cardinality, may be an asterisk (*) for "more than one" or "many," or an explicit number, or a set of numbers, or a range. The indicator strings shown in the figure have the following meanings:

0..*   may be zero, one, or more
1..*   may be one or more
0..1   may be zero or 1
1..1   must be exactly one

Composed of/Part of. Additional symbols denote where each object in one class *is composed of* one or more objects in the second class. Each object in the second class must be *part of* one and only object in the first class. A diamond symbol is placed on the relationship line next to the parent or "composed of" class to indicate actions on the connected classes. If the association is mandatory, a solid diamond symbolizes deletion of all children classes when the corresponding parent class gets deleted. If the association is optional, an open diamond denotes that the parent class may be deleted without affecting the children classes. Unified Modeling Language does not address the restricted rule in which deletion of the parent is not permitted if children classes exist.

Constraints. A dashed or broken line between two relationship lines represents a constraint. Note the dashed line between the relationship lines connecting Product and Service to LineItem. Annotations on these dashed lines indicate the type of constraint as follows:

Annotation {xor} or {or}: Each instance of the base entity must be or may be related to either an instance of one entity or an instance of the other entity, but not to instances of both.
Annotation {ior}: Each instance of the base entity must be or may be related to either an instance of one entity or to an instance of the other entity or to instances of both.

Unique Identifiers. In object-orientation, unique identifiers are not generally indicated. This representation will be part of modeling that involves behavior of objects. When the behavior of objects in a class needs to locate a specific instance of another class, the attribute used to locate the instance will be shown next to the entity that needs it.

However, stereotype parameters described above may be used to designate attributes and relationship that make up unique identifiers. Refer to Figure 2-12 and note the marks ≪ident≫ in front of attribute names.

Supertypes and Subtypes. Separate rectangular boxes represent subtypes, each connected to the corresponding supertype box by relationship lines. Each instance of a subtype is an instance of a supertype.

When each instance of the supertype must be an instance of one of the subtypes (complete) and when an instance of a supertype may not be an instance of more than one subtype, as seen in Figure 2-12, the supertype/subtype relationship is marked {disjoint, complete}. UML does not force this constraint. The subtype structure could be {overlapping, incomplete} or any other combinations of the other two.

UML for Data Modeling: Comments. Unified Modeling Language has several advantages over the other data modeling techniques. The method provides a solid basis for design. UML is essentially a design tool. Many of its components and representations lack the generality and simplicity for use as a communication tool with domain experts.
Here are a few comments:

- Attributes may be expressed in greater detail.
- The idea of a small flag to contain descriptive text enhances representation of difficult business rules governing relationships.
- Constraints between relationships that could not be expressed in other techniques may be adequately denoted in this method.
- UML methodology for optionality and cardinality is quite expansive to accommodate complex upper limits.
- It allows overlapping and incomplete subtypes.
- It permits multiple inheritance and multiple type hierarchies.
- It seems to contain too many unnecessary symbols for distinguishing kinds of relationships.
- The handling of unique identifiers is incomplete.

UML in the Development Process

In the 1980s and early 1990s, several methods and tools appeared in the industry for analysis, design, and implementation of object-oriented systems. UML attempts to unify, consolidate, and enhance these various techniques into one language for the entire system development process.

One aspect of the system development process deals with the modeling of the data structures and relationships that would support the system. However important, this is just one part of the entire development. Modeling the data content alone does not constitute the whole development. You have to model how the various data structures would be used and produce information to run the many business processes.

We have seen the usefulness of UML as an approach to modeling the data structures and relationships by means of class diagram. In this section, we will trace the application of UML to other aspects of system development. You need to model how the system and how the data in the system will be used. You need to model the functionality to be provided by the system. Let us follow the use and application of UML in the complete development life cycle to a reasonable extent.

Use case diagrams illustrate the system's functions. Once the functions are explored and modeled, object class diagrams describe the relevant data structures and relationships. We have already discussed class diagrams at some length. Integration diagrams provide models of how groups of objects collaborate in some function or behavior. A sequence diagram, one form of an interaction diagram, portrays the sequence in which messages flow and behaviors ensue. A collaboration diagram displays the layout of objects showing how they are statically connected and interact with one another. Another useful tool to describe the behavior of a system is the set of state diagrams, especially

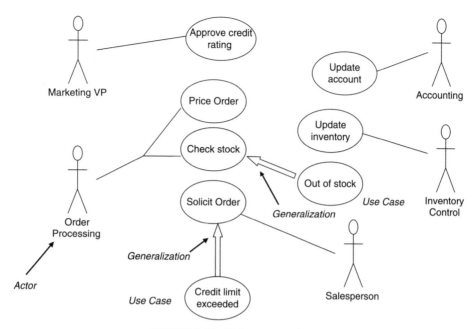

FIGURE 2-13 UML use case diagram.

the behavior of objects across use cases. When you need to describe workflow, particularly where behavior has much parallel processing, activity diagrams come in handy. Closer to deployment and system implementation are deployment diagrams and component diagrams. These physical diagrams model the implementation features.

We have mentioned some of the important tools in UML to model the entire system development life cycle. However, as data modeling is the primary thrust of this textbook, process modeling facilities in UML are not within our scope. Nevertheless, in the next few sections, we will present an example of each of the leading techniques in UML. However, the physical diagrams are excluded from our discussions.

Use Case Diagram. Figure 2-13 shows an example of a use case diagram.

Note the role of actors and their behaviors. Notice the functions represented in the diagram. Observe how generalizations and extensions are used and shown in the diagram.

Sequence Diagram. In Figure 2-14, you may review an example of a UML sequence diagram.

Note the objects shown as boxes at the top of dashed vertical lines. These lines are called the lifelines of the object. Each lifeline symbolizes the life of the object during the specific interaction. Notice the arrows between two lifelines representing the messages.

Collaboration Diagram. Figure 2-15 displays an example of a collaboration diagram.

In this version of an interaction diagram, sequence numbers indicate the order of execution of the messages. More spatial arrangement of a collaboration diagram enables it to display other components and explanations more easily.

State Diagram. State diagrams may be used to depict the behavior of a system. You may want to draw a state diagram for each of the significant objects in a system. Each state

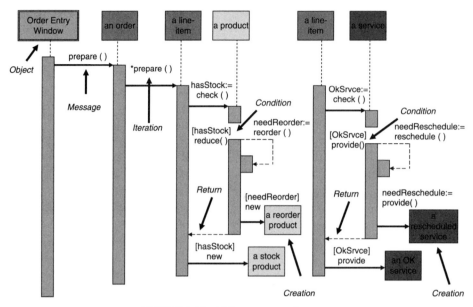

FIGURE 2-14 UML sequence diagram.

diagram would describe all possible states for an object resulting from various events that reach the object.

State diagrams come in different flavors. Figure 2-16 shows one example of a state diagram.

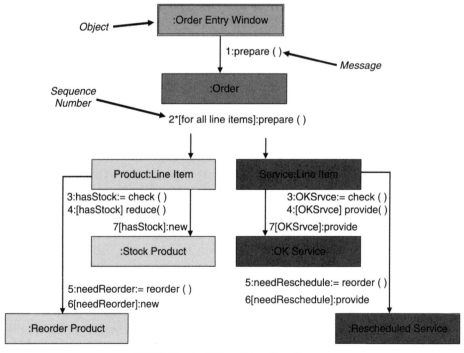

FIGURE 2-15 UML collaboration diagram.

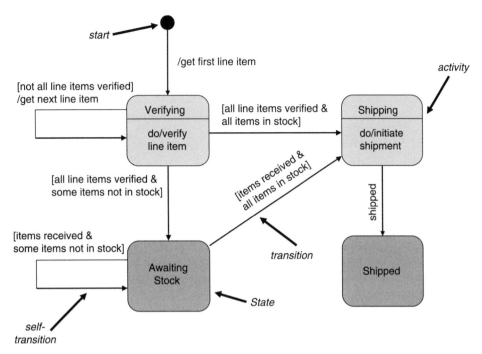

FIGURE 2-16   UML state diagram.

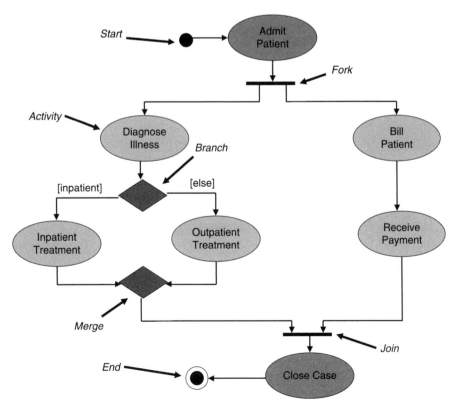

FIGURE 2-17   UML activity diagram.

Activity Diagram. Figure 2-17 illustrates the concept of an activity diagram. You may want to use activity diagrams for analyzing a use case, understanding a workflow, working with a multithreaded application, or for describing a complex sequential algorithm.

Note the core symbol for an activity state or activity in the form of an elongated circle. Note the various junctions of fork, merge, join, and branch. Note also the start and end points in an activity diagram signifying the range of the activities.

CHAPTER SUMMARY

- A data model defines the rules for the data structures and relationships. Different modeling techniques work with varying structuring rules and constraints.
- There are four modeling approaches: semantic modeling, relational modeling, entity-relationship modeling, and binary modeling.
- The Peter Chen (E-R) modeling technique is still widely used even after three decades. It can represent business entities, their attributes, and the relationships among entities. Enhanced E-R technique includes representations of supertype and subtype entities.
- The information engineering modeling technique, developed by Clive Finkelstein of Australia and enhanced by James Martin of the United States, is another popular methodology. A data model created using this technique is fairly concise.
- Many United States government agencies use the IDEF1X modeling technique. Although a good design methodology for data modelers, this technique produces models that are not easily intelligible to users.
- Richard Barker's modeling technique has ways of differentiating between types of entities and types of attributes. A data model created using this method is well suited for use as a communication tool with the users.
- Object-role modeling techniques have been perfected. The role or relationship is the primary modeling concept. ORM can describe constraints and business rules well. Perhaps this is the most versatile and descriptive of all techniques.
- Although XML is not exactly a data modeling methodology, a few data modelers use XML for modeling purposes. However, the proper use of tags provides an excellent method to describe, organize, and communicate data structures.
- Unified Modeling Language is an object-modeling methodology. UML may be used for data modeling. Its strength lies in the ability to represent application functions as well. UML consolidates techniques for modeling data and processes into one unified language for the entire system development life cycle.

REVIEW QUESTIONS

1. True or false:
   A. In semantic modeling approach, the concept of type plays a significant role.
   B. The earliest version of the Chen (E-R) modeling technique provided for maximum and minimum cardinalities.
   C. The IE modeling method has no provision to show attributes.
   D. The IDEF1X model displays attributes and identifiers outside the entity boxes.

    E. Richard Barker's notation does not distinguish between different kinds of attributes.

    F. In ORM, the relationship or role is the primary modeling concept.

    G. XML has very limited data modeling capabilities.

    H. Enhanced E-R modeling technique includes supertypes and subtypes.

    I. The IDEF1X model is easily understood by nontechnical users.

    J. UML class diagrams are suitable for data modeling.

2. Explain what is meant by semantic modeling. How does the concept of type play an important role in this method?

3. Describe how the E-R model represents entities. Draw a partial E-R model diagram to show examples of entities.

4. How does the E-R modeling technique handle generalization and specialization of entity types? Give two examples.

5. Describe how the IE method represents cardinality and optionality in relationships. Give an example to illustrate this.

6. Explain the representation of relationships in the IDEF1X modeling technique. How would you show the relationship between CUSTOMER and ORDER in this model?

7. How does the Richard Barker's method represent the "exclusive OR" constraint? Give an example.

8. How are attributes represented in the ORM technique? Draw a partial ORM model showing the attributes for STUDENT and COURSE.

9. Draw a UML class diagram for the student registration example shown in Figure 2-2. Describe the components.

10. Name any four types of diagrams in UML used in the system development process. Give examples for two of the types of diagrams.

II

DATA MODELING
FUNDAMENTALS

3

ANATOMY OF A DATA MODEL

CHAPTER OBJECTIVES

- Provide a refresher on data modeling at different information levels
- Present a real-world case study
- Display data model diagrams for the case study
- Scrutinize and analyze the data model diagrams
- Arrive at the steps for creating the conceptual data model
- Provide an overview of logical and physical models

In Chapter 1, we covered the basics of the data modeling process. We discussed the need for data modeling and showed how a data model represents the information requirements of an organization. Chapter 1 described data models at different information levels. Although an introductory chapter, it even discussed the steps for building a data model. Chapter 1 has given you a comprehensive overview of fundamental data modeling concepts.

As preparation for further study, Chapter 2 introduced the various data modeling approaches. In that chapter, we discussed several data modeling techniques and tools, evaluating each and comparing one to the other. Some techniques are well suited as a communication tool with the domain experts and others are more slanted toward the database practitioners for use as a database construction blueprint. Of the techniques covered there, entity-relationship (E-R) modeling and Unified Modeling Language (UML) are worth special attention mainly because of their wide acceptance. In future discussions, we will adopt these two methodologies, especially the E-R technique, for describing and creating data models.

In this chapter, we will get deeper into the overall data modeling process. For this purpose, we have selected a real-world case study. You will examine the data model for

Data Modeling Fundamentals. By Paulraj Ponniah
Copyright © 2007 John Wiley & Sons, Inc.

a real-world situation, analyze it, and derive the steps for creating the data model. We intend to make use of E-R and UML techniques for the case study. By looking at the modeling process for the case study, you will understand a practical approach on how to apply the data modeling steps in practice.

First, let us understand how to examine a data model, what components to look for, and learn about its composition. In particular, we will work on the composition of a conceptual data model. Then, we will move on to the case study and present the data model diagrams. We will proceed to scrutinize the data model diagrams and review them, component by component. We will examine the anatomy of a data model.

This examination will lead us into the steps that will produce a data model. In Chapter 1, you had a glimpse of the steps. Here the discussion will be more intense and broad. You will learn how each set of components is designed and created. Finally, you will gain knowledge of how to combine and put all the components together in a clear and understandable data model diagram.

DATA MODEL COMPOSITION

Many times so far we have reiterated that a data model must act as a means of communication with the domain experts. For a data modeler, the data model is your vehicle for verbalizing the information requirements with the user groups. You have to walk through the various components of a data model and explain how the individual components and the data model as a whole represent the information requirements of the organization. First, you need to point out each individual component. Then you should be describing the relationships. After that, you show the subtle elements. Overall, you have to get the confirmation from the domain experts that the data model truly represents their information requirements.

How can you accomplish all of this? In this section, we will study the method for scrutinizing and examining a data model. We will learn what to look for and how to describe a data model to the domain experts. We will adopt a slightly unorthodox approach. Of course, we will start with a description of the set of information requirements. We will note the various business functions and the data use for the functions. However, instead of going through the steps for creating a data model for the set of information requirements, we will present the completed data model. Using the data model, we will try to describe it as if we are communicating with the domain experts. After that, we will try to derive the steps of how to create the data model. We will accomplish this by using a comprehensive case study. So, let us proceed with the initial procedure for reviewing the set of components of a data model.

Models at Different Levels

You will recall the four information levels in an organization. Data models are created at these four information levels. We went through the four types of data models: external data model, conceptual data model, logical data model, and physical data model. We also reasoned out the need for these four types of data models.

The four types of data models must together fulfill the purposes of data modeling. At one end of the development process for a data system is the definition and true representation of the organization's data. This representation has to be readable and understandable so that the data modelers can easily communicate with the domain experts. At the other end of the development process is the implementation of the data system. In order to do this, we need a blueprint with sufficient technical details about the data. The four types of data models address these two separate challenges. Let us quickly revisit the four types of data models.

Conceptual Data Model. A conceptual data model is the highest level of abstraction to represent the information requirements of an organization. At this highest level, the primary goal is to make the representation clear and comprehensible to the domain experts. Clarity and simplicity dictate the underlying construct of a conceptual data model. Details of data structures, software features, and hardware considerations must be totally absent in this type of data model.

Essentially, the data model provides a sufficiently high-level overview of the basic business objects about which data must be stored and available in the final data system. The model depicts the basic characteristics of the objects and indicates the various relationships among the objects. Despite its simplicity and clarity, the data model must be complete with all the necessary information requirements represented without any exceptions. It should be a global data model for the organization. If ease of use and clarity are prime goals, the conceptual data model must be constructed with simple generic notations or symbols that could be intuitively understood by the user community.

External Data Model. At the conceptual level, the data model represents the information requirements for the whole organization. This means that the conceptual data model symbolizes the information requirements for the entire set of user groups in an organization. Consider each user group. Each user group has a specific set of information requirements. It is as if a user group looks at the total conceptual data model from an external point of view and indicates the pieces of the conceptual data model that are of interest to it. Then that part of the conceptual data model is a partial external data model specific for that user group. What about the other user groups? Each of the other groups has its own partial data model.

The external data model is the set of all the partial models of the entire set of user groups in an organization. What happens when you combine all the partial models and form an aggregate? The aggregate will then become the global conceptual model. Thus, the partial models are a high-level abstraction of the information requirements of individual user groups. Similar to the conceptual data model, the external data model is free from all complexities about data structures and software and hardware features. Each partial model serves as a means of communication with the relevant user group.

Logical Data Model. The logical data model brings data modeling closer to implementation. Here the type of database system to be implemented has a bearing on the construction of the data model. If you are implementing a relational database system, the logical data model takes one specific form. If it is going to be a hierarchical or network database system, the form and composition of the logical data model differs. Nevertheless, still considerations of specific DBMS (particular database software) and hardware are kept out.

As mentioned earlier in Chapter 1, if you are implementing a relational database system, your logical model consists of two-dimensional tables called relations with columns and rows. In the relational convention, data content is perceived in the form of tables or relations. Relationships among the tables are established and indicated through logical links using foreign key columns. More details on foreign keys will follow later on.

Physical Data Model. A physical data model is far removed from the purview of domain experts and user groups. It has little use as a means of communication with them. At this information level, the primary purpose of the data model is to serve as a construction blueprint, so it has to contain complex and intricate details of data structures, relationships, and constraints. The features and capabilities of the selected DBMS have enormous impact on the physical data model. The model must comply with the restrictions and the general framework of the database software and the hardware environment where the database system is being implemented.

A physical data model consists of details of how the database gets implemented in secondary storage. You will find details of file structures, file organizations, blocking within files, storage space parameters, special devices for performance improvements, and so on.

Conceptual Model: Review Procedure

In this chapter, we are going to concentrate mainly on the conceptual data model. Once we put together the conceptual data model correctly, we can arrive at the lower level models by adopting standard transformation techniques. Therefore, understanding conceptual modeling ranks higher in importance.

In Chapter 1, we introduced the components of a conceptual data model and reviewed some examples. You know the main parts of the model, and that all the parts hang together in a model diagram. In this chapter, we intend to review conceptual data model diagrams in greater detail. We will be reviewing model diagrams drawn using E-R and UML techniques.

Let us say we are presented with a conceptual data model diagram. How could we go about scrutinizing the diagram and understanding what the diagram signifies? What are the information requirements represented by the diagram? What do the components signify? Are there any constraints? If so, how are they shown in the diagram? On the whole, how will the domain experts understand the diagram and confirm that it is a true representation?

In Chapter 1, you noted the various symbols used to represent data model components. Chapter 2 expanded the meaning of the notations as prescribed in various modeling techniques. At this time, let us formulate a systematic approach to reviewing a data model diagram. Let us consider an E-R data model diagram. The systematic approach would render itself to be adopted for other modeling techniques as well. We will apply the formulated systematic approach to the data model diagrams to be presented in the next section for the case study.

First and foremost, we need to make a list of all the various notations used in the diagram and the exact nature of the symbols. What does each notation signify? What does it represent? What is the correlation between an element in the real-world information requirements and its representation in the data model diagram? Essentially, a database contains data about the business entities or objects of an organization. What are the business entities for the organization? So, we look for the representations of business entities or objects in the data model diagram. The business entities in a company are all connected in some way or other. Customers place orders. Clients buy at auctions. Passengers make reservations on airline flights. The business objects denoting customers and orders are related. Similarly, the business objects of passengers and flights are related. Therefore, the next logical step in the review of a data model diagram would involve the examination of relationships among objects. Pursuing this further, we can formulate a systematic approach to the examination and description of a data model.

Let us summarize these steps:

Symbols and Meanings. Study the entire data model diagram. Note the symbols and their meanings.

Entity Types. Observe and examine all the entity types or objects displayed, one by one.

Generalization/Specialization. Notice if any superset and subsets are present. If they are shown, examine the nature and relationships between each group of subsets and their superset.

Relationships. Note all the relationship lines connecting entity types. Examine each relationship. Note the cardinalities and any constraints.

Attributes. Inspect all the attributes of each entity type. Determine their meanings.

Identifiers. Check the identifier for each entity type. Verify the validity and uniqueness of each identifier.

Constraints. Scrutinize the entire diagram for any representations of constraints. Determine the implication of each constraint.

High-Level Description. Provide an overall description of the representations.

Conceptual Model: Identifying Components

Before proceeding to the comprehensive case study in the next section, let us take a simple small conceptual data model diagram. We will study the diagram and examine its components using the systematic approach formulated in the previous section. This will prepare you to tackle the larger and more comprehensive model diagrams of the case study. Figure 3-1 shows the conceptual data model diagram for a magazine distributor.

Let us examine the conceptual data model diagram using a systematic approach.

Symbols and Meanings. The model diagram represents the information requirements using the E-R modeling technique. Note the square-cornered boxes; these represent the entity types. You find six of them indicating that information relates to six business objects. Observe the lines connecting the various boxes. A line connecting two boxes indicates that the business objects represented by those two boxes are related; that is, the instances within one box are associated with instances within the other. The diamond or rhombus placed on a relationship line denotes the nature of the association. Also, note the indicators as a pair of parameters at either end of a relationship line. These are cardinality indicators for the relationship.

Notice the ovals branching out from each entity boxes. These ovals or ellipses embody the inherent characteristics or attributes for the particular entity type. These ovals contain the names of the attributes. Note that the names in certain ovals for each entity type are

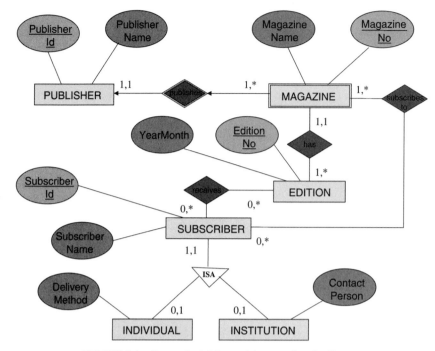

FIGURE 3-1 Conceptual data model: magazine distributor.

underscored. The attributes for each box with underscored names form the identifier for
that entity type.

In the model diagram, you will observe two subset entity types as specializations of the
supertype entity types. Although the initial version of the E-R model lacked provision for
indicating supersets and subsets, later enhancements included these representations.

Entity Types. Look at the square-cornered boxes in the data model diagram closely. In
each box, the name of the entity type appears. Notice how, by convention, these names are
printed in singular and usually in uppercase letters. Hyphens separate the words in multiword names. What does each entity type box represent? For example, the entity type box
PUBLISHER symbolizes the complete set of publishers dealing with this magazine distri-
buting company. You can imagine the box as containing a number of points each of which
is an instance of the entity type—each point indicating a single publisher.

Notice the name of one entity type MAGAZINE enclosed in a double-bordered box.
This is done to mark this entity type distinctly in the diagram. MAGAZINE is a dependent
entity type; its existence depends on the existence of the entity type PUBLISHER. What
do we mean by this? For an instance of the entity type MAGAZINE to exist or be present
in the database, a corresponding instance of the entity type PUBLISHER must already
exist in the database. Entity types such as MAGAZINE are known as weak entity types;
entity types such as PUBLISHER are called strong entity types.

Generalization/Specialization. Notice the entity type boxes for INDIVIDUAL and
INSTITUTION. These are special cases of the entity type SUBSCRIBER. Some subscribers are individuals and others are institutional subscribers. It appears that the data model

wants to distinguish between the two types of entities. Therefore, these two types of subscribers are removed out and shown separately. INDIVIDUAL and INSTITUTION are subtypes of the supertype SUBSCRIBER. When we consider attributes, we will note some of the reasons for separating out subtypes. Note also that an instance of the supertype is an instance of exactly one or the other of the two subtypes.

Observe how the connections are made to link the subtypes to the supertype and what kinds of symbols are used to indicate generalization and specialization. The kinds of symbols vary in the different CASE tools from various vendors.

Relationships. Note the direct relationships among the various entity types. The relationship lines indicate which pairs of entity types are directly related. For example, publishers publish magazines; therefore, the entity types PUBLISHER and MAGAZINE are connected by a relationship line. Find all the other direct relationships: MAGAZINE with EDITION, SUBSCRIBER with MAGAZINE, SUBSCRIBER with EDITION.

The model diagram shows two more relationship lines. These are between the supertype SUBSCRIBER and each of the subtypes INDIVIDUAL and INSTITUTION. Observe the special symbols on these relationship lines indicating generalization and specialization.

The names within the diamonds on the relationship lines denote the nature of the relationships. Whenever the model diagram intends to indicate the nature of the relationships, verbs or verb phrases are shown inside the diamonds. For example, the verb "publishes" indicates the act of publishing in the relationship between PUBLISHER and MAGAZINE. However, some versions of the data model consider relationships as objects in their own right. In these versions, relationship names shown inside the diamonds are nouns. Sometimes these would be concatenations of the two entity type names, for example, something like the compound word publisher-magazine.

Let us consider the cardinality and optionality depicted in the relationships. The second parameter in the pair indicates the cardinality; that is, how many occurrences of one entity type may be associated with how many of occurrences of the other entity type. The first parameter denotes the optionality; that is, whether the association of occurrences are optional or mandatory. The business rules dictate the assignment of cardinality and optionality parameters to relationships. By reviewing these parameters, you can know the business rules governing the relationships.

Figure 3-2 lists all the relationships and their cardinalities and optionalities. Study the interpretation of each pair of parameters and the business rule each pair represents in the data model diagram.

Attributes. Review the attributes indicated for each entity type. Because this is a simple example just to illustrate the examination of a data model, only a few attributes are shown. In the real world, many more attributes for each type will be present. A database is simply a storehouse of values for all the attributes of all the entity types.

Each attribute name is shown in the noun form within an oval. Usually, they are specified in mixed case, compound words being separated by hyphens. However, some conventions allow multiword names to be written together with no spaces or hyphens in-between; the separation is done by capitalizing each word in a multiword name.

An E-R diagram does not indicate whether values for a particular attribute are mandatory or optional. In other words, from the diagram you cannot infer if every instance of entity type must have values for a specific attribute.

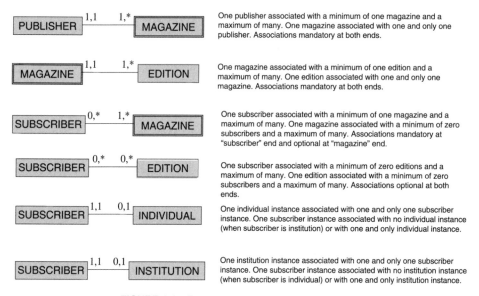

FIGURE 3-2 Relationships: cardinality/optionality.

As this is a conceptual data model at the highest level of abstraction, the model diagram does not specify the size, data type, format, and so on for the attributes. Those specifications will be part of the next lower level data models.

Identifiers. Although the inventor of the E-R modeling technique recognized the role of attributes in forming unique identifiers for entity types, he did not provide any special notation to indicate identifiers. The model diagrams would show identifiers as one or more attributes with oval symbols and spouting out of entity type boxes.

Later enhanced versions of the E-R modeling technique indicate identifiers by underscoring the attribute names. For example, PublisherId indicates an identifier.

Note the identifier for the weak entity type MAGAZINE. Its identifier consists of two attributes: the identifier PublisherId of the strong entity type PUBLISHER concatenated with its own identifier MagazineNo. This indicates the dependency of the weak entity type on the strong entity type for identifying individual occurrences of MAGAZINE.

Constraints. The "exclusive OR" is a common case of a relationship constraint. With this constraint, one instance of a base entity type must be related to instances with one other entity, but with not more than one entity. The E-R modeling technique has no provision to signify the "exclusive OR" constraint.

Nevertheless, in our data model diagram, we do not see any entity type with relationship lines connecting to more than one other entity type. Therefore, the "exclusive OR" situation does not arise in this case.

High-Level Description. After scrutinizing and studying the data model diagram, what can we say about the real-world information requirements it portrays? What overall remarks can we make about the magazine distribution business and its data requirements?

The following few comments apply:

- The organization distributes magazines from different publishers. One publisher may be publishing more than one of the magazines being distributed. No magazine can exist without a publisher.
- Magazine editions are distributed. Any particular edition relates to one and only one magazine. In the initial stage before publication of editions, data about a magazine may be set up to get it started.
- Subscribers subscribe to magazines. A subscriber may subscribe to one or more magazines. On the other hand, a magazine may be subscribed to by one or more subscribers.
- A subscriber may be an individual or an institution, but not both.
- Subscribers receive the appropriate magazine editions. This is the distribution or fulfillment of editions.

CASE STUDY

We derived a method for examining and studying a data model. Then we applied the method to a simple data model and studied the model. Now we want to expand our study to a larger, more complex set of information requirements that approximate real-world situations to a great extent. We will take a comprehensive case study and present the data model diagrams using two modeling techniques: E-R and UML. The data models will be based on the set of information requirements for the case study.

We will then use the method derived earlier and examine the data models. Our examination will result in a description of what information requirements are represented in the models. The examination and study themselves will prompt us into steps that are necessary to create the data models. We will walk through these for creating the data models and learn the process of designing and creating the data models.

First, the description of the case study.

Description

The case study deals with a world-class, upscale auctioneer known as Barnaby's. The company finds buyers for rare and expensive art and other objects. These objects or property items range anywhere from Van Gogh's multimillion-dollar paintings to distinguished 100-karat diamonds owned by princesses. The owners or dealers of the property items who bring them to Barnaby's for auctions are known as consignors. The buyers purchase the property items by bidding for them at the respective auctions.

Barnaby's collects a commission from the consignors for their services and a buyer's premium from the buyers for making the property items available for sale at auctions. The commission and the buyer's premium are calculated as percentages of the selling price on a published sliding scale.

Many of the consigned property items are one-of-a-kind; there are no two versions of Van Gogh's *Irises*. Incidentally, this single 16″ by 20″ painting has been sold for more than $40 million at auction. Barnaby's unique service extends to appraising a property item, ensuring that it is genuine and not a fake, and suggesting high and low estimates of its value. For this purpose, Barnaby's has a band of world-class experts in each area, for example, in contemporary paintings, Chinese jade, Florentine vases, European jewelry, and in many, many more similar specialties. The company has more than 100 such specialty departments.

Barnaby's runs its worldwide business from its headquarters in New York and its main branch offices in leading cities in the United Kingdom, Europe, Asia, Africa, and Australia. Consignors can bring their property items to any of the worldwide offices. The company holds its auctions at nearly 25 sites in various parts of the world. A property item may be transferred from the office where it was consigned to the auction site where it is likely to sell and fetch the best price.

A property item that is received at a particular Barnaby's office moves through various stages until it is sold at an auction and delivered to the buyer. At each stage, Barnaby's employees perform various functions to move the property item toward sale. Data is required or collected at these stages for the employees to perform the functions and conduct the company's business. Our modeling task is to capture these data requirements in the form of conceptual data models that can be used for communicating with the domain experts and getting their confirmation.

Let us record the different stages in the movement of property items and arrive at the set of information requirements that need to be modeled.

Initial Receipting. The property item consigned for sale arrives at Barnaby's. The company's receiving department examines the property item, collects basic information such as ownership, high and low estimates of the value as determined by the consignor, the reserve price below which consignor does not want to sell, and notes down the condition of the property item. The receiving department prints a formal receipt and forwards it to the consignor. Many times consignors send more than one property item, and a single receipt may cover all these several items.

The receiving employee notes down the particular property department that will handle the property for inclusion in their auctions. The employee then transfers the property item to that department. If more than one property item will be consigned together, the employee transfers the different items to the various appropriate departments.

Appraisal. The property department receives the property from the receiving department, acknowledges the transfer, and examines the condition of the property. If the property item needs some minor repairs, the department will transfer the property item to the restoration department or to an outside restorer. The transfer is also documented. On the other hand, if the department feels that the property item is not saleable, the department will return it to the consignor with a note saying it has "no sale value" (NSV).

The department experts then scrutinize the object very carefully, verify its authenticity, compile its provenance, and, if necessary, revise the high and low estimates. If the reserve price is not at the right level, the experts discuss this with the consignor and revise it.

If the property department in the office of original receipting thinks that a property item would sell better at an auction at a different site, then the department will transfer the property item to that site for further processing.

Restoration. Those property items needing restoration or repairs are acknowledged based on the transfer documents sent from the property department. After restoration, a property item is sent back to the original department for further action.

Restoration and repairs takes several forms and may be done at different levels of severity. Provision is made to get the restoration done at the proper places, within the company or outside.

Cataloguing. This function prepares a property item to be included in a sale catalogue and be ready for sale at an auction. The department cataloguers add catalogue texts and other information to the property item. The data added includes: a proper description of the property item, firmed up high and low estimates, confirmed reserve price, edited provenance information, and any additional text that will help in the sale of the item.

At this stage, the property item is ready to be included in a particular auction. The property department checks their inventory to ensure that all catalogued items are there, readily available, and in top condition for sale.

Sale Assignment. An auction sale consists of several lots that are assigned to be sold at that auction. Usually, an auction runs into more than one session. Sale lots are assigned to be sold in specific sessions. Thus, sale assignment refers to the assignment of a lot to a particular sale and session.

The property department assigns a lot number to each catalogued property item. It then includes that lot in a specific session of a particular auction sale. Each sale lot is an object originally receipted as a property item on the initial receipt. A link, therefore, exists between a sale lot and the initial receipt and item on the receipt.

The catalogue subscription department prints attractive catalogues for every sale and mails them to regular subscribers or for one-time purchasers of catalogues. Potentially, buyers and consignors are part of catalogue subscribers and one-time buyers of catalogues.

Sale at Auction. Buyers may purchase lots by bidding for them from the auction floor or by calling the auction staff during the auction or by sending in absentee bids in advance. The highest bidder gets the sale lot. The auctioneer accepts the highest bid by lowering down his or her gavel or hammer. The hammer price is the sale price for the sold lot. This price forms the basis for consignor commission and buyer's premium.

In order for a prospective buyer to participate in an auction, the buyer must first register for the auction and obtain a paddle. A paddle is small flat device with a handle like a ping-pong racquet. The paddles are numbered with a number prominently painted on each paddle. Prospective buyers raise their paddles during the auction to indicate that they are bidding for the lot. A sold lot at an auction is thus associated with a specific paddle number in that auction. A paddle number is also assigned to each absentee bid.

After a lot has been assigned to a sale, these are the alternative disposal options: the assigned lot may be withdrawn from the sale by the consignor for valid reasons or questions of authenticity; the lot may be sold to the highest bidder; the lot may be passed and withdrawn from the auction because of total lack of interest by potential buyers; the lot may be "bought in" (BI) by the auctioneer on behalf of the consignor because the highest bid for it did not reach the reserve price.

Processing of Sold Items. Sold lots are delivered to the buyer using the requested shipment method. For cash sales, money is collected before shipment. This includes lot hammer price due to the consignor and buyer's premium due to Barnaby's. The company bills those buyers purchasing on credit and processes the amounts through Buyers Receivable Accounts.

The amounts due to the consignors are handled through Consignor Payable Accounts. Hammer price monies received on cash sales are passed on to the consignors. For credit sales, hammer price monies are passed on to the consignors only after they are collected from the buyers. On sold items, consignor commission amounts based on the hammer prices are collected from the consignors.

Disposal of Unsold Items. Barnaby's adopts a few options for disposing unsold lots. Sometimes the company would determine that the unsold lot may do well in a future auction at the same site or at another site. Then the property item is reassigned to the new sale.

If the company deems that the property item does not have another chance of being sold, it returns the item to the owner ("returned to owner"; RTO). Barnaby's may collect expenses it incurred on processing the item from the consignor. This is based on prior agreement with the consignor. A transfer document covers the return of the property item to the consignor.

E-R Model

Close study and consideration of the business functions described above enables you to come up with a list of required data elements. These data elements support those business functions. End-users in the various departments carrying out the business functions either record the data elements in the data system or use the data elements to perform the functions.

The set of data elements that support the business functions performed by a department forms the data view or external schema for that department. The set of data elements in the external schema or external model provides all that the department needs from the final data system. That is the external view of the data system for that department as if it stands outside the data system and views the system.

When you combine or integrate all the data views of every user group, you arrive at the total conceptual data model, modeling the entire information requirements of relevant business domains in the organization. What do we mean by relevant business domains? In the above description of the case study, we have considered the auction processing of Barnaby's. Apart from this primary major process, the company performs several other auxiliary processes. For example, the company prints terrific, glossy catalogues for all the auctions and runs a catalogue subscription business. Clients bring high-value art and other objects to get them appraised for insurance; the company runs a property appraisal business. Companies such as Barnaby's are also involved in upscale real estate business to cater to the needs of their very wealthy clients. In our data model, we do not consider these auxiliary business functions. These are not part of the business domain considered for modeling.

After integrating all the external models, we will obtain the conceptual data model. Such a data model using the E-R modeling technique is now presented to you for study and review. Figures 3-3 through 3-5 show the conceptual data model for the auction system.

Examine the data model diagram closely. You know the symbols used in the E-R modeling technique. Look for the various notations and understand what each component in the diagram represents. Use the systematic method derived earlier to scrutinize the data model diagram.

Entity Types. Note all the square-cornered boxes. Take each box and understand the entity type it represents. What types of entities are these? Tangible, concepts, people, or things? Are there any weak entity types indicated in the diagram?

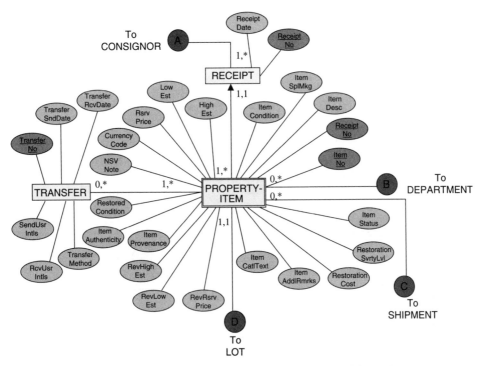

FIGURE 3-3 Barnaby's auction system: E-R data model, part 1.

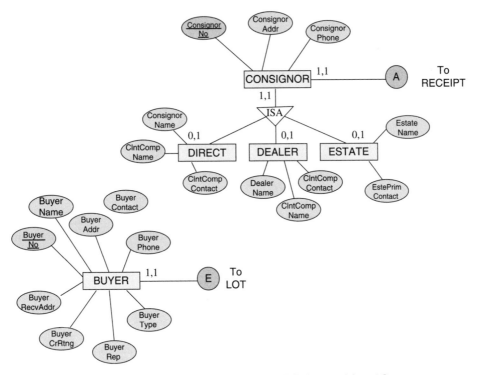

FIGURE 3-4 Barnaby's auction system: E-R data model, part 2.

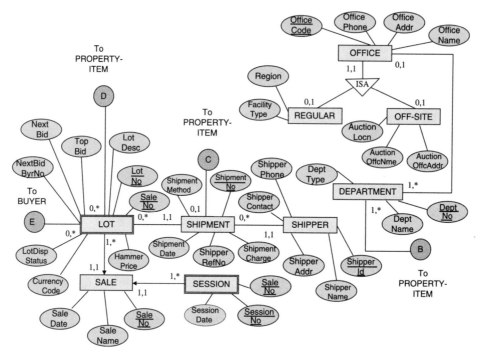

FIGURE 3-5 Barnaby's auction system: E-R data model, part 3.

Generalization/Specialization. Notice supersets and their subsets. What type of specialization does each represent? Complete, overlapping, or partial?

Relationships. Note all the relationship lines connecting entity types. Examine each relationship. Make a note of the cardinalities. Look at the minimum cardinality indicators. What business rules or constraints do these denote? Do these business rules make sense?

Attributes. Go back to each entity type box. Inspect all the attributes attached to each entity type box. Determine their meanings. Is each attribute name precise to convey the correct meaning?

Identifiers. Check the identifier for each entity type. Verify the validity and uniqueness of each identifier. Note the identifiers where new arbitrary attributes are introduced to form the identifiers.

Constraints. Scrutinize the entire diagram for any representations of constraints. Determine the implication of each constraint.

High-Level Description. Looking at each component and the overall data model diagram, come up with a high-level description of information requirements represented by the data model.

UML Model

In Chapter 2, you were introduced to the UML data modeling technique. In order to illustrate the facilities of the UML modeling technique, we now present the UML data model for the information requirements of the Barnaby's auction processing.

As you remember, object classes in UML represent what corresponds with entity types in E-R modeling. Because of its ability to model all aspects of system development process, UML has several types of modeling diagrams. Class diagrams are what we are primarily interested in for data modeling. Recall the other types of diagrams in UML such as use case diagrams, sequence diagrams, collaboration diagrams, state diagrams, activity diagrams, and so on. We will not get into these other types of diagrams here. To present a data model, use of class diagrams and application of use case diagrams is sufficient.

For our case study, we will consider only the class diagram. Figures 3-6 through 3-8 show this class diagram for your careful study and review.

Entity Types. Note all the square-cornered boxes. Each of the boxes represents an object class. Note each object class and match it up with the representation in the E-R model shown earlier. What types of object classes are these? Is the class diagram complete? Typical UML representation of an object class shows a box separated into three sections. Note the top section in each box displaying the name of the class. Observe how the class names are printed—singular nouns in upper case. The bottom section contains the behavior of the object class—the interactions with other classes. For our purposes, the bottom sections are blank and, therefore, are not shown.

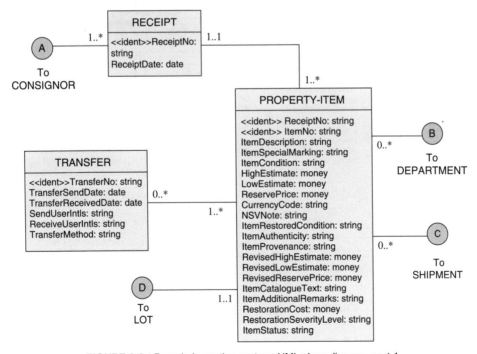

FIGURE 3-6 Barnaby's auction system: UML class diagram, part 1.

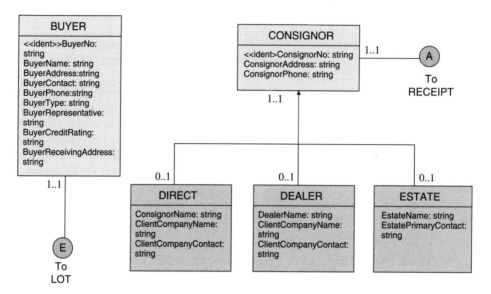

FIGURE 3-7 Barnaby's auction system: UML class diagram, part 2.

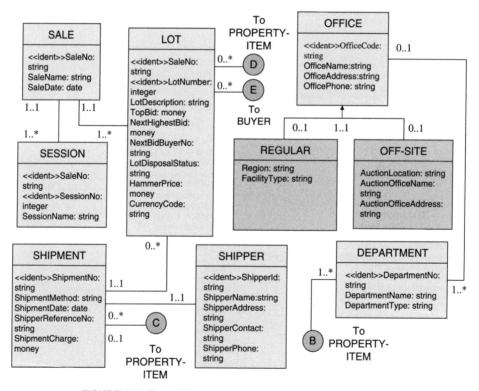

FIGURE 3-8 Barnaby's auction system: UML class diagram, part 3.

Attributes. Unlike the E-R diagram, the UML class diagram presents the attributes of an object class within the box representing the class itself. Observe the middle section within each object class box. You will note the list of attributes. Inspect all the attributes in each box. Understand their meanings. UML has additional capabilities to provide more information about each attribute. Note the parameters qualifying each attribute.

Relationships. Note all the relationship lines connecting the object classes. These indicate the associations between the various classes. Each end of an association line connects to one class. Association ends denote roles. You may name the end of an association with a role name. Customarily, labels may used at the end of association lines to indicate role names. As our data model is kept simple, labels for role names are not shown. Further, an association end also has multiplicity indicating how many objects may participate in the specific relationship. Note the multiplicity indicators (0..*, 1..1, 1..*, and so on) placed at the ends of association lines. Compare these with cardinality indicators in the E-R model.

Identifiers. As you know, UML does not indicate identifiers of object classes explicitly. We can derive the attributes that participate in the identifier by noting the parameter ≪ ident≫ placed in front of an attribute name within the object class box.

Generalization/Specialization. Notice the subsets connected to the superset by the "isa" relationship. The combinations of the words "disjoint/overlapping/complete/incomplete" indicate how subtypes relate to their superset. Usually, such indications are included in the UML class diagram.

Constraints. A broken line connecting two relationship lines would indicate a constraint imposed on the relationship. Usually, you will see the annotations {or}, {xor}, or {ior} placed on this broken line to describe the constraints of entity instances being inclusive or exclusive.

High-Level Description. Compare your overall understanding of the information requirements as derived from the UML diagram with your understanding from the E-R diagram. In which areas does the UML technique provide more information? On which aspects is it lacking?

CREATION OF MODELS

You have now reviewed the data models for Barnaby's auction processing based on two modeling techniques: E-R and UML. You have noticed that the two model diagrams portray the information requirements in more or less similar fashion, but you have also observed the essential differences between the two approaches.

Now we will address the task of analyzing how the data models were created. Given the statements about the business operations and information required to carry out these operations, how do you go about designing and creating the model? We had already looked at the methodology for performing data modeling for limited examples. However, we now want to review the process more systematically in a wider context. For our purposes

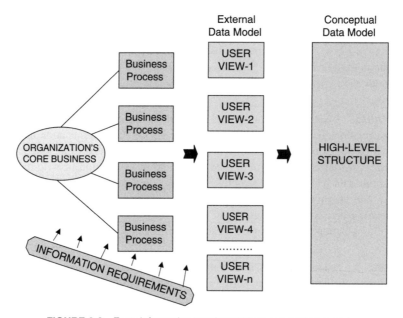

FIGURE 3-9 From information requirements to conceptual model.

here, we will consider creating a data model for information requirements using the E-R modeling technique. Creating a UML data model would be a similar process. You can attempt to derive the UML model on your own.

As you know, a conceptual data model portrays the information for the entire domain of interest. On the other hand, an external data model comprises the individual user views of the various user groups making up the entire domain of interest. Thus, it makes sense to prepare the individual data views and then arrive at the conceptual data model by combining all the user views. This will be our general methodology. See Figure 3-9 summarizing the steps from information requirements to conceptual data model.

User Views

Let us begin with the business processes described earlier. These business processes support Barnaby's auction processing. As a property item travels through the various departments and the business processes get performed, the item reaches the final stages when it is either sold or unsold. Let us track the data requirements for each of these processes. Let us make a list of the data items that either get generated during each process or are needed for the process to complete.

Here are the business processes: initial receipting, appraisal, restoration, cataloguing, sale assignment, sale at auction, sold item processing, unsold items disposal. Figures 3-10 through 3-12 show the list of data items for these business processes.

Who performs these business processes? The various user departments. The collection of user views of data for these departments forms the external data model. From the data items for the different business processes, let us derive the user views for the various departments.

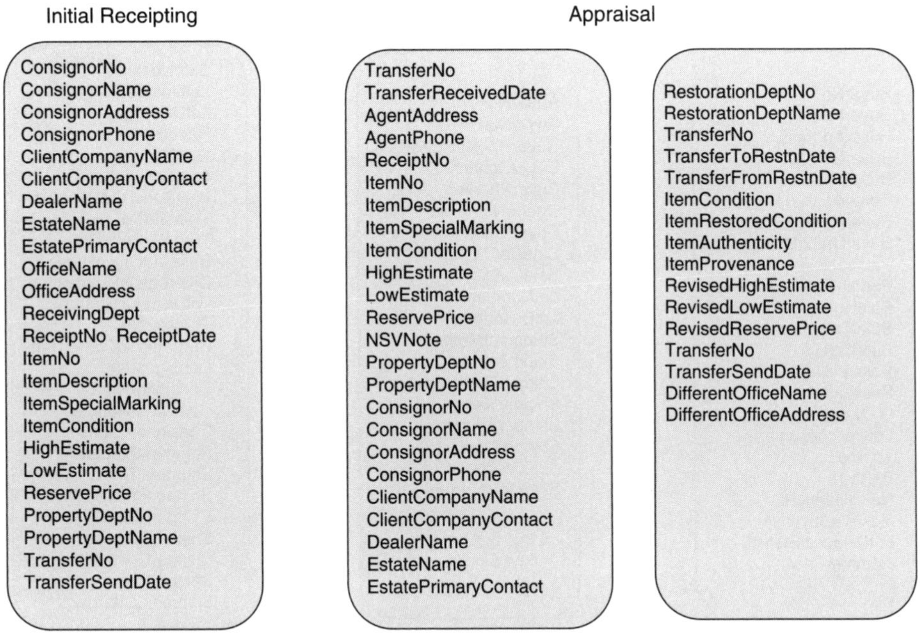

Initial Receipting

Appraisal

ConsignorNo
ConsignorName
ConsignorAddress
ConsignorPhone
ClientCompanyName
ClientCompanyContact
DealerName
EstateName
EstatePrimaryContact
OfficeName
OfficeAddress
ReceivingDept
ReceiptNo ReceiptDate
ItemNo
ItemDescription
ItemSpecialMarking
ItemCondition
HighEstimate
LowEstimate
ReservePrice
PropertyDeptNo
PropertyDeptName
TransferNo
TransferSendDate

TransferNo
TransferReceivedDate
AgentAddress
AgentPhone
ReceiptNo
ItemNo
ItemDescription
ItemSpecialMarking
ItemCondition
HighEstimate
LowEstimate
ReservePrice
NSVNote
PropertyDeptNo
PropertyDeptName
ConsignorNo
ConsignorName
ConsignorAddress
ConsignorPhone
ClientCompanyName
ClientCompanyContact
DealerName
EstateName
EstatePrimaryContact

RestorationDeptNo
RestorationDeptName
TransferNo
TransferToRestnDate
TransferFromRestnDate
ItemCondition
ItemRestoredCondition
ItemAuthenticity
ItemProvenance
RevisedHighEstimate
RevisedLowEstimate
RevisedReservePrice
TransferNo
TransferSendDate
DifferentOfficeName
DifferentOfficeAddress

FIGURE 3-10   Barnaby's: data items for business processes, part 1.

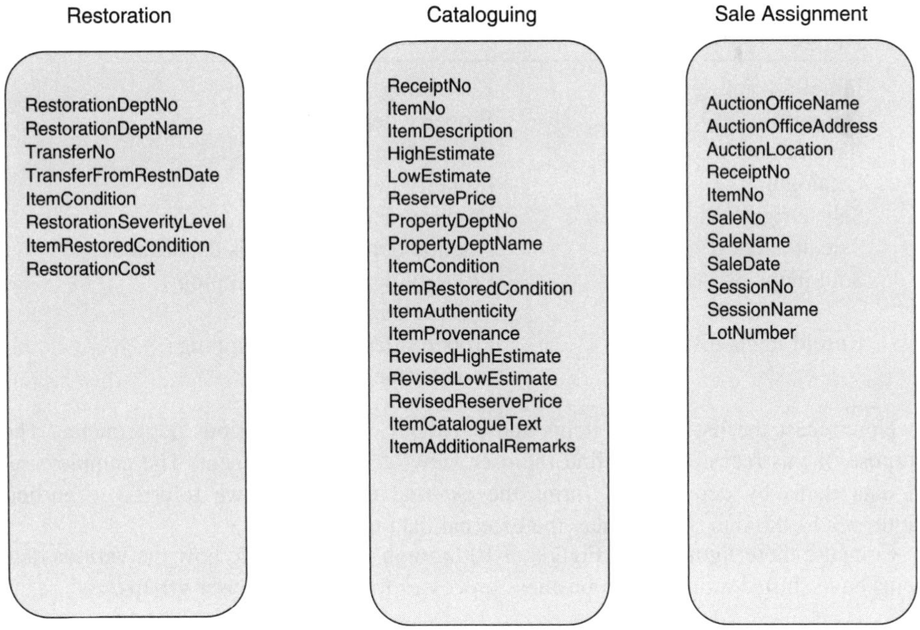

Restoration

Cataloguing

Sale Assignment

RestorationDeptNo
RestorationDeptName
TransferNo
TransferFromRestnDate
ItemCondition
RestorationSeverityLevel
ItemRestoredCondition
RestorationCost

ReceiptNo
ItemNo
ItemDescription
HighEstimate
LowEstimate
ReservePrice
PropertyDeptNo
PropertyDeptName
ItemCondition
ItemRestoredCondition
ItemAuthenticity
ItemProvenance
RevisedHighEstimate
RevisedLowEstimate
RevisedReservePrice
ItemCatalogueText
ItemAdditionalRemarks

AuctionOfficeName
AuctionOfficeAddress
AuctionLocation
ReceiptNo
ItemNo
SaleNo
SaleName
SaleDate
SessionNo
SessionName
LotNumber

FIGURE 3-11   Barnaby's: data items for business processes, part 2.

Sale at Auction	Sold Items Processing	Unsold Items Disposal
BuyerNo BuyerName BuyerAddress BuyerContact BuyerPhone DealerName BuyerRepresentative BuyerCreditRating PaddleNo PaddleType SaleNo SaleName SaleDate SessionNo SessionName LotNumber LotDescription TopBid BidType NextHighestBid NextBidBuyerNo LotDisposalStatus HammerPrice	BuyerNo BuyerName BuyerReceivingAddress BuyerContact BuyerPhone DealerName BuyerRepresentative SaleNo SaleDate LotNumber LotDescription ShipmentMethod ShipmentDate ShipperReferenceNo ShipperName ShipperAddress ShipperContact ShipperPhone ShipmentCharge	SaleNo LotNumber LotDescription ReceiptNo ItemNo ItemDescription ItemSpecialMarking TransferNo TransferSendDate DifferentOfficeName DifferentOfficeLocation LotDisposalStatus TransferNo ReturnedToOwnerDate ConsignorNo ConsignorName ConsignorAddress ConsignorPhone ShipmentMethod ShipmentDate ShipperReferenceNo ShipperName ShipperAddress ShipperContact ShipperPhone ShipmentCharge

FIGURE 3-12 Barnaby's: data items for business processes, part 3.

Match the business processes with the specific departments. The following is the business process and department list:

Business Process	Performing Department
Initial receipting	Receipting department
Appraisal	Property department
Restoration	Restoration department
Cataloguing	Property department
Sale assignment	Property department
Sale at auction	Auction department, bids department
Sold items processing	Property department, shipping department
Unsold items disposal	Property department, shipping department

Now recast the list of data items and put them under the various departments. The purpose of this recasting is to find the user view of each department. The complete set of data items by departments forms the external data model we referred to earlier. Figures 3-13 through 3-18 display the external data model.

Compare these figures with Figures 3-10 through 3-12 and note how the various data items have shifted around from business processes to the various user groups.

View Integration

We have so far completed the tasks to arrive at the external data model from the statements and analysis of the information requirements. The next task relates to the combination or

Receipting
Department

USER
VIEW

EXTERNAL DATA MODEL (Partial)

ConsignorNo
ConsignorName
ConsignorAddress
ConsignorPhone
ClientCompanyName
ClientCompanyContact
DealerName
EstateName
EstatePrimaryContact
OfficeName
OfficeAddress
ReceivingDept
ReceiptNo
ReceiptDate
ItemNo
ItemDescription
ItemSpecialMarking
ItemCondition
HighEstimate
LowEstimate
ReservePrice
PropertyDeptNo
PropertyDeptName
TransferNo
TransferSendDate

FIGURE 3-13   Barnaby's: external model, part 1.

Property
Department

USER
VIEW

EXTERNAL DATA MODEL (Partial)

TransferNo
TransferSendDate
ReceivedDate
AgentAddress
AgentPhone
ReceiptNo
ItemNo
ItemDescription
ItemSpecialMarking
ItemCondition
HighEstimate
LowEstimate
ReservePrice
NSVNote
PropertyDeptNo
PropertyDeptName
ConsignorNo
ConsignorName
ConsignorAddress
ConsignorPhone
ClientCompanyName
ClientCompanyContact
DealerName
EstateName
EstatePrimaryContact
RestorationDeptNo
RestorationDeptName

TransferTo
RestnDate
TransferFromRestnDate
ItemRestoredCondition
ItemAuthenticity
ItemProvenance
RevisedHighEstimate
RevisedLowEstimate
RevisedReservePrice
DifferentOfficeName
DifferentOfficeAddress
ItemCatalogueText
ItemAdditionalRemarks
AuctionOfficeName
AuctionOfficeAddress
AuctionLocation
SaleNo SaleName
SaleDate
SessionNo
SessionName
LotNumber BuyerNo
BuyerName
BuyerReceivingAddress
BuyerContact
BuyerPhone

DealerName
BuyerRepresentative
LotDescription
ShipmentMethod
ShipmentDate
ShipperReferenceNo
ShipperName
ShipperAddress
ShipperContact
ShipperPhone
ShipmentCharge
DifferentOfficeLocation
LotDisposalStatus
ReturnedToOwnerDate
ConsignorNo
ConsignorName
ConsignorAddress
ConsignorPhone
ShipmentMethod
ShipmentDate
ShipperReferenceNo
ShipperName
ShipperAddress
ShipperContact
ShipperPhone
ShipmentCharge

FIGURE 3-14   Barnaby's: external model, part 2.

Restoration
Department

USER
VIEW

EXTERNAL DATA MODEL (Partial)

RestorationDeptNo
RestorationDeptName
TransferNo
TransferFromRestnDate
ItemCondition
RestorationSeverityLevel
ItemRestoredCondition
RestorationCost

FIGURE 3-15   Barnaby's: external model, part 3.

Auction
Department

USER
VIEW

EXTERNAL DATA MODEL (Partial)

BuyerNo
BuyerName
BuyerAddress
BuyerContact
BuyerPhone
DealerName
BuyerRepresentative
BuyerCreditRating
PaddleNo
PaddleType
SaleNo
SaleName
SaleDate
SessionNo
SessionName
LotNumber
LotDescription
TopBid
BidType
NextHighestBid
NextBidBuyerNo
LotDisposalStatus
HammerPrice

FIGURE 3-16   Barnaby's: external model, part 4.

Bids
Department

EXTERNAL DATA MODEL (Partial)

USER
VIEW

BuyerNo
BuyerName
BuyerAddress
BuyerContact
BuyerPhone
DealerName
BuyerRepresentative
BuyerCreditRating
PaddleNo
PaddleType
SaleNo
SaleName
SaleDate
SessionNo
SessionName
LotNumber
LotDescription
TopBid
BidType
NextHighestBid
NextBidBuyerNo
LotDisposalStatus
HammerPrice

FIGURE 3-17   Barnaby's: external model, part 5.

Shipping
Department

EXTERNAL DATA MODEL (Partial)

USER
VIEW

BuyerNo
BuyerName
BuyerReceivingAddress
BuyerContact
BuyerPhone
DealerName
BuyerRepresentative
SaleNo
SaleDate
LotNumber
LotDescription
ShipmentMethod
ShipmentDate
ShipperReferenceNo
ShipperName
ShipperAddress
ShipperContact
ShipperPhone
ShipmentCharge

ReceiptNo
ItemNo
ItemDescription
ItemSpecialMarking
TransferNo
TransferSendDate
DifferentOfficeName
DifferentOfficeLocation
LotDisposalStatus
ReturnedToOwnerDate
ConsignorNo
ConsignorName
ConsignorAddress
ConsignorPhone

FIGURE 3-18   Barnaby's: external model, part 6.

DATA GROUPS

CONSIGNOR	PROPERTY-ITEM	OFFICE	SALE
ConsignorNo	ItemNo	OfficeName	SaleNo
ConsignorName	ItemDescription	OfficeAddress	SaleName
ConsignorAddress	ItemSpecialMarking	AuctionLocation	SaleDate
ConsignorPhone	ItemCondition	AuctionOfficeName	SessionNo
ClientCompanyName	HighEstimate	AuctionOfficeAddress	SessionName
ClientCompanyContact	LowEstimate	DifferentOfficeName	
DealerName	ReservePrice	DifferentOfficeAddress	**LOT**
EstateName	NSVNote		LotNumber
EstatePrimaryContact	ItemRestoredCondition		LotDescription
	ItemAuthenticity	**DEPARTMENT**	TopBid
	ItemProvenance	ReceivingDepartment	NextHighestBid
RECEIPT	RevisedHighEstimate	PropertyDeptNo	NextBidBuyerNo
ReceiptNo	RevisedLowEstimate	PropertyDeptName	LotDisposalStatus
ReceiptDate	RevisedReservePrice	RestorationDeptNo	HammerPrice
	ItemCatalogueText	RestorationDeptName	
	ItemAdditionalRemarks		
	RestorationCost	**TRANSFER**	**SHIPMENT**
	RestorationSeverityLevel	TransferNo	ShipmentMethod
		TransferSendDate	ShipmentDate
	BUYER	TransferReceivedDate	ShipperReferenceNo
	BuyerNo	AgentAddress	ShipperName
	BuyerName	AgentPhone	ShipperAddress
	BuyerAddress	TransferToRestnDate	ShipperContact
	BuyerContact	TransferFromRestnDate	ShipperPhone
	BuyerPhone	ReturnedToOwnerDate	ShipmentCharge
	DealerName		
	BuyerRepresentative		
	BuyerCreditRating		
	BuyerReceivingAddress		

FIGURE 3-19   Barnaby's: integrated data groups.

integration of all the user views that are part of the external data model. Let us integrate the user views.

As we perform the process of view integration, you will note that data groups form rather naturally. What do we mean by this? When you combine data items from the various data views, you tend to put all data items about a property item in one group, all data items about a consignor in another group, all data items about a buyer in yet another group, and so on. You actually tend to form data groups. Of course, while forming each data group, you will eliminate duplicates, that is, by not recording the same data item more than once in a data group. As you assemble the data items and form data groups, you may name each data group to suggest what business object might be described by the attributes of the data items. Now consider Figure 3-19, which presents the data groups formed by integrating the user views. Each group has a suggested object name. Notice these names and determine if the names make sense.

Entity Types

Go back to Figure 3-19 and examine the data groups carefully. What does each data group represent? Does not each group represent data items that describe some entity type or business object? Identify these data types and derive a first iteration of the entity types for the data model. Let us represent this initial set of entity types by square-cornered boxes and present them in Figure 3-20.

Communication with Domain Experts.   Remember, the conceptual data model is a vehicle for communication with the domain experts and for obtaining their confirmation of its correctness. This communication process is not just a one-time conversation after you complete the data model. It is an ongoing process until the final diagram is firmed up.

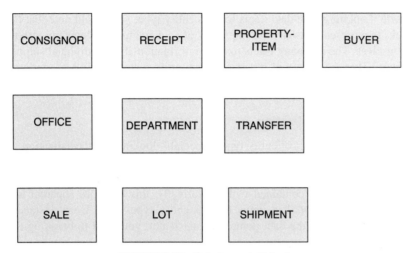

FIGURE 3-20   Data types: initial set.

Let us pursue the discussions with the domain experts about the suggested initial entity types as shown in Figure 3-20. The results of the discussions are indicated below.

Receipt. Although property items seem to have independent existence, however, within Barnaby's data system, a property item makes its appearance only after it is receipted. Each property item is associated with a receipt under which it was received. Within Barnaby's data system, a property item needs a corresponding receipt for its existence. Therefore, in the data model, PROPERTY-ITEM must be designated as a weak entity type dependent on the strong entity type RECEIPT.

Department. This entity type represents various departments within the Barnaby's offices. Some are administrative departments; some are functional departments; others such as the departments that provide expertise in specific areas of art are specialty departments. Nevertheless, all the departments may be represented by a single entity type.

Buyer. Most of the buyers are direct buyers; they or their representatives are either present at the auctions or send absentee bids or call in phone bids. Some of the buyers are dealers in art who buy for resale. However, there is no need to symbolize the dealers with a separate entity type. All buyers may be represented by a single entity type.

Transfer. Transfers of property items take place in a variety of situations. This entity type as shown can accommodate all the various transfers from one location to another, within the company or to the outside.

Session. This entity type depends on the entity type SALE for its existence. Usually, the sessions are simply numbered in sequence within a particular sale. Therefore, SESSION entity type is a weak entity type depending on the strong entity type SALE.

Lot. Lots are numbered sequentially from "001" onward for each sale. A lot has no existence without its corresponding sale. LOT will be symbolized as a weak entity type depending on the strong entity type SALE.

Shipment. Looking at the data items for this entity type, you would note that the entity type seeks to represent not only the shipments of sold and unsold items but also the shippers themselves. The company wants to keep information about individual shippers in its data system. Therefore, we will separate out an entity type SHIPPER to represent information about individual shipping companies.

Specialization/Generalization

Let us review the initial set of entity types especially looking for specialization and generalization of entity types. If you find that a particular entity type contains other similar entity types, then this is a case of generalization. That is, the entity type is the superset of the other entity types contained within. Normally, this becomes apparent when you examine the initial set of data items for the entity type. Does every instance of the entity type have each of the data items present? If not, you need to break up the entity type into subtypes.

On the other hand, are there similar entity types that are shown separately and distinctly? Can these form subtypes of a supertype entity? If so, you have case of specialization that can be put together in supertype–subtype relationship.

Let us look at the initial set of entity types. Our investigation would produce the following results.

Consignor. Barnaby's primarily deals with three types of consignors: direct consignor, dealers who sell property items on behalf of their clients, and estates usually of deceased collectors. Therefore, we need to introduce a superset CONSIGNOR with subsets of DIRECT, DEALER, and ESTATE.

Office. This entity type represents the various Barnaby's offices. Most of the time, auctions are held at an office that houses a number of departments. Sometimes, auctions are held at off-site locations like an old princely castle where the entire contents are catalogued and auctioned off. Some auctions are held at seasonal locations, for example, St. Moritz, known as the millionaire's ski town in Switzerland. A temporary office is set up at such off-site locations. The OFFICE entity type can, therefore, be a supertype with subtypes of REGULAR and OFF-SITE.

Relationships

After reviewing and recasting the entity types, we now arrive at the following entity types to be part of the conceptual data model:

CONSIGNOR, DIRECT, DEALER, and ESTATE
OFFICE, REGULAR, and OFF-SITE, DEPARTMENT
RECEIPT and PROPERTY-ITEM
TRANSFER
BUYER
SALE, SESSION, and LOT
SHIPPER, SHIPMENT

Let us look for direct relationships among the entity types.

First, let us mark the supertype–subtype relationships. Here are these: supertype CON-SIGNOR with subtypes DIRECT, DEALER, and ESTATE; supertype OFFICE with sub-types REGULAR and OFF-SITE.

Next, note the strong and weak entity types respectively: RECEIPT and PROPERTY-ITEM; SALE and SESSION; SALE and LOT.

Let us record the remaining direct relationships as follows:

CONSIGNOR to RECEIPT (one-to-many)

PROPERTY-ITEM to LOT (one-to-many)

BUYER to LOT (one-to-many)

SHIPPER to SHIPMENT (one-to-many)

SHIPMENT to LOT (one-to-many)

SHIPMENT to PROPERTY-ITEM (one-to-many)

OFFICE to DEPARTMENT (one-to-many)

TRANSFER to PROPERTY-ITEM (many-to-many)

DEPARTMENT to PROPERTY-ITEM (many-to-many)

Draw a preliminary data model diagram showing the entity types, the relationship lines, and the cardinality indicators. Also show the optionality conditions of the relationship using minimum cardinality indicators (see Fig. 3-21).

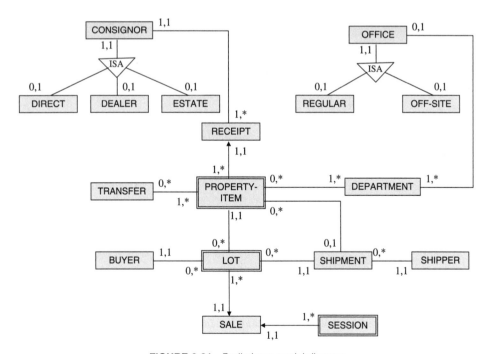

FIGURE 3-21 Preliminary model diagram.

Attributes

Revisit Figures 3-19 and 3-20 to scrutinize the list of data items for each entity type. These data items refer to the attributes for the entity types. Based on our review, we will have to revise the list of attributes as follows:

Consignor. In this superset, retain only the common attributes. Other attributes specific to particular subsets must be removed to the subset entity types DIRECT, DEALER, or ESTATE.

Office. Retain the common attributes in the superset OFFICE. Include specific attributes in the subset entity types REGULAR and OFF-SITE.

Receipt. This strong entity type sustains the existence of the corresponding weak entity type PROPERTY-ITEM. Most of the attributes are found in PROPERTY-ITEM. Add a few more attributes to RECEIPT such as ShipmentType, ReceiverInitials, and so on.

Property-Item. Include attribute CurrencyCode to indicate the currency in which estimates and reserve prices are recorded. As the property item moves through various stages before being offered for sale, it is important to know the current status of the property item. For this purpose, add attribute ItemStatus.

Department. Combine the attributes as generic attributes for all types of departments. Add a few more relevant attributes. Include DepartmentType attribute to indicate the type of department: receiving, shipping, property, restoration, and so forth.

Buyer. This entity type represents all types of buyers. Add BuyerType attribute to denote the type of buyer after removing the specific attribute DealerName.

Transfer. This entity type refers to a concept, not something tangible—the transfer function itself. It represents all transfers from various locations to other locations. Remove specific attributes such as TransferToRestnDate, TransferFromRestnDate, and ReturnedToOwnerDate. Include attributes SendUserIntls and ReceiveUserIntls. Remove AgentAddress and AgentPhone, which seem to be redundant. Include TransferMethod to indicate how the property item was transferred.

Session. Separate out the attributes describing this entity type from entity type SALE.

Lot. The HammerPrice is determined in the local currency. So, add CurrencyCode attribute to indicate the currency.

Shipment. Remove the attributes describing the shipper.

Shipper. Include the attributes ShipperName, ShipperAddress, ShipperContact, and ShipperPhone.

Identifiers

Many of the entity types have attributes that can be used as unique identifiers. For the other entity types, we need to add surrogate attributes that can be used as unique identifiers.

Here is the set of attributes already present that can be used as identifiers:

Entity Type	Identifier
CONSIGNOR	ConsignorNo
RECEIPT	ReceiptNo
BUYER	BuyerNo
TRANSFER	TransferNo
SALE	SaleNo

The following entity types do not have attributes that can be used as identifiers. Therefore, add attributes that can be used as identifiers as follows:

Entity Type	Identifier
OFFICE	OfficeCode
SHIPMENT	ShipmentNo
SHIPPER	ShipperId

A weak entity forms its identifier as the concatenation of its partial identifier with the identifier of the corresponding strong entity type. Listed below are the weak entity types and their concatenated identifiers:

Weak Entity Type	Concatenated Identifier
PROPERTY-ITEM	ReceiptNo, ItemNo
SESSION	SaleNo, SessionNo
LOT	SaleNo, LotNumber

The following subtypes inherit their identifiers from the corresponding supertypes:

Subtype	Supertype	Identifier
DIRECT	CONSIGNOR	ConsignorNo
DEALER	CONSIGNOR	ConsignorNo
ESTATE	CONSIGNOR	ConsignorNo
REGULAR	OFFICE	OfficeCode
OFF-SITE	OFFICE	OfficeCode

Refer to Figures 3-22 and 3-23. These figures now display all the entity types with their attributes and identifiers. Observe the identifiers marked with underscores. Note how the figures reflect all the revisions we have discussed earlier.

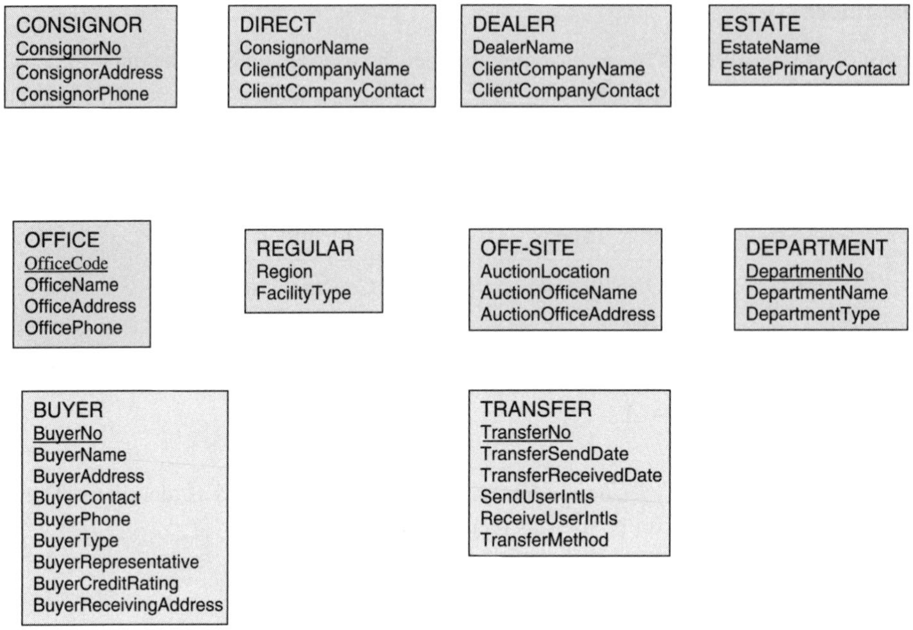

CONSIGNOR
ConsignorNo
ConsignorAddress
ConsignorPhone

DIRECT
ConsignorName
ClientCompanyName
ClientCompanyContact

DEALER
DealerName
ClientCompanyName
ClientCompanyContact

ESTATE
EstateName
EstatePrimaryContact

OFFICE
OfficeCode
OfficeName
OfficeAddress
OfficePhone

REGULAR
Region
FacilityType

OFF-SITE
AuctionLocation
AuctionOfficeName
AuctionOfficeAddress

DEPARTMENT
DepartmentNo
DepartmentName
DepartmentType

BUYER
BuyerNo
BuyerName
BuyerAddress
BuyerContact
BuyerPhone
BuyerType
BuyerRepresentative
BuyerCreditRating
BuyerReceivingAddress

TRANSFER
TransferNo
TransferSendDate
TransferReceivedDate
SendUserIntls
ReceiveUserIntls
TransferMethod

FIGURE 3-22 Entity types, attributes, and identifiers, part 1.

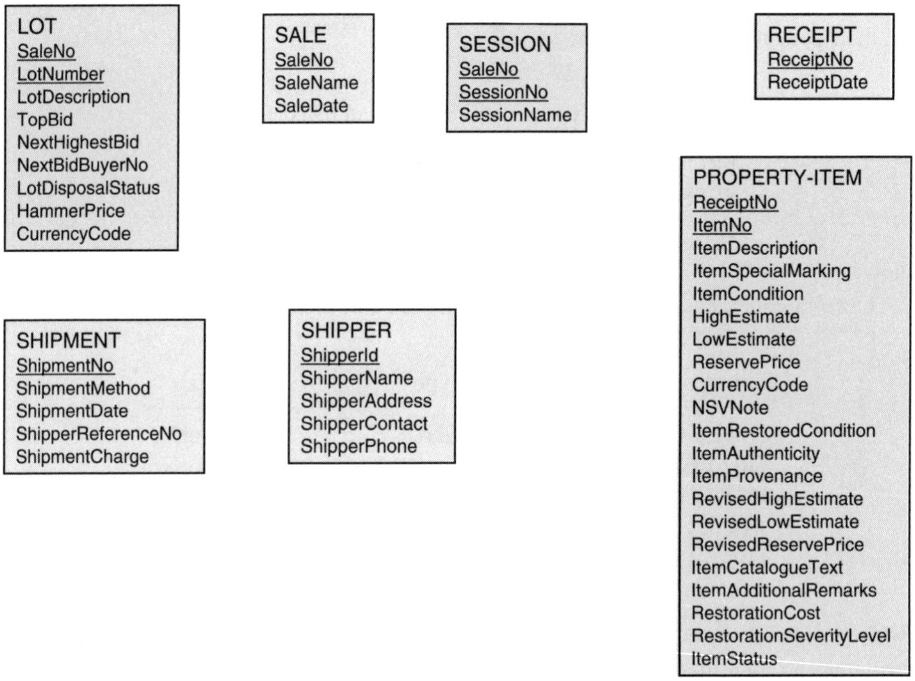

LOT
SaleNo
LotNumber
LotDescription
TopBid
NextHighestBid
NextBidBuyerNo
LotDisposalStatus
HammerPrice
CurrencyCode

SALE
SaleNo
SaleName
SaleDate

SESSION
SaleNo
SessionNo
SessionName

RECEIPT
ReceiptNo
ReceiptDate

PROPERTY-ITEM
ReceiptNo
ItemNo
ItemDescription
ItemSpecialMarking
ItemCondition
HighEstimate
LowEstimate
ReservePrice
CurrencyCode
NSVNote
ItemRestoredCondition
ItemAuthenticity
ItemProvenance
RevisedHighEstimate
RevisedLowEstimate
RevisedReservePrice
ItemCatalogueText
ItemAdditionalRemarks
RestorationCost
RestorationSeverityLevel
itemStatus

SHIPMENT
ShipmentNo
ShipmentMethod
ShipmentDate
ShipperReferenceNo
ShipmentCharge

SHIPPER
ShipperId
ShipperName
ShipperAddress
ShipperContact
ShipperPhone

FIGURE 3-23 Entity types, attributes, and identifiers, part 2.

Review of the Model Diagram

Go back and refer to Figures 3-3 through 3-5, which display the E-R data model diagram for Barnaby's auction processing. Also, please go back to the set of information requirements narrated earlier. We have arrived at the E-R model from these information requirements following a standard modeling procedure. Having gone through this procedure, step by step, you are now in position to appreciate and understand the various components of the model. Now you know how the different symbols have been used to represent the data elements and their relationships.

Let us walk through the diagram quickly and observe the components:

Entity Types. Now notice all the square-cornered boxes representing entity types. Observe the entity types PROPERTY-ITEM, SESSION, and LOT shown as boxes enclosed by double lines. As you know, these are the weak entity types.

Generalization/Specialization. Notice supersets CONSIGNOR and OFFICE and their corresponding subsets DIRECT/DEALER/ESTATE and REGULAR/OFF-SITE. E-R modeling technique in its original version does not distinguish between the types of specialization such as complete, overlapping, or partial. Some later practitioners, however, have come up with special notations for these. We will consider these in later chapters.

Relationships. Note all the relationship lines connecting entity types. Note the maximum cardinality indicators denoting one-to-many and many-to-many relationships. Observe the relationships as indicated between supersets and their subsets. See how the subsets inherit the relationships from their supersets. For example, CONSIGNOR is related to RECEIPT, therefore, DEALER is related to RECEIPT. Next, look at the minimum cardinality indicators. What do you infer from these about optional and mandatory conditions of the relationships? Here are a few comments on some of the relationships:

CONSIGNOR to RECEIPT (One-to-Many). One or more receipts associated with one consignor; one receipt associated with not more than one consignor; some consignors may not be associated with any receipt; every receipt associated with a consignor.

PROPERTY-ITEM to LOT (One-to-Many). One property item associated with one or more lots (same property item might be unsold at one auction and then offered at another, and so on); some property items may not be associated with any lot (property item not yet assigned to a sale with a lot number); every lot associated with at least one property item.

BUYER to LOT (One-to-Many). One buyer associated with one or more lots; some buyers not yet associated with any lots (registered, but not yet successful at an auction); each lot associated with one and only one buyer; all lots must be associated with buyers.

SHIPPER to SHIPMENT (One-to-Many). One shipper associated with one or more shipments; every shipment associated with one and only one shipper; some shippers not associated with any shipments yet.

SHIPMENT to LOT (One-to-Many). One shipment associated with one or more lots; some lots not associated with any shipments (lots hand-carried by buyers themselves).

SHIPMENT to PROPERTY-ITEM (One-to-Many). One shipment associated with one or more property items; some items not associated with any shipments (NSV items taken back by the consignors themselves).

OFFICE to DEPARTMENT (One-to-Many). One office associated with one or more departments; each department not associated with more than one office; some departments not associated with offices (such as outside departments or locations used for restoration).

TRANSFER to PROPERTY-ITEM (Many-to-Many). One transfer relates to one or more property items (group transfers); every transfer must be associated; one property item may be related to no transfers at all; a property item may participate in many transfers (over time).

Attributes. Inspect all the attributes attached to each entity type box. Especially, note how the subsets inherit attributes from their corresponding supersets.

Identifiers. Check the identifier for each entity type. Verify the validity and uniqueness of each identifier. Note the identifiers where new arbitrary attributes are introduced to form the identifiers.

Constraints. The initial version of E-R modeling technique does not indicate constraints.

High-Level Description. Looking at each component and the overall data model diagram, come up with a high-level description of information requirements represented by the data model.

LOGICAL MODEL: OVERVIEW

The data model diagram so far discussed relates to the conceptual data model. At this level, as you know, the main purpose is to represent the information requirements correctly and in a readable manner for communication with the domain experts. This level of model does not serve the purpose of implementation. It can hardly be used as a blueprint for implementation.

The logical data model at the next lower level of abstraction is closer to being a blueprint. The logical model, therefore, depends on what type of database system you want to implement. Necessarily, the logical model for a relational database system would differ from that for, say, a hierarchical database system.

In our discussions, we will assume a relational database system. As such, the logical data model in our consideration would be the one for this type of database system. Chapter 7 covers the logical data model in more detail. At this stage, we just want to review the components of a logical data model for a relational implementation. Also, we want to highlight the steps for proceeding from the conceptual model to the logical model.

Model Components

First, consider the components of the logical data model. The logical data model for a relational database system may be termed a relational data model. A relational data model perceives data as in the form of two-dimensional tables or relations. Therefore, the components of a relational model would be the components of a two-dimensional table. Without getting into relational theory and the mathematical foundations of the relational model, let us review its parts.

Relation or Table. A relation or a table is the primary data modeling concept of the relational model. What is a two-dimensional table? It is a collection of columns and rows. For example, consider a table consisting of data about consignors. Call this the CONSIGNOR table. This table consists of columns and rows holding pieces of data about consignors. The concept of mathematical relation forms the basis for the data structure in the relational data model. A relation is visualized as a two-dimensional table with rows and columns containing only atomic values. Figure 3-24 shows an example of the CONSIGNOR table.

The following features of a relation are relevant:

- A relation is a table representing data about some business object.
- A relation is not just any random table, but a table whose rows and columns conform to certain relational rules.
- A relation consists of a specific set of named columns and an arbitrary number of rows.
- Each row contains a set of data values.
- Table names and column names provide meaning to the data contained in a table.

Columns. Note the following remarks about the columns in a relation:

- Each column indicates a specific attribute of the business object or entity type.
- The column heading is the name of the attribute.
- No two columns in a table may have the same name because the column names refer to the attributes in a relational model.
- For each row, the values of the attributes are shown in the appropriate columns.
- Each attribute takes its value from a set of allowable values for that attribute.

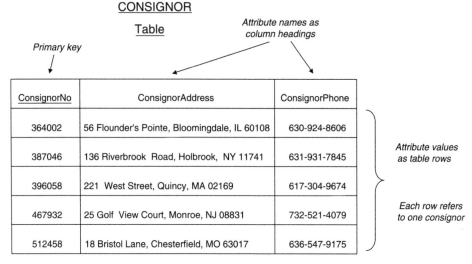

FIGURE 3-24 CONSIGNOR relation or table.

Rows. Each row holds the values of attributes for a single occurrence of a business object. Notice each row in the CONSIGNOR table. Each row contains the attribute values for a single consignor. In a relation, each row represents one instance of the object.

Each column for that row indicates one piece of data describing a single occurrence of the object. Take a particular row in the CONSIGNOR table. Look at the values in the columns for this row. What are these values? These are the values of attributes for that specific consignor.

Primary Key. One or more attributes in a relation get designated as the primary key for the relation. Underscoring the column names denotes the primary key attributes.

The values in the primary key columns for a particular row uniquely identify that row. Note the column values for ConsignorNo. This column cannot contain duplicate values in the CONSIGNOR table. If you have duplicate values, then the rows, that is, individual consignors, cannot be uniquely identified.

Relationships. In the E-R data model diagram for Barnaby's, notice the one-to-many relationship between entity types CONSIGNOR and RECEIPT. How does a relational model indicate a relationship between two tables?

Consider Figure 3-25 showing CONSIGNOR and RECEIPT tables.

Relationships are established in the tables logically:

- Two related tables are linked logically through what are known as foreign keys.
- A new column, called the foreign key column, is added to the table on the "many" side. Note the new column ConsignorNo in the RECEIPT table.
- To link a specific row in the "parent" table to one or more rows in the "child" table, place the value in the primary key column for that row in the "parent" table as the value in the foreign key column of the corresponding rows in the "child" table. Observe the values in the foreign key column, namely, ConsignorNo in the

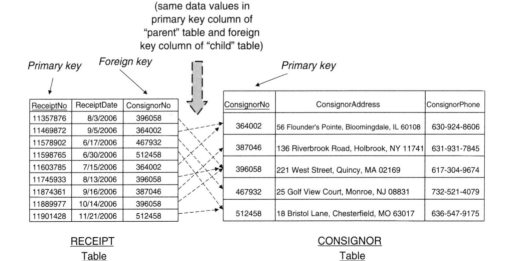

FIGURE 3-25 CONSIGNOR and RECEIPT tables: relationship.

RECEIPT table. Note how these values match up the values in the primary key column in the CONSIGNOR table.

- A foreign key column in the "child" table need not have the same name as the corresponding primary key column in the "parent" table. However, the data types and length must match between the primary key and the foreign key.

Transformation Steps

Now let us turn our attention to the transformation of the conceptual data model into a logical data model. In our case, the relational data model is the logical data model.

Note the following major components of a conceptual data model and a relational data model.

E-R Data Model

Entity types
Attributes
Identifiers
Relationships
Generalization/specialization (superset/subset)

Relational Data Model

Relations or tables
Rows
Columns
Primary keys
Foreign keys

The transforming task comes down to mapping the components of the conceptual data model to the components of the relational data model. Let us walk through the transformation or mapping process.

Entity Types. Let us begin with the most obvious component—entity type in the E-R data model. What is an entity type? If *consignor* is something Barnaby's is interested in storing information about, then *consignor* is an entity type represented in the conceptual data model. The set of all consignors in the organization about whom data must be captured in the proposed relational database system is the entity type CONSIGNOR.

Note the following points about the transformation from conceptual E-R model to relational model:

- Entity type is transformed into a relation.
- Name of the entity type becomes the name of the relation.
- The entity instances viewed as present inside the entity type box transform into the rows of the relation.
- The complete set of entity instances becomes the total set of rows of the relation or table.
- In the transformation, nothing is expressed about the order of the rows in the transformed relation.

Attributes. Entities have intrinsic or inherent characteristics. So, naturally the next component to be considered is the set of attributes of an entity type.

Make note of the following points with regard to the transformation of attributes:

- Attributes of an entity type are transformed into the columns of the corresponding relation.
- The names of the attributes become the names of the columns.
- The domain of values of each attribute translates into the domain of values for the corresponding column.
- In the transformation, nothing is expressed about the order of the columns in the transformed relation.

Identifiers. In the conceptual data model, each instance is uniquely identified by values of one or more attributes. These attributes together form the identifier for the entity type.

Note the following points on the transformation of identifiers:

- The set of attributes forming the identifier becomes the primary key columns of the relation.
- If there is more than one attribute, all the corresponding columns are indicated as primary key columns.
- Because the primary key columns represent identifiers, the combined values in these columns for each row is unique.
- No two rows in the relation can have the same values in the primary key columns.
- Because identifiers cannot have null values, no part of the primary key columns can have null values.

Relationships. The E-R data modeling technique has notable ways for representing relationships between two entity types. Wherever you perceive direct associations between instances of two entity types, the two entity type boxes are connected by lines with a diamond in the middle containing the name of the relationship. How many instances of one entity type are associated with how many instances of the other? The indication about the numbers is given by cardinality indicators, especially the maximum cardinality indicator. The minimum cardinality indicator denotes whether a relationship is optional or mandatory.

You know that a relational data model establishes relationships between two relations through foreign keys. Therefore, transformation of relationships as represented in the E-R model involves mapping of the connections and cardinality indicators into foreign keys. Note the following summary on the transformation of relationships.

One-to-One Relationships

- When two relations are in one-to-one relationship, place a foreign key column in either one of the two relations. Values in foreign key columns for rows in this table match with primary key values in corresponding rows of the related table.
- The foreign key attribute has the same data type, length, and domain values as the corresponding primary key attribute in the other table.
- It does not really matter whether you place the foreign key column in one table or the other. However, to avoid wasted storage space, it is better to place the foreign key column in the table that is likely to have less number of rows.

One-to-Many Relationships

- When two relations are in a one-to-many relationship, place a foreign key column in the relation that is on the "many" side of the relationship. Values in foreign key column for rows in this table match with primary key values in corresponding rows of the related table.
- The foreign key attribute has the same data type, length, and domain values as the corresponding primary key attribute in the other table.

Many-to-Many Relationships

- Create a separate relation, called an intersection table. Use both primary keys of the participating relations as the concatenated primary key for the intersection table. The primary key of the intersection table contains two attributes: one attribute establishing the relationship to one of the two relations and the other attribute linking the other relation.
- Each part of the primary key of the intersection table serves as a foreign key.
- Each foreign key attribute has the same data type, length, and domain values as the corresponding primary key attribute in the related table.
- The relationship of the first relation to the intersection relation is one-to-many; the relationship of the second relation to the intersection relation is also one-to-many. In effect, transformation of many-to-many relationship is reduced to creating two one-to-many relationships.

Generalization/Specialization. The superset entity types transform into relations; similarly, the subset entity types convert into relations. The identifier and attributes of the superset entity type migrate as columns to the relations representing the corresponding subtypes.

Relational Model

Study Figures 3-26 through 3-28 showing the relational data model for Barnaby's. This relational model is the result of transformation of the E-R model displayed earlier in Figures 3-3 through 3-5.

```
RECEIPT (ReceiptNo, ConsignorNo, ReceiptDate)
        Foreign Key:     ConsignorNo REFERENCES CONSIGNOR
PROPERTY-ITEM (ReceiptNo, ItemNo, ShipmentNo, ItemDescription,
        ItemSpecialMarking, ItemCondition, HighEstimate, LowEstimate,
        ReservePrice, CurrencyCode, NSVNote, ItemRestoredCondition,
        ItemAuthenticity, ItemProvenance, RevisedHighEstimate,
        RevisedLowEstimate, RevisedReservePrice, ItemCatalogueText,
        ItemAdditionalRemarks, RestorationCost, RestorationSeverityLevel,
        ItemStatus)
        Foreign Keys:    ReceiptNo REFERENCES RECEIPT
                         ShipmentNo REFERENCES SHIPMENT
TRANSFER (TransferNo, TransferSendDate, TransferReceivedDate,
        SendUsrIntls, ReceiveUsrIntls, TransferMethod)
ITEM-TRANSFER (ReceiptNo, ItemNo, TransferNo)
        Foreign Keys:    ReceiptNo, ItemNo REFERENCES
                         PROPERTY-ITEM
                         TransferNo REFERENCES  TRANSFER
```

FIGURE 3-26 Barnaby's auction system: relational model, part 1.

CONSIGNOR (<u>ConsignorNo</u>, ConsignorAddress, ConsignorPhone)
DIRECT (<u>ConsignorNo</u>, ConsignorName, ConsignorAddress, ConsignorPhone,
    ClientCompanyName, ClientCompanyContact)
    Foreign Key: ConsignorNo REFERENCES CONSIGNOR
DEALER (<u>ConsignorNo</u>, DealerName, ConsignorAddress, ConsignorPhone,
    ClientCompanyName, ClientCompanyContact)
    Foreign Key: ConsignorNo REFERENCES CONSIGNOR
ESTATE (<u>ConsignorNo</u>, EstateName, ConsignorAddress, ConsignorPhone,
    EstatePrimaryContact)
    Foreign Key: ConsignorNo REFERENCES CONSIGNOR
BUYER (<u>BuyerNo</u>, BuyerName, BuyerAddress, BuyerContact, BuyerPhone,
    BuyerType, BuyerRepresentative, BuyerCreditRating,
    BuyerReceivingAddress)
OFFICE (<u>OfficeCode</u>, OfficeName, OfficeAddress, OfficePhone)
REGULAR (<u>OfficeCode</u>, OfficeName, OfficeAddress, OfficePhone, Region,
    FacilityType)
    Foreign Key: OfficeCode REFERENCES OFFICE
OFF-SITE (<u>OfficeCode</u>, OfficeName, OfficeAddress, OfficePhone, AuctionLocation,
    AuctionOfficeName, AuctionOfficeAddress)
    Foreign Key: OfficeCode REFERENCES OFFICE

FIGURE 3-27 Barnaby's auction system: relational model, part 2.

Take some time to go over these three figures and note the statements, line by line. These figures represent the relational data model using a standard notation. Study the statements for each table or relation. Notice the relation or table names shown in upper case. Note how the column names are shown within parentheses for each relation. See how the notation indicates primary key columns with underscores. Specially make a note of the foreign key clauses. Refer to the dependent or weak entity types and their corresponding strong entity types. Observe how the primary keys are formed for the weak entity types.

DEPARTMENT (<u>DepartmentNo</u>, OfficeCode,DepartmentName, DepartmentType)
    Foreign Keys: OfficeCode REFERENCES OFFICE,*NOT NULL*
        OfficeCode REFERENCES REGULAR,*NOT NULL*
        OfficeCode REFERENCES OFF-SITE,*NOT NULL*
DEPARTMENT-ITEM (<u>DepartmentNo</u>, <u>ReceiptNo</u>, <u>ItemNo</u>)
    Foreign Keys: ReceiptNo, ItemNo REFERENCES PROPERTY-ITEM
        DepartmentNo REFERENCES DEPARTMENT
SALE (<u>SaleNo</u>, SaleName, SaleDate)
LOT (<u>SaleNo</u>, <u>LotNo</u>, ReceiptNo, ItemNo, BuyerNo, ShipmentNo, LotDescription,
    TopBid, NextHighestBid, NextBidBuyerNo, LotDisposalStatus,
    HammerPrice, CurrencyCode)
    Foreign Keys: SaleNo REFERENCES SALE
        ReceiptNo, ItemNo REFERENCES PROPERTY-ITEM
        BuyerNo REFERENCES BUYER
        ShipmentNo REFERENCES SHIPMENT
SESSION (<u>SaleNo</u>, <u>SessionNo</u>, SessionName)
    Foreign Key: SaleNo REFERENCES SALE
SHIPPER (<u>ShipperId</u>, ShipperName, ShipperAddress, ShipperContact,
    ShipperPhone)
SHIPMENT (<u>ShipmentNo</u>, ShipperId, ShipmentMethod, ShipmentDate,
    ShipperReferenceNo, ShipmentCharge)
    Foreign Key: ShipperId REFERENCES SHIPPER

FIGURE 3-28 Barnaby's auction system: relational model, part 3.

PHYSICAL MODEL: OVERVIEW

From the prior discussions, you know the purpose of the logical data model. You have reviewed the steps; and you have learned the steps and tasks of the process. First, you model the information requirements by creating a conceptual data model. Then you transform the conceptual data model into a logical data model such as the relational or hierarchical or network data model. As the relational data model is superior to the others and because it is widely used, we emphasized the relational data model in our discussions.

Remember, a conceptual data model is a generic data model. It has no relational or hierarchical or network flavor. A conceptual data model does not consist of tables with rows and columns; only a relational data model does. Only when you move from a conceptual data model to a logical data model such as the relational data model will you represent and perceive data as contained in two-dimensional tables or relations.

From the relational data model, we proceed to the physical data model to represent the information requirements in physical hardware storage. Conceptual models and relational models are not representations of how data is actually stored. Actual data is going to reside on physical storage, and the physical model stipulates how, where, and which data gets stored in physical storage. The emphasis here is exclusively on relational databases. When we discuss any aspect of a physical model, assume that the discussion refers to relational databases.

In order to store and manage data on physical storage, the representation of the logical model must be transformed into a representation for actual data storage. Why is this necessary? Computer systems do not store data in the form of tables with columns and rows; they typically store data in a different way. Computer storage systems store data as files and records. Physical model is at the lowest level of abstraction for implementing the database on physical storage. Therefore, in physical data modeling, you are concerned with the features of the storage system on which your database will reside. Further, you are also concerned with the functions, features, and facilities of the DBMS selected to manage your database.

Model Components

When you finish with physical modeling, what is the collective set of components you expect to produce? When you create a physical data model, what is the set of components that are expected to emerge? What major components make up the physical model of your database system? Here is a list of the essential components:

File Organization. For each file in the physical model, the method or technique for arranging the records of the file on physical storage.

Indexes. Types and list of index files to improve data access.

Integrity Constraints. Constraints or rules in the form of data edit rules and business rules; rules for enforcement of referential integrity on inserts and deletes.

Data Volumes. Sizing for each data and index file.

Data Usage. Analysis of expected data access paths and access frequencies.

Data Distribution. Strategy for providing data to users by means of centralized or partitioned or replicated database systems.

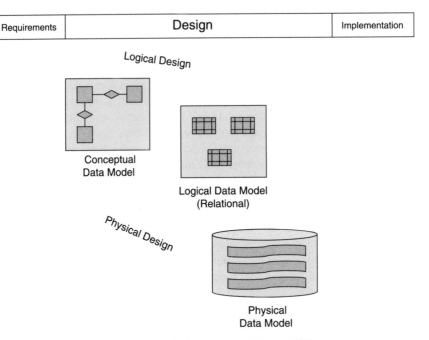

FIGURE 3-29   Physical modeling in overall modeling.

Transformation Steps

Our scope of discussions excludes intricate details of physical modeling. Therefore, let us conclude here with two figures about physical data models.

Refer to Figure 3-29 that shows the transition from conceptual data model to relational data model and thereafter to physical data model. The figure gives some overall indications on the components in the models at these three levels.

Figure 3-30 indicates the mapping of components between a relational data model and a physical data model.

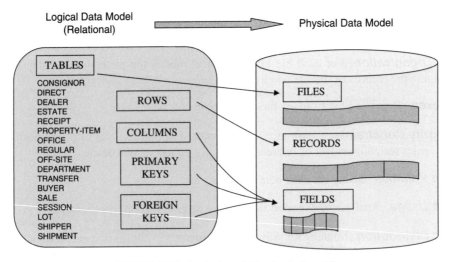

FIGURE 3-30   Logical model to physical model.

CHAPTER SUMMARY

- Data models created at the four information levels in an organization: external data model, conceptual data model, logical data model, and physical data model.
- Each type of model fulfills specific purposes: conceptual model, the highest level of abstraction, is used for discussion with domain experts and user groups; external model, a set of partial models for individual user groups, describes information relevant to individual user groups; logical model, specified for the type of database system, is closer to programmers and analysts; physical model, the lowest level with details of software and hardware, is used as the database blueprint.
- Studying a data model includes examination of the symbols and meanings for the components: entity types, relationships, attributes, identifiers, constraints, and generalization/specialization.
- Studying a given data model helps learning the steps for creating data models. Note the E-R and UML models for the case study—Barnaby's auction system.
- The general methodology for creating a conceptual data model: create individual external models and aggregate the partial models.
- Review entity type and look for generalization and specialization. Define supertype and subtype entities.
- Note direct relationships.
- List all attributes for each entity type.
- Mark the identifier for each entity type.
- Draw the model diagram and review it for completeness and accuracy.
- A logical model for a relational database system consists of two-dimensional tables.

REVIEW QUESTIONS

1. Match the column entries:

1. Generalization	A. All subsets present
2. User view	B. Restrictive rules
3. Entity type	C. Dependent entity type
4. Minimum cardinality	D. Bulk of database content
5. Complete specialization	E. Partial model
6. Weak entity type	F. No duplicate values
7. Constraints	G. Combines partial models
8. Attribute values	H. Supersets
9. View integration	I. Indicates optionality
10. Primary key column	J. Transforms into relation

2. List the steps for studying a given data model. What are supersets and subsets?
3. What are direct relationships among entity types? How do you identify these in a model diagram as opposed to noting indirect relationships?

4. Why are identifiers important? What purpose does an identifier serve in an entity type?

5. Refer to Figures 3-3 through 3-5. List all the relationships with their cardinalities.

6. For Barnaby's auction system, list all the supersets and their subsets. What type of specialization does each represent? Explain.

7. Compare the E-R model and the UML class diagrams for Barnaby's auction system. List the similarities and differences.

8. List the steps for creating a conceptual data model. Describe each step briefly.

9. Name the relational tables in the logical data model for Barnaby's auction system.

10. Pick any one-to-many relationship from the logical data model for Barnaby's auction system. Explain how the linkage is established through the foreign key.

4

OBJECTS OR ENTITIES IN DETAIL

CHAPTER OBJECTIVES

- Provide an in-depth discussion of entities or business objects
- Show how to identify and define entity types
- Present categories of entity types and their application
- Explore dependencies between entity types
- Review generalization and specialization thoroughly
- Scrutinize special cases and exceptions
- Learn relevant advanced concepts
- Conclude with an entity validity checklist

After the discussions in the previous chapter, you are very familiar with several aspects of a data model. You understand the various components that make up a conceptual data model. We presented a comprehensive real-world data model. You went through the model, component by component. You can recognize the significance of the different components.

Using the data model as a basis, you also studied the steps and the tasks needed to arrive at the various components and then the complete data model itself. This process reinforced your comprehension of the concepts behind each type of component. You reviewed the method for identifying business objects or entity types; you explored the attributes and the identifiers; you scrutinized the relationships and their implications. Now we have come to a point where you need to strengthen your comprehension of individual component types even further.

In this chapter, you will launch an in-depth study of business objects or entity types. As this is a primary modeling concept, it is proper that we begin our in-depth study with

Data Modeling Fundamentals. By Paulraj Ponniah
Copyright © 2007 John Wiley & Sons, Inc.

business objects. Then we will move on to other components. In the subsequent chapters, we will discuss attributes and then relationships.

We will embark on the intense study of business objects as part of a conceptual data model. As you know, this model, being at the highest level of abstraction and devoid of technical details, renders itself to understanding easily both for the domain experts and IT personnel. Your understanding of business objects as part of the conceptual model can easily be shifted to the logical and physical models in later chapters.

Our study will use the E-R modeling technique to explore the features of the components. You already know how the E-R modeling technique presents business objects or entity types. Although this discussion may use other modeling techniques, we want to stay with E-R technique because of its wider use and also because it has been in practice longer than most of the other techniques.

ENTITY TYPES OR OBJECT SETS

What are entities? What are entity types? Can we think of these as objects and object sets? How do you recognize objects in the context of the information content you want to model? Are there different categories of entity types? We want to explore these questions in detail.

When you consider the information that an organization needs for carrying out its various business processes, when you break down this information into small elements, you arrive at pieces of data about things the organization is interested in. For an organization such as a bank, the information is about its customers, about its checking, savings, and loan accounts, its various promotional products, and so on. For a medical center, the information is about its patients, health care procedures, its laboratory services, the medical personnel, and so on. The type of information and the type of things about which information is needed depends on the particular organization and its domain of operations.

What are these things about which an organization needs information? How can we classify them? Are these individual things or groups of similar things? Take the case of a medical center. Look at individual patients. Each patient is separate and unique. The medical center needs to keep information about each patient. When you model the information about patients, do you have to model information about each patient as separate components? Let us define precisely what we mean by things about which an organization needs to keep information.

Comprehensive Definition

Because business objects and their representation in a data model are of paramount importance to an organization, we need to emphasize the clear understanding of the concept. Only then you will be able to identify the relevant business objects and proceed further in creating a data model. The business objects form the initial set of components to begin the process of data modeling.

If you are creating a data system for an airlines company, you need to collect and store information about the fleet of aircraft, the flight routes, the passenger reservations, and so on. Again, if you are implementing a data system for a car dealership, you need information on the inventory, the specific models your company sells, the promotions, and so on. Are these—aircraft, flight route, reservation, inventory, vehicle model, promotion—the business objects to be represented in a data model?

We need to get a clear understanding of what constitutes a business object. Should a business object be tangible? What about concepts that are intangible? What about business events about which we need information? Are events business objects? Should they be modeled? If so, how?

Definition Guidelines. Before attempting a precise and comprehensive definition of an entity in data modeling, let us develop a few guidelines. The guidelines should suggest to us the necessary ingredients in a good definition. We would need guidance on how to produce a good definition. What are the considerations?

Here are a few guidelines for a good definition of an entity:

Clarity. The definition must be very clear and unambiguous. Readers of the definition must understand the definition statements in one way and in only one way. The definition must not mislead readers.

All-Inclusive. The definition must be comprehensive enough to include all relevant and important aspects of an entity.

Succinctness. At the same time, the definition must be concise and to the point. It must not be couched in unnecessary verbiage.

Precision. The definition must be clear-cut to mean exactly what it says.

Description. The definition must be able to describe an entity as adequately as possible.

Contextual. The definition must define an entity only in the context of the information for an organization or its appropriate domains being modeled.

Significance. Notice if any superset and subsets are present. If they are shown, examine the nature and relationships between each group of subsets and their superset.

Illustration. If necessary, the definition must include a few examples for further clarification.

With the above guidelines in mind, if you refer to how various authors and data modeling experts define an entity or business object, you will notice a few different versions. If you ask practicing data modelers for a definition, they would offer a few more variations.

Here is a sample of various definitions of an entity from authors and data modeling experts:

- A thing that can be distinctively identified.
- Means anything about which we store information. For each entity type, certain attributes are stored.
- Any distinguishable object that is to be represented in the database.
- Represents some "thing" that is to be stored for later reference. The term entity refers to the *logical* representation of data.

- Any distinguishable person, place, thing, event, or concept about which information is kept.
- May be an object with a physical existence (a particular person, car, house, or employee) or it may be an object with conceptual existence (a company, a job, or a university course).
- A "thing" or "object" in the real world that is distinguishable from all other objects.
- Is a person, place, thing, or concept that has characteristics of interest to the enterprise and about which you want to store information.
- Is an object in the real world that is distinguishable from other objects.
- Is some item in the real world that we wish to track.

Defining Entities or Business Objects. Taking into considerations the various definitions mentioned above, can we formulate a proper definition of an entity? What can we say about an entity? Reading the above definitions, you can detect the following underlying, common themes in them:

- An entity is a thing or object or concept.
- It is something in the real world.
- It is distinguishable from other objects.
- It is something about which an organization is interested and wants to store information about and keep track of it.
- An entity is a single thing that may considered as part of a group of similar things.

Following the guidelines for definition and also considering the common themes in a variety of definitions, let us arrive at a workable definition.

Definition of an Entity. An entity is a single distinguishable business object such as a person, place, thing, event or concept, part of a group of similar objects, relevant to an organization about which the organization is interested in storing and using information.

Let us examine this definition using an example. An airline business is interested in storing and using information about all its passengers. Therefore, according to the definition, each passenger about whom the organization wants to store information is an entity. What can we say about this entity?

- Each passenger is an entity or business object for the airline company.
- This entity is a person.
- Each entity called passenger is part of the group known as passengers with similar characteristics.
- However, each passenger is uniquely identifiable. Passenger Mary Jones is unique and different from passenger Sylvia Rodriguez.
- The entity is relevant to the airline company. The company wants to store information about the entity.

At this stage, let us make the distinction between physical and conceptual entities. You have noted from our discussions that some of the entities mentioned may be seen, heard, or touched—things that are tangible. However, examples of some other entities indicate that these entities cannot be seen or experienced. These are intangible. Nevertheless, both categories are things of interest to an organization. Your data model will include both categories.

Physical Entities. Things with physical existence: an employee, an automobile, a building, equipment, or an aircraft.

Conceptual Entities. Things with existence as concepts: a university course, a visit to the doctor, an invoice, a bank account, an aircraft type.

Entity Types. So far in our discussion, we have indicated one particular thing of interest to an organization as an entity. An entity is a single thing. One customer is a "thing" that an organization is interested in. Of course, there would be thousands of customers for an organization. So, data modelers make the distinction and refer to the notion that refers to the collection of entities as an entity type. Entities are individual "things," whereas entity types refer to the group of entities.

Figure 4-1 illustrates the two notions of entity types and entities.

Note the two examples shown in the figure:

Entity types: EMPLOYEE, DEPARTMENT

Entity: Individual occurrences of each entity type

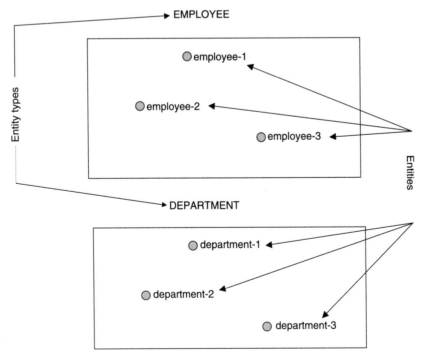

FIGURE 4-1 Entity types and entities.

Illustrations with Examples. Having defined entities and entity types, let us list a few examples to illustrate the concepts. We will list some typical organizations, state their core businesses, and present examples.

Refer to the columns shown in Figure 4-2. The first column lists examples of types of organizations. In the second column, you will read about the core business of each organization type. The third and fourth columns present examples of entity types and entities each organization type will be interested in. When you examine the E-R data models for these organization types, you will notice the listed entity types shown as square-cornered boxes.

Identifying Entity Types

Having successfully defined entities and entity types, you now have a clearer notion of what constitutes business objects for an organization and what needs to be included in your data model. You have noted that when we say an entity, we mean an individual thing, and that an entity type refers to a collection of similar individual things. If you represent an entity type using a box in the model diagram, then you can imagine entities as represented by single points within that box.

The next consideration relates to identification of entities and entity types within an organization. We know that entities are those things of interest to the organization for the purpose of collecting and storing information. But what are these things of interest? Who is going to tell you? How do you find out? Are there any methodologies to ascertaining entities? Are there any guidelines? Let us explore.

Identification Guidelines. Of course, the identification of entities occurs during the requirements definition phase in the data system development life cycle. You work very closely with the domain experts. You carefully study each business process and scrutinize the data needs for each process. You come across many entities or business objects. You are able to inventory the various data elements being used or needed.

ORGANIZATION TYPE	CORE BUSINESS	ENTITY TYPES	ENTITIES
Airline	Provide air transportation	AIRPLANE, AIRPLANE TYPE, FLIGHT SCHEDULE, AIRPORT, PASSENGER	Planes in the fleet, types of planes, domestic and foreign airports, economy passengers, arrival times
Car Dealership	Sell cars/vans/trucks	VEHICLE, CUSTOMER, SALESPERSON, LOAN, LEASE, MANUFACTURER	Cars in the inventory, leases to customers, car manufacturers, corporate customers, vehicle types
Department Store	Sell consumer goods	CUSTOMER, PRODUCT SALE, DEPARTMENT, SALES-PROMOTION	Walk-in customers, women's coats, men's shoes, holiday discounts, television sets, garden equipment
University	Provide higher learning	STUDENT, FACULTY, COURSE, CLASS, REGISTRATION	Full-time students, adjunct faculty members, data modeling course, spring semester
Medical Center	Provide health care	PATIENT, PHYSICIAN, PROCEDURE, APPOINTMENT, ADMISSION, ROOM-BED	Same-day-surgery patients, ER residents, neonatal ward, inpatient admissions, ICU rooms
Computer Consulting	Run consulting projects	CLIENT, CONSULTANT, PROJECT, FEE-SCHEDULE, ASSIGNMENT	Foreign clients, full-time consultants, data modeling project, assignments of part-time consultants

FIGURE 4-2 Examples of entity types and entities.

Of the multitude of data elements, which ones qualify to be modeled and which ones to be ignored? Let us work out a few guidelines. Guidelines are not methodologies for identification of entities; whatever methodology is serviceable, the guidelines will have to influence the methodology. The guidelines should prompt you in your decision either to include or exclude a type of entity in the data model. Here are a few guidelines for identifying entity types:

Scope. Entity type must be within the scope of the information domain that is being modeled within the organization.

Relevant, Not Redundant. It must be of immense interest to the organization—something about which the organization wants to collect and store information for running its business.

Representation. It must represent a set of similar individual things.

Distinctiveness. It must be some set of individual things where each instance or occurrence of individual things within the set can be readily and uniquely identified.

Conceptual Integrity. It must represent a single concept that embraces a set of similar things with cohesive characteristics.

Approaches to Identification. Different data modelers advocate a variety of approaches for identifying entity types. As you become more and more adept at data modeling, you will compile a set of techniques that works for you and produces a methodology for yourself. We need to reiterate that whatever approach you might take, it must be completely grounded in proper requirements definition. This phase is where you begin the process of identifying entity types. This is where you decide what to include and what to ignore.

At this point, we want to suggest two basic approaches to the process of identifying entity types. For either approach, you need to go through the requirements definition phase. You have to complete the usual tasks of reviewing business operations, studying all relevant business processes, poring over pertinent documents, conducting interviews, meeting with all groups of stakeholders in the organization, and so on. All of these must be done quite thoroughly for identifying entity types.

The first method is a meticulous, systematic approach. As you go through the various business processes, you document all the data elements involved. Then you will use the collection of data elements to proceed to the identification process.

The second approach is more intuitive. Based on your completed requirements definition phase, you try to come up with a list of entity types that must be present in your data model. For small data systems, this method is likely to have better results.

Process-Oriented Method. This method is more rigorous and systematic than other methods. Usually, where the model tends to be large and complex, this method proves to be effective. In the past chapters, we have hinted at this method. Now let us examine this method in more detail.

Every company exists for the purpose of fulfilling its core business. For example, the core business for a banking business may be expressed by the following statement: help customers manage their finances by providing banking services. The bank would fulfill its core business by performing a number of individual business processes. The marketing department would perform business processes relating to marketing and sales functions. The loan department would perform business processes pertaining to loans and mortgages. The sum total of all the processes enables the bank to fulfill its core business of providing banking service to its customers.

While performing each of the many processes, the relevant user would collect data elements or use data elements collected in other processes. As you observe and study each process, you can list all the data elements applicable to that process. Recall that the set of data elements for all the processes in a department forms a partial external data model. This method of identifying entity types makes use of the principle of aggregating all partial external models.

Study Figure 4-3. This figure shows the various business processes for a bank and the data elements associated with each process.

The next task in the method aggregates or combines all the data elements and forms groups. Figure 4-4 shows how this is done.

As soon as the data groups are formed, you examine each group and see if that group of data elements describes something of interest to the bank. You pose questions based on the guidelines mentioned earlier. Is something that is being described within the scope of what you are modeling? Is it relevant? Is that something representative of a set of similar individual things? Can each unit in the set be uniquely identified?

One by one, you will be able to identify the business object sets or entity types. These entity types will form the basic components in your data model. Figure 4-5 indicates how the entity types are derived from the data groups.

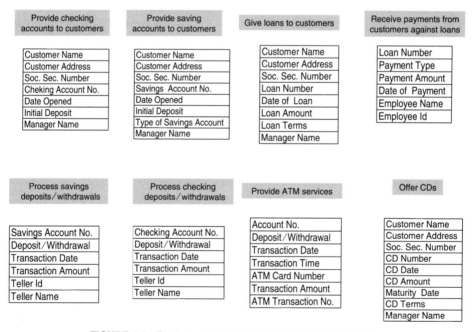

FIGURE 4-3 Banking business: processes and data elements.

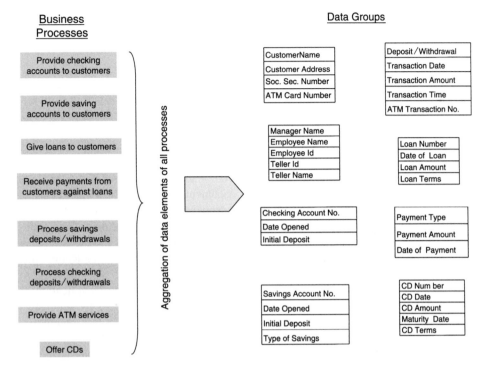

FIGURE 4-4   Banking business: data aggregation.

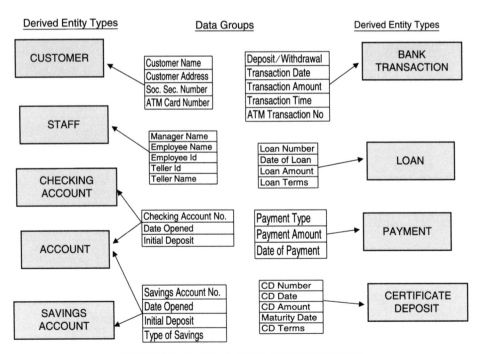

FIGURE 4-5   Banking business: deriving entity types.

After we derive the entity types, we go ahead and classify the entity types into categories before proceeding further with the data model. Depending on the category, additional effort will be warranted. In a way, this method is process-oriented because we examine the various processes to determine the entity types.

Data-Oriented Method. This is somewhat an intuitive method. Based on everything you have studied and documented during the requirements phase plays a key role in supporting the intuition. Here is how this method works.

Based on the various business operations, the data modeler comes up with an initial set of entity types. He tabulates the list and maybe even puts down some characteristics for each entity type within each box. That is the end of the first iteration. Using this initial crude diagram, the data modeler revisits the documented information requirements and reviews the initial set with the domain experts. Now he or she is performing the second iteration. The set of entity types gets refined. Then the modeler moves on to the next iteration. After a few iterations, the data modeler will be able to produce a good working set of entity types that must be included in the data model. Figure 4-6 gives an indication of the iterations and shows the outputs of each iteration.

After a few iterations before concluding the activity of entity type identification, the data modeler must validate the outputs with the domain experts and by referring to some major business processes. However, if you are modeling a large and complex set of information requirements, this method may not produce a complete set of entity types. Even after filling out other components in the data model, you may have to go back to keep refining the data model a few times.

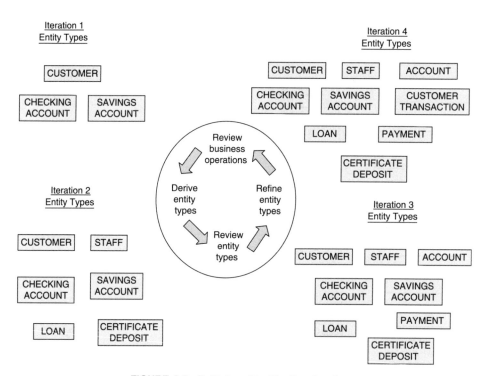

FIGURE 4-6 Entity type identification: iterations.

Homonyms and Synonyms

Homonyms and synonyms could cause problems in properly identifying entity types. These could be problematic not only for entity types but also for attributes and, sometimes, for other data model components. At this time, let us discuss homonyms and synonyms for entity types. Why is detecting homonyms and synonyms important in data modeling? If you do not detect and resolve them, the resulting data model could be seriously flawed. Homonyms and synonyms cause misunderstandings and make the data model less precise.

Generally, homonyms and synonyms cause problems when the scope of the data model is fairly wide. This is especially the case, when multiple data modelers undertake to look at partial requirements and come up with partial data models. At the time of consolidating the partial models, if homonyms and synonyms are not reckoned with, your integrated data model will be flawed. So, let us briefly discuss the implications.

Homonyms. Two words or phrases that are spelt the same way or have similar sounds constitute homonyms. For two words or phrases with similar spelling or sound to be homonyms, they must refer to different business objects or entities. These different objects may have completely different characteristics or may share some characteristics but differ from each other in many other ways.

Homonyms sneak into a data model because of several reasons. Homonyms can be quite prevalent when many teams of data modelers create partial models that will eventually be combined. In such situations, two or more entity types are referred to by the same or similar names. In this case, if unresolved, the consolidated data model will show more than one entity types with similar names. What will happen in this situation? The final review will reveal more than one entity type with similar names. At that time, because of confusion, only one entity type will be retained in the data model and others discarded. This is a case of nonreconciled homonyms.

Another type of problem relates to implied homonyms. Here, homonyms are embodied in a single entity type. In this case, only one entity type is identified. However, if you carefully notice, within its definition itself, you will understand that there are really two entity types to be modeled. You need to separate out the two entity types. Let us consider examples of these two cases of homonyms with ways to resolve them.

Nonreconciled Homonyms. See Figure 4-7 for an example. Note the definitions. The definitions really tell us that these are homonyms that cannot be allowed on the data model without resolving them. Note also the different identifiers. The figure illustrates how the homonyms are reconciled.

Contained in One Entity Type. Figure 4-8 shows a single box to represent an entity type. After reading the definition, it becomes clear that, in fact, this actually should be made to represent two distinct entity types. Observe how the figure presents the resolution.

Synonyms. These are the opposite of homonyms. Here, two different words or phrases that are spelled differently or sound differently are synonyms provided they refer to the same business object or entity. Synonyms are more prevalent than homonyms. Synonyms result from different departments or user groups calling the same thing by different names over time. These departments must have been working separately, each using its own

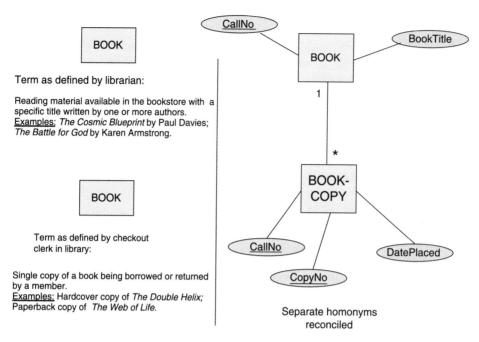

FIGURE 4-7 Nonreconciled homonyms.

terminology. One department may refer to workers as *employees* whereas another department may call them *associates*.

Resolution of synonyms is harder than that of homonyms. Homonyms may be tracked with comparative ease because of similarly spelled names or similar sounding words. But

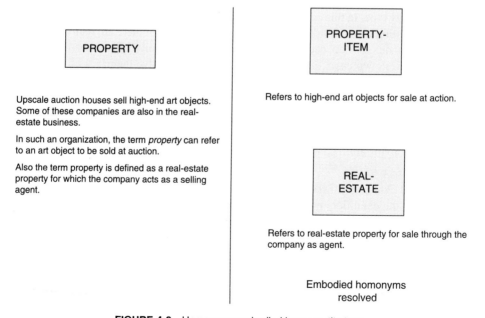

FIGURE 4-8 Homonyms embodied in one entity type.

in the case of synonyms, you will have to sift through hundreds of terms to detect them. During the initial iterations of the data modeling process, as soon as you suspect that two entity types could be synonymous, put them through a thorough examination.

Determine the degree of similarity between two entity types by studying the following:

- Definition of the entity types
- Attributes of the two entity types (however, the attributes may themselves have different names)
- Identifier for each of the two entity types
- Relationship of each entity type with other entity types

Just like homonyms, if synonyms are not resolved, the resulting data model will be imprecise and have redundancies. Data consistency and data integrity could also be compromised.

Figure 4-9 presents a set of unsolved synonyms and also indicates how these synonyms are resolved.

Category of Entity Types

In the rest of this chapter, we will explore the various categories of entity types in detail. Therefore, at this point, we just want to express that a data model will contain different categories of entity types. All entity types shown in a data model represent a set of similar business objects. You know that a CUSTOMER entity type symbolizes the set of all the individual customers of an organization. An ORDER entity type represents

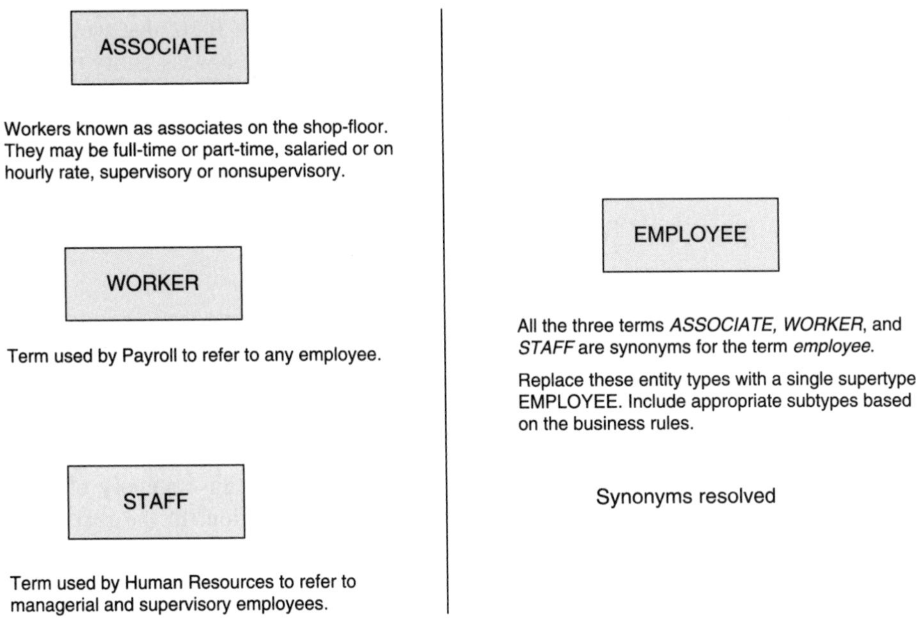

ASSOCIATE

Workers known as associates on the shop-floor. They may be full-time or part-time, salaried or on hourly rate, supervisory or nonsupervisory.

WORKER

Term used by Payroll to refer to any employee.

STAFF

Term used by Human Resources to refer to managerial and supervisory employees.

EMPLOYEE

All the three terms *ASSOCIATE, WORKER,* and *STAFF* are synonyms for the term *employee.*

Replace these entity types with a single supertype EMPLOYEE. Include appropriate subtypes based on the business rules.

Synonyms resolved

FIGURE 4-9 Resolution of synonyms.

the set of all the orders received by an organization. Similarly, an ORDER-DETAIL entity type denotes the set of all the line-item details of all the orders.

However, variation in categories of entity types arise based on a few differences in conditions and functions. Some entity types are different because of existence conditions. Another entity type is different because of its special function in a certain type of relationship. Some entity types may be derived from other general entity types. Let us list the major categories of entity types.

Weak Entity Type. This entity type represents a set of individual entities that cannot exist by themselves in a database. A weak entity type needs another strong entity type in the data model. A weak entity type depends on the related strong entity type for its existence. Without the presence of strong entities and the association with these entities, weak entities cannot stand on their own in the data system.

Here are a few examples:

Weak Entity Type	Related Strong Entity Type
ORDER-DETAIL	ORDER
INVOICE-DETAIL	INVOICE
STATEMENT-ITEM	VENDOR-STATEMENT
ORDER	CUSTOMER
EMPLOYEE-DEPENDENT	EMPLOYEE

Regular or Strong Entity Type. Entity occurrences that can exist in the database on their own form a strong or regular entity type. Most entity types you find in a data model are of this category. They are not dependent on other entity types for their existence. When you identify an entity type to be included in the data model, you need to verify whether the entity occurrences can have independent existences. If so, that would be a strong entity type. Otherwise, the identified entity type would be a weak entity type that would need another strong entity type for its existence.

In addition to the strong entity types noted above, the following are a few more examples of regular entity types:

Strong or Regular Entity Type
STUDENT
FACULTY
COURSE
TEXTBOOK
EXAM-TYPE

Supertypes and Subtypes. As you already know, you find this category of entity types in a data model because of generalization and specialization. In the real world, business objects occur that are special cases of other types of business objects. On the other hand, when you examine certain sets of business objects, you will discover that these can be separated out into subsets of similar business objects. Such entity types are categorized as subtypes and supertypes.

Note the following examples of supertypes and the corresponding subtypes of entities:

Supertype	Subtypes
PASSENGER	ECONOMY, BUSINESS, FIRST
PERSON	MALE, FEMALE
RENTAL-PROPERTY	MOUNTAIN, BEACH
STOCKHOLDER	INSTITUTIONAL, INDIVIDUAL
BANK-ACCOUNT	CHECKING, SAVINGS, LOAN

Association or Intersection Entity Type. If you have two entity types in many-to-many relationship, in a conceptual data model diagram you can show these two entity types and mark their relationship as many-to-many. In a data model at the conceptual data model, expressing many-to-many relationships is perfectly standard. However, when you want to transform the conceptual data model into a logical model for relational databases, you run into a problem. In a relational model, the two entity types transform into two relational tables. But when you try to transform the many-to-many relationship using foreign keys, you have to address the question of where to place the foreign key—in the first table, or the second table, or in both.

The intersection entity type resolves this problem. In order to transform a many-to-many relationship, you have to introduce a new entity type, called the intersection entity type, into your data model. You may do this in the conceptual data model itself in preparation of its transformation into a relational model down the line. Chapter 7 covers this topic in more detail. At this point, take a look at Figure 4-10 showing an example of intersection entity type.

Aggregation Entity Type. Consider three entity types: WAREHOUSE, SHIP-METHOD, and ORDER. When you want to identity a particular shipment and describe it, you need to include warehouse, shipping method, and order data. A shipment of a specific order takes place from a particular warehouse and using a certain shipping method. Therefore, we need an entity type SHIPMENT to indicate the three-way relationship among WAREHOUSE, SHIP-METHOD, and ORDER. The identifier for this new

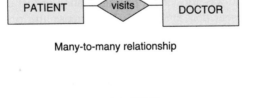

Many-to-many relationship

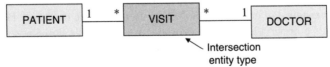

Many-to-many relationship resolved through an intersection entity type

FIGURE 4-10 Intersection entity type.

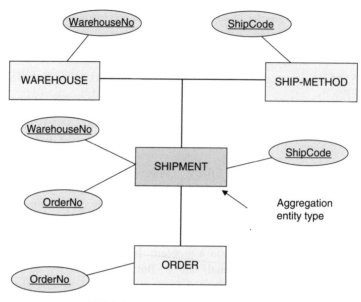

FIGURE 4-11 Aggregation entity type.

entity type SHIPMENT has to be the aggregation of the identifiers of the three related enti-ties. Aggregation entity type denotes three-way, four-way, and sometimes, higher degree relationships.

Figure 4-11 illustrates the formation of an aggregation entity type for the above three-way relationship:

EXPLORING DEPENDENCIES

Earlier in this chapter we reviewed methods for identifying entity types. As soon as you identify an entity type, you need to recognize which category the entity type would belong to. Depending on the category, your representation of that entity type will vary from others. By taking into account the category and proper representation of the entity type, you are paving the way for correct implementation of that entity type in the final database. Proper representation enables you to impose the right constraints in the implemented database.

One aspect of such scrutiny relates to exploring dependencies. What do we mean by that? Let us say that you have identified an entity type called ORDER. Examine the indi-vidual entities being represented by this entity type. These individual entities or business objects are single orders. Now, ask the question. Does the existence of a single order depend on the existence of entities of another entity type in the database? Does the exist-ence of an order number 1234 depend on the existence of the corresponding customer number 2244 in the database? If you delete customer number 2244 from the database, does that mean that you have to delete order number 1234 also from the database to pre-serve data integrity? The answers to these questions determine the dependency of ORDER entity type on CUSTOMER entity type. This is the process of exploring dependencies of entity types.

Let us say you determine that ORDER entity type is dependent on CUSTOMER entity type. Your representation of these two entity types and their relationship will be different from how you will show other entity types and relationships. Differentiation in this respect achieves two purposes. Your data model will reflect the information requirements truly; proper constraints will be imposed on the implemented database.

Dependent or Weak Entity Types

Let us pursue the example of CUSTOMER and ORDER entity types. Let us suppose that when you gather the information requirements, you find out more details about customers and orders. You determine how orders are received and how they are recorded. You note what is allowed to happen when orders are received from new customers.

Two cases are possible. In both cases, ORDER entity type is dependent of CUSTOMER entity type for its existence.

Some Independent Orders. In this case, independent orders are allowed to exist in the database even if it is for a short while. If an order is received from a new customer before the customer data is recorded in the database, the order processing department wants to record the order in the database and get a head-start on the fulfillment of the order. Later on, when the customer data is recorded in the database, the connection between order and customer will be made.

How do you distinguish this condition in the data model? You will make the distinction by means of a minimum cardinality indicator on the relationship between the two entity types. Still the data model will show ORDER as a weak entity type depending on the corresponding strong entity type CUSTOMER. If a customer occurrence gets deleted from the database, all of the pertinent order occurrences must be deleted from the database.

Every Order Dependent. On the other hand, the organization does not permit any orders to be recorded in the database before the relevant customer data is recorded. Even for a new customer, first the customer data must be recorded and then the order must be recorded. The order processing department must ensure this sequence of data entry.

In this case, the data model will simply show ORDER as a weak entity type depending on the corresponding strong entity type CUSTOMER. There is no need to distinguish the relationship further with minimum cardinality indicators.

Figure 4-12 illustrates these two cases of weak entity types.

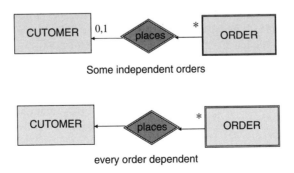

FIGURE 4-12 Dependence and partial independence.

Classifying Dependencies

We have discussed that a weak entity type depends on its corresponding strong entity type. The question arises whether all dependencies are of the same type. Are they different? If we are able to differentiate between the types of dependencies, could we then classify the weak entity types? What are the implications of the classification? How do they influence your ability to use your data model as a communication tool for discussion with domain experts? What effect does the classification have on the use of the data model as a blueprint for implementation?

Weak entities may be classified into two groups based on how exactly they depend on their corresponding strong entities. If ORDER is dependent on CUSTOMER, what exactly is the nature of the dependency? Examining a number of weak entities and their dependencies, we can establish that we can put weak entities into two classifications. Let us discuss these groupings.

ID Dependency. Entities in some weak entity type cannot be uniquely identified by their own attributes. The entities in such entity types will have to be identified by means of their association with entities in the corresponding strong entity types. Let us take a few examples.

Suppose we have a weak entity type ORDER-LINE. Each entity in this entity type represents a line-item of the corresponding order. The line-items will contain product, quantity, and price data. The line-items on every order will usually be numbered sequentially beginning with "01" and proceeding with higher numbers depending on how many line-items there are on the order. The entities in every ORDER-LINE entity type will have the same sequence numbers. None of the attributes—line item number, product, quantity, or price—can be used as an identifier for ORDER-LINE entity type. What is the solution?

Each entity in ORDER-LINE weak entity type can be uniquely identified only through its association with the relevant entity in the corresponding ORDER strong entity type. If you want to identify and locate the third line-item on order number 123456, then you can use the concatenation of "123456" and "03" for purposes of identification. Thus, the entities in ORDER-LINE depend on the entities in ORDER for identification. This is ID (identification) dependency. The dependency of weak entity type ORDER-LINE on strong entity type ORDER is an ID dependency.

Let us consider another example. Here, the weak entity type is CHILDREN depending on strong entity type of EMPLOYEE. The relationship is established to associate children with their parents for insurance coverage. The attributes of CHILDREN are name of child, age, type of insurance, and, perhaps, a generic sequence number similar to the one used for order line-items. None of the attributes of CHILDREN is of any use as a unique identifier. CHILDREN entity type has to depend on entity type EMPLOYEE for identification. This is also a case of ID dependency.

Because the strong entity type identifies the corresponding weak entity type, the strong entity type is also known as an identifying entity type. The relationship between the strong entity type and the weak entity type is called an identifying relationship.

Existence Dependency. Let us revisit the above two examples. We determined that the dependency of ORDER-LINE on ORDER is an ID dependency. Similarly, CHILDREN depends on EMPLOYEE for identification. The weak entity types need their corresponding strong entities for identification. But ID dependency also implies existence dependency.

Entities in ORDER-LINE cannot exist in the database without their relevant entities in ORDER. The existence of entities in ORDER-LINE depends on the existence of corresponding entities in ORDER. If certain orders get deleted from the database, their corresponding line-items must also be deleted. The line-items cannot exist in the database on their own. The dependency is not only ID dependency, it is also existence dependency.

Similarly, the dependency of CHILDREN on EMPLOYEE is both ID dependency and existence dependency. Entities of CHILDREN cannot exist in the database without the existence of their corresponding entities in EMPLOYEE. If an employee is deleted from the database, all the corresponding children must also be removed from the database.

Although ID dependency implies existence dependency, the converse need not be true. Consider a data model where two entity types are represented. One entity type is CUSTOMER and the other is CREDIT-CARD. This model needs to show credit card information for each customer. In the database, we need to record credit card data for each customer. A customer may have more than one credit card. Examine these two entity types. Entities in CREDIT-CARD cannot exist unless their corresponding entities in CUSTOMER also exist. So, this is existence dependency. However, examine the attributes of CREDIT-CARD: CardNo, CardType, ExpirationDate, and IssuedBy. In this case, clearly CardNo can uniquely identify entities in CREDIT-CARD. These entities do not have to depend on the corresponding entities in CUSTOMER for identification. Thus, this not ID dependency.

Representation in the Model

Let us illustrate the dependencies by showing how they are indicated in data model diagrams. Carefully note the following figures. Observe the strong and weak entities and

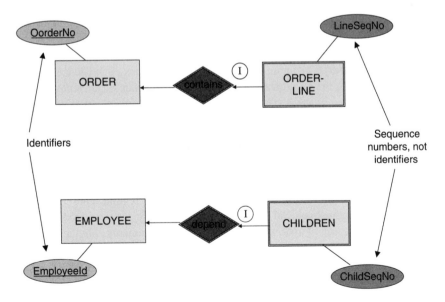

FIGURE 4-13 ID dependency.

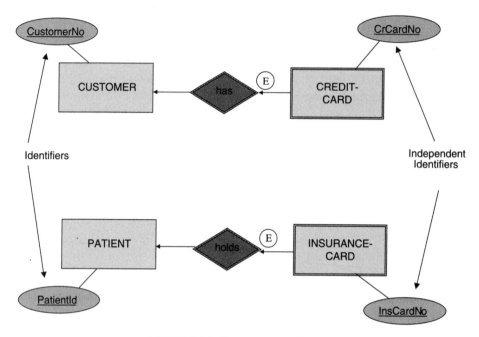

FIGURE 4-14 Existence dependency.

the relationship lines with arrowheads. Notice the double boxes symbolizing weak entity types. Also, in the case of ID dependencies, make a note of the discriminator attributes in the weak entity types. These are just partial identifiers. By themselves, they cannot uniquely identify occurrences of weak entities. Identification is possible only when the discriminators are combined with the identifiers of the strong entity type.

ID Dependency. Figure 4-13 shows two examples of ID dependency. Note the letter "I" on the relationship line indicating ID dependency.

Existence Dependency. Figure 4-14 shows two examples of existence dependency. Note the letter "E" on the relationship line indicating existence dependency.

GENERALIZATION AND SPECIALIZATION

A true data model must reflect every aspect of real-world information. If there are peculiarities about certain business objects, then the model must represent those special conditions. If some relationships are different from the regular ones, then the data model must portray those special relationships. A realistic data model should display everything about the set of real-world information requirements. Frequently, you will find that some of the attributes and relationships are the same for more than one object. Generalization and specialization of object sets is a common occurrence when you observe business objects in the real world.

Take the case of modeling the real-world information for a medical center. One of the main business objects to be modeled is the PATIENT entity type. Think about coming up with a model for this entity type. Modeling any object requires considerations of the possible and relevant attributes for the object. Also, you must consider the relationships that instances of this object have with instances of other objects. As you proceed to model the entity type PATIENT, you realize that there are inpatients, outpatients, and emergency room patients. Your model must include all these patient categories. Now examine these patient categories for attributes. You notice that all these three categories of patients have common attributes such as PatientID, PatientName, Address, Diagnosis, and so on. But, you also realize that each category of patients has attributes that are not common to the other two categories of patients. For example, inpatients have attributes such as AdmissionDate, DischargeDate, LengthOfStay, TypeOfMeals, and so on, that are not shared by outpatients and E-R patients. Further, inpatients are related to another entity type in the model, namely, ROOM. Inpatients may be transferred from one room to another.

You see that there is something special about the three categories of patients in the way they share their attributes and in the manner in which some attributes are specific to each category. Clearly, all patients in the medical center cannot be modeled with one entity type PATIENT. Then what are the options? You can opt to model the patients with three separate entity types INPATIENT, OUTPATIENT, and ERPATIENT. If you make this choice, then your model will repeat several attributes and perhaps relationships for each of the three entity types.

Step back and look at the four entity types PATIENT, INPATIENT, OUTPATIENT, and ERPATIENT. It appears as though an entity type PATIENT is a supertype object and that the other three are subtypes whose attributes and relations may be derived from the supertype object. You will find it best to use these four objects in your data model to truly represent the real-world information in the case of the medical center. Figure 4-15 explains the need for this method of representation in the model.

What you have noticed is the concept of generalization and specialization in a data model. This concept enables special types of objects to be represented in a data model. As you examine the information requirements of any business, you will observe these types of objects.

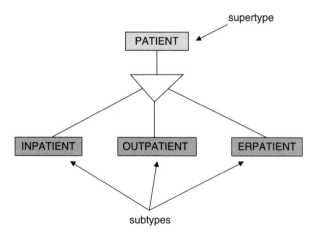

FIGURE 4-15 PATIENT object: supertype and subtypes.

The initial version of the E-R modeling technique lacked provision for generalization and specialization. However, later versions called enhanced entity relationship (EE-R) techniques included these concepts and presented symbols for the representations.

Why Generalize or Specialize?

Generalization structures enable the data modeler to partition an entity type into subsets. Each subset is a part of the whole. For example, trucks, cars, ships, and airplanes may be considered as subtypes of the supertype called vehicle. This modeling structure preserves cohesiveness in a model.

Attributes: Common and Variable. Sharing of attributes results in a supertype and subtype representation. Each subtype may share most of its attributes with all the other subtypes. These shared attributes may then be grouped together as the attributes of the supertype. Further, certain attributes of each subtype may be different. Variation in attributes necessitates representation of multiple subtypes in a model.

Variations in attributes produce subtypes. In the case of trucks, cars, ships, and airplanes, each of these have specific attributes to make them distinct. Because of these variable attributes, you have to show these four distinct subtypes in your model.

At the same time, these four entity types have a number of common attributes. They all represent objects that are used in transportation. The common attributes can, therefore, be included in the supertype entity type as a generalized entity type. Generalization structures enable the data modeler to partition an entity type into subsets.

Relationships: Common and Variable. Similar to sharing of attributes, sharing of relationships results in a supertype and subtype representation. Most of the relationships with other entity types may be shared among all the subtypes. These shared relationships may then be regarded as the relationships of the supertype with the other entity types. Again, some of the relationships of each subtype may be different. Variation in relationships makes it necessary to represent multiple subtypes in a model.

For example, all subtypes INPATIENT, OUTPATIENT, and ERPATIENT may have a relationship with another entity type called SERVICE. Thus, this relationship may be generalized as a relationship between SERVICE and the supertype PATIENT. But, on the other hand, only inpatients have associations with an entity type called ROOM. So, you need to represent this variation by separating out inpatients into a distinct subtype INPATIENT.

Effect of Generalization/Specialization. When attributes and relationships are shared among entity types, if you represent the shared concepts with several entity types, you will be unnecessarily introducing duplicate descriptions in your data model. Generalization avoids such duplication. You will be representing significant semantic content in a concise form.

Generalization hierarchies improve the stability of the data model by allowing changes to be made only to those entity types germane to the changes. They simplify the model by reducing the number of entity types, attributes, and relationships. Generalization and specialization make the data model more readable.

When to be Used. Generalization and specialization should be used when

- A large number of entity types appear to be of the same type
- Attributes are repeated for multiple entity types
- Relationships with other entity types are repeated for multiple entity types
- The model is continually evolving

Supertypes and Subtypes

We looked at the example of *car* being a subset of the superset known as *vehicle*. When you come to think of this, is *car* an instance of the set *vehicle* or is it a subset of *vehicle*? How do you make the determination? You have to examine the natural use of the set of *cars*. Is this a distinct set within the set of vehicles? Or is *car* considered as just another *vehicle*?

Defining criteria indicating whether one set is a subset of another superset:

- How the domain experts or users define the set
- The similarities and differences in the definitions
- What the users think about the member of the set
- The number of members in the set
- Inferences from sample data

In practice, how do you notice these special entity types while modeling the information requirements? You may adopt the top-down or the bottom-up approach. You may look at several entity types and realize that these may be subtypes of some supertype entity. Conversely, you may examine an entity type and determine that it would break down into subtypes.

Let us explore these two approaches.

Generalization. Generalization proceeds from the recognition of common features of attributes and relationships of individual entity types. It is a bottom-up approach where you minimize differences among similar entity types. You suppress the differences to arrive at the common features and name an entity type with these common features.

Create boxes in the data model to represent every possible category of business objects. Examine the objects and determine if some of these may be subtypes of some other business object. Suppress the differences between the subtypes, identify the common attributes and relationships. Generalize to define the supertype.

Figure 4-16 illustrates the generalization approach for medical center patients.

Specialization. Specialization results from emphasizing differences among attributes and relationships among similar objects. It is a top-down approach where you recognize differences among similar entity types. You magnify relevant differences to arrive at a set of distinct entity types and define these as the subtypes of the original entity type that gets represented as the supertype.

Create boxes in the data model for only the high-level business objects. That is, ignore any possible variations in the set of attributes for instances within each high-level object.

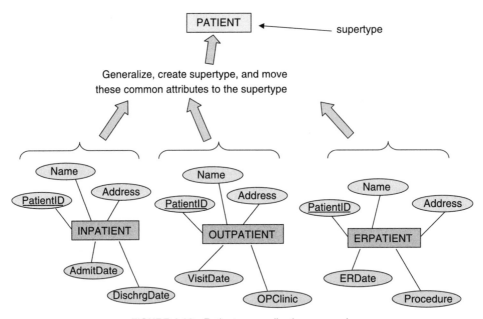

FIGURE 4-16   Patient: generalization approach.

In the case of a medical center, first you will come up with the PATIENT entity type. Then examine the instances within the object and note the differences in the sets of attributes for the instances. Separate out the instances that possess the same set of attributes as a special subtype for the supertype PATIENT.

Figure 4-17 illustrates the specialization approach for medical center patients.

Generalization Hierarchy

Refer back to Figure 4-17 showing the subtypes and the supertype representing patients in a medical center. As certain attributes for a subtype are derived from the supertype, the supertype and its subtypes form a hierarchy in the arrangement of these entity types in a data model. The hierarchical, top-down arrangement with the supertype box above the subtype boxes gives indication of how the supertype provides the common attributes to the subtypes in real-world situations.

That figure shows two levels of the hierarchy, PATIENT at the higher level and the other three subtypes one level down. Sometimes, you will come across more than two levels in the generalization/specialization hierarchy. Figure 4-18 shows three levels in the hierarchy for POLICY and shows levels of subtypes for insurance policies.

What about the instances in the supertype and each of the subtypes? The set of instances within the supertype is a collection of all the instances in the lower level subtypes. If a particular instance is present in subtype AUTOPOLICY, then that instance also exists in the supertype POLICY. Cardinality indicator "1,1" between the supertype and each subtype will be shown to signify this.

There is no theoretical limit to the number of levels in a generalization hierarchy. However, more than three or four levels are comparatively rare in practice. More levels

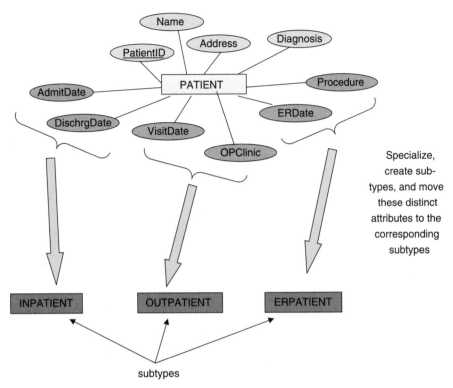

FIGURE 4-17 Patient: specialization approach.

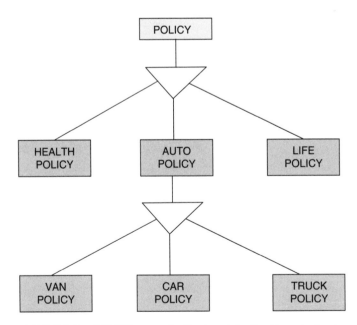

FIGURE 4-18 POLICY: generalization/specialization hierarchy levels.

become cumbersome and unwieldy representations in a data model defeating the whole purpose of the structure itself.

Inheritance of Attributes

A significant feature of a supertype and its subtypes is the inheritance of the attributes by each subtype from the supertype. These are the attributes that are common to all the subtypes. In the case of the objects for a medical center as discussed earlier, all the subsets share common attributes such as PatientID, PatientName, Address, and Diagnosis. Because the subtypes share these attributes, there is no point in repeating these as attributes of each of the subtypes. In a data model diagram, you may, therefore, show these as attributes of the supertype. The principle of inheritance of attributes by the subtypes from the supertype implies that each of the subtypes has these attributes. In addition, each subtype may have other attributes specific only to that subtype.

Figure 4-19 illustrates the principle of inheritance of attributes by the subsets. Note the common attributes shown at the supertype level. Also, observe the attributes specific to individual subtypes.

Inheritance of Relationships

Let us take an example of a company leasing vehicles to customers. A lease agreement covers a particular leasing arrangement with a customer. Examining the information requirements, you can come up with two initial entity types, namely, VEHICLE and AGREEMENT. Of course, there would be other entity types. But let us consider these two entity types for now. Over a period of time, the same vehicle would relate to different lease agreements. That is, when a vehicle comes out of one lease agreement, it would be

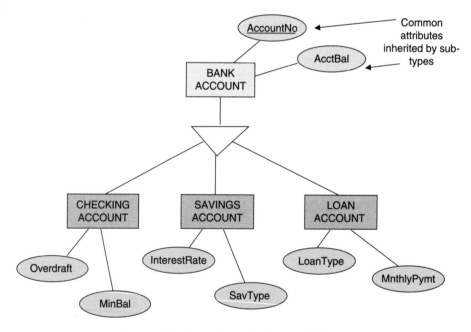

FIGURE 4-19 Subtypes: inheritance of attributes.

leased to another customer or the same customer with a new lease agreement. You note that a direct relationship exists between the entity types AGREEMENT and VEHICLE.

Examine the instances of the entity type VEHICLE. Do all the instances have the same attributes? You quickly notice that cars, trucks, and vans that are leased have common attributes. More importantly, each of these three types has specific attributes not shared with the other two types. You have now come across the situation of supertype and sub-types in the information requirements. VEHICLE is the supertype and CAR, TRUCK, and VAN are the subtypes.

What about the association of the instances of VEHICLE with instances of AGREE-MENT? In the same way, do instances of CAR have associations with instances of AGREEMENT? They do because cars are covered by lease agreements. You note that if the supertype VEHICLE has a relationship with another entity type AGREEMENT, then its subtype CAR also has the same relationship with the entity type AGREEMENT.

Figure 4-20 illustrates this principle of inheritance of relationships by the subtypes from the supertype. Note that each of the subtypes inherits the relationship with the entity type AGREEMENT.

Constraints

A supertype represents a set of entities. These entities in the superset are grouped by sub-types. Thus each entity in any subtype must have the same entity as part of the supertype. The converse is not necessarily true: every entity in the supertype may not have the same entity in some subtype. The existence of entities of the superset in the subsets depends on the conditions of business. The rules of the particular business govern this. The business rules impose certain constraints on the generalization structure and features.

Let us examine the existence conditions that are determined by the business rules. The rules determine the nature of generalization/specialization. Let us classify these constraints.

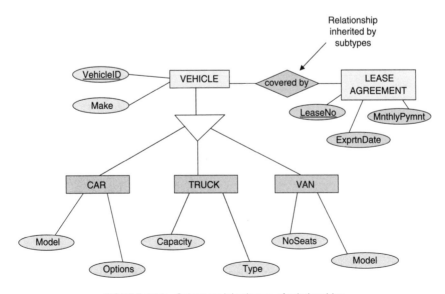

FIGURE 4-20 Subtypes: inheritance of relationships.

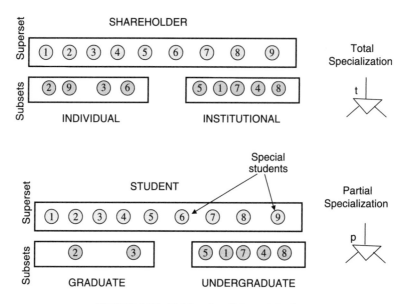

FIGURE 4-21   Total and partial specialization.

Total/Partial. See examples shown in Figure 4-21.

Total Specialization. All subtypes are defined. Every entity in the supertype must be a member of a subtype. This is represented by a double relationship line emanating from the supertype.

Partial Specialization. Not all subtypes are known, defined, or chosen to be defined. Some entities in the supertype may not be a member of any of the subtypes. This is represented by a single relationship line drawn from the supertype.

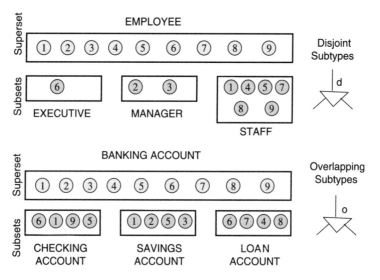

FIGURE 4-22   Disjoint and overlapping subtypes.

Disjoint/Overlapping. See Figure 4-22 for examples.

Disjoint or Exclusive. Each instance of supertype must be an instance in one and only one subtype; marked with a "d" on the relationship line.

Overlapping or Inclusive. Instances of supertype can be instances of any or all of the subtypes; marked with an "o" on the relationship line.

Possible Combinations. The above two sets of constraints may be combined to be shown in the data model to reflect the true nature of the governing business rules. Possible combinations of the constraints are as follows:

- Disjoint, total
- Disjoint, partial
- Overlapping, total
- Overlapping, partial

Design Constraints. These are meant to have the generalization structure of your data model portray information requirements very precisely. Sometimes, a discriminator attribute is introduced in the supertype. The values in the discrimator attribute would be used to break down the entities into subtypes. So, we can have the following two cases:

Condition- or Predicate-Defined. The predicate value is written on the relationship line; discriminator attribute to contain the proper predicate value. Subtype entities are generated based on predicate value. See Figure 4-23.

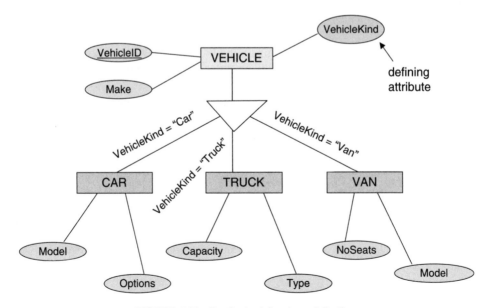

FIGURE 4-23 Predicate-defined specialization.

User-Defined. No discriminator attribute; user is responsible to create entities in the subtypes.

Rules Summarized

Let us conclude our discussion of generalization and specialization by highlighting some general rules:

Subtype Distinctiveness. Each subtype must have at least one distinct non–key attribute or at least one distinct relationship with another entity type.

Supertype Justification. For a supertype to be defined, a large number of entities must be of the same type, attributes must be repeated for multiple entities, and the model is in an evolving state.

Entity Occurrences. Every entity in the supertype must be an entity of one or more of its subtypes.

Relationship. The supertype is in a one-to-one relationship with each of its subtypes.

Subtype Discriminator. If the subtypes are predicate-defined, the supertype contains a subtype discriminator as an additional attribute to establish which subtype each entity is associated with.

Mutual Exclusivity. All subtypes governed by the same discriminator need not be mutually exclusive.

Nested Generalization Hierarchy. A subtype may become a supertype in another generalization hierarchy.

Supertype Limits. There is no theoretical limit to the number of levels in a generalization hierarchy; but too many levels will impose the presence of multiple discriminators.

Relationship Dependency. A subtype cannot be a child entity type in any other identifying relationship.

Dependent Entity Types. Generalization hierarchies may be present for associative and aggregation entity types just as if they were regular entity types.

SPECIAL CASES AND EXCEPTIONS

Most of the entity types you will come across in real-world situations are regular entity types such as CUSTOMER, EMPLOYEE, DEPARTMENT, and so on. We discussed such entity types in detail. We also reviewed a few of the other entity types. We studied supertypes and subtypes at length. We examined association entity types. You also learned about aggregation entity types.

We are now at a point to complete our study of entity types by considering a few exceptions and special cases. More than being exceptions, these present special situations in real-world modeling. Recursive structures are not that rare. You will see them in almost every data model. We will visit recursive structures in this section and also later on when we discuss relationships in Chapter 6. Conceptual and physical entity types must be recognized and need special treatment in a data model.

Sometimes you will be run into a quandary as to how to treat a specific modeling construct—as an attribute or as a separate entity type. Relationships also pose similar questions in certain circumstances. We will explore these situations.

Recursive Structures

EMPLOYEE is a fairly common entity type in many real-world information requirements. Think about the instances for this entity type. Every employee in the organization will be represented by an instance. In the set of instances, you will find workers who supervise other workers. An instance representing a supervisor associates with those instances of employees under his or her supervision. What you find here is that instances of an entity type associate with instances of the same entity type. Associations recur within the same entity type among its own members. These are recursive associations. This type of relationship is a recursive relationship. Your data model must be able to indicate entity types participating in recursive relationships.

Figure 4-24 shows examples of a recursive structure in a data model.

Note how the relationship line from an entity type is linked back to itself. Cardinalities may vary with recursive relationships just like it does with regular relationships. Observe the different sets of cardinality indicators represented in the figure.

Conceptual and Physical

Assume that you are asked to model the information requirements for an airline company. Very quickly you realize that AIRCRAFT must be one of the business objects in your data model. You will represent this as an entity type in your data

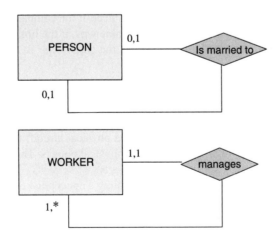

FIGURE 4-24   EMPLOYEE: recursive structure.

model. Now, examine the requirements of the company with regard to the entity type AIRCRAFT. The company's fleet consists of many aircrafts. Each of these aircrafts has a serial number, a certain number of seats, the date the aircraft was placed in service, the chief mechanic responsible to service the plane, and so on. The company needs to keep track of all the planes in its fleet. Notice also that the company uses different types of aircraft like Boeing 747, MD 11, Airbus 321, and so on. The company needs to keep track of the aircraft categories used in its fleet as well. What are Boeing 747, MD11, Airbus 321, and so on? Are these aircrafts? No, these are categories of aircraft, not the physical aircraft themselves. In this case of information requirements for the airline company, you find two kinds of related business objects. One is the object AIRCRAFT and the other AIRCRAFT-CATEGORY.

Now, consider the information requirements for a library. The library has to keep track of individual copies of books so that it will know which particular copy is out with a member. Each copy is marked with a call number. Further, the library must also have a catalogue of books available for the members. These are not the actual copies of the books, but the titles. So, in this case, you see the need for two related objects in your data model: BOOK and BOOK-COPY. The two are not the same. They will have to be represented by separate entity types in the data model. The instances within each entity type are different. In the case of the entity type BOOK, the instances are the individual titles; for the entity type BOOK-COPY, the instances are individual copies of the books.

Consider just one more example. An appliance store needs to keep track of individual units of each appliance. Also, the store has to maintain a list of the kinds of appliances available in the store. Here, you note the need for two related entity types in the data model: APPLIANCE-UNIT and APPLIANCE-CATEGORY.

Physical Objects. The entity types like AIRCRAFT, BOOK-COPY, and APPLIANCE-UNIT are representations of physical objects. A physical object refers to tangible object that you can see, touch, or feel. These are physical things. You need to have entity types symbolizing physical objects in your data model, whenever the information requirements call for keeping track of individual, physical things.

What about the instances within the entity type indicating a physical object? Each instance represents a particular physical thing. The instances within the entity type AIRCRAFT are the physical aircraft in the company's fleet. If the company owns 100 aircraft, 100 instances exist within the entity type. In the same way, if the library has a total inventory of 10,000 physical copies of various books, the entity type BOOK-COPY contains these 10,000 instances.

Conceptual Objects. AIRCRAFT-CATEGORY, BOOK, and APPLIANCE-CATEGORY do not represent any tangible things. You cannot touch or see an AIRCRAFT-CATEGORY. What you can see is a physical aircraft that is of the Boeing 747 category. So, these are not representations of physical objects. The objects represented by these are conceptual; these are conceptual objects.

What kinds of instances does an entity representing a conceptual object contain? These instances are not physical things. Each instance within the entity type BOOK refers to a particular title in the library. The library may have the book *A Brief History of Time* by Stephen Hawking. This title will be an instance of the entity type denoting the conceptual object BOOK in the data model. If the library holds four copies of this book, then you will

CONCEPTUAL OBJECT   PHYSICAL OBJECT

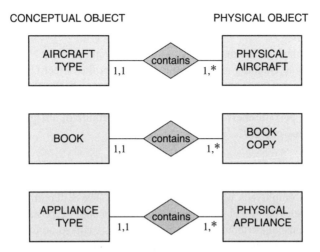

FIGURE 4-25   Data model diagrams: conceptual and physical objects.

have four corresponding instances in the entity type representing the physical object
BOOK-COPY.

Data Model Diagram. Figure 4-25 presents the data model diagrams for the three
examples discussed.

Note the relationships between the conceptual object and the corresponding physical
object in each example. Also, observe the cardinality indicators and understand the association of the instances.

Assembly Structures

What is a bill-of-materials structure? You come across bill-of-materials processing
(BOMP) in manufacturing. In manufacturing of automobiles, an assembly of a major
part consists of several subassemblies; each subassembly in turn may be broken down

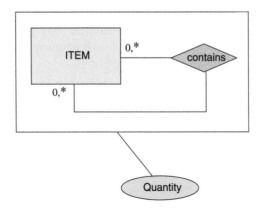

FIGURE 4-26   Assembly structure.

further. Assembly structures are cases of recursive relationships where the associations recur at many levels.

Figure 4-26 displays an example of an assembly structure.

Notice the attribute Quantity shown in the diagram for the object ITEM. This attribute Quantity does not represent quantities of individual instances of the object. Quantity indicates units for the various recursive associations. How many units for the combinations of part number 1 with part numbers 4, 5, and 6? It is an attribute of an aggregate entity type consisting of just one object.

Entity Type Versus Attribute

Consider the set of employees working in departments. These departments have department numbers. When you model this, you will include an entity type called EMPLOYEE. There would be the usual attributes such as name, address, and so on for the EMPLOYEE entity type. Now what about the department in which each employee works in? How do you indicate this aspect in your data model? Let us also consider the fact that an employee may be working in a particular department during a specific duration. If the information suggests that you need show the duration also, how should your data model represent that?

Frequently, you will be faced with questions of this nature. What are the options for representation in the data model? The simplest solution is to show DeptNumber as an attribute for the entity type. In this simplest resolution, all we know about each department is the DeptNumber. What if we need to indicate other data about departments such as Dept-Name, DeptLocation, and DeptManagerName in the data model? Then a simple representation of DeptNumber as an attribute of the entity type EMPLOYEE will be inadequate.

Further, if you represent DeptNumber as an attribute and nothing else in the data model, what about the duration an employee works in a department? If you have to represent the duration also in your data model, then the simple representation of DeptNumber as an attribute of EMPLOYEE will be incomplete.

The ultimate question is whether department data can be represented just using attributes of a different entity type, namely, EMPLOYEE. Or, if this is inadequate and the data model will not truly represent the information requirements, then DEPARTMENT must be represented as a separate and distinct entity type with relationship to EMPLOYEE. Department data—attribute or entity type? The conditions and business rules of the information requirements will dictate how this should be handled in a data model.

Figure 4-27 shows the representation of department data as a separate entity type because of the need for complete information about departments and durations.

Entity Type Versus Relationship

In the case discussed above, we were faced with the options of either representing data as an attribute or as a separate entity type. Here we will address another type of question—whether to represent data as a relationship or as separate entity types. Frequently, you may run into situations such as these.

Let us take an example where you need to represent managers and the departments they manage. This can easily be set up in a data model using MANAGER and DEPARTMENT entity types and showing the relationship between them. However, when you explore the data requirements further, you will come across managers who manage more than one

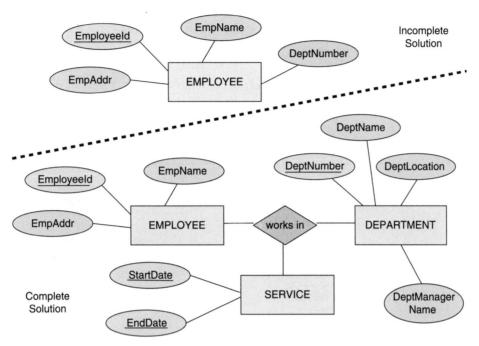

FIGURE 4-27   Department as separate entity type.

department. Now think about this additional requirement. Still you can represent this by making the relationship between MANANGER and DEPARTMENT as a one-to-many relationship. The representation will hold. But, what about the fact that a manager managing many departments may have separate budgets for each department he or she manages? Also, you may need to show the date from which each manager started managing each department. Thus, the simple representation showing MANAGER, DEPARTMENT, and the relationship between them may not be adequate in a data model. You will have to create another entity type to show the attributes such as Budget and StartDate for each (manager, department) pair.

Thus, we are faced with the options about proper representation. Should the information requirements be represented as a relationship between two object types? Or, should the requirements be represented by introducing another entity type? Management data—relationship or another entity type?

Figure 4-28 shows the representation of management data as a separate entity type because of the need for complete information about managers and their departments.

Modeling Time Dimension

Think of the values of attributes stored in the database. Normally, the values stored are the current values. What values do you find for the Address attribute of CUSTOMER entity type? The current address of each customer. As a customer's address changes, the new address replaces the old address in the database. In the same way, what values will be stored in the ProductUnitCost and ProductUnitPrice attributes of PRODUCT entity type?

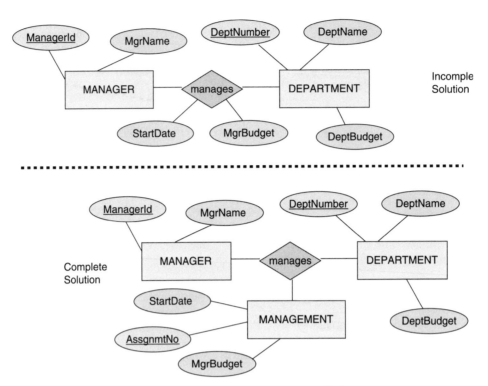

FIGURE 4-28 Management as separate entity type.

Assume that just the current costs and current prices are stored in the database for the products. What happens if an old invoice to a customer has to be recalculated and reprinted? What happens when you want to calculate the profit margin for the past quarter using the unit cost and unit price? If there had been no intervening price or cost changes, you can perform these tasks without any problems. What you notice is that ProductUnitCost and ProductUnitPrice are time-dependent data elements and that your data model must include historical entity types to keep track of the changes.

Figure 4-29 indicates how historical entity types are included in the data model. Note why ProductNo and EffectiveDate are used together to form the primary key for the historical entity types.

Categorization

While discussing generalization and specialization, you have noticed that a supertype may be subdivided into multiple subtypes. The entities within a supertype occur within the subtypes. One supertype, many subtypes. Every subtype has only one supertype related to it. An entity in a subtype can be an entity of only one supertype.

However, in some situations you may find the need to create models with more than one supertype associated with one or more subtypes. Here we do not have one distinct supertype. We have multiple supertypes. This is different from our earlier discussion on generalization and specialization. When a subtype is related to more than one supertype, we call

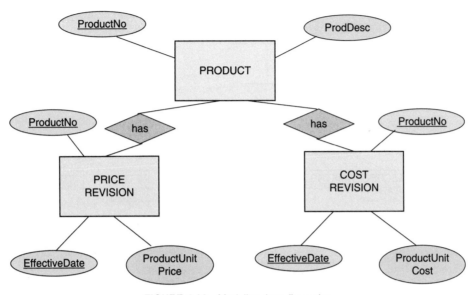

FIGURE 4-29   Modeling time dimension.

the subtype a category. Categorization is the modeling of a single subtype with a relationship involving two or more specific supertypes.

But before we look at categorization, let us consider an example that will lead us up to that topic. This is the notion of shared subtype. Shared subtypes give rise to multiple inheritance.

Shared Subtype. Consider trainees in an organization. Trainees are part of the total employees in the organization. Observe that the set of employees may form subsets of supervisors, secretaries, IT personnel, marketing personnel, finance personnel, manufacturing personnel, and trainees. How do you model this so far? You can make EMPLOYEE as the supertype with SUPERVISOR, SECRETARY, INFOTECH, MKTNG, FINANCE, MANUFACTURE, TRAINEE as subtypes. This is straightforward specialization.

Now, let us say we need to model information technology trainees distinctly because they have particular attributes not shared by other types of trainees. So, you create a distinct entity type IT-TRAINEE which will be a subtype of INFOTECH and TRAINEE subtypes. A subtype with more than one supertype–subtype relationship is called a shared subtype. An entity of IT-TRAINEE must be an entity of INFOTECH and TRAINEE subtypes. As a result, IT-TRAINEE inherits the attributes of INFOTECH and TRAINEE. In addition, IT-TRAINEE has its own attributes. This is called multiple inheritance.

Figure 4-30 shows the portion of the data model illustrating shared subtype and multiple inheritance.

Categories. Consider the relationship between a subtype and its supertype. In all the examples considered on generalization and specialization so far, every such relationship has one supertype. For example, in the relationship between IT-TRAINEE and INFOTECH, INFOTECH is the supertype and IT-TRAINEE is the subtype. In this relationship,

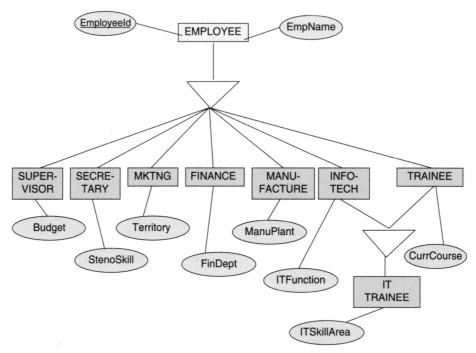

FIGURE 4-30 Shared subtype and multiple inheritance.

only one supertype is involved. Similarly, in the relationship between IT-TRAINEE and TRAINEE, only one supertype TRAINEE is involved.

However, in some situations, the modeling of the supertype–subtype relationship may involve two distinct supertypes. In such cases, the subtype is known as a category. Let us review the entity types shown in Figure 4-31.

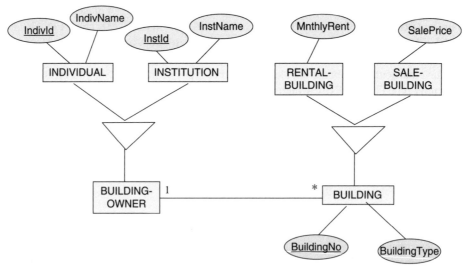

FIGURE 4-31 Example of categorization.

The figure shows two categories OWNER and BUILDING. The OWNER category relates to two distinct supertypes INDIVIDUAL and INSTITUTION. The BUILDING category is associated with two distinct supertypes SALE-BUILDING and RENTAL-BUILDING. Note the symbols on the relationship lines.

A category entity type has selective inheritance. For example, each entity in BUILDING-OWNER inherits only the attributes of INDIVIDUAL or the attributes of INSTITUTION, but not both.

ENTITY VALIDATION CHECKLIST

At the completion of a portion of the data modeling activity, it is always a good practice to validate your work against a checklist. This enables you to ensure that you have not overlooked any particular step or missed any specific component. You need to go back and review the model as it evolves against information requirements.

Entities and entity types are primary model components. We collect and store data about things. Your model must truly represent the entities about which you need to collect and store data. You have to ensure that your model so far is complete; you must ascertain that your model is free of errors. You need to confirm whether the model up to this point represents the information requirements completely and correctly.

In this section, let us enumerate the items for validation of entities in the form of checklists. The first checklist relates to completeness of the entity types; the second deals with correctness of the defined entity types.

Completeness

Requirements Review. Compare the model with requirements and ensure that all entity types are defined.

Dependent Entity Types. Review each entity type to check for dependencies; ensure that all weak entities and their corresponding strong entities are named and defined.

Association Entity Types. Wherever intersection or association entity types are necessary to resolve many-to-many relationships, ensure that they are defined and indicated.

Generalization/Specialization. Review individual entity types to check if each may be a supertype or a subtype; make certain that all supertypes and subtypes are completely defined.

Category Subtypes. Scrutinize each subtype to check whether it has a relationship with two distinct supertypes; make sure all category subtypes are defined.

Attributes as Entity Types. Examine attributes and ensure all those needed to be defined as entity types are expressed properly.

Relationships as Entity Types. Examine relationships and make sure all those that must be defined as entity types are modeled properly.

Entity Names. Review all entity type names and resolve vague abbreviations and non-standard acronyms.

Entity Descriptions. Ensure that each entity is described completely in a supplementary document to the data model diagram.

Estimates. Estimate current and future number of occurrences for each entity type and record in the design documentation. This is useful for the logical and physical design of the database.

Correctness

Entity Type Representations. Ensure that each entity represents a true business object in the real-world domain of the organization that is being modeled.

Entity Type Names. Ensure that all entity types have the names spelled and shown in proper case according to the accepted standard in the organization. The general convention for entity type names is to record them in uppercase and use singular nouns. The name of each entity type should accurately indicate which business object that name stands for. It must be a name that users accept as easily and correctly understood.

Entity Descriptions. Ensure that the modelers have noted each entity type correctly according to acceptable standards and usage of the entity type by the users.

Entity Documentation. Ensure that each entity is noted completely in a supplementary document to the data model diagram.

Homonyms and Synonyms. Review the complete list of entity type names, side by side. Check suspected homonyms and synonyms. Guarantee that these are completely resolved.

Weak Entity Types. Scrutinize each weak entity type and the strong entity type on which it is dependent. Verify the notations in the data model diagram and make sure that the symbols are correct. Check the weak entity type's discriminator for correctness. Ensure that the data model diagram correctly shows the type of dependency—existence, identification, or both.

Association or Intersection Entity Types. Check each association entity type between two entity types. Verify that the association entity correctly resolves the many-to-many relationship between the two original entity types.

Generalization/Specialization. Carefully examine each generalization/specialization structure. Verify each set of subtypes to ensure that they are subtypes of the indicated supertype. Review the relationships. Especially make certain that the proper notations are correctly shown in the model diagram.

Category Subtypes. Verify each category subtype and ensure that it is a true category entity type. Check the correctness of its supertype–subtype relationships with two distinct supertypes.

CHAPTER SUMMARY

- An entity is a single distinguishable business object such as a person, place, thing, event, or concept, part of a group of similar objects, relevant to an organization, and about which the organization is interested in storing and using information.
- An entity may be physical or conceptual.
- An entity type refers to a collection of similar entities.
- Methods for identifying entity types: process-oriented and data-oriented.
- Homonyms and synonyms must be resolved while identifying entity types.
- Various entity types: weak, regular or strong, super, sub, association or intersection, aggregation.
- Dependent entity types—dependency may be partial or complete; dependency may be ID dependency or existence dependency.
- Subsets inherit attributes and relationships from their corresponding superset. Specialization may be (a) total or partial and (b) disjoint or overlapping.
- Recursive structures consists of entities within an entity type having associations with entities with other entities within the same entity type.
- A data model may consist of physical objects such as book-copy and conceptual objects such as book.
- Assembly structures as in manufacturing consist of recursive structures.
- Historical entity types are needed to include the time dimension in a data model.
- After defining entity types for a data model, use an entity validation checklist to verify completeness and correctness.

REVIEW QUESTIONS

1. True or false:
   A. In a data model, only tangible business objects must be represented.
   B. Intersection entity types are introduced in a data model to resolve many-to-many relationships.
   C. For weak entity types, ID dependency implies existence dependency.
   D. Only three levels of generalization hierarchy can be present in a data model.
   E. For disjoint specialization, instances of supertype can be instances of any or all of the subtypes.
   F. In all recursive relationships, the cardinality must be one-to-one.
   G. Historical entity types are needed to represent the time dimension in a data model.
   H. Aggregation entity types can represent four-way relationships.

      I. Resolution of synonyms is easier than that for homonyms.

      J. In a recursive entity type, entities within the entity type may be associated with other entities within the same entity type.

2. Enumerate the guidelines for a good definition of an entity. Using these guidelines, define an entity for an organization.

3. Distinguish between entities and entity types using examples.

4. What are two common methods for identifying entity types for an organization? Describe one of the methods with an example.

5. What are homonyms and synonyms in entity types? How could these cause problems in identifying entity types properly?

6. What are the two types of dependencies of weak entity types on their corresponding strong entity types? Describe one of the two types with an example.

7. Discuss the need for generalization and specialization in data modeling. Explain with examples of supersets and subsets.

8. Subsets inherit attributes and relationships from their corresponding superset. Explain this statement with an example.

9. Give an example of an overlapping partial specialization. Describe the entities in the representation.

10. What are conceptual and physical objects? When is it necessary to represent these in a data model? Explain the relationship between a conceptual object and a physical object with an example.

5

ATTRIBUTES AND IDENTIFIERS IN DETAIL

CHAPTER OBJECTIVES

- Provide an in-depth discussion of attributes and identifiers
- Explore the nature and definition of attributes
- Discuss attribute domains in detail
- Study how constraints work for attributes
- Classify attributes by various types
- Establish the need and role of identifiers
- Present types of keys and the governing rules
- Conclude with an attribute validation checklist

Open up the database of an organization and look at the data content. What you will find is a huge collection of values. Some of these will be in text form; others in numeric format; and still others in complex formats depending on the type of data stored. What are these values?

If CUSTOMER is one of the business objects about which data is collected and stored, then you will find data values for data elements such as customer name, customer address, customer phone number, and so on. If ORDER is another business object in your database, then you will observe data values for such data elements such as order number, order date, order amount, and shipping method. What are these data values? You know that customer name, customer address, and customer phone describe the business object CUSTOMER. These are attributes of the business object. Similarly, order number, order date, order amount, and shipping method are attributes of the business object ORDER. So, the data values you find stored in the database are values of the attributes of the

Data Modeling Fundamentals. By Paulraj Ponniah
Copyright © 2007 John Wiley & Sons, Inc.

business objects. Apart from a few other types of data stored in a database, attribute values form the bulk of the data content.

Attributes, therefore, stand out as important components of a data model. What is the true nature of an attribute? How should we understand the role of an attribute in terms of entity types and relationships? What set of values can an attribute of a business object take? Can the value sets be shared among different attributes? Are attributes subject to constraints or restrictions or rules? If so, what types of constraints? Are all attributes of a business object of the same type? If different, how can we differentiate them and depict them in a data model?

We will address such questions in detail. In the previous chapters, you have been exposed to various examples of attributes. In Chapter 3, when we considered a case study example, you reviewed the attributes of the different entity types. Now, we want to explore attributes and make an in-depth study.

ATTRIBUTES

What do we mean by an attribute of a business object? What are values for an attribute? We consider CustomerName as an attribute of a business object or entity type we call CUSTOMER. What does the term CustomerName imply in terms of an entity type known as CUSTOMER? Is it a placeholder to contain values for customer names? Is it a common characteristic of all entities known as customers in that business? How is the term CustomerName used when we access the database for customer names? We wish to explore these questions in detail.

When you take into account the various components of a data model, attribute ranks high as an important building block. As the leading component whose values fill up the data content in a database, attributes deserve serious study. Let us get a clear understanding of attributes.

Properties or Characteristics

Every business object possesses certain properties or characteristics that are relevant to the information requirements. These characteristics describe the various instances of an object set. For example, *last name* Jones describes an instance of the object EMPLOYEE. Similarly, if that employee was hired on 10/1/2006, *hire date* is another attribute describing that instance of the object.

Figure 5-1 shows attributes of an object STUDENT. Note the names of the attributes written inside the ellipses or ovals. Observe how these are characteristics or descriptors of the individual instances of the object set.

So, what are attributes?

Inherent Characteristics. Consider the data elements StudentID, StudentName, SocSecNo, StudentPhone, and StudentMajor. These data elements are associated with the object STUDENT. They are innate or natural or intrinsic or inherent properties of STUDENT. Next, think of a particular course for which a student has enrolled. CourseNo is also a data element associated with the object STUDENT. If so, is CourseNo also an attribute of the object STUDENT? Compare the two data elements StudentName and CourseNo. StudentName is a natural characteristic of the object STUDENT, whereas CourseNo does not indicate a basic property of the object. CourseNo does not describe

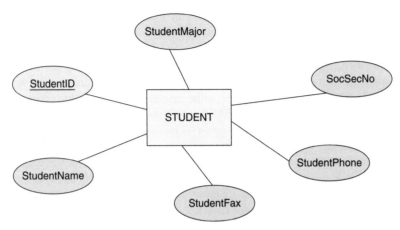

FIGURE 5-1 STUDENT object: attributes.

some intrinsic property of STUDENT, but only its relationship with another object called COURSE. Therefore, CourseNo does not qualify to be an attribute of STUDENT.

Distinct Characteristic. An attribute is a distinct and specific characteristic of an entity type that is of interest to the organization.

Indicates Data. An attribute of an entity type designates the nature of the data that is maintained in the database for that entity type.

Describes Entity. An attribute is a simple, separate, distinct, singular property that describes an entity.

Grouping of Entities. In our prior discussions on entities and entity types, you must have observed that a group of entities were put together and called an entity type because those entities were similar. Customer entities are grouped together as CUSTO-MER entity type for the reason that the entities share common characteristics. If one customer entity possesses the characteristics of name, address, and phone, then another customer entity also has these characteristics; yet another customer entity also shares these characteristics. Common characteristics or attributes determine whether a number of entities or "things" may be grouped together as one type. Thus, attributes play a key role in the formation of entity types.

An entity set is a set of entities of the same type that share the same properties or attributes. An entity set is represented by a set of attributes that are descriptive properties possessed by each member of an entity set.

Ownership by Entity. Go back to the data elements StudentID, StudentName, SocSecNo, StudentPhone, and StudentMajor. These data elements are associated with the entity type STUDENT. They are innate or natural or inherent properties of STUDENT. These attributes are "owned" by the entity type STUDENT.

In a database, there may be hundreds of attributes. Every one of these attributes is "owned" by some entity type. Each attribute has a name that uniquely identifies it with a description that can be clearly interpreted. An attribute "owned" by an entity type may be either a key attribute or a non–key attribute. Key attributes serve as identifiers for the entity type (more about key attributes in a later section). Non–key attributes constitute the bulk of the data content. These non–key attributes describe the entity type.

Attributes of Relationships. Until now, we have been considering attributes insofar as they apply to entity types. However, in certain cases, attributes may be needed to describe relationships as well. Let us look at the case of employees being assigned to projects. Here we have two entity types EMPLOYEE and PROJECT in a many-to-many relationship. One employee may be assigned to one or more projects; one project may be carried out by one or more employees.

Think about the types of data that must be collected and stored in the database. For example, you would have to store start date and the duration for each employee on the projects that person has worked on. What are these values? These are values for start date and duration. These are values for attributes known as StartDate and AssignmentDuration. But which entity types "own" these attributes?

StartDate for an employee does not make sense; nor does it make sense for a project. Similarly, AssignmentDuration does not make sense for employee or project by themselves. However, StartDate has meaning for an employee working on a project; the attribute StartDate makes sense only when you consider the association of the employee with a specific project. StartDate has to be an attribute of the relationship between EMPLOYEE and PROJECT, not an attribute of either entity type apart from the relationship.

Figure 5-2 shows the relationship and its attributes.

Mapping Between Sets. Another way to look at attributes: attributes are mappings between an entity set or a relationship set with a set of values. Let us examine this aspect of attributes. Suppose you look at the data content in a database. Let us say we find a number of values in text format indicating names of persons. This is a set of values. Let us say also we find a number of values indicating Social Security numbers. Now we understand that the first set of values is names of students and the second set of values is Social Security numbers of students.

A particular name (John Silverstein) and a specific Social Security number (111-44-3456) are those of a certain student. What is the mapping or connection here? The specific student entity from the set of students maps into the values "John Silverstein" and "111-44-3456." How is the mapping done between entity and the values? It is done through what we call attributes. The attributes StudentName and SocialSecurityNumber provide the mapping between the set of values for names and Social Security numbers and the set of student entities.

An attribute associates an entity set with a set of values. A value set in a database gets interpreted in the context of a set of entities.

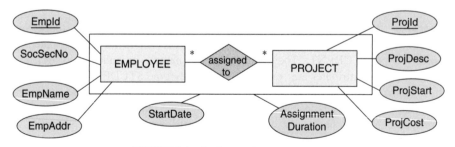

FIGURE 5-2 Attributes of a relationship.

Attributes as Data

Most people, even many data modelers, think of attributes as data. This is only partially true. Representations of attributes exist in the database as values in the form of text, codes, numeric measures, and even images. In advanced systems, complex values in the form of audio and video compositions may exist representing attributes.

When you represent an attribute with an oval in a data model diagram, you are expressing the representation of specific data values from a designated set. The attribute Customer-Phone is manifested in the database as several valid phone numbers stored as data. Your data model showing the attribute CustomerPhone depicts this representation of data values of valid phone numbers.

Attributes as Data Holders. Consider the attributes of STUDENT entity type: StudentId, StudentName, SocSecNo, StudentPhone, StudentMajor, and StudentFax. Figure 5-3 shows a set of values for these attributes. Examine these values.

The values such as "Networking," "Web Design," "Engineering," and so on are manifestations of the data model component known as StudentMajor. What is this data model component? What does the name StudentMajor point to? You may think of it as the name for a data holder that contains data values such as mentioned. The representation of an attribute in a data model is the depiction of a data holder.

Attributes of a single entity hold values that describe that specific entity. For example, look at the values for the student, Kristin Rogers. The attributes StudentId, StudentName, SocSecNo, StudentPhone, StudentMajor, and StudentFax hold data values "111245," "Kristin Rogers," "214-56-7835," "516-777-9584," "Networking," and "516-777-9587," respectively, for this student.

Attributes Indicate Data Storage. When you designate an attribute for an entity type, your data model shows this attribute. For example, when you name an attribute Student-Phone for the entity type STUDENT, you are expressing that the database stores phone numbers as data for each student.

The assignment of an attribute for an entity type makes the statement about data storage of values for that attribute in the database. For each entity, a value is to be stored for that attribute. Each entity may have its own value for the attribute to be stored in the database.

Entity as Attribute–Value Pairs. Once again, let us review the attributes of STUDENT entity type: StudentId, StudentName, SocSecNo, StudentPhone, StudentMajor, and StudentFax. What can we say about each entity in the set? In particular, how can we describe the entity representing Kristin Rogers?

STUDENT

StudentID	StudentName	SocSecNo	StudentPhone	StudentMajor	StudentFax
111245	Kristin Rogers	214-56-7835	516-777-9584	Networking	516-777-9587
121365	Rob Smith	123-44-5546	718-312-4488	Web Design	
123456	Mary Williams	101-54-3838	212-313-1267	Networking	212-313-1267
234754	Shaina Gonzales	213-36-7854	212-126-3428	Social Science	
388910	Andrew McAllister	311-33-4520	718-567-4321	Engineering	718-567-4322
400500	Kassy Goodman	512-22-8542	732-346-5533	Programming	732-346-5538
511675	Rob Smith	111-22-3344	908-212-5629	Liberal Arts	908-212-5630

FIGURE 5-3 STUDENT entity type: attribute values.

This particular entity may be described as a set of attribute–value pairs as follows:

(StudentId, 111245),
(StudentName, Kristin Rogers),
(SocSecNo, 214-56-7835),
(StudentPhone, 516-777-9584),
(StudentMajor, Networking),
(StudentFax, 516-777-9587).

Thus, each entity may be described by a set of (attribute, value) pairs, one pair for each attribute of the entity type.

Attribute Values

Take a few samples of the values of the attributes shown in Figure 5-3. Examine the data values shown in each column. We want get a clear understanding of attribute values as applicable to any entity type.

First of all, when you consider the attribute values for one single entity or instance of the entity type, you will note the values are specific and unique for that entity. Second, the data values for a specific entity instance may themselves change over time.

Unique Values for an Instance. Look at one set of values shown in one row of Figure 5-3. These values for the attributes StudentID, StudentName, SocSecNo, and StudentPhone relate to one student, a specific instance of the entity type STUDENT. These attributes do not relate to any random instance of the entity type; they relate to one particular student.

Let us say, this student is Mary Williams. Then these attributes are characteristics of Mary Williams. If you observe a specific instance of the entity type STUDENT, namely Mary Williams, then you will note a unique and specific set of values for the attributes. This unique set of values describes Mary Williams. In the data model, each instance of an entity type possesses a unique set of values for its attributes.

However, this does not mean a value for any attribute may not be repeated for other students. In fact, look at the value for the attribute StudentMajor. For Mary Williams, the value is "Networking." This value applies to Mary Williams. It may also apply to other students as well. Other students may also have the value "Networking" as the value for the attribute StudentMajor.

Changeable Values. You have noted that each instance of an entity type is described by a unique set of values for its attributes. Review the unique set of values for the attributes describing the instance Mary Williams in Figure 5.3. Let us say Mary marries John Pearson and changes her name to Mary Pearson. Also, she changes her phone number. What are the implications?

What you notice is that although each instance is described by a unique set of values for its attributes, these values may change over time. The values for StudentName and StudentPhone would change, but still the instance refers to the same student. Again, after the changes, a unique set of values for the attributes describes the student Mary Pearson. It is important to note that values of the attributes for an object instance may change, but the instance itself remains the same.

Names and Descriptions

Attributes in a data model are indicated by their names. In the E-R data model, the attribute names are shown within the ovals that represent the attributes. Attribute names and their descriptions are intended to provide a clear understanding of the nature of the data we want to store about each entity of an entity type.

The data model diagram displays the attribute names. Attribute descriptions are written in an accompanying requirements definition document.

Attribute Names. Following are a few guidelines for choosing and assigning a name for an attribute.

Nouns. Use a noun in the form of a single or compound word. Use minimum number of words. Avoid the use of special characters such as *, #, @, and so on.

Logical Not Physical. In choosing a name, conform to logical considerations, not physical characteristics of the attribute.

Naming Standards. Follow the naming standards and conventions of your organization.

Synonyms and Homonyms. Resolve all issues relating to synonyms and homonyms before finalizing the attribute names.

Clarity. Pick a name that is clear, precise, and self-explanatory.

CASE Tool. If a CASE tool is being used for data modeling, be guided by the requirements of the CASE tool for assigning attribute names.

In Line with Description. Do not let the attribute name contradict the attribute description.

To Be Avoided. In the attribute name, avoid abbreviations, acronyms, plural words, possessive forms of nouns, articles, conjunctions, prepositions, and verbs.

Attribute Descriptions. Attribute descriptions provided in the supplementary documentation enable clear thinking about the attributes. The descriptions present the rationale for each attribute and explain the reason and role of the attribute.

A good attribute description supplements the meaning derived from the name of the attribute. It builds on the name and enhances the understanding. The description must be concise. If any technical terms are used in the descriptions, these terms must be explained.

While writing an attribute description, do not simply rephrase the name. The description must be able to stand alone by itself. A few examples may be used, but a description by means of just examples is incomplete. Dictionary meaning of the attribute name is not a good description. Avoid technical jargon in the description.

ATTRIBUTE DOMAINS

In our discussions on attributes, you have noted the use of the term domain. Each attribute is related to a specific domain. A set of data values constitute a domain. Value sets may be a set of integers, a set of valid phone numbers, a set of valid zip codes, and so on. The data set or domain for a particular attribute provides values for individual entities.

When you examine the domain for an attribute, you get to know more about the attribute. Domain information describes an attribute further. We will study the information that may be obtained from a domain. We will look at examples of attributes and their domains. We will also study special cases of domains.

Definition of a Domain

First let us get a clear understanding of an attribute domain. What are the characteristics of a domain? How do the values in a domain apply to attributes?

What about the nature of the values in a domain? How do they depend on the attribute itself? First let us define a domain.

What Is an Attribute Domain? An attribute domain is a set of values that may be assigned to an attribute. A domain defines the possible, allowable, potential values of an attribute. As noted earlier, a domain is simply a set of values.

When you relate a set of values to an attribute, the set of values becomes the domain for that attribute. Make a list of all the department numbers in your organization. This list of values of department numbers becomes the domain for an attribute called DeptNo. When you link a set of values to an attribute, then the set of values takes a special role of containing allowable values for the attribute.

Every attribute has values for each of the entities for which it is an attribute. If you have an entity type known as DEPARTMENT and it has an attribute DeptName, then this attribute has different values for the various occurrences of the entity type. Each department has a specific department name. The set of possible department names constitutes the domain for DeptName.

Every attribute must, therefore, have a domain consisting of at least two values. Most attributes have domains consisting of large number of values. We understand that attribute is a term used to indicate a business fact that can have values from a given domain.

Examples of Attribute Domains. Let us now consider the example of an entity type and its possible attributes.

Entity type:	EMPLOYEE
Attributes:	EmployeeID, SocSecNo, EmpName, EmpZip, Salary, HireDate

Examine the values of each of these attributes. You will note that the values for a particular attribute are from a definite set of values. For example, the values for EmployeeID may be any number with six digits. That means, the set of values from which the value of EmployeeID for a particular instance of object EMPLOYEE is the set of numbers from 000001 to 999999. This is the domain of values for the attribute EmployeeID.

Domain of an attribute is, therefore, the set of legal or allowable values for that attribute. In the case EmployeeID, the attribute domain is the set of numbers from 000001 to 999999. Attribute domains are sets based on natural limitations as for numbers or characters of the alphabet. Mostly, business rules determine attribute domains.

Each attribute has its own domain for its values. Here are some examples of domains for the above attributes:

EmployeeID:	Set of numbers from 000001 to 999999
SocSecNo:	Set of legal 9-digit Social Security numbers
EmpName:	Any text up to 45 characters
EmpZip:	Set of legal zip codes
Salary:	Currency value from 000000.00 to 999999.99
HireDate:	Legal values for date greater than January 1, 1900

Domain Information

In the above example, you have looked at several examples of domains. Again, remember each domain is a value set. You can examine the values in each domain.

For example, when you scrutinize the domain for the attribute Salary, what information about the attribute does this domain convey to you? The values tell you that salary values are numeric and that salary values must fall within a certain range. What about the domain for HireDate? Here you note that the values for this attribute must have a correct date format and that the dates must be after January 1, 1900.

How do you set up the domain for an attribute? Generally, the nature of the attribute itself determines the contents of the domain. Beyond this, business rules regarding the attribute shapes the contents of the domain. For example, for the attribute HireDate, the set of values must be numeric and in date format. The nature of this attribute determines this general aspect of the domain. In this organization, all employees were hired after January 1, 1900. Therefore, no HireDate can be before January 1, 1990. This is a business rule. And this business rule determines the special aspect of the domain. Sometimes, the data type is known as the general domain and specific values, ranges, and so on are referred to as the specific domain.

Domain Information Content. Having reviewed the examples of domains, what information should attribute domains include? What should we be able to understand by reviewing the definition and contents of a domain?

Domain information must include the following.

Data Type. Type of data such as text, numeric, character, integers, audio, and video.

Format. Input and display formats for numeric data such as groupings with comma separation.

Length. Length for text data and formats such as long integer.

Distinct Formats. Specific formats such as currency and date.

Specific Values. Discrete values such as "Office," "Store," and "Warehouse" for attribute BuildingType in a data model for a retail organization.

Range. Range of values with inclusive or exclusive terminal values such as A001 to D999 for DeptNo attribute.

Constraints. Exclusions or exceptions in a set of domain values.

Nulls. Stipulation whether null is valid as part of the domain.

Default Values. Default value to be assigned for an attribute where input value is missing or unavailable.

Attribute Values and Domains

As you already know, each attribute of the various entities of an entity type gets its values from a set of allowable values. This set of legal values forms the domain of values for the attribute.

In order to firm up our understanding of attributes and domains, let us consider one more example of attributes and domains. Figure 5-4 displays examples of attributes and respective domains for entity type ORDER.

Note how the domain for each attribute consists of a set of allowable values. Notice how the two attributes OrderDate and ShipmentDate share the same domain. A domain

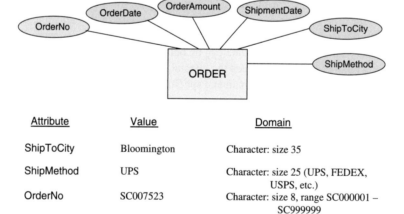

Attribute	Value	Domain
ShipToCity	Bloomington	Character: size 35
ShipMethod	UPS	Character: size 25 (UPS, FEDEX, USPS, etc.)
OrderNo	SC007523	Character: size 8, range SC000001 – SC999999
OrderAmount	4675.00	Numeric, range 0 – 99999.99
OrderDate	15NOV2006	Valid date, range 01JAN1920 –
ShipmentDate	17NOV2006	Valid date, range 01JAN1920 –

FIGURE 5-4 Attributes and domains for ORDER entity type.

of values may apply to several attributes of an entity type. However, each attribute takes its values from a single domain.

Split Domains

Quite often, domain values enable us to divide them into subsets so that we could distinguish between instances of attributes. Take the example of an entity type EMPLOYEE. In this organization, employees have to be distinguished and categorized into married or single groups. You can use values of an attribute known as MaritalStatus and split the domain into two groups.

All employee entities with "M" as the value for MaritalStatus will fall into one category and those with the value "S" will be in the other category. We are splitting the domain into two subsets and making use of the splitting to categorize the employees. At the same time, MaritalStatus represents a single business concept. Each attribute must represent a single concept.

We may achieve the same categorization by using two separate attributes MarriedIndicator and SingleIndicator in the EMPLOYEE entity type. Here, "Y" in MarriedIndicator or SingleIndicator will allow us to group married employees and single employees. However, if we do so, we will be splitting a logically complete domain into two separate attributes. We will be separating a single concept and the model will not reflect single concepts as single attributes. This will be an incorrect method of splitting domains.

Figure 5-5 shows incorrect and correct methods for domain split.

Misrepresented Domains

Every domain must represent the business rules correctly. The data model must reflect the information requirements and the business rules exactly. Sometimes, data modelers tend to misrepresent domains, mix them up, and produce incorrect data models.

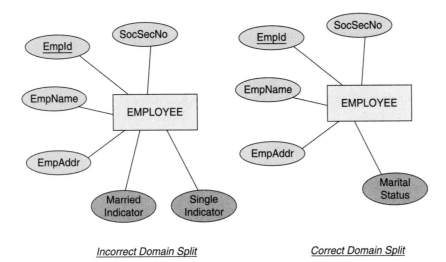

Incorrect Domain Split   *Correct Domain Split*

FIGURE 5-5   Incorrect and correct domain split.

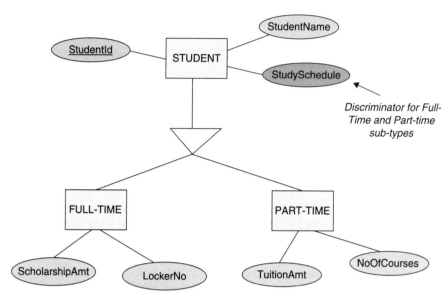

FIGURE 5-6 Model not matching requirements.

Consider the data model for a university. One of the major entity types is STUDENT. For this particular data model, two business rules need to be taken into account:

- The university has both full-time and part-time students.
- Some students receive scholarships, others do not.

The resulting data model must incorporate these business rules. Essentially, you need to separate out student into groups as full-time and part-time students, as well as students with scholarships and those without scholarships. How do you do that? You have to use domain values to indicate which group a student belongs to. Here is how the data modeler presented the partial model. Figure 5-6 displays the incorrect representation.

What is wrong with the figure? The data modeler implicitly assumed that no part-time students receive scholarships. In this model, two different concepts *study schedule* and *tuition payment* are mixed. These attributes need separate value domains; however, the domains are misrepresented in the model. Two domains have been mixed together using a single attribute StudySchedule. We will look at how this case of mixed domains could be resolved.

Resolution of Mixed Domains

We have to separate out the domains into two and express the two concepts separately. For this purpose, we need to express the two distinct concepts with two separate attributes StudySchedule and TuitionPayment. Then each of these attributes will have a separate domain.

Figure 5-7 indicates a resolution to the problem of mixed domains. Examine how the problem is resolved with two separate attributes.

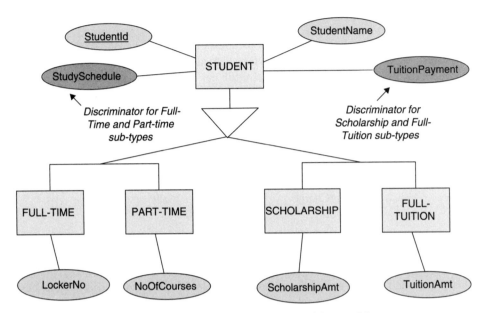

FIGURE 5-7 Resolution of misrepresented data model.

CONSTRAINTS FOR ATTRIBUTES

Constraints are rules or restrictions imposed on attributes. This is mainly done through imposing restrictions on the values in the domains. While reviewing examples of attributes and domains, you have already come across some of the constraints.

Constraints portray special aspects of the business rules. They provide character to the attributes. Later on, in the development of the database, constraints get implemented by means of facilities provided in the DBMS. In this section, let us summarize some of the ways of imposing constraints on attributes.

Value Set

You may specify constraints for an attribute by allowing only distinct values in the domain. Every entity is allowed to use only values from this restricted value set for the particular attribute.

Note the following examples for this kind of constraint:

Attribute	Domain
EmployeeGender	"Male"/"Female"
ApplicanceColor	"White"/"Black"/"Silver"/"Beige"
EmploymentStatus	"Full-time"/"Part-time"
StudentZip	Valid Zip Codes
CreditCardNumber	Valid 10-digit card number

Range

This is a common method of imposing constraints. You do not provide specific values to be part of the domain; instead, you give a range of values for the attribute. Each entity uses a value within the range for the particular attribute.

Here are a few examples for range of domain values used as constraints:

Attribute	Domain
HourlyWage	From 5.00 to 50.00
EmployeeDOB	Greater than 1/1/1930
WeeklyWorkHours	0.00 > and < = 80.00
ShipmentCharge	4.99 to 24.99
ExamScore	0 to 100

Type

Data type governs all attribute values. Data type constraints are either stated explicitly or they are implied. We have already seen some examples of data types such as numeric, text, and so on.

In addition to data type, domain constraints include the lengths of the character strings for text data and number of digits for numeric data. Note the following examples:

Attribute	Domain
YearlySalary	Numeric, long integer
DaysWorked	Numeric
CustomerName	Text up to 60 characters
ProductDesc	Text up to 45 characters
CityName	Text up to 65 characters

Null Values

Consider the attribute StudentFax for an entity type STUDENT. What about the values of this attribute for the various entity instances? If Mary Pearson has a fax machine, then that fax number will be the value for StudentFax for her.

On the other hand, if Rob Smith does not have a fax machine, then what about the value for StudentFax for Rob Smith? We then say that the attribute StudentFax for Rob Smith has a *null* value. If an object instance has no value for one of its attributes, then this attribute has a null value for that instance. Null values are not blanks or spaces. Null value for an attribute in an entity instance indicates the absence of a value for that attribute in that instance.

Null values for attributes play a significant role in databases. The value of an attribute for a particular instance of an object may be set to null if a value is not available, missing, or genuinely absent. In a database, null values may not be permitted for certain attributes. Using appropriate language commands, you can check for null values in attributes for object instances.

An attribute may have a null value for an instance of a entity type when

- this attribute is not applicable for that entity instance, or
- the actual value is missing or unavailable at input, or
- it is unknown whether a value exists for that entity instance.

TYPES OF ATTRIBUTES

Mostly, a particular attribute of a single entity has only one value at any given time. For example, the value of the attribute ProjectDuration for a single entity of the entity type PROJECT has a value of 90 days. At any given time, this is the only value for that attribute. However, in real-world situations, you will come across attributes that may have more than one value at the same time. You will also notice other types of variations in attributes.

In this subsection, we will describe such variations in the types of attributes. As you know, the data model must reflect real-world information correctly. The E-R modeling technique provides for representation of different attribute types. Let us go over a few examples.

Single-Valued and Multivalued Attributes

Note the following examples of single-valued and multivalued attributes. Observe the values of attributes for a single entity. These are the values at a given point in time.

Single-Valued

Entity type:	EMPLOYEE
Attribute:	EmployeeJob
Attribute value for single entity:	Salesperson
Entity type:	EMPLOYEE
Attribute:	EmployeeDOB
Attribute value for single entity:	24JAN2006

Multivalued

Entity type:	AUTOMOBILE
Attribute:	ExteriorColor
Attribute values for single entity:	Beige, Gold (two-tone color)
Entity type:	CUSTOMER
Attribute:	CustomerPhone
Attribute values for single entity:	732-888-1234, 732-888-3456, 732-889-5566

Figure 5-8 illustrates how single-valued and multivalued attributes are represented in a data model diagram with different notations for the two types.

Simple and Composite Attributes

This is another variation in attribute types. In real-world information, you will notice that some attributes may be divided further into smaller units. The smaller units are known as simple or atomic attributes, whereas the larger units are called composite attributes. Most of the attributes in real-world information, however, are simple attributes. Your data model has to represent these variations. Note the examples presented below.

Composite

Entity type:	CUSTOMER
Composite attribute:	CustomerAddress
Component simple attributes:	Street, City, State, Zip

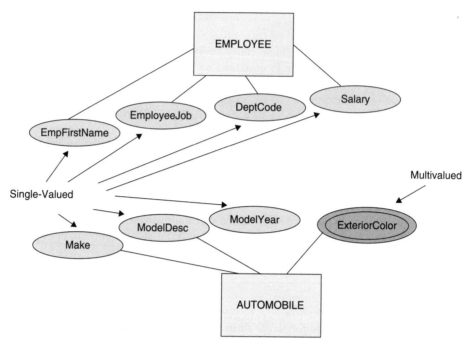

FIGURE 5-8 Single-valued and multivalued attributes.

Composite

Entity type:	EMPLOYEE
Composite attribute:	EmployeeName
Component simple attributes:	FirstName, LastName, MidInitial

Simple

Entity type:	LOAN ACCOUNT
Simple attribute:	LoanAmount
Entity type:	EMPLOYEE
Simple attribute:	SocialSecNumber

Figure 5-9 shows the notations used for representing composite attributes. Note how the composite attribute branches into the simple attributes that are its components. Especially observe how the attribute CustomerAddress may be broken down further into simple attributes.

Attributes with Stored and Derived Values

In later phases of database development, you will transform the data model into the physical structure of how data gets stored in the database. From our discussion of attributes, you must have realized that the physical data stored in the database consists of values of the attributes of the complete set of all the entities. Stored data is really values of the attributes.

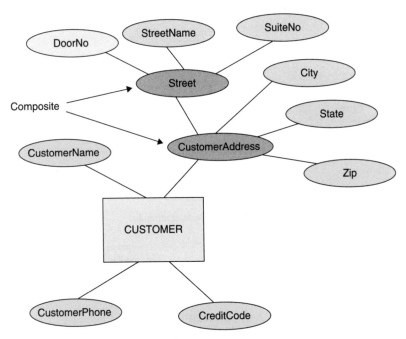

FIGURE 5-9 Composite attribute.

If you have a CUSTOMER entity type with CustomerName, CustomerAddress, and Phone as the attributes, then your database stores the values of these attributes for all the customer entities in your organization. These are attributes where values are stored in the database.

Sometimes, you would want to calculate and derive values from the values of one or more attributes and store the derived values in separate attributes. These are attributes containing derived values. Look at the following examples.

Attributes with Derived Values

Entity type:	EMPLOYEE
Derived attribute:	LengthOfEmployee
Attribute derived from:	EmployeeStartDate (and today's date)
Entity type:	PRODUCT
Derived attribute:	ProfitMargin
Attributes derived from:	UnitPrice and UnitCost

Figure 5-10 illustrates how a derived attribute is represented in an entity-relationship data model.

Optional Attributes

In some entity types, a good number of entity occurrences may not have values for specific attributes. So, for such entity instances, the database will contain nulls for those attributes. Simply, these attributes are not applicable to those entity instances.

Figure 5-11 shows CUSTOMER entity type with its attributes. Various attributes have different data value domains, and individual instances of the entities will pick up data

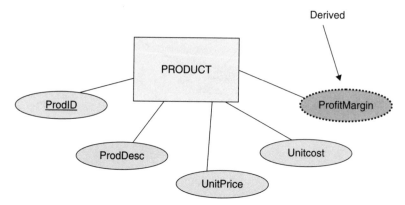

FIGURE 5-10   Derived attribute.

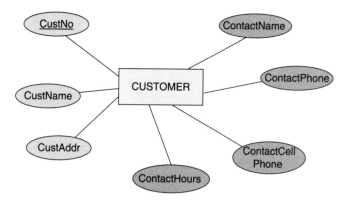

FIGURE 5-11   Optional attributes for CUSTOMER.

values from the domains for their attributes. However, notice the following attributes: ContactName, ContactPhone, ContactCellPhone, and ContactHours. These attributes relate to the contact persons for individual customers.

Not all customers have separate contact persons. Maybe only about a third of the customers have contact persons. Therefore, for about two-thirds of the entity instances of

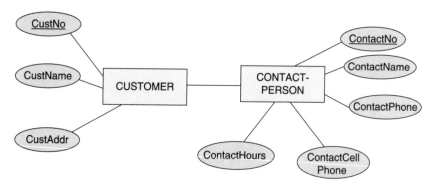

FIGURE 5-12   Resolution of optional attributes.

CUSTOMER, these attributes will have null values. These attributes are optional attributes. Resolve this situation by splitting these attributes from CUSTOMER and creating another entity type CONTACT-PERSON as shown in Figure 5-12.

IDENTIFIERS OR KEYS

Identifiers are attributes whose values enable us to uniquely identify individual occurrences of an entity type. If you have a CUSTOMER entity type, this represents the complete set of customers. The representation of the entity type in a data model portrays the entire set of customers. But in a database, we are interested in specific customers. Which customers live in Dayton, Ohio? Which customers bought for more than $100,000 last year? Who is the customer that sent order number 123456?

We need a method for identifying individual entities. In our earlier discussions, we have covered entity identifiers. Now we would like to get into more details.

Need for Identifiers

Go back to Figure 5-3 displaying sample attributes for the entity type STUDENT. You have noted that the set of values in each row describes a single instance. But, do you know which set describes a particular instance? If asked what is the address of Rob Smith, how can you find the address from the database? You can go through all instances of entity type STUDENT and check for the name value Rob Smith and then find the value for the address. What if there are three students in the university with the same name Rob Smith? Which Rob Smith are we referring to?

You need a method to identify a particular instance of an entity type. Obviously, values of an attribute may be used to identify particular instances. You tried to do that by looking for STUDENT instances with value "Rob Smith" for the attribute StudentName. However, you could not say for sure that you found the correct student because of the possibility of duplicate values for this attribute. On the other hand, if you had used values of the attribute StudentID, you could uniquely identify the student. What is the address of the student with StudentID 123456? It is Mary Williams; nobody else has that StudentID. Therefore, values of the attribute StudentID can be used to uniquely identify instances of STUDENT.

Attributes whose values can be used to uniquely identify instances of an entity type are known as identifiers. They are also known as keys for the entity type. Now, review the attributes for the entity type STUDENT. StudentName, StudentPhone, or StudentMajor cannot be used to identify instances uniquely. This is because these may have duplicate values in the set of instances for the entity type. Therefore, any attribute that is likely to have duplicate values does not qualify to be a key or identifier for an entity type.

Definitions of Keys

Let us define a few versions of key that are applicable to entity types. These definitions will help you to appreciate the differences and apply them correctly.

Candidate Key. A candidate key is an attribute or group of attributes whose values uniquely identify individual occurrences of an entity type.

In the example for STUDENT entity type, either of the attributes StudentID or SocSecNo qualifies to be a key. Values of either attribute will uniquely identify individual occurrences of STUDENT entities. Such attributes are known as candidate keys—candidates to become the key.

Primary Key. One of the candidate keys is chosen to serve as the unique identifier for the entity type. The selected candidate key becomes the primary key.

For the STUDENT entity type, you can choose either StudentID or SocSecNo to be the identifier. If you choose SocSecNo, then this attribute becomes the primary key for the entity type.

Composite Key. For some entity types, one attribute alone will not be enough to form the identifier. You may have to use the combination of two or more attributes as the identifier. A primary key consisting of more than one attribute is known as a composite key.

For example, for an entity type PROJECT-ASSIGNMENT representing the assignment of employees to projects, the combination of attributes ProjectId and EmployeeNo—a composite key—is needed to form the identifier.

Superkey. If a set of attributes is chosen to serve as the primary key and if there are superfluous attributes in the combination, then such a key is known as a superkey. A superkey contains redundant attributes.

For example, the attributes StudentID and StudentName together can serve as the primary key for STUDENT. However, StudentID by itself is sufficient to form the key; StudentName in the key is superfluous.

Natural Key. Natural key consists of attributes that represent some characteristics found in the real world. For example, check numbers and credit card numbers are real-world attributes.

If you form the primary key using such attributes, your key is a natural key. Commonly, entity types use natural keys.

Surrogate Key. In many cases, natural keys are not consistent or stable enough for use as primary keys. Some natural keys may be unduly long. In these situations, a new attribute called the surrogate key or artificial key is introduced in the entity type.

Values generated manually or by the computer system are used for the surrogate key attribute. For example, you can have autogenerated invoice numbers as values for the surrogate key InvoiceNum of the entity type INVOICE.

Guidelines for Identifiers

Refer back to our discussion of null values for attributes. Can an attribute with null values qualify to be a key? If null values are permitted for an attribute, then many instances of the object may have null values for this attribute. That means this attribute is useless for identifying those instances for which the attribute has null values. Attributes for which null values are allowed cannot be used as keys.

Let us summarize a few important guidelines for choosing primary keys.

Optional Attributes. Optional attributes may have null values for individual entity instances. Therefore, do not include optional attributes in the primary key of an entity type.

Single Attribute. Adopt the *smallest key* rule. If a single attribute will suffice, do not use a composite primary key. If a single attribute is not enough to form the primary key, use the minimum number of attributes to form the key.

Stable Attribute. Choose an attribute such that its value will not change or become null for the lifetime of each entity instance.

Uniqueness. For primary key, choose an attribute that will have a unique value for each individual instance of the entity type. No two instances may have the same value for the chosen attribute.

Definitive. Choose an attribute for which a value exists for every instance of the entity type at creation time such that an entity occurrence cannot be created unless a primary key value also exists.

Length. Choose the candidate key that has the minimum length.

Single-Valued Attribute. Choose a single-valued attribute for primary key. A multivalued attribute, by definition, may have multiple values for the same entity instance; therefore, it cannot serve as the primary key.

Built-in Meanings. Avoid any candidate key where values of parts of the attribute may have built-in meanings. For example, ProductNumber where part of the attribute indicates the production plant number is not a good candidate key. When another plant begins to manufacture this product, the product number for the same product will have to be changed. In other words, the primary key values must be "factless."

Key in Generalization Hierarchy

In a generalization hierarchy, the primary key is inherited by the subtype entities. The hierarchy may consist of several levels, yet the primary key values trickle down from the supertype at the highest level.

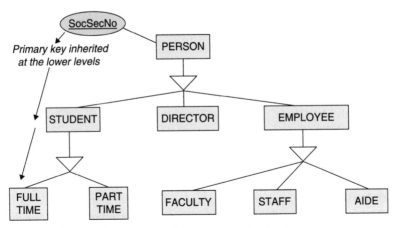

FIGURE 5-13 College data model: multilevel generalization.

Figure 5-13 illustrates a multilevel generalization hierarchy in a college data model.

Notice the primary key attribute SocSecNo for the supertype PERSON at the highest level. Observe the entity types at the second level. For each of these entity types, the primary key attribute is still SocSecNo. As it is implied, the primary key in not explicitly shown in the model diagram. The primary key attribute gets inherited by the entity types at the next two lower levels also.

ATTRIBUTE VALIDATION CHECKLIST

Thus far in this chapter, we covered many topics on attributes in detail. We reviewed formal definitions of attributes. We elaborated on attribute domains. We looked at the types of constraints relating to attributes. We studied various types of attributes and noted how these are represented in a data model. We reviewed key attributes in sufficient depth.

During the data modeling process, at each stage, you need to check the data model for completeness and correctness. Data modeling is an iterative process. After defining the entity types, the next major activity refers to the representation of attributes and identifiers.

We now present a checklist of items for validation of attributes. Two checklists are presented: one to verify completeness and the other to verify correctness of attributes. Use these checklists to complete the review process for attributes.

Completeness

Requirements Review. Go over the requirements for each entity type and make sure all attributes are completely defined.

Attribute Names. Review each attribute name and ensure that it represents a single business fact in the real world. Rewrite vague abbreviations and nonstandard acronyms.

Attribute Descriptions. Provide descriptions for all attributes as needed in the supplementary documentation.

Domains. Ensure that the domain is clearly indicated for each attribute.

Constraints. Wherever business rules are present in the requirements relating to attributes, ensure that these are properly noted in the definition of the domains. Use supplementary documentation.

Composite Attributes. Make certain that all composite attributes are identified and represented in the data model diagram.

Multivalued Attributes. Review each entity type for multivalued attributes. Mark multivalued attributes in the data model diagram with proper notation.

Derived Attributes. Wherever needed, ensure that derived attributes are shown in the data model diagram. Also, verify that the derivation rules are recorded in the supplementary documentation.

Optional Attributes. Verify that all optional attributes are noted and documented as notes in the data model diagram and in the supplementary documentation.

Primary Key. Ensure that every entity type has an assigned primary key.

Surrogate Key. Wherever there is a need for a surrogate key, make sure a separate attribute is defined for the corresponding entity type and marked as primary key. Also, document how values for the surrogate key are generated.

Correctness

Attribute Representation. Ensure that each attribute represents a single fact about the organization.

Attribute Names. Make sure that all attribute names are spelled and shown in proper case according to the accepted standard in the organization. Use the same standard such as separating words in the names with hyphens, underscores, or embedded uppercase letters, and so on. Review each attribute name and ensure that it represents a single business fact in the real world.

Attribute Descriptions. Ensure that each attribute description correctly supplements and describes the attribute name. Make sure descriptions exist for all attributes except the very obvious ones where the meaning can be clearly inferred from the attribute name itself.

Homonyms and Synonyms. Review the complete list of attribute names. Scan for homonyms and synonyms and resolve these.

Domains. Review the domain for each attribute and make sure that the domain is appropriate and conforms to the requirements. Ensure that each domain contains at least two data values.

Constraints. Review the expressions of constraints through domain definitions and ensure correctness.

Composite Attributes. Go over all composite attributes and ensure that they are properly broken down and shown in the data model diagram.

Multivalued Attributes. Verify representations of multivalued attributes in the data model diagram for correctness.

Derived Attributes. Check representations of derived attributes in the data model diagram. Verify derivation rules.

Optional Attributes. Verify documentation of optional attributes and ensure that these are truly optional.

Primary Key. Check each primary key attribute. Ensure that each primary key attribute will contain unique values that will last for the lifetime of the entities. Double check and ensure that the primary key attribute is not an optional attribute. Make sure that the primary key does not contain any superfluous attributes. Review all candidate keys for each entity type and make certain that the most suitable candidate key is chosen as the primary key.

CHAPTER SUMMARY

- Attribute values form the bulk of the data content in a database.
- Attributes are distinct, intrinsic, and inherent characteristics of an entity type. An attribute designates the nature of data for an entity type; an attribute describes an entity type.
- An attribute associates an entity set with a set of values.
- Each entity may be described by a set of (attribute, value) pairs, one pair for each attribute of the entity type.
- A set of allowable or legal values for an attribute constitutes the domain for that attribute.
- Domain information includes data type, format, length, specific value, range, constraints, use of nulls, and default values.
- Attribute types: single-valued and multivalued, derived and stored, optional attributes.
- Identifiers signify unique instances of entity types. One of the candidate keys is chosen as the primary key for the entity type.

REVIEW QUESTIONS

1. Match the column entries:

1. Attributes	A. Actual value missing
2. Default values	B. Artificial key
3. Constraint on attribute	C. More than one attribute
4. Null value	D. Data holders
5. Composite attribute	E. Integer
6. Surrogate key	F. No duplicate values
7. Composite key	G. Extra unnecessary attributes
8. Data type	H. Range of domain values
9. Primary key	I. Made up of simple attributes
10. Superkey	J. Part of domain information

2. Discuss in detail what attributes are and what their features are. Use some examples to enable the discussion to be understood.

3. Explain with an example how a relationship can have attributes.

4. Stipulate any five criteria for selecting names for attributes.
5. What is an attribute domain? Describe clearly with examples.
6. List the types of information to be included in the domain definition.
7. What are split domains? Describe the correct method for domain split with an example.
8. Name four types of constraints for attributes. Give examples for any two types.
9. Distinguish between stored and derived attributes. Give two examples.
10. List any six guidelines for choosing the primary key.

6

RELATIONSHIPS IN DETAIL

CHAPTER OBJECTIVES

- Study various aspects of relationships in detail
- Explore the nature and definition of relationships
- Discuss relationships for dependent entity types
- Examine structural constraints for relationships
- Provide in-depth coverage of cardinality and nullability
- Investigate potential problems and study solution options
- Review several design issues and resolutions
- Conclude with a relationship validation checklist

We have reviewed entities in detail; entities are business object instances about which an organization collects and stores information. We made an in-depth study of attributes; these represent the data content about the entities. Entities or business objects do not simply exist in isolation. In the real world, business objects interact with one another. This interaction produces types of useful information for an organization.

Consider a question: Which are the orders placed by a specific customer? Here the information can be derived only when you consider the interaction between the entity representing that customer with the entities denoted by that customer's orders. Another question: Which are flights taken by a passenger in a frequent-flier program? This is pertinent information needed by an airlines company administering a frequent-flier program. Interaction or relationship between passenger entities and entities representing flights provides the required information.

Entity types and their attributes provide static information. In isolation, you can obtain information about customers only and nothing else from the attributes of CUSTOMER

Data Modeling Fundamentals. By Paulraj Ponniah
Copyright © 2007 John Wiley & Sons, Inc.

entity type. Similarly, by themselves, the attributes of ORDER entity type provide information about orders only. Only when you make use of the relationships between customer and order entities you can obtain more dynamic and useful information.

In this chapter, we will explore relationships in greater detail. Although we have covered relationships among entity types earlier, this is a more elaborate and intensive study. We will walk through potential problems in modeling relationships and examine some critical design issues.

RELATIONSHIPS

Consider an order entry process. This is a typical process in most organizations. Examine the information requirements for an order entry process. Apart from others, three entity types feature prominently in the information requirements. The information requirements are about CUSTOMER, ORDER, and PRODUCT. Each entity type has its own set of attributes. If your data model represents just the three entity type and their attributes, then the model will not be a true representation of the information requirements. Of course, in the real-world situation, you have these three entity types. But, that is not the whole story. These three entity types do not just remain in seclusion from one another. The business process of order entry takes place on the basis of associations between the three sets of entities. Accordingly, the data model must reflect these associations.

Customers place orders; orders contains products. At a basic level, CUSTOMER entity type and ORDER entity type are associated with each other. Similarly, the entity type ORDER and the entity type PRODUCT are linked to each other. As you know, such links and associations are represented as relationships in data model diagrams.

Associations

We expressed that relationships in data model diagrams symbolize associations or logical links. Let us inspect the associations among the three entity types CUSTOMER, ORDER, and PRODUCT. Figure 6-1 shows a data model diagram with these entity types.

First, observe the relationship between CUSTOMER and ORDER. The relationship symbol indicates that the relationship exists because in the real-world situation, a customer *places* an order. The action of placing an order forms the basis for the relationship. A relationship name is an action word—usually a single verb. Relationships indicate interaction between objects. They represent associations between objects and the types of action that govern the associations.

Next, review the relationship between ORDER and PRODUCT. Here the action is not very apparent; nevertheless, it is the action of an order containing products. The association of ORDER with PRODUCT rests on the fact that orders are for products; that is, orders contain products. The verb or action word in this case is *contains*.

Role of Relationships. In Figure 6-1, look at the relationship symbol between CUSTOMER and ORDER. Does the symbol indicate the linkage between the two boxes representing the two objects or individual entity instances within each of the two boxes? Figure 6-2 illustrates this important distinction.

The relationship indicated between two entity type boxes is actually the associations between specific instances of one entity type with particular occurrences of another

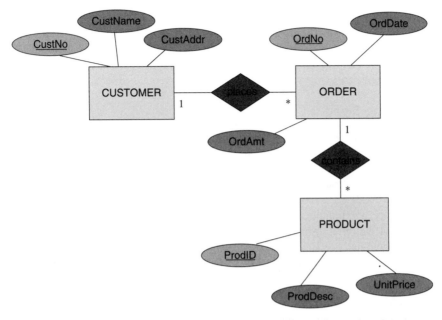

FIGURE 6-1   Relationships: CUSTOMER, ORDER, PRODUCT.

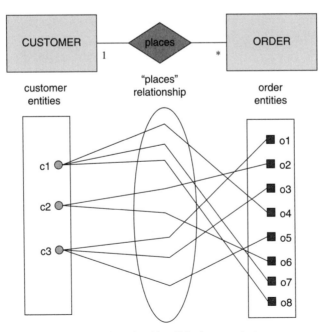

FIGURE 6-2   Relationships: links between instances.

entity type. Take a little time to grasp the significance of the meaning and role of relationships symbolized in data model diagrams. The connection shown between two entity type boxes simply indicates that the instances are related with one another. The name of the relationship as written within the diamond applies to each link between instances.

Relationship: Two-Sided

Consider a relationship between two entity types PROJECT and EMPLOYEE. This relationship represents associations between project entities and employee entities. You may select one project entity and look for the employee entities associated with that project entity. Here you proceed to review the relationship from one side of the relationship, namely, the PROJECT entity type. You may also study the associations by choosing one employee entity and find the project entities associated with that employee entity. This is the other side of the relationship.

Every relationship has two sides to it. Figure 6-3 illustrates the two-sided nature of the relationship between PROJECT and EMPLOYEE.

Relationship from PROJECT. Let us review the relationship from the PROJECT side. Note the association lines connecting individual instances of the two entity types. From this side of the relationship, each project consists of certain employees.

Take specific examples. Look at one project instance that has the ProjectName "Design." Trace the association lines. These lines connect the "Design" project with employee instances of "Mary Brown," "Samuel Raymo," and "Tabitha Daniels." That means the design project consists of three employees Mary Brown, Samuel Raymo, and

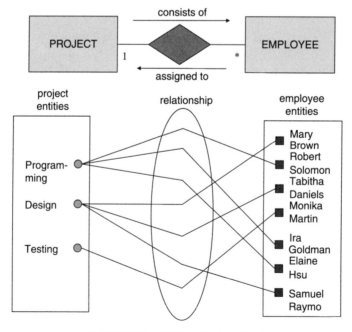

FIGURE 6-3 Relationship: two-sided.

Tabitha Daniels. Tracing the relationship from PROJECT helps find employees working on particular projects.

Later on, when the data model gets implemented, searches for employees working on a specific project will make use of the relationship from this side. Also, when you examine the relationship from this side, you understand the cardinality of how many employees may be associated with one project.

Relationship from EMPLOYEE. Now look at the relationship from the other side, namely, from EMPLOYEE. Note the association lines connecting individual instances of EMPLOYEE and PROJECT. For this side of the relationship, each employee is assigned to a certain project.

Let us check specific instances. Look at the employee instance Robert Solomon. Trace the association line. This line connects the instance to the project instance "Programming." There are no other association lines from the employee instance Robert Solomon. What does this mean? It conveys the information that the employee is assigned to one project. This is different from looking at the relationship from the other side.

We therefore note that the relationship is a one-to-many relationship as seen from the PROJECT side. One project may have one or many employees. On the other hand, one employee is assigned to only one project.

Relationship Sets

When we consider an entity type, we refer to the set of entities of the same type. For example, the EMPLOYEE entity type refers to a set of employees. This is a set of instances with similar attributes. The notion of a set may be extended to relationships as well.

Take an example of the relationship between entity types EMPLOYEE and DEPART-MENT. Find the associations between employee entities and department entities. Concentrate on one association such as Jerry Stone working in Sales Department. This association is one instance of several such associations between employee instances and department instances. Figure 6-4 shows the relationship between the two entity types and the associations among the individual instances.

Let us list the associations shown in the figure: (Sales—Jerry Stone), (Sales—Martha Johnson), (Finance—Rudy Brunner), (Finance—Ashlee Thomas), and so on.

What are these associations? These associations form a set of pairs. What does this set of associations indicate? The relationship between the entity types DEPARTMENT and EMPLOYEE may be reckoned as a set of the associations noted above. A relationship between two entity types constitutes a set of associations between entities of the first entity type and entities of the second entity type.

Double Relationships

In the relationships considered so far, the entities of one entity type are associated with entities of the other entity type in only one way. For example, in the relationship between EMPLOYEE and DEPARTMENT, the relationship indicates employees working in departments or, looking at it from the other side, departments having employees. Nevertheless, the relationship expresses only one type of relationship.

Sometimes, two entity types may have dual relationships. That is, entities of one entity type may be associated with entities of another entity type based on one type of

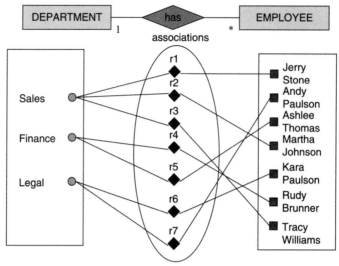

Set of associations   { r1, r2, r3, r4, r5, r6, r7 }

Set of   { Sales—Jerry Stone, Sales—Martha Johnson, Sales—Tracy Williams,
associations as Finance—Rudy Brunner, Finance—Ashlee Thomas,
entity pairs   Legal—Kara Paulson, Legal—Andy Paulson }

FIGURE 6-4   Employee and department: relationship and associations.

association. Again, entities for the same two entity types may be associated with each other based on a different criterion for the relationship.

Let us review a few examples of dual relationships.

Professor–Student Dual Relationship. Consider two entity types PROFESSOR and STUDENT. A professor entity may be associated with a student entity when the professor is teaching a class where the student is in the class. This is one type of relationship between the two entity types.

In another case, a professor entity may be associated with a student entity in the sense of the professor being a dissertation advisor for the student. Here, although the professor and student entities are related, the relationship is of a different nature.

See Figure 6-5 illustrating the dual relationship.

Customer–Address Dual Relationship. Take another example for considering dual relationship. Look at the requirements for relating orders with billing and shipping addresses. Customers place orders, and for the orders there could be billing and shipping addresses. For some orders, no such separate addresses may exist.

The entity types in question are CUSTOMER, ORDER, and ADDRESS. Here addresses are not reckoned as attributes of customers; addresses have separate existence. When residential, billing, and shipping addresses may apply to customers, you gain advantage by not expressing the addresses as attributes. If you do so, you will have to permit nulls and allow empty spaces on many customer instances that do not have such separate addresses.

Figure 6-6 shows the entity types and the relationships.

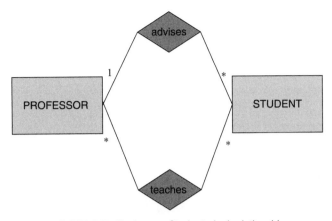

FIGURE 6-5 Professor–Student: dual relationship.

Observe how address and order entities are related in a dual relationship. A specific address entity may be related to one or more order entities where the address is the billing address. Again, some other address entity may be associated with one or more order entities where the address is the shipping address.

Relationship Attributes

When we discussed attributes in detail in the previous chapter, we presented attributes as descriptors of entities. An entity type has descriptive attributes. Values of each attributes describe particular entities. If an entity type WATER-HEATER in a model for an appliance store has attributes SerialNo and Color, then for each water heater in the store, there are distinct values for SerialNo and Color. The entity type WATER-HEATER

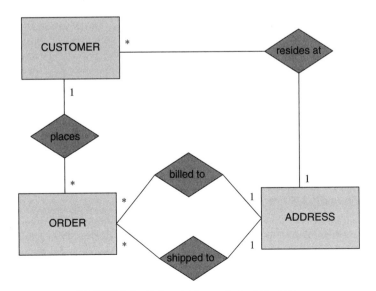

FIGURE 6-6 Order–Address: dual relationship.

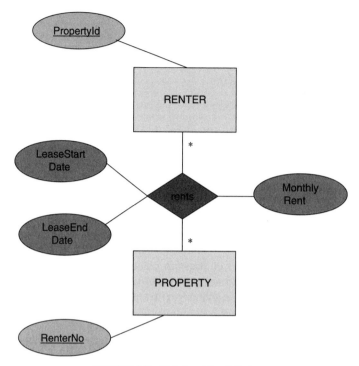

FIGURE 6-7 Relationship attributes.

comprises the set of all water heaters in the store. Values for attributes SerialNo and Color are associated with each member of this set.

Earlier, we considered relationships as being sets. The members of this relationship set consist of pairs indicating entities from participating entity types. Take an example of two entity types RENTER and PROPERTY for a real estate rental organization. A relationship "rents" exists between these two entity types. This relationship forms a set of pairs of entities, one from each entity type—(renter1 to property3), and so on. Each of these pairs itself has specific values such LeaseStartDate, LeaseEndDate, and MonthlyRent. What are these specific values? These values describe each pair in the relationship set. These are attributes for the relationship between entity types RENTER and PROPERTY.

Figure 6-7 illustrates attributes for relationships themselves.

Note the relationship between RENTER and PROPERTY and the attributes for the relationship apart from the attributes of the entity types themselves.

DEGREE OF RELATIONSHIPS

From the examples of relationships seen so far, you note that entity types are related in twos or threes. That is, instances of two entity types are associated with each other, or instances of three entity types are associated to form a combination.

The degree of a relationship in a data model refers to the number of entity types that participate in the relationship. A three-way relationship is a ternary relationship with degree three; two-way, a binary relationship with degree two; one-way, a unary relationship with degree one. A unary relationship is also known as a recursive relationship as the entities of the same entity type associate with one another. Relationships with degree four are known as quaternary relationships. These are quite rare. Mostly, real-world situations contain binary relationships.

When you examine a relationship and note the degree of the relationship, the degree specifies how members of the relationships are constituted. Each relationship symbolizes a relationship set. As we mentioned earlier, the relationship between two entity types forms a set consisting of entity pairs, one entity from the first entity type pairing with one entity from the second entity type. Thus a binary relationship indicates a set of entity pairs. If the binary relationship has an attribute, then each entity pair in the relationship set pertains to a specific value for this attribute.

What about a ternary relationship? How is this relationship constituted? A ternary relationship set contains triplets of entities formed by one entity from each of the three participating entity types. Thus, if the ternary relationship has an attribute, then each entity triplet in the relationship set points to a particular value for this attribute.

We may extend the notion of constituents of a relationship set to quaternary relationships and relationships with degrees higher than four. This is the main point about relationship degrees. The degree determines how members of the relationship set are formed—whether they are entity pairs, triplets, quadruplets, and so on.

Let us examine a few examples of relationships with varying degrees When you look at each example, observe how the relationship set for the example gets formed.

Unary Relationship

As you already know, a unary relationship links an entity type with itself. Entities of a single entity type associate with entities within itself. For forming an association, we take an entity of the single entity type and revert back to the same entity type to find the associative entity.

In a unary relationship, the relationship set consists of entity pairs, taking entities from the same entity type. In the relationship pair, entities from the same entity types recur. In the entity pair, an entity is taken for an entity type, and again another entity is picked from the same entity type. Therefore, the name recursive relationship applies to a unary relationship.

Figure 6-8 illustrates unary relationship with two examples.

In each example, explore how entity pairs from the same entity type form the relationship set. Also, note the attributes in each unary relationship. We expressed that relationships in data model diagrams symbolize associations or logical links.

Binary Relationship

You have seen several examples of binary relationships. When you scrutinize any data model, you will notice that most of the associations are binary relationships. Providing another example of a binary relationship may strike you as being redundant. Nevertheless, we want to show a common example of a binary relationship between STUDENT and COURSE. However, in this example we want to examine the contents of the relationship.

Figure 6-9 shows the binary relationship.

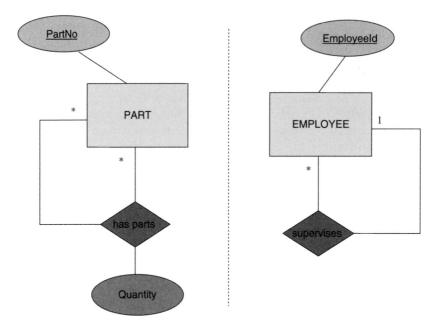

FIGURE 6-8 Unary relationship: examples.

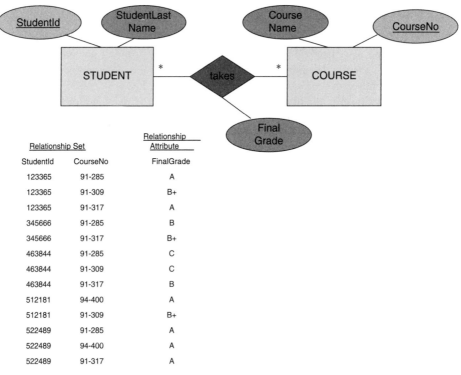

FIGURE 6-9 Binary relationship and relationship set.

Carefully examine the figure with the binary relationship. In particular, review the members of the relationship set. As you know, the pairs made up of student and course entities form the set. Note each member and values of the attribute for this relationship.

Ternary Relationship

Although binary relationships outnumber other types of relationships in a data model, you will have occasion to design ternary relationships. When you run into attributes that depend on three entities, one from each of three entity types, representing a three-way relationship becomes essential.

Let us consider two examples. The first example relates to product shipments. Usually, shipments involve entities from more than two entity types. This example covers the entity types PRODUCT, VENDOR, and WAREHOUSE.

The second example deals with doctors, patients, and offices. In a group practice having several locations, doctors may see patients in any of the offices of the group practice. Therefore, the date and time of an appointment depend on entity triplets from DOCTOR, PATIENT, and OFFICE. Here you find a ternary relationship.

See Figure 6-10 for the two examples of ternary relationship. Note the attributes of the relationships and how the attribute values depend on triplets formed by entities from each of the three entity types.

Quaternary Relationship

You may rarely run into a relationship with four participating entity types. Such a representation becomes necessary only when attribute values rely on entities from four independent entity types. This does not happen too often in real-world situations.

Let us look at one example of a quaternary relationship. A company procures loans to its clients from lending institutions for properties. Agents bring this business to the

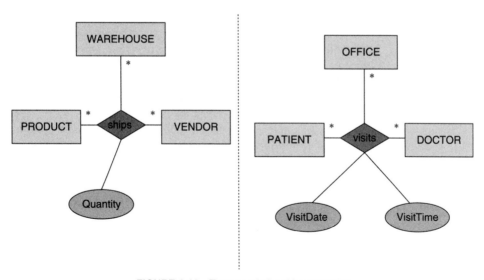

FIGURE 6-10 Ternary relationship: examples.

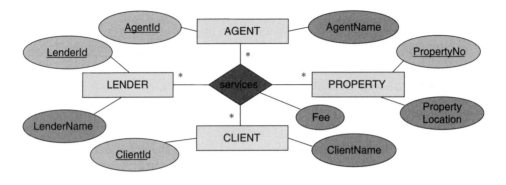

AgentId	LenderId	ClientId	PropertyNo	Fee
11	123	98	333	1000
22	234	76	111	2000
33	345	87	222	1500

FIGURE 6-11   Quaternary relationship and relationship set.

company. The company charges a small fee for its services based on specific considerations of the type of property, lending institution, and rates for agents. The fee relates
to the client, property, lending institution, and agent. We note a four-way relationship.

Figure 6-11 illustrates the quaternary relationship with four participating entity types.
The figure also shows the quadruplets that make up the relationship set and their corresponding values for fee.

STRUCTURAL CONSTRAINTS

Constraints are restrictions or rules that apply to any component of a data model. If the data
model represents real-world information requirements accurately, it must portray all
aspects of the requirements including any business rules that govern the information
content. Business rules may apply to the way each entity type gets constituted. Several
business rules affect attributes and their values. Now, we want to consider how business
rules in an organization influence relationships among entity types.

Let us work with a familiar example. In any organization, different types of projects
exist. Employees get assigned to the project. When you symbolize the assignment of
employees to projects, you create entity types of PROJECT and EMPLOYEE. The
relationship between these two entity types expresses the assignment of employees to
projects. Associations between employee entities and project entities exist.

With regard to these associations, the business rules may give rise to different scenarios.
How are these two types of entities related? How many entities of one type may be associated
with how many entities of the second type? Should every employee entity be associated with
one or more of the project entities? What about the opposite direction of the association?

Figure 6-12 indicates the relationship between PROJECT and EMPLOYEE expressing
some possible scenarios about the associations of individual entities.

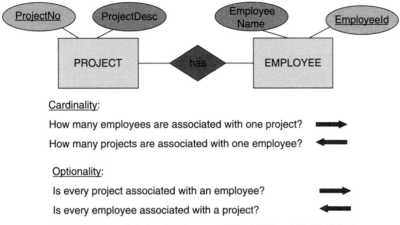

Cardinality:

How many employees are associated with one project?

How many projects are associated with one employee?

Optionality:

Is every project associated with an employee?

Is every employee associated with a project?

FIGURE 6-12   Relationship between PROJECT and EMPLOYEE.

When you study the types of questions that arise regarding the associations, you will note that business rules can impose two types of constraints on relationships. The first relates to the question: How many of one entity type with how many of another entity type—one, none, several? This type of constraint, as you know, relates to the cardinality of relationship—deals with numbers of associated entities. The second type of constraint relates to the question: Whether an entity must be part of an association or not? This constraint tells about whether the association is optional or mandatory. This constraint type is known as optionality constraint. It is also called participation constraint because it indicates whether individual entities may or may not participate in the relationship. Sometimes, the term nullability constraint also refers to this type of constraint.

We will note some examples of these two types of relationship constraints. In the next section, we will elaborate on the cardinality and participation constraints with more examples using the concept of maximum and minimum cardinalities.

Cardinality Constraint

Business rules stipulate how many of an entity type may be associated with how many of a second entity type. The cardinality indicators placed on the relationship line denotes the cardinality constraint. Let us revisit the three common types of cardinality constraint: one-to-one, one-to-many, and many-to-many.

As you already know, a relationship between two entity types actually indicates the nature of associations or links between individual instances of the two entity types. Only occurrences of individual entities are connected—that is what the relationship line between two entity types symbolizes. Let us review an example for each of the three types of cardinality constraint.

Cardinality Constraint: One-to-One.   Take the example of executives responsible to administer company divisions. This responsibility differs in various organizations. When you create a data model to show this relationship, you have to replicate the business rule governing the administration in your organization.

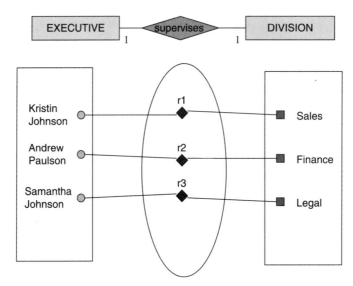

FIGURE 6-13 Cardinality constraint: one-to-one.

Let us consider a business rule about the administration of divisions and its representation a data model.
Business rule:

In the organization, one executive is responsible for one division and not more than one division. Also, one division is supervised by one executive and not by more than one executive.

Representation of relationship constraint:

Each executive entity is associated with one division entity and not with more than one division entity. Each division entity is associated with one executive entity and not with more than one executive entity.

Figure 6-13 represents the one-to-one cardinality constraint. Note the individual associations between entities shown in the diagram.

Cardinality Constraint: One-to-Many. For an example of this type of constraint, let us consider the information requirements for an airlines company where you have to account for individual planes in the fleet by airplane type. Your model must reflect the relationship between AIRPLANE-TYPE and AIRPLANE. The entity type AIRPLANE-TYPE represents the various types of airplanes in the fleet such as Boeing 767, Boeing 747, Airbus 311, and so on whereas the entity type AIRPLANE includes the individual planes in the fleet.

In this case, the business rule is fairly obvious. The associations between type entities and plane entities must follow the basic business rule about types and instances.
Business rule:

In the airline company, one airplane type may have one or several planes of this type. On the other hand, every single plane belongs to only one airplane type.

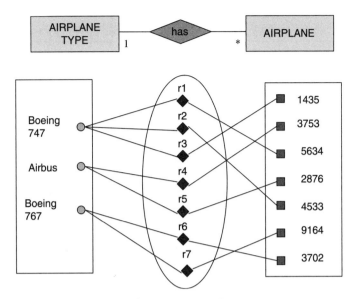

FIGURE 6-14   Cardinality constraint: one-to-many.

Representation of relationship constraint:

Each airplane type entity is associated with one or many plane entities. Each plane entity is linked to one and only one airplane type entity.

Figure 6-14 represents the one-to-many cardinality constraint. Observe the individual associations between entities shown in the diagram. Notice how one type entity gets linked to one or more of the plane entities. From the other side, one plane entity gets connected to one and only one type entity. One-to-many constraint from one side of the relationship implies many-to-one constraint from the other side of the relationship.

Cardinality Constraint: Many-to-Many. This type of constraint is quite common in real-word situations. Take the familiar example of students enrolled in courses. Your model must reflect the relationship between STUDENT and COURSE entity types. For a specific student, you must be able to ascertain which courses he or she is enrolled in. Also, the database implementation should provide information on students enrolled for a particular course.

The business rule in the university dictates how students may enroll in a course. Usually, there are no restrictions as to the number of courses a student may enroll in. However, your data model must reflect the actual business rule governing the specific situation about enrollment.

Business rule:

In the university, one student may enroll in one or more courses. Also, one course may have one or more students.

Representation of relationship constraint:

Each student entity is associated with one or more course entities. Each course entity is linked to one or more student entities.

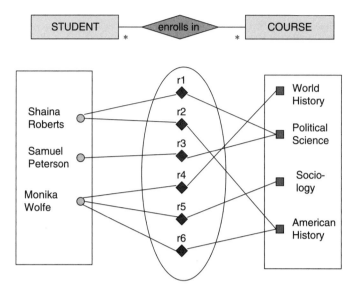

FIGURE 6-15   Cardinality constraint: many-to-many.

Figure 6-15 shows the many-to-many cardinality constraint. Pay attention to the individual associations between entities shown in the diagram. Notice how one student entity connects to one or more of the course entities. Also, the same type of linkage happens from the other side, too. From the other side, one course entity gets connected to one or many student entities. Many-to-many constraint is a symmetrical constraint on the relationship from either side, though the exact numbers of associated entities may vary.

Participation Constraint

Other terminology also refers to participation constraints. Participation constraints deal with whether participation of individual entities in a relationship between entity types is mandatory or optional. Participation constraints are also known as optionality in the relationship.

Let us reconsider the relationship between EMPLOYEE and PROJECT and examine if participation constraint could apply to this relationship. In this relationship, employee instances or occurrences associate with project occurrences. Suppose the relationship between PROJECT and EMPLOYEE is one-to-many. This means one project entity is associated with one or more employee entities, and one employee entity is associated with one and only one project entity. This is the cardinality constraint.

In addition to stipulating the numbers or cardinalities, the business rule for the relationship may include another type of constraint. For example, the business may specify whether employee entities need to participate in the relationship. Two cases arise regarding the participation. We will examine the two cases.

Partial Participation. It is likely that in an organization, some employees belong to special cadres or work on routine operations. Such employees will not be working on projects. Our data model must reflect this information about the relationship in addition to the cardinality.

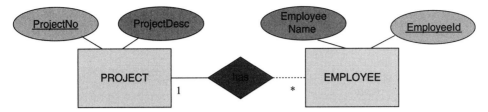

FIGURE 6-16   Participation constraint: partial participation.

We need to show how employee entities are associated with project entities both in terms of numbers and participation. The data model must represent how participation applies to the relationship. Let us review the business rule relating to partial participation.
Business rule:

In the company, one project has at least one employee assigned to it. Some employees may not be working on any project at all.

Representation of relationship constraint:

Every project entity is associated with at least one employee entity. An employee entity may not be associated with any project entity; if associated, an employee entity is linked to only one project entity.

Figure 6-16 shows the relationship between EMPLOYEE and PROJECT indicating partial participation of employee entities. The diagram denotes the partial participation by means of a broken line meaning that the participation of entities from the EMPLOYEE end is partial or optional. However, from the PROJECT end, the participation is not partial. Every project entity participates in the relationship. Indication of partial participation with broken lines is one method of representation. Other symbols such as single line for partial participation and double lines for total participation are also in usage.

Total Participation. In this case, there are no exceptions; every employee works on some project. This is typical of consulting companies where every employee is working on one or more client projects. The data model must reflect this information about the relationship in addition to the cardinality.
Our data model has to show how employee entities are associated with project entities both in terms of numbers and participation. The data model must represent how participation applies to the relationship. Let us review the business rule relating to total participation.
Business rule:

In the company, one project has at least one employee assigned to it. Every employee works on one or more projects.

Representation of relationship constraint:

Every project entity is associated with at least one employee entity. Every employee is linked to at least one project entity.

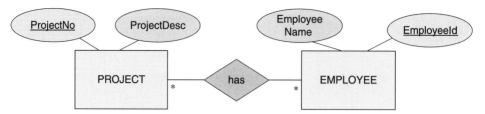

FIGURE 6-17 Participation constraint: total participation.

Figure 6-17 shows the relationship between EMPLOYEE and PROJECT indicating total participation of employee entities. The diagram denotes the total participation by means of a solid line meaning that the participation of entities from the EMPLOYEE end is total or mandatory. Also, from the PROJECT end, the participation is total. Every project entity participates in the relationship.

DEPENDENCIES

In Chapter 4, we covered weak entities that depend on strong or regular entities for their existence. We will now revisit existence conditions for entities and also study relationships between entity types in this context.

Exploring relationships in terms of entity existence conditions has a strong impact on implementation of these in the database. When we study transformation of conceptual data model into a logical data model, especially the relational framework, you will grasp the significance of existence-dependent relationships.

Entity Existence

In a data model, entity types represented by rectangular boxes in the E-R technique do not present themselves as isolated and separate. You know that entity types participate in relationships. However, the relationships do not always determine whether entity types may exist independently.

As we have already seen earlier, many entity types do exist independently irrespective of their relationships with other entity types. Most of the entity types fall into this category. However, you will note occasions when some entity types need other entity types for their existence. Let us review some examples.

Independent Existence. Let us say you have a data model for a university. Two important entity types are COURSE and INSTRUCTOR. The COURSE entity type represents all the courses offered in the university. Similarly, the INSTRUCTOR entity type comprises all the instructors that teach the courses.

In fact, these two entity types are related because instructors teach courses. Individual instructor entities associate with distinct course entities. Take a specific example: instructor Kassia Silverton teaches Data Modeling course. Irrespective of this association, the instance of INSTRUCTOR, namely, Kassia Silverton, will exist in the database. In the same manner, the instance of COURSE, namely, Data Modeling, will exist in the database independent of the association.

We can say that the entity instances of the two entity types INSTRUCTOR and COURSE exist independent of each other. Also, the associations between entities of these two entity types have no bearing on the existence of the entities. INSTRUCTOR and COURSE entity types have independent existence.

Dependent Existence. Now take another example of entity types for a mortgage company. Two important entity types we can consider would be LOAN and PAYMENT. The PAYMENT entity type represents payments by mortgage customers toward their loans. The LOAN entity type symbolizes mortgage loans given to the customers.

Examine the entity instances of the two entity types. Specifically, look at one loan to a customer and a payment from the customer. Let us use concrete values. A payment with PaymentSequence 77345 dated 9/15/2006 for $1500 is received against loan number 12345. Now review the existence of these two entity instances.

Loan 12345 will exist in the database whether the Payment 77345 is received or not. In other words, this loan instance will exist irrespective of the existence of any payment instance. All loan instances have independent existence. LOAN is an independent entity type.

Now, turn your attention to the payment instance with PaymentSequence 77345. This is a payment against Loan 12345. Without Loan 12345, Payment 77345 has no meaning—has no existence. Payment 77345 can exist only if Loan 12345 exists in the database and there is a relationship expressed between these two entities. PAYMENT is a dependent entity type. We have covered such entity types, also known as weak entity types, earlier.

One more example of existence dependency. Observe the nature of two entity types CLIENT and ACCOUNT. ACCOUNT entity type includes client accounts holding accounts-receivable data where debits and credits are recorded. These two entity types are related because accounts transactions associate with client instances. Think about the individual instances of the two entity types. If an account transaction number 113345 relates to client 54321, can that transaction exist in the database without the existence of client 54321 in the database? The transaction will have no relevance without the existence of the client instance. Thus CLIENT is an independent entity type; ACCOUNT is a dependent entity type.

Relationship Types

In the examples of independent and dependent entity types, you have noted the relationships. In the example of INSTRUCTOR and COURSE, the relationship is between two independent entity types. The other two examples of LOAN and PAYMENT as well as CLIENT and ACCOUNT express relationships between an independent entity type and a dependent entity type. These relationships differ from the first relationship between INSTRUCTOR and COURSE.

Based on the existence conditions of entity types, we can divide relationships into two types. The first type connects a dependent entity type to an independent entity type. The second relationship type links two independent entity types.

Can there be a third type relating two dependent entity types? Obviously, this relationship cannot be present. Dependent entity types, by definition, cannot exist by themselves. Each dependent entity type requires an independent entity type for its existence.

The two relationship types are named as follows:

Identifying Relationship. Occurs between a dependent entity type and an independent entity type where the entity instances of the independent entity type identify entity instances of the dependent entity type.

Nonidentifying Relationship. Occurs between two independent entity types where there is no necessity for entity instances of one entity type to identify entity instances of the other entity type.

Identifying Relationship

Let us study identifying relationships as these appear to be a special kind of relationship. We will note various aspects of an identifying relationship with an example. Remember, in this type of relationship, entity occurrences of an independent, strong entity type identify entity instances of a dependent, weak entity type.

Take the case of a library that has to keep track of books and copies of books. Here we have two entity types: BOOK and COPY. BOOK represents entity instances of various book titles. Instances of copies of books form the entity type COPY. If you think about the entity instances of these entity types, you will determine that instances of COPY depend on the instances of BOOK for their existence. Therefore, the two entity types form an identifying relationship.

Figure 6-18 illustrates the identifying relationship between the two entity types. The diagram also gives an indication of the relationship set. Note the special notations to

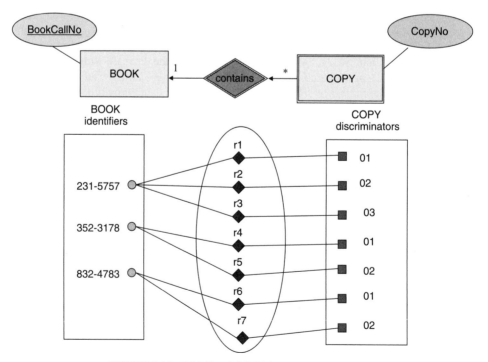

FIGURE 6-18   BOOK and COPY: identifying relationship.

indicate the identifying relationship. Observe the figure carefully and note the following remarks about identifying relationships.

Relationship Set. Examine the relationship set consisting of entity pairs formed by book and copy entities. Each entity pair has a book entity and a copy entity shown as a combination. If the library has three copies of a specific book, then the relationship contains three entity pairs, each pair formed by the same book entity instance with the three copy instances.

Relationship set gives us a clear indication how entity instances combine to constitute the relationship. Relationship sets for identifying relationships do not differ from those for nonidentifying relationships. So, no special treatment is warranted by such relationship sets.

Identifiers. Identifiers of entity types in identifying relationships present an essential difference. As you know, the identifier of the independent entity type provides identification for the dependent entity type. The value of the identifier BookCallNo for a specific book instance identifies all the occurrences of copy instances. This is how the dependent entities establish their existence. The independent entity type shares its identifier with its dependent entity type.

For example, note the book with BookCallNo "231-5757" and all the copies of this book. All copies of every book are numbered serially as 01, 02, 03, and so on. How do instances of copies with serial numbers 01, 02, and 03 get identified in the identifying relationship? Each of the copies gets identified by the concatenated values 231-575701, 231-575702, 231-575703, and so on. These are the values for the identifier of COPY entity type.

Participation Constraint. We had reviewed participation constraints of relationships in an earlier section. Participation constraint refers to whether entities of one entity type must necessarily participate in the relationship. Participation of entities of one entity type in a relationship may be partial or total. Total participation designates that every entity instance must participate in associations with instances of the other entity type. Partial participation implies optional condition—not all instances need to participate.

In an identifying relationship, what is the nature of the participation? Does every book instance participate in the relationship? The answer would depend on the business rule. If you need to record book information in the database before actual copies arrive in the library, then the participation could be partial.

However, look at the other side. What about the participation constraint for copy instances? Can a copy instance exist without the corresponding book instance and the association between them? Of course, not. If there is copy instance, then that instance must necessarily be part of an association with the corresponding book instance. Thus, for the COPY entity type, the participation constraint has to be total participation.

Benefits. Having considered identifying relationships in some detail, you might derive some benefits from the establishment of such relationships. Specifically, identifying relationships provide the following benefits.

Easy Access. You can access all dependent entity occurrences once you locate the instance of their independent entity type.

Data Integrity. Sharing of primary identifier between the dependent and independent entity types enforces existence dependency.

Nonidentifying Relationship

A typical nonprofit organization runs its operations using volunteers. Volunteers serve on various committees for rendering services. VOLUNTEER and COMMITTEE would be two relevant entity types. Let us examine the relationship between these two entity types.

A volunteer may serve on one or more committees. A committee may consist of one or more volunteers. Can entities of each of these two entity types exist independently? What about participation constraints? Note the following about the relationship between entity types VOLUNTEER and COMMITTEE:

Relationship Type. Nonidentifying type because each of the two entity types has independent existence.

Identifiers. Each entity type has its own independent identifier; no identifier sharing.

Cardinality. Many-to-many relationship.

Optionality. Optional association at VOLUNTEER end and mandatory association at COMMITTEE end. However, depending on the business rules, if committees may be allowed without any members yet, associations at COMMITTEE end may also be optional.

MAXIMUM AND MINIMUM CARDINALITIES

Earlier, we briefly discussed cardinality constraints and participation constraints as applicable to relationships between entity types. We looked at a few examples. You have noted how these two types of constraints are shown in a data model. Cardinality indicators such as 1 or * denote one or many while representing one-to-one, one-to-many, or many-to-many relationships. You have also noticed that broken or solid lines provide a method for denoting partial or total participation.

Maximum and minimum cardinality indicators also provide a method for representing the cardinality and optionality constraints. We will explore a detailed example to review these constraints. Maximum and minimum cardinality indicators are expressed as a pair of indicators placed with or without parentheses and located on the relationship line at both ends. The second indicator, the maximum cardinality indicator, denotes the cardinality constraint; the first indicator, the minimum cardinality indicator, symbolizes the participation constraint.

Recall how the minimum cardinality indicator expresses the optional or mandatory nature of a relationship. Placing a "0" as the minimum cardinality indicator near an entity type indicates that some of the entities of that entity type may not participate in the relationship. That means the relationship is optional for that entity type. Let us explore the notion of optional and mandatory nature of relationships further.

Consider a real-world situation of employees working in departments. Normally, every employee is assigned to a department, and every department will have employees. But, this may not always be true. Newer employees may not be assigned to a department yet; some

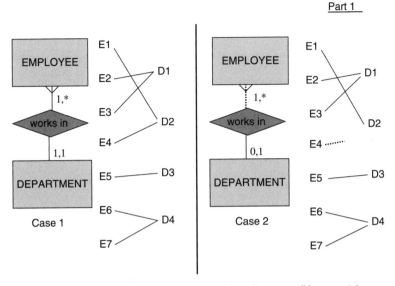

FIGURE 6-19   Relationship: optional and mandatory conditions, part 1.

employees on special assignments may not be part of the conventional departments. On the other hand, some special departments may have been created for costing raw materials and equipment with no human resources being part of the departments. In this case, such departments do not have employees associated with them. Your data model must be able to represent such exceptional conditions found in real-world information requirements. Follow along to learn how these conditions are represented in the data model.

Four cases arise based on the exception conditions. Figure 6-19 illustrates the first two cases; Figure 6-20 the next two cases. Note the minimum and maximum cardinality

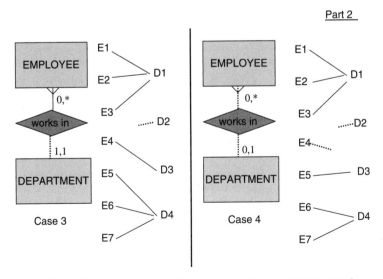

FIGURE 6-20   Relationship: optional and mandatory conditions, part 2.

indicators shown in ease case. Also, note each dotted line indicating that the relationship on that side is optional.

Let us review these four cases in some detail. As you will observe, minimum cardinality indicator denotes the optional or mandatory nature of the relationship—whether it is partial participation or full participation in the relationship by the specific entity type. Pay special attention to the figure while we discuss the four cases in detail.

Mandatory Conditions: Both Ends

Consider the case where the relationship is mandatory at EMPLOYEE and DEPART-MENT ends.

Case 1

A department must have at least one employee, but it may have many employees.

Note minimum cardinality indicator 1 and maximum cardinality indicator * near EMPLOYEE entity type.

Meaning of Minimum Cardinality Indicator 1. Each department entity is associated with at least one employee entity. That is, the minimum number of employee instances associated with one department entity is 1. Notice the solid relationship line next to DEPART-MENT indicating that the relationship on this side is mandatory and that every department entity participates in the relationship.

*Meaning of Maximum Cardinality Indicator *.* A department entity may be associated with many instances of employee.

An employee must be assigned to at least one department, and he or she can be assigned to only one department.

Note minimum cardinality indicator 1 and maximum cardinality indicator 1 near DEPARTMENT entity type.

Meaning of Minimum Cardinality Indicator 1. Each employee entity is associated with at least one department entity. That is, the minimum number of department instances associated with one employee entity is 1. Notice the solid relationship line next to EMPLOYEE indicating that the relationship on this side is mandatory and that every employee entity participates in the relationship.

Meaning of Maximum Cardinality Indicator 1. An employee entity can be associated with one instance of department at most.

Optional Condition: One End

Consider the case where the relationship is optional at EMPLOYEE end.

Case 2

A department must have at least one employee, but it may have many employees.

Note minimum cardinality indicator 1 and maximum cardinality indicator * near EMPLOYEE entity type.

Meaning of Minimum Cardinality Indicator 1. Each department entity is associated with at least one employee entity. That is, the minimum number of employee instances associated with one department entity is 1. Notice the solid relationship line next to DEPARTMENT indicating that the relationship on this side is mandatory and that every department entity participates in the relationship.

*Meaning of Maximum Cardinality Indicator *.* A department entity may be associated with many employee entities.

> Every employee may not be assigned to a department; if assigned, he or she can be assigned to only one department.

Note minimum cardinality indicator 0 and maximum cardinality indicator 1 near DEPARTMENT entity type.

Meaning of Minimum Cardinality Indicator 0. Some employee entities may not be associated with any department entities. Not every employee entity is associated with a department entity. That is, the minimum number of department instances associated with one employee entity is 0. Not every employee entity participates in the relationship. Notice the dotted or broken relationship line next to EMPLOYEE entity type indicating that the relationship on this side is optional and that not every employee entity participates in the relationship. A broken or dotted line denotes partial participation in the relationship.

Meaning of Maximum Cardinality Indicator 1. An employee entity can be associated with one instance of department at most.

Optional Condition: Other End

Consider the case where the relationship is optional at DEPARTMENT end.

Case 3

> Every department may not have employees; if it has, a department can have many employees.

Note minimum cardinality indicator 0 and maximum cardinality indicator * near EMPLOYEE entity type.

Meaning of Minimum Cardinality Indicator 0. Some department entities may not be associated with any employee entities. Not every department entity is associated with employee entities. That is, the minimum number of employee instances associated with one department entity is 0. Not every department entity participates in the relationship. Notice the dotted or broken relationship line next to DEPARTMENT entity type indicating that the relationship on this side is optional and that not every department entity participates in the relationship. A broken or dotted line denotes partial participation in the relationship.

Meaning of Maximum Cardinality Indicator *. A department entity may be associated with many employee entities.

> An employee must be assigned to at least one department, and he or she can be assigned to only one department.

Note minimum cardinality indicator 1 and maximum cardinality indicator 1 near DEPARTMENT entity type.

Meaning of Minimum Cardinality Indicator 1. Each employee entity is associated with at least one department entity. That is, the minimum number of department instances associated with one employee entity is 1. Notice the solid relationship line next to EMPLOYEE indicating that the relationship on this side is mandatory and that every employee entity participates in the relationship.

Meaning of Maximum Cardinality Indicator 1. An employee entity can be associated with one instance of department at most.

Optional Conditions: Both Ends

Consider the case where the relationship is optional at EMPLOYEE and DEPARTMENT ends.

Case 4

> Every department may not have employees; if it has, a department can have many employees.

Note minimum cardinality indicator 0 and maximum cardinality indicator * near EMPLOYEE entity type.

Meaning of Minimum Cardinality Indicator 0. Some department entities may not be associated with any employee entities. Not every department entity is associated with employee entities. That is, the minimum number of employee instances associated with one department entity is 0. Not every department entity participates in the relationship. Notice the dotted or broken relationship line next to DEPARTMENT entity type indicating that the relationship on this side is optional and that not every department entity participates in the relationship. A broken or dotted line denotes partial participation in the relationship.

> Every employee may not be assigned to a department; if assigned, he or she can be assigned to only one department.

Note minimum cardinality indicator 0 and maximum cardinality indicator 1 near DEPARTMENT entity type.

Meaning of Minimum Cardinality Indicator 0. Some employee entities may not be associated with any department entities. Not every employee entity is associated with a department entity. That is, the minimum number of department instances associated with one employee entity is 0. Not every employee entity participates in the relationship.

Notice the dotted or broken relationship line next to EMPLOYEE entity type indicating that the relationship on this side is optional and that not every employee entity participates in the relationship. A broken or dotted line denotes partial participation in the relationship.

Meaning of Maximum Cardinality Indicator 1. An employee entity can be associated with one instance of department at most.

SPECIAL CASES

We have covered various types of relationships up to now. You have looked at examples of relationships involving a single entity type, two entity types, and more than two entity types. We had used the term *degree* to denote the number of entity types that participate in a relationship. You had also noted that relationships of varying degrees could have attributes attached to them.

We have also examined relationship sets. A relationship set consists of members formed by combining entity occurrences from the participating entity types. Members of a relationship set indicate how individual instances of entity types associate with one another.

You also studied business rules and how they apply to cardinality and optionality conditions in the relationships between entity types. Cardinality indicates how many instances of one entity type may associate with instances of the related entity type. Optionality or nullability denotes if all or some instances will participate in a relationship.

Some relationships present unique arrangements of entity types in a data model. They arise out of special conditions in the information requirements of an organization. We will consider some important special cases. Although special, these are by no means infrequent. Studying how to deal with such special cases will enhance your data modeling skills.

Gerund

The first special case we want to look at is the use of a gerund. What is a gerund? Let us first understand this special case.

We come across instances where many-to-many relationships themselves have attributes. The question arises then whether the relationship is a relationship or an entity type because it has attributes. This is where you may have to use a gerund.

In English grammar, the word *writing* is a gerund; the word is derived from the verb *to write* but it behaves like a noun. Similarly, if a relationship behaves like an entity type, that entity type may be termed a gerund.

Consider a three-way many-to-many relationship among three entity types CUSTOMER, PRODUCT, and WAREHOUSE. The real-world situation of shipping products to customers from different supply warehouses gives rise to this type of ternary relationship. As you know, in the E-R technique normally a diamond symbol denotes this relationship.

However, actually, the relationship appears to be an entity type. The relationship behaves like an entity type because it has two attributes ShipNumber and NoOfUnits. It is a gerund. When do you, as a data modeler, represent a relationship as a gerund and specify the relationship as an entity type to be represented in the E-R technique by a

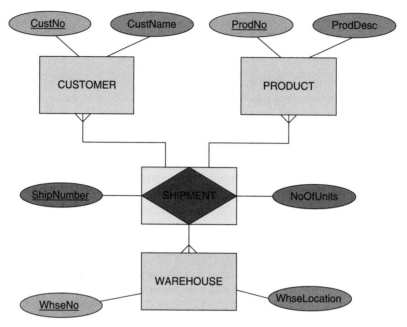

FIGURE 6-21 Representing a gerund in the E-R technique.

box? You need to represent a relationship as an entity type if the relationship truly has specific attributes.

Figure 6-21 illustrates the gerund as the entity type SHIPMENT, based on the relationships among three distinct entity types CUSTOMER, PRODUCT, and WAREHOUSE.

Aggregation

This special case is similar to the case of gerunds. This may be taken as an extension of the concept of gerunds. Aggregation attempts to resolve the issue of expressing relationships of relationships.

Let us take a specific example. An internal consulting unit of an organization runs projects for departments within the company. A project may relate to one or more departments. Special user representatives are assigned as liaison personnel for projects of different departments.

Think about the relationship. A relationship "performed for" exists between entity types DEPARTMENT and PROJECT. This relationship has a relation set consisting of entity pairs formed by entity instance pairs, one from each of these two entity types.

Now see how the relationship "liaises" fits in. Is this relationship entity type USER-REP has with either DEPARTMENT or PROJECT by themselves? A representative does not liaise with entity instances of either DEPARTMENT or PROJECT. The "liaises" relationship set, therefore, associates with "performs" relationship set.

For the purpose of defining a relationship set "liaises," we introduce the notion of aggregation, a feature of the enhanced E-R technique. Aggregation enables you to express that a relationship participates in another relationship. A box enclosed by broken lines (a dashed box) symbolizes aggregation. Figure 6-22 presents aggregation for the above example.

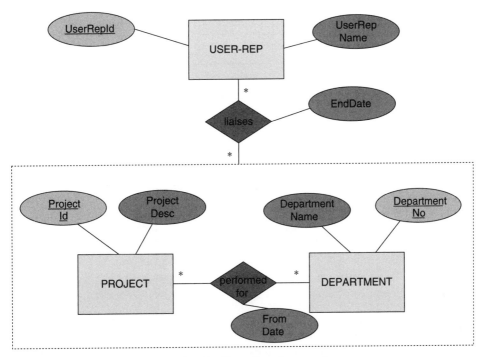

FIGURE 6-22 The notion of aggregation.

We have used the notion of aggregation for the example of DEPARTMENT, PROJECT, and USER-REP. We adopted aggregation to express the relationships between the two relationships "performed for" and "liaises." Why is there a need to use aggregation? Why not make "performed for" a ternary relationship? Why aggregate? This is because there are actually two separate and distinct relationships, each with its own attributes. Note the attribute FromDate of "performed for" relationship and the attribute EndDate for "liaises" relationship. These are attributes of two different relationships and, therefore, using a ternary relationship will not work.

Access Pathways

Next we will examine two cases of relationships where access pathways between entity occurrences could pose problems. What are access pathways? Access pathways lead from an entity occurrence of one entity type to an entity instance of a second related entity type. The access pathways could lead to difficulty when three entity types are present and related.

Walk through a common example of customers ordering products. CUSTOMER, ORDER, and PRODUCT entity types constitute the partial data model. The relationships among these three entity types are as follows: CUSTOMER to ORDER, one-to-many; ORDER to PRODUCT, many-to-many.

Figure 6-23 represents the relationships.

Study the entity occurrences and the lines linking the associated occurrences shown in the figure. The lines connecting entity instances form the access pathways. For example, if you want to know the orders and products bought under each order for a specific customer,

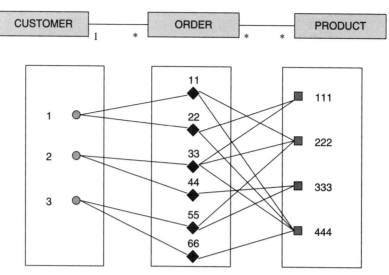

FIGURE 6-23   Relationships and access pathways.

you start with entity occurrence for that customer, follow the links to the corresponding order occurrences, and then continue on the links to the product occurrences from each order occurrence. On the other hand, you can trace back on the links from product occurrences to the customer occurrences.

In the above example, the access paths are clear—not ambiguous, not missing. You can proceed from one entity type and trace the access paths with no difficulty. The correct design of the data model enables you to create correct access paths. However, if the data model is not constructed correctly from information requirements, problems could arise with regard to the access paths among entity occurrences. Two types of problems need to be addressed: access paths ambiguous and access paths missing. We will examine two such special cases.

Ambiguous Access Pathways.   Let us say you have to create a data model for a college campus. Your partial data model must show computers in the various buildings of the campus. Computers with specific serial numbers are set up in classrooms. Each building in the campus has many classrooms. You have understood the information requirements as follows: campus buildings have computers; classrooms are in campus buildings.

You come up with entity types BUILDING, COMPUTER, and CLASSROOM. You also determine the relationships and cardinality indicators: BUILDING to COMPUTER, one-to-many; BUILDING to CLASSROOM, one-to-many. Then you draw the model diagram as shown in Figure 6-24, which results in ambiguous access pathways among entity occurrences.

The figure also shows access pathways between instances of the three entity types. Now, try to trace some pathways. Let us say, we want to find out in which classroom is computer C1 placed? So, trace the access pathway from C1. You find that it is in building B1. From building B1 follow the link to the classroom. But from B1 there are links to two classrooms R4 and R5. Remember, the relationship between BUILDING to CLASS-ROOM is one-to-many. We are not sure whether computer C1 is placed in classroom R4 or R5. The access pathway is ambiguous.

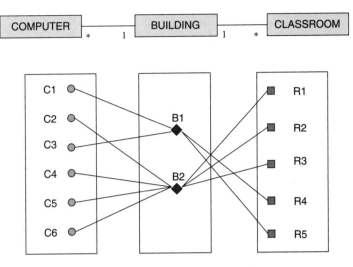

FIGURE 6-24 Ambiguous access pathways.

Usually, the problem of this kind occurs when the data modeler does not comprehend the relationships completely and correctly. When you run into possible ambiguous access pathways, you can resolve the problem by recasting the relationships. Figure 6-25 illustrates resolution of ambiguous access pathways.

Missing Access Pathways. This type of problem occurs when you have incorrect modeling of relationships with partial participation of entity occurrences. Here the access pathway stops in the middle without going all the way.

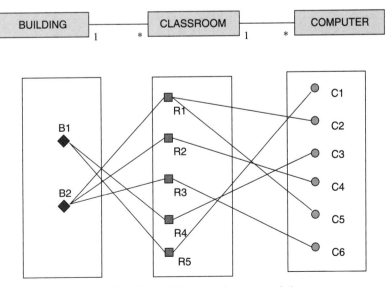

FIGURE 6-25 Ambiguous pathways: resolution.

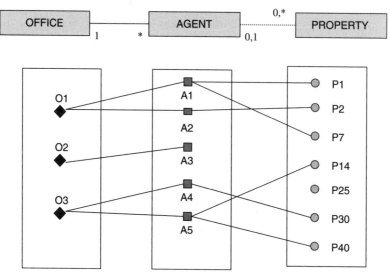

FIGURE 6-26 Missing access pathways.

Let us consider an example. Take the case of a real estate agency. The agency has many branch offices, and properties that come up for sale are allocated to branch offices based on proximity. At each branch, one or more real estate agents work and liaise with the buyers. A branch office assigns each property to a specific agent as soon as all the paperwork is completed. Until the paperwork is completed, a particular property awaits assignment of an agent.

Based on the requirements definition, you determine the entity types as OFFICE, AGENT, and PROPERTY. You also decide on the relationships and cardinality indicators: OFFICE to AGENT, one-to-many; AGENT to PROPERTY, one-to-many. You examine

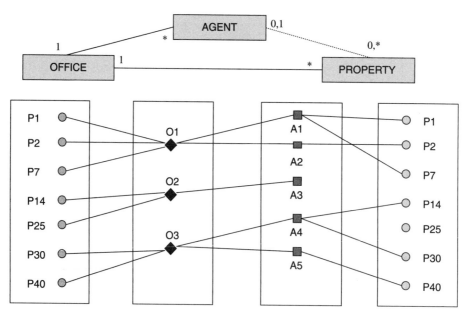

FIGURE 6-27 Missing pathways: resolution.

the relationships and find that the relationship AGENT to PROPERTY has participation constraints. At both ends, the associations are optional. There could be some agents just started and no properties allocated to them yet. There could be some properties where the paperwork has not been completed and, therefore, not yet allocated. You may draw the model diagram as shown in Figure 6-26, which results in missing access pathways among entity occurrences.

Observe the access pathways between instances of the three entity types. Now, try to trace some pathways. Let us say, we want to find out which branch office is responsible for property P25? You find that no link is present from property P25. Presumably, this property has not been allocated to an agent because the paperwork is still pending. The part of the access pathway for this property instance to an office instance is missing. Apparently, the data model is faulty.

Again, this type of problem results from unclear understanding of the relationships and their constraints. You can resolve the problem of missing access pathways by revising the relationships. Figure 6-27 shows the resolution of missing access pathways.

DESIGN ISSUES

Our detailed discussion on relationships will not be complete without looking at some design issues. As you study and understand the information requirements and begin to prepare the data model, a few questions about denoting relationships are likely to arise. Is this a relationship or should there be another entity type to represent requirements accurately? Should the data model show an aggregation or just a relationship? Are the one-to-one or one-to-many relationships indicated properly? These issues affect the design of the data model.

Your ultimate goal consists of making your data model represent the information requirements truly and completely. Relationships and their representation are major factors in proper design of a data model. In this section, we are highlighting a few significant and common issues you will be faced with in your data modeling projects. Study each issue carefully, understand the exact nature of the issue, and then explore the options to be applied in your data modeling efforts.

Relationship or Entity Type?

This is a fairly common design issue. You have to decide whether representation of information requirements by means of a relationship between two entity types will do. Or do you have to introduce another entity type to complete the picture? Here the decision is between using a relationship or another entity type.

Let us look at an example of customers and bank accounts. You will represent this in the data model with entity types CUSTOMER and BANK-ACCOUNT showing a relationship "has" indicating customers having bank accounts. One customer may have one or more bank accounts. Now, let us say, you have to indicate the StartDate in the data model. You may show this as an attribute of the relationship. So far, the two entity type boxes and the relationship between them will be sufficient.

Next, suppose you have to fit in another piece of information—Balance. This attribute indicates to total balance for the customer adding up all the accounts if the customer has more than one bank account. Obviously, this is not an attribute of the relationship between

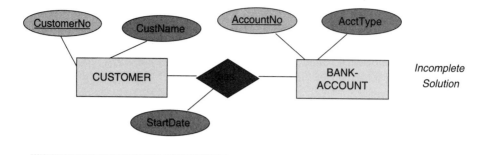

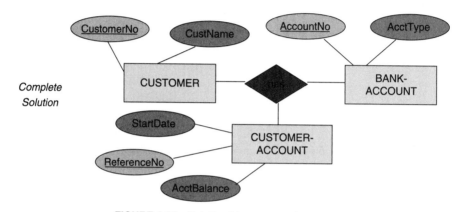

FIGURE 6-28   Relationship versus entity type.

CUSTOMER and BANK-ACCOUNT. The members of this relationship set are pairs consisting of single customer entity instances and single account entity instances.

When you face a design issue such as this, you have to examine the nature of the attributes and make your decision as to whether to show just a relationship or to include another entity type. Figure 6-28 shows the two configurations.

Ternary Relationship or Aggregation?

When you run into three-way relationships, this design issue may confront you. At that time, you need to decide whether to introduce aggregation or stay with a ternary relationship. The information requirements of the real-world situation will dictate the choice. In many situations, ternary relationships will be adequate to represent the requirements in the data model.

We have already looked at this issue partially when we covered aggregation earlier. Go back and look at Figure 6-22 and study why aggregation was introduced in that example. Mostly, the decision to choose between aggregation and ternary relationship rests on the presence of a relationship that relates to a relationship set or to an entity set or a second relationship set. Sometimes, the choice is further guided by the need to express relationship constraints.

Binary or N-ary Relationship?

In the earlier sections, you have seen examples of ternary and quaternary relationships. Relationships of higher degrees with more than four participating entity types may also be present in a data model based on information requirements. Generally, you can break up higher degree (or *N*-ary, where *N* is any number greater than 4) relationships and replace them with a set of binary relationships. This is a design issue.

Binary relationships can be simpler and easier to understand. When you walk through a data model with domain experts and user groups, you will find it less complicated to discuss and to confirm the requirements. When you have ternary or quaternary relationships, you will find it hard to explain the composition of relationship sets. With higher degree relationships, the difficulty increases even more.

However, if you restrict your data model to contain only binary relationships, you may have to face other types of problems. As you break down a higher degree relationship, you will have to create additional entity sets, more binary relationship sets, and identifying attributes. This increase in data model components may add to the complexity. Other the other hand, if you leave the *N*-ary relationship in the data model, you may be able to show the participation of several entity types with different participation constraints.

Therefore, whenever you are faced with higher degree relationships, consider the options carefully. First, you have to decide if you can leave the higher degree relationship intact in the data model. This may be the wise choice in some cases. If you have to replace the higher degree relationship with multiple binary relationships, clearly define the additional entity types, relationships, and extra identifying attributes.

Figure 6-29 shows a quaternary relationship and its break-down into binary relationships. Study the figure carefully to understand the choices. Observe how the binary relationships represent the original quaternary relationship.

One-to-One Relationships

A one-to-one relationship associates one instance of the first entity type to one instance of the second entity type. Whenever you design a one-to-one relationship, you need to

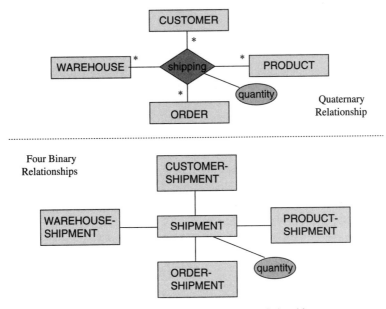

FIGURE 6-29 Quaternary into binary relationships.

consider a few questions about the relationship. Here the main issue is whether to preserve the relationship and keep the two entity types intact in the data model. The other choice is merging of the two entity types into a single entity type and including all the attributes of both entity types in the merged entity type.

Let us work with a generic example. Some data modeling practitioners advocate the elimination of one-to-one relationships altogether. Most database systems support one-to-one relationships. It is up to you to make the choice depending on the particular situations. Let us examine the generic example and offer some suggestions. This example consists of two generic entity types A and B with a one-to-one relationship between them. Consider the possible cases in terms of participation constraints.

Mandatory at Both Ends. Each instance of A associates with an instance of B. From the other side, each instance of B associates with an instance of A. When you look at an instance of A and the corresponding instance of B, the attributes of this association will be combination of the attributes of both A and B.

Usually, this means that representation of the requirements as two separate entity types is unnecessary. Combine the two entity types into one with a meaningful entity name. The identifier of either of A or B can serve as the identifier for the merged entity type. The attributes of the merged entity type will consist of the complete set of attributes from both A and B.

Optional at One End. In this case, two possibilities exist. The relationship at the A end is mandatory and it is optional at the B end. Or the converse may be true. In either case, the relationship is mandatory at one end and optional at the other end. As these are symmetrical, we can consider one possibility and apply the discussion to the other possibility.

Let the relationship be optional at the A end and mandatory at the B end. This means not all instances of A participate in the relationship. For some instances of A there are no corresponding instances of B. This is the case where A could represent customers and B represent contact persons for the customers. Not all customers may have distinct contact persons.

Assume that you want to merge the two entity types into one as you did in the previous case. Then, for many instances of the merged entity types, values of attributes of B will be null. If you have a much larger number of A occurrences compared with B occurrences, this is not a recommended option. You can leave the two entity types in your conceptual data model. So, consider your particular situation and make the decision on this design issue.

Optional at Both Ends. This possibility refers to the case where not all instances of either A or B may participate in the relationship. If you take a particular instance of A, it may not be part of the relationship. Again, considering a particular instance of B, it may not participate in the relationship.

Let us say you want to merge the two entity types and eliminate the one-to-one relationship. What you will find is as follows: some merged entity instances will lack the attribute values of B and other merged entity instances will not have the attribute values of A. So, there will be many partial entity instances.

In general, merging of entity types is not advisable in this case. You want to avoid many entity occurrences with the likely prospect of having a lot of null values for the attributes.

Ascertain the participation constraints and if you have optional conditions at both ends, choose to leave the relationship in the data model.

One-to-Many Relationships

Sometimes, participation constraints may lead to design issues in one-to-many relationships as well. Let us look at a specific example. In a product warehouse, some of the products need industry standard certification. Other products do not. The certification procedure designates the quality rating for the products that need certification. In order to represent this business requirement, you start designing entity types and relationships.

You will come up with entity types CERTIFICATION and PRODUCT. Note these two will form a one-to-many relationship. What about the participation constraints? At either end, participation of entity instances is optional. We know that some products do not need certification; these product instances will not participate in the relationship. Similarly, there may some certification scores for which there are no products yet.

When you are faced with this type of issue, carefully examine if the data model depicts the business rules correctly. Later on, when you transform your conceptual data model into a logical data model for implementation, you may run into problems for linking related entity instances. Figure 6-30 shows the one-to-many relationship and possible way of eliminating the optional condition on the CERTIFICATION side. You will note that products are separated out into certified products and others.

Circular Structures

Occasionally, you will run into what are known as circular structures or circular references. You will create three entity types A, B, and C; you will then find A as the parent of B, B as the parent of C, and C as the parent of A. Each relationship tends to be a one-to-many relationship. This is a cyclical set of relationships.

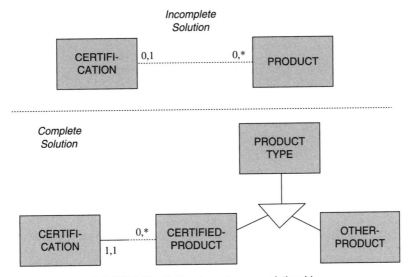

FIGURE 6-30 Optional one-to-many relationship.

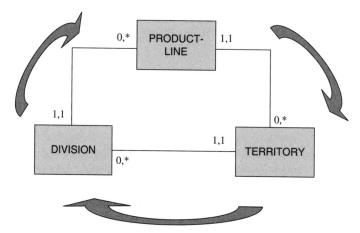

FIGURE 6-31 Circular structure.

If the business requirements are not transmitted correctly, this is a likely result. Possibly, parent–child relationships are reversed. Or a many-to-many relationship could have been mistaken as a one-to-many relationship. Nevertheless, circular structures cause problems and must be resolved.

Let us work out a partial data model for a manufacturing company. Each of its production divisions supplies different product lines. Each product line gets sold in multiple territories. Each territory relates to one or more divisions. Create a data model with entity types DIVISION, PRODUCT-LINE, and TERRITORY. Establish the three one-to-many relationships. Figure 6-31 presents this circular structure.

First, we want to reverse the cyclical progression of relationships. A better approach would be to introduce additional entity types and resolve the circular structure of parent–child relationships. Then we want to make each relationship amplified and clarified. Figure 6-32 illustrates a refinement of the circular structure. Note the additional entity types and new relationships introduced in the data model.

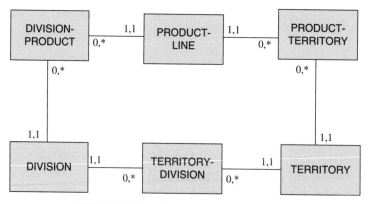

FIGURE 6-32 Refinement of circular structure.

Redundant Relationships

As you go through iterations in the data modeling process, you will come across redundant relationships. In your review, you will specifically look for such redundancies and eliminate them. When you show two dependency paths between the same two entity types, in effect, you create a triad involving a redundant relationship. Typically, you will see a set of three entity types tangled as a triad with a redundant relationship.

Let us take an example. A supermarket has various departments such as paper goods, meat, dairy, and so on. Each of these departments offers product types. Products belong to product types. These entities form various relationships. Now consider the entity types DEPART-MENT, PRODUCT-TYPE, and PRODUCT. DEPARTMENT to PRODUCT-TYPE is a one-to-many relationship; PRODUCT-TYPE to PRODUCT is also a one-to-many relationship. You create the data model showing these relationships. Then you realize the departments and products are also associated in one-to-many relationship. So, you add another relationship line between DEPARTMENT and PRODUCT. This last relationship is redundant and you have created a triad. You have to resolve by eliminating the redundant relationship.

Figure 6-33 illustrates the triad and its resolution. Note how the redundant relationship gets removed.

Multiple Relationships

At times, two entity types may be related to each other in multiple ways. Two or more types of associations are possible between entity instances. A manufacturing plant may serve both as a production unit as well as a storage area for products. In this case, two entity types BUILDING and PRODUCT may be used to represent the entities as well as two types of relationships between them. You probably want to represent the relationships with two relationships lines, one representing the "produces" relationship and one the "stores" relationships.

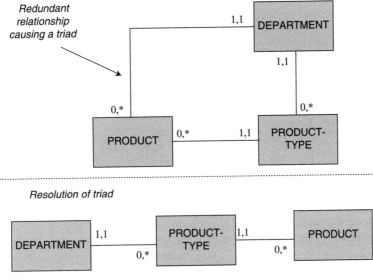

FIGURE 6-33 Triad and its resolution.

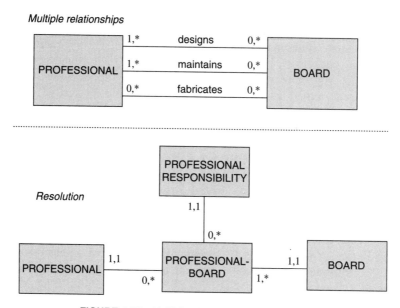

FIGURE 6-34 Multiple relationships and resolution.

When you have multiple relationships between the same two entity types, represented with multiple relationship lines, problematic consequences may follow. The cardinalities and participation constraints may be in conflict among the multiple relationships. Sometimes, multiple relationships may tend to represent process logic. A data model should be devoid of process logic representation. Representation of multiple relationships may also result in the data model becoming confusing and vague.

If you encounter situations with multiple relationships between the same two entity types, carefully scrutinize the cardinalities and participation constraints. If you trace any conflicts, resolve multiple relationships. If you note that process logic is being interjected into the data model, again look for ways of resolving multiple relationships. This is a significant design issue for relationships.

Let us present an example of multiple relationships and the resolution. Figure 6-34 shows multiple relationships between circuit boards and professionals who design, maintain, and fabricate them. Note the entity types PROFESSIONAL and BOARD and observe the three types of relationships between them. Also, study the resolution achieved by the introduction of two other entity types.

RELATIONSHIP VALIDATION CHECKLIST

Our detailed discussions of relationship are about to end. So far, in this chapter, we covered several topics. We revisited the concept of relationship as associations of individual entity occurrences. This led us to the concept of relationship sets. A relationship set consists of combinations of single entity instances taken one from each participating entity type. If relationships themselves have attributes, then the attribute values relate to members of the relationship sets.

We reviewed useful examples of binary, ternary, and quaternary relationships. The degree of a relationship determines how individual entity instances combine to make the relationship set. The significance of cardinality and optionality constraints on relationships cannot be overemphasized. Participation constraints play an important role in representing relationship properly in a data model.

We brought the discussions to completion by considering special cases and important design issues. You looked at several types of situations where resolution of relationships becomes necessary. You have gone over examples of resolutions.

As you go through the data modeling process, at each stage, you need to check the data model for completeness and correctness. Again, remember that data modeling is an iterative process. After defining the entity types and their attributes, defining of relationships follows. You may even begin representing relationships as soon as you have the first cut of the entity types. In the iterative process, you may refine the model by adding or modifying previously included relationships.

What follows is a task list for validation of relationships as represented in your data model. Two checklists are presented: one to verify completeness and the other to verify correctness of relationships. These checklists should come in handy to conduct the review process for relationships.

Completeness

Requirements Review. Go over the information requirements for each relationship shown in the data model. Ensure that no relationships are missing. Regroup entity types by pairs and make sure that no relationship between qualifying pairs is left undefined.

Relationship Names. Review each verb or verb phrase that indicates a relationship either recording within the diamond symbol or written over the relationship line. Think of connotation of each verb phrase and ensure that all relationships are properly described.

Relationship Descriptions. Provide clarifications for all relationships and descriptions of cardinality and participation constraints in the supplementary documentation.

Cardinality Constraints. Go through every relationship. Be certain that the cardinality indicators are shown for each end of each relationship line.

Optionality Constraints. Wherever business rules indicate participation constraints, make sure these constraints are represented in the data model.

Identifying Relationships. Search for all weak entity types. Wherever you have noted weak entity types, ensure the presence of identifying relationships.

Gerunds. Make certain that all gerunds are identified and represented in the data model.

Aggregations. Review pairs of entity types to verify if any aggregations are necessary. If so, aggregate the qualifying entity types.

Correctness

Relationship Representation. Ensure that each relationship represents the associations correctly.

Relationship Verb Phrases. Make sure that all verbs or verb phrases used to specify relationships reflect the exact nature of the associations. Ensure that the verbs or verb phrases are not vague or ambiguous.

Relationship Attributes. Wherever attributes are shown for relationships, make sure these attributes are truly attributes of the relationships and not of any of the participating entity types.

Cardinality Constraints. Go over each maximum cardinality indicator or any other notation used to signify cardinality constraint. Make sure that these represent cardinalities correctly.

Participation Constraints. Verify each minimum cardinality indicator or any other corresponding notation. Ensure each optional or mandatory condition accurately reflects the business rules.

Gerunds. Validate each gerund and justify formation of the gerund.

Aggregation. Review each aggregation to verify its correctness in terms of the grouping of entity types and relationships. Make sure the correct decision has been made to represent the aggregation instead of a ternary relationship.

Access Pathways. Check access pathways to proceed from each entity instance and trace through associated entity instances in the related entity types, one after the other in sequence. Make sure that the pathways are unambiguous and present. If any pathway is ambiguous or missing, recast the entity types and relationships to resolve potential problems.

Relationship Review. Review each relationship to ensure that it need not be replaced by an entity type.

N-ary Relationships. Check each higher degree relationship to determine if these should be broken up into binary relationships.

One-to-One Relationships. Verify each one-to-one relationship for participation constraints. If necessary, merge participating entity types into a single entity type.

One-to-Many Relationships. Check each one-to-many relationships with optional participation at both ends of the relationships. If necessary, resolve problematic one-to-many relationships.

Circular Structures. Look for circular structures. If found, resolve these.

Triads. Carefully examine the data model for triads. If found, remove the redundant relationships.

Multiple Relationships. Scrutinize binary relationships. If you suspect multiple relationships between the participating entity types, resolve this design issue.

CHAPTER SUMMARY

- Relationships between two entity types are associations between specific instances of one entity type with particular occurrences of another entity type.
- Every relationship has two sides to it with respective cardinalities.
- A relationship between two entity types constitutes a set of associations between entities of the first entity type and entities of the second entity type.
- A relationship itself may have attributes apart from the attributes of participating entity types.
- The degree of a relationship in a data model refers to the number of entity types that participate in the relationship.
- Three common types of cardinality constraints of relationships are one-to-one, one-to-many, and many-to-many.
- Participation constraint refers to whether instances of one entity type need to participate in associations with instances of another entity type. Participation may be partial or total.
- Identifying and nonidentifying relationships are two types of relationships. An identifying relationship is between a weak entity type and its corresponding strong entity type.
- Minimum cardinality indicator denotes optional or mandatory nature of a relationship.
- Aggregation is used to resolve the issue of expressing relationships of relationships.
- Triads must be resolved. A triad consists of redundant relationships.

REVIEW QUESTIONS

1. True or false:
   A. A relationship constitutes a set of associations between entities of two entity types.
   B. Quaternary relationships are the most common form of relationship in real-world situations.
   C. Cardinality constraint refers to the numbers of entities participating in a relationship.
   D. Total participation also means mandatory nature of the relationship.
   E. A weak entity type sometimes may have independent existence.
   F. Minimum cardinality indicator of "0" means mandatory relationship.

G. Merging of entity types in a one-to-one relationship is not advisable when the relationship is optional at both ends.

H. Only some relationships have two sides.

I. In a ternary relationship, the relationship entity set consists of triplets.

J. Ambiguous access pathways can usually be resolved by recasting the relationships.

2. A relationship is two-sided. Explain this statement with an example.

3. Show with an example how a relationship itself can have attributes.

4. What is a ternary relationship? Give an example.

5. Give two examples of many-to-many relationships. Describe the associations of entities in each example.

6. What is partial participation in a relationship? Explain with an example.

7. Give an example with optional conditions at both ends of the relationship. Describe the associations of entities.

8. What is a gerund in terms of relationships? How do you identify a gerund? Provide an example.

9. What is the problem of missing pathways in relationships? Describe with an example.

10. What are circular structures in relationship representation? Give an example and show how to refine a circular structure.

DATA MODEL
IMPLEMENTATION

7

DATA MODELING TO DATABASE DESIGN

CHAPTER OBJECTIVES

- Make the transition from data modeling to database design
- Focus on the relational data model as the logical model of choice
- Study significant fundamentals of the relational model
- Examine the leading transition approaches
- Provide in-depth coverage of the model transformation method
- Walk through transformation of each model component

In an earlier chapter, we reviewed the different information levels that exist in an organization. You need to model the information requirements of the organization at these levels to satisfy different purposes. We looked at data models at the different information levels. We started with an introduction to the conceptual data model. This is at the highest level of abstraction. A conceptual data model serves as a communication tool to converse about and confirm information requirements with domain experts.

Elaborate coverage of the conceptual data model spread over the previous chapters. This data model provides the initial expression and representation of the data content of the eventual database. Therefore, we studied the components of the conceptual data model in great detail. However, we now need to proceed further on the path toward database design and implementation. The next step in the process consists of creating a logical data model. Naturally, the logical data model has to be derived from the conceptual data model. The steps following logical data modeling consummate in designing the physical details and implementing the database.

Data Modeling Fundamentals. By Paulraj Ponniah
Copyright © 2007 John Wiley & Sons, Inc.

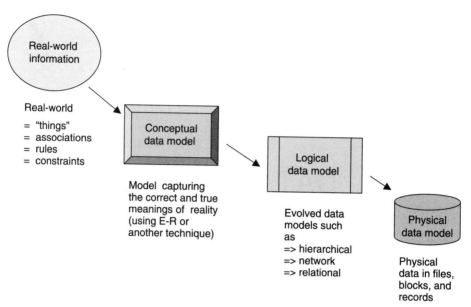

FIGURE 7-1 Data models at different levels.

For us, the relational data model will be the logical model of choice. As you know, the logical data model is to serve as a blueprint for database construction. We have selected the relational model because this has proved to be superior to other models such as hierarchical and network models. Relational databases are the most popular ones, and these work based on the relational data model.

Figure 7-1 shows the data models at different levels. Note how the figure illustrates the transition from one level to the next.

Before we deal with the transition of a conceptual to a relational data model, we need to cover the fundamentals of the relational model in sufficient detail. We have to study the various components of that model so that you may appreciate the transition steps. After the comprehensive coverage of the fundamentals, we will move into the mapping and transformation of model components from conceptual to logical. This method is the model transformation method.

We will also consider another method for creating a relational data model—a more traditional or informal method. That method has elements of intuition, and trial and error. We will do a quick review of the data normalization method. In a way, this is relational data modeling from scratch.

The above figure shows physical data modeling as a final modeling step. Physical data modeling comes very close to implementation. Specific target DBMS and hardware configurations directly influence physical design. Considerations of specific commercial DBMSs or hardware components do not fall within the scope of our discussions in this book. Therefore, we will exclude physical data modeling from our scope. You may consult the several good books available on database design and implementation to learn about that topic.

RELATIONAL MODEL: FUNDAMENTALS

The relational model uses familiar concepts to represent data. In this model, data is perceived as organized in traditional, two-dimensional tables with columns and rows. You find the rigor of mathematics incorporated into the formulation of the model. It has its theoretical basis in mathematical set theory and first-order predicate logic. The concept of a relation comes from mathematics and represents a simple two-dimensional table.

The relational model derives its strength from its simplicity and the mathematical foundation on which it is built. Rows of a relation are treated as elements of a set. Therefore, manipulation of rows may be based on mathematical set operations. Dr. Codd used this principle and provided two generic languages for manipulating data organized as relations or tables.

A relation or two-dimensional table forms the basic structure in the relational model. What are the implications? In requirements gathering, you collect much information about business objects or entities, their attributes, and relationships among them. You create a conceptual data model as a replica of information requirements. All of these various pieces of information can be represented in the form of relations. The entities, their attributes, and even their relationships are all contained in the concept of relations. This provides enormous simplicity and makes the relational model a superior logical data model.

Basic Concepts

We will begin our examination of the relational data model by studying its basic concepts. You need to review the inherent strengths of this model so that you can appreciate why it is so widespread. Having grounding in solid mathematics, data represented as a relational model renders itself for easy storage and manipulation.

Simple modeling concepts constitute the data model. When you need to transform a conceptual data model into a relational data model, the transition becomes easy and straightforward. We will also note how the mathematical concept of a relation serves as the underlying modeling concept.

Strengths of the Relational Model. Before we proceed to explore the relational model in detail, let us begin with a list of its major strengths. This will enable you to appreciate the superiority of the model and help you understand the features in a better light. Here is a summary of the strengths:

Mathematical Relation. The model uses the concept of a mathematical relation or two-dimensional table to organize data; rests on solid mathematical foundation.

Mathematical Set Theory. The model applies the mathematical set theory for manipulation of data in the database. Data storage and manipulation depend on a proven and precise approach.

Disciplined Data Organization. The model rests on a solid mathematical foundation; data organization and manipulation are carried out in a disciplined manner.

Simple and Familiar View. The model provides a common and simple view of data in the form of two-dimensional tables. Users can easily perceive how data is organized; they need not be concerned with how data is actually stored in the database.

Logical Links for Relationships. Other data models such as hierarchical and network use physical links to relate entities. If two entities such as CUSTOMER and ORDER are related, you have to establish the relationship by means of physical addresses embedded within the stored data records. In striking contrast, the relational model uses logical links to establish relationships. This is a major advantage.

Mathematical Foundation. We have mentioned that the relational model rests on a solid mathematical foundation. Specifically, in a relational model, the principles of matrix theory apply. Relational model tables are similar to mathematical matrices arranged as rows and columns. Thus, concepts of matrix manipulations can be applied to the rows and columns in a relational table.

Again, the principles and operations of mathematical set theory may be applied to the relational data model. The rows of a relational table are analogous to members of a mathematical set. If you need to work with data rows in two relational tables, you may consider these as members of two sets and apply set operations.

Figure 7-2 illustrates how mathematical principles can apply to relational tables. First, notice the similarity between elements placed in a mathematical matrix and data in the form of a relational table. Next, look at the two sets and their representations. Individual entity instances may be taken as members of sets.

Single Modeling Concept. As mentioned earlier, a relation or table is the primary data modeling concept in the relational mode. A table is a collection of columns that describe a thing of interest to the organization. For example, if COURSE is a conceptual thing of interest in a university, then a two-dimensional table or relation will represent

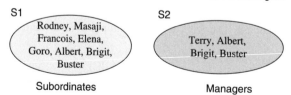

Mathematical matrix or relation				Data arranged as a relation or table			
a1	a2	a3	a4	E10	Charles	418	D200
b1	b2	b3	b4	E20	Mary	236	D300
c1	c2	c3	c4	E30	Eldon	179	D300
d1	d2	d3	d4	E40	Paul	522	

Mathematical sets: S1 (x1, x2, x3, x4, x5, x6, x7, x8)   S2 (y1, y2, y3, y4)

Entities considered as elements of sets:
S1 – Set of subordinates   S2 – Set of managers

S1 Rodney, Masaji, Francois, Elena, Goro, Albert, Brigit, Buster

S2 Terry, Albert, Brigit, Buster

Subordinates   Managers

FIGURE 7-2 Mathematical foundation of relational model.

RELATION

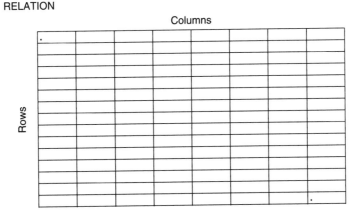

FIGURE 7-3 Relation or two-dimensional table.

COURSE in the relational data model for the university. Figure 7-3 shows a plain two-dimensional table whose format represents an entity or object.

Note the following features about a relation or two-dimensional table:

- Relation is table, representing data about some entity type or object.
- Relation is not any random table, but one that conforms to certain relational rules.
- Relation consists of a specific set of columns that can be named and an arbitrary number of rows.
- Each row contains a set of data values.
- Table names and column names are used to understand the data. The table or relation name indicates the entity type; the column names, its characteristics.

Structure and Components

As we have been repeatedly saying, the relational data model possesses a simple structure. What can you say about a simple two-dimensional table? The table has rows; the table has columns. Somehow, the usual components of a data model—entity types, attributes, relationships, and so on—must be mapped to the simple structure of a relational table.

Let us go over the basic form of a relational table. We will note which part of the table would represent what component of a data model. What are the meanings of the rows, columns, column headings, and the data values in the rows and columns? Which ones are the attributes, attribute values, identifiers, and relationships?

Relation or Table. In the relational data model, a table stands for an entity type. Each entity type in a conceptual data model gets represented by a separate table. If you have 15 entity types in your conceptual data model, then usually the corresponding relational model will contain 15 tables. As we will see later, additional tables may be become necessary. Nevertheless, an entity type in a conceptual model maps into a table or relation.

See Figure 7-4 representing the entity type called EMPLOYEE. The name of the table is the name of the entity type.

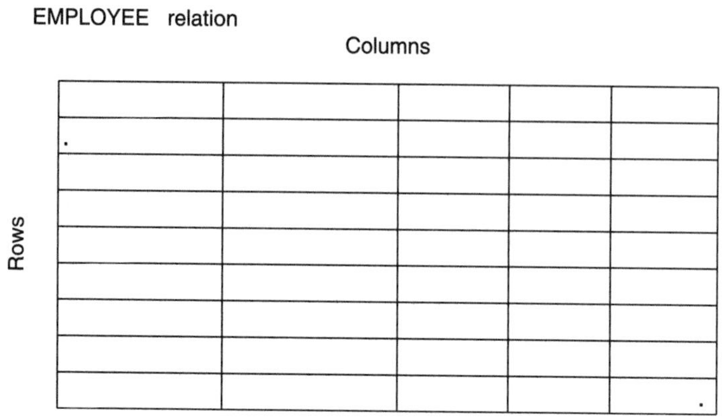

EMPLOYEE relation

Columns

FIGURE 7-4 Employee relation or table.

Columns as Attributes. Figure 7-5 presents a relation representing an entity type EMPLOYEE.

Make note of the following about the columns in a relation as illustrated in the figure.

- Each column indicates a specific attribute of the relation.
- The column heading is the name of the attribute.
- In the relational model, the attributes are referred to by the column names and not by their displacements in a data record. Therefore, no two columns can have the same name.
- For each row, the values of the attributes are shown in the appropriate columns.
- For a row, if the value of an attribute is not known, not available, or not applicable, a null value is placed in the specific column. A null value may be replaced with a correct value at a later time.
- Each attribute takes its values from a set of allowable or legal values called the attribute domain. A domain consists of a set of atomic values of the same data type and format.
- The number of columns in a relation is referred to as the degree of the relation.

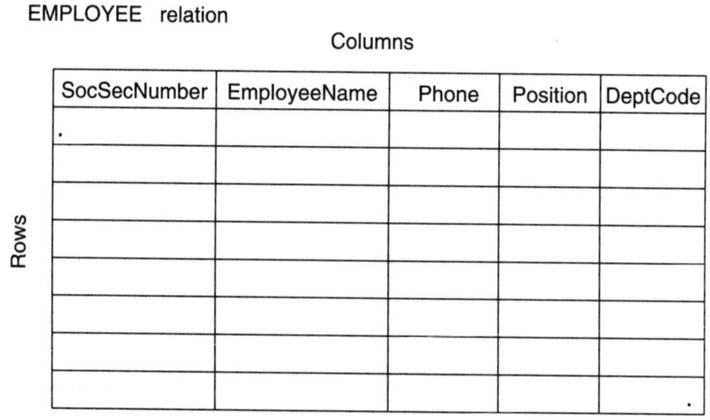

EMPLOYEE relation

Columns

SocSecNumber	EmployeeName	Phone	Position	DeptCode

FIGURE 7-5 Employee relation: attributes.

Rows as Instances. Rows, also referred to by the mathematical name of tuples, indicate the occurrences or instances of the entity type represented by a relation. In a relation, each row represents one instance of the entity type. Each column in that row indicates one piece of data about the instance.

Figure 7-6 shows the rows or tuples for the EMPLOYEE relation.

If there are 10,000 employees in the organization, the relation will contain 10,000 rows. The number of tuples in a relation is known as the cardinality of the relation. For an EMPLOYEE relation with 10,000 rows, the cardinality is 10,000.

Now, because a relation is considered as a mathematical set, this EMPLOYEE relation is a set of 10,000 data elements. Manipulation of data in the EMPLOYEE relation, therefore, becomes a set operation. Each row represents a particular employee. Look at the row for the employee Carey Smith. Note the value shown under each column in this row. Each of the values in the columns describes the employee Carey Smith. Each value represents one piece of data about the employee. All data for the employee is contained in the specific row.

Primary Key. As mentioned above, in a relation, each tuple represents one instance of the relation. In an EMPLOYEE relation with 10,000 rows, each row represents a particular employee. But, how can we know which row represents an employee we are looking for? In order to identity a row uniquely, we can use the attribute values. We may say that, if the value of the attribute EmployeeName is "Carey Smith," then that row represents this particular employee. What if there is another Carey Smith in the organization? Thus, you need some attribute whose values will uniquely identify individual tuples. Note that the attribute SocSecNumber can be used to identify a tuple uniquely.

Given below are definitions of keys or identifiers in a relation:

Superkey. A set of columns whose values uniquely identify each tuple in a relation; however, a superkey may contain extra unnecessary columns.

Key. A minimal set of columns whose values uniquely identify each tuple in a relation.

Composite Key. A key consisting of more than one column.

Candidate Key. A set of columns that can be chosen to serve as the key.

EMPLOYEE relation

Columns

SocSecNumber	EmployeeName	Phone	Position	DeptCode
214-56-7835	Robert Moses	516-777-9584	Programmer	501
123-44-5546	Kassia Raj	718-312-4488	Analyst	
101-54-3838	Andrew Rogers	212-313-1267	Manager	408
213-36-7854	Samuel Prabhu	212-126-3428	Controller	201
311-33-4520	Kaitlin Jones	718-567-4321	Assistant	
512-22-8542	Carey Smith	732-346-5533	Senior VP	301
111-22-3344	Amanda Lupo	908-212-5629	Executive VP	101
122-65-5378	Tabitha Williams	215-576-4598	DBA	501

Tuples OR rows

FIGURE 7-6 Employee relation: rows.

Primary Key. One of the candidate keys actually selected as the key for a relation.

Surrogate Key. A key that is automatically generated for a relation by the computer system; for example, CustomerNumber, generated in sequence by the system and assigned to CUSTOMER rows. Surrogate keys ensure that no duplicate values are present in the relation. Surrogate keys are artificial keys.

Relationship Through Foreign Keys. You have noted earlier that the relational model is superior to other conventional data models because it does not use physical links to establish relationships. The relational model uses logical links. How is this done? What is a logical link?

Figure 7-7 presents two relations EMPLOYEE and DEPARTMENT. Obviously, these two relations are related to each other because there are associations between employees and departments. One or more employees are assigned to a particular department; an employee is assigned to a specific department.

Observe the links shown between tuples in EMPLOYEE relation to corresponding tuples in DEPARTMENT relation. The DeptCode attribute in EMPLOYEE relation is called a foreign key attribute. Especially, note the value of the foreign key attribute and the value of the primary key attribute of the related row in the other relation.

Let us summarize how relationships are established in the relational data model.

- Relationships in the relational data model are established through foreign keys, not physical pointers.
- The logical link between a tuple in the first relation to a tuple in a second relation is established by placing the primary key value in the tuple of the first relation as the

DEPARTMENT relation

DeptCode	DeptName	DeptLocation
101	Administration	New York
201	Finance	Chicago
301	Marketing	Atlanta
303	Sales	Boston
408	Production	Detroit
501	Information Technology	San Francisco

LOGICAL LINKS

EMPLOYEE relation

SocSecNumber	EmployeeName	Phone	Position	DeptCode
214-56-7835	Robert Moses	516-777-9584	Programmer	501
123-44-5546	Kassia Raj	718-312-4488	Analyst	
101-54-3838	Andrew Rogers	212-313-1267	Manager	408
213-36-7854	Samuel Prabhu	212-126-3428	Controller	201
311-33-4520	KaitlinJones	718-567-4321	Assistant	
512-22-8542	Carey Smith	732-346-5533	Senior VP	301
111-22-3344	Amanda Lupo	908-212-5629	Executive VP	101
122-65-5378	Tabitha Williams	215-576-4598	DBA	501

FIGURE 7-7 Department and employee relations: relationship.

foreign key value in the corresponding tuple of the second relation. The first relation may be referred to as the parent relation and the second as a child.

- If tuples of a relation are related to some other tuples of the same relation, then the foreign key attribute is included in the same relation. This is a recursive relationship. For example, in an EMPLOYEE relation, some tuples representing employees may be related to other tuples in the same relation representing supervisors.
- Foreign key attributes need not have the same names as the corresponding primary key attributes.
- However, a foreign key attribute must be of the same data type and length of the related primary key attribute.

In the above figure, you notice that some tuples show null values for the foreign key attributes. What is the significance of the null values?

Optional Relationship. Consider a tuple in EMPLOYEE relation with null value in the foreign key column. This shows that the specific tuple is not linked to any tuple in DEPARTMENT relation. This means that this particular employee is not assigned to any department. He or she could be a new employee not yet assigned to a department or an employee on special assignment not tied to a specific department. Null value in the foreign key column indicates the nature of the relationship. Not all employees need be associated with a department. Null values in foreign key indicate an optional relationship between the two relations.

Mandatory Relationship. In EMPLOYEE relation, suppose that null values are not allowed in the foreign key. This requires specific discrete values to be present in all the tuples of this relation. Every tuple in EMPLOYEE relation, therefore, points to a related tuple in DEPARTMENT relation. In other words, every employee must be related to a department. If null values are not allowed in the foreign key, the relationship between the two relations is a mandatory relationship.

Relational Model Notation. Figure 7-8 gives an example of relational tables. Figure 7-9 presents a standard notation used to represent this relational data model.
Note the following description of the notation:

- Notation for each relation begins with the name of the relation. Examples: WORKER, ASSIGNMENT, BUILDING, SKILL.
- For each relation, the column names are enclosed within parentheses. These are the attributes for the relation.
- Primary key attributes are indicated with underscores. Examples: BuildingID, SkillCode.
- Statements immediately following the notation of a relation indicate the foreign key within that relation. Example: Foreign Keys: SkillCode references SKILL.
- The foreign key statement includes the name of the foreign key and the name of the parent relation.
- Note the foreign key SupvID indicating a recursive relationship.

WORKER relation

WorkerNo	Name	HourlyRate	SkillCode	SupvId
1111	Morris	24.50	ELE	
1287	Vitale	20.00	MAS	
3917	Nagel	18.00	ROF	
4467	Hart	20.50	ELE	1111
5179	Grasso	22.50	PLM	

BUILDING relation

BuildingID	Address	Type	Status
H245	135 Green Street	House	S1
H267	212 Tices Road	House	S4
O123	295 Hillside Avenue	Office	S2
O156	15 Camner Terrace	Office	S3
T451	23 Oaks Drive	Townhouse	S5

SKILL relation

SkillCode	SkillType	WklyHrs
MAS	Masonry	35
FRM	Framing	40
ROF	Roofing	35
ELE	Electric	35
PLM	Plumbing	40

ASSIGNMENT relation

WorkerNo	BuildingID	StartDate	DaysWorked
1111	H245	15-Mar	10
1287	O123	15-Feb	8
5179	T451	1-Mar	7
4467	O156	15-Apr	15
1287	H267	1-Apr	9

FIGURE 7-8 Relational tables.

Data Integrity Constraints

It is essential that a database built on any specific data model must ensure validity of data. The data structure must be meaningful and be truly representative of the information requirements. Constraints are rules that make sure proper restrictions are imposed on the data values in a database. The purpose is to regulate and ensure that the data content is valid and consistent. For example, in order to preserve the uniqueness of each tuple in a relation, the constraint or rule is that the primary key has unique values in the relation. Another example is a domain constraint that requires that all values of a specific attribute be taken from the same set or domain of permissible values.

As mentioned earlier, a relational data model consists of tables or relations that conform to relational rules and possess specific properties. We will now discuss the constraints and properties that ensure data correctness and consistency in a relational data model. First, let

WORKER   (WorkerNo, Name, HourlyRate, SkillCode, SupvID)
Foreign Keys: SkillCode references SKILL
                       SupvID references WORKER

ASSIGNMENT   (WorkerNo, BuildingID, StartDate, DaysWorked)
Foreign Keys: WorkerNo references WORKER
                       BuildingID references BUILDING

BUILDING   (BuildingID, Address, Type, Status)

SKILL   (SkillCode, SkillType, WklyHrs)

FIGURE 7-9 Relational data model: notation.

us establish the reasons for ensuring data integrity. A database is said to possess data integrity if the data values will provide a correct and valid representation of the characteristics of the entities or objects. Data integrity includes consistency of data values. Data values derived from one business process must match up correctly with the same values derived from another process.

Why Data Integrity? Let us summarize the reasons for data integrity and examine how the relational data model must ensure data integrity

- In a mathematical set, no two elements can be the same. Similarly, in the relational model that is based on set theory, no two rows can be exactly the same.
- Each tuple must represent one specific entity. There must be no ambiguity in identification of the tuple for each specific entity.
- The values in all tuples for any single attribute must be of the same data type, format, and length. There must not be variations, confusion, or unpredictability in the values for every attribute.
- The columns must be identified only by names and not by position or physical order in a relation.
- A new row may be added anywhere in the table so that the content does not vary with the order of the rows or tuples in a relation.
- The model should express relationships correctly and without any room for exceptions.
- The data model must consist of well-structured relations with minimum data redundancy.
- Data manipulations in a relational database must not result in any data inconsistencies.

First, we will consider the basic relational properties that support data integrity and data consistency. Next, we will address three special cases that further enhance data integrity.

Basic Relational Properties. Following is a list of the significant relational properties that govern the relations in a relational model.

Row Uniqueness. Each row or tuple is unique—no duplicate rows with the same set of values for the attributes are allowed. No two rows are completely identical.

Unique Identifier. The primary key identifies each tuple uniquely.

Atomic Values. Each value of every attribute is atomic. That is, for a single tuple, the value of each attribute must be single-valued. Multiple values or repeating groups of attributes are not allowed for any attribute in a tuple.

Domain Constraint. The value of each attribute must be an atomic value from a certain domain.

Column Homogeneity. Each column gets values from same domain.

Order of Columns. The sequence of the columns is insignificant. You may change the sequence without changing the meaning or use of the relation. The primary key may be in any column, not necessarily in the first column. Columns may be stored in any sequence and, therefore, must be addressed by column names and not by column positions.

Order of Rows. The sequence of the rows is insignificant. Rows may be reordered or interchanged without any consequence. New rows may be inserted anywhere in the relation. It does not matter whether rows are added at the beginning, or middle, or at the end of a relation.

Entity Integrity. Consider the relation EMPLOYEE. The rows in the relation represent individual employees in an organization. The rows represent real-world entities. Each row represents a specific employee. Similarly, a row in the relation CUSTOMER stands for a particular customer. In other words, each tuple or row in a relation must be uniquely identified because each tuple represents a single and distinct entity. Entity integrity rule in the relational data model establishes this principle for an entity.

But, how is a specific row or tuple in a relation uniquely identified? As you know, the primary key serves this function. The primary key value of each tuple or row uniquely identifies that row. Therefore, entity integrity rule is a rule about the primary key that is meant to identify rows uniquely. The rule applies to single relations.

Entity integrity rule

No part of the primary key of any tuple in a relation can have a null value.

Figure 7-10 presents three relations EMPLOYEE, PROJECT, and ASSIGNMENT. Relations EMPLOYEE and PROJECT have primary keys with single attributes; two attributes make up the primary key for the ASSIGNMENT relation. The figure explains how violation of entity integrity rule affects the integrity of the data model.

Note the null values present in a few rows, and because of these rows the entity integrity rule is violated in the relation. If two or more rows have nulls as primary key values, how can you distinguish between these rows? Which row denotes which specific entity? In the case of the relation ASSIGNMENT, even if part of the primary key contains nulls for any rows, the entity integrity rule is violated.

Referential Integrity. You have noted that foreign keys establish relationships between tables or relations. The value placed in the foreign key column of one table for a specific row links to a row with the same value in the primary key column in another table. Figure 7-11 shows two relations DEPARTMENT and EMPLOYEE.

Note how the values in the foreign key column DeptNo in EMPLOYEE relation and in the primary key column DeptNo in DEPARTMENT relation link related rows in the two relations. In the figure, employee Charles is assigned to department Accounting; employee Eldon, to Marketing. What about employee Mary who is supposed to be assigned to department D555? But, the database does not have department D555. Look at the row for employee Paul. This row has a null value in the foreign key column. Is this allowed? What do nulls in foreign key columns indicate? You know that nulls in foreign key columns denote optional relationships. That means employee Paul is not assigned to any department.

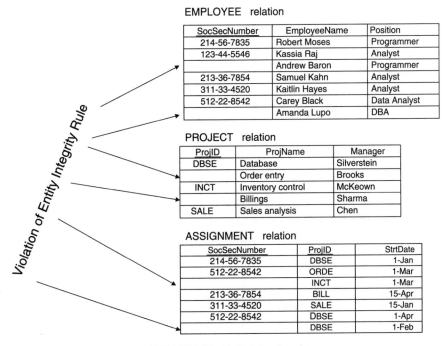

EMPLOYEE relation

SocSecNumber	EmployeeName	Position
214-56-7835	Robert Moses	Programmer
123-44-5546	Kassia Raj	Analyst
	Andrew Baron	Programmer
213-36-7854	Samuel Kahn	Analyst
311-33-4520	Kaitlin Hayes	Analyst
512-22-8542	Carey Black	Data Analyst
	Amanda Lupo	DBA

PROJECT relation

ProjID	ProjName	Manager
DBSE	Database	Silverstein
	Order entry	Brooks
INCT	Inventory control	McKeown
	Billings	Sharma
SALE	Sales analysis	Chen

ASSIGNMENT relation

SocSecNumber	ProjID	StrtDate
214-56-7835	DBSE	1-Jan
512-22-8542	ORDE	1-Mar
	INCT	1-Mar
213-36-7854	BILL	15-Apr
311-33-4520	SALE	15-Jan
512-22-8542	DBSE	1-Apr
	DBSE	1-Feb

Violation of Entity Integrity Rule

FIGURE 7-10   Entity integrity rule.

When one relation is related to another through foreign key values, the references of the relationship must be clearly indicated. There should not be any ambiguities. A foreign key value must clearly indicate how that row is related to a row in the other relation. Referential integrity rule addresses the establishment of clear references between related tables. Referential integrity rule, therefore, applies to sets of two relations.

Referential integrity rule

The value of a foreign key in a table must either be null or be one of the values of the primary key in the related table.

EMPLOYEE relation

EmpNo	EmpName	Phone Ext.	DeptNo
E10	Charles	418	D200
E20	Mary	236	D555
E30	Eldon	179	D300
E40	Paul	522	

DEPARTMENT relation

Dept No	DeptName	Location
D100	Engineering	West
D200	Accounting	South
D300	Marketing	East

FIGURE 7-11   Referential integrity rule.

Functional Dependencies. Let us use EMPLOYEE, PROJECT, and ASSIGNMENT relations shown in Figure 7-10 to examine the concept of functional dependency. The notion of functional dependency in a relation arises because the value of one attribute in a tuple determines the value for another attribute. Let us look at some examples.

In the EMPLOYEE relation of Figure 7-10, note the tuple with key value 213-36-7854. This determines that the tuple represents a distinct employee whose name is Samuel Kahn and whose position is Analyst. Now, look at the tuple with key value 311-33-4520. This key value uniquely identifies an employee whose name is Kaitlin Hayes and whose position also happens to be Analyst. Let us inspect the dependencies.

Values of which attribute determine values of other attributes? Does the value of the primary key uniquely and functionally determine the values of other attributes?

- Key value 213-36-7854 uniquely and functionally determines a specific row representing Samuel Kahn with position Analyst.
- Key value 311-33-4520 uniquely and functionally determines a specific row representing Kaitlin Hayes with position Analyst.

Let us ask the questions the other way around. Does the value of the attribute Position uniquely and functionally determine the value of the primary key attribute?

- Attribute value Analyst does not uniquely determine a key value—in this case, it determines two values of the key, namely, 213-36-7854 and 311-33-4520.

What you see clearly is that the value of the primary key uniquely and functionally determines the values of other attributes, and not the other way around.

Let us express this concept using a functional dependency notation,

FD: SocSecNumber $\rightarrow$ EmployeeName
FD: SocSecNumber $\rightarrow$ Position

In the ASSIGNMENT relation, two attributes SocSecNumber and ProjectID together make up the primary key. Here, too, the values of the other attribute in a tuple are uniquely determined by the values of the composite primary key.

FD: SocSecNumber, ProjID $\rightarrow$ StrtDate

The discussion of functional dependencies leads to another important rule or constraint about the primary key of a relation.

Functional dependency rule

Each data item in a tuple of a relation is uniquely and functionally determined by the primary key, by the whole primary key, and only by the primary key.

TRANSITION TO DATABASE DESIGN

From the discussion so far, you have captured the significance of the relational data model. You have understood how it stands on a solid mathematical foundation and is, therefore, a disciplined approach to perceiving data. The view of data in the form of the common two-dimensional tables adds to the elegance and simplicity of the model. At the same time, relational constraints or rules, to which the two-dimensional tables must conform, ensure data integrity and consistency.

Commercial relational database management systems are implementations of the relational data model. So, in order to develop and build a relational database system for your organization, you need to learn how to design, put together a relational data model, and make the transition to database design. Although the model appears to be simple, how do you create a relational data model from the requirements? The previous chapters covered details of creating data models. We went through the methods and steps for creating a conceptual data model using the E-R modeling technique. Now, the task is to create a relational data model, which is not the same as one of designing the conceptual data model. Why do you need to create a relational data model? If you are developing a relational database system, then you require your information requirements represented in a relational data model. Let us explore the methods for creating a relational data model.

Design Approaches

From the previous chapters, you know how to create a conceptual data model from the information requirements. A conceptual data model captures all the meanings and content of information requirements of an organization at a high level of abstraction. Being a generic data model, a conceptual data model is not restricted by the structure and format rules of the conventional data models such as hierarchical, network, or relational data models. Representing information requirements in the form of a conceptual data model is the proper way to start the data modeling process.

Well, what are the steps between creating a conceptual data model and the implementation of a relational database system for your organization? You know that the conceptual data model, if created correctly, will represent every aspect of the information that needs to be found in the proposed database system. The next steps depend on the extent and complexity of your database system. Let us examine the options.

Database practitioners adopt one of two approaches to design and put together a relational data model. The relational data model must, of course, truly represent the information requirements. In the simplest terms, what is a relational data model? It is a collection of two-dimensional tables with rows and columns, and with relationships expressed within the tables themselves through foreign keys. So, in effect, designing and creating a relational data model reduces to creating the proper collection of two-dimensional tables.

Figure 7-12 presents the two design approaches for creating a relational data model.

Note how in one approach, you go through the steps of creating a conceptual data model first and then transform the conceptual model into a relational data model. The other approach appears to be a short-cut method bypassing the conceptual data model. In this approach, you go to the task of creating the relational data model straight from requirements definitions. However, you may still want a conceptual data model to serve as the communication vehicle between data modelers and user groups. Let us examine the basics of the two approaches.

Conceptual to Relational Model

The first method shown in Figure 7-12 takes you through the conceptual data model. In this approach, first you complete the conceptual data model. For creating the conceptual data

1. Semantic modeling approach *(used for large, complex databases)*:
    *   Create semantic data model
    *   Transform semantic model to relational model

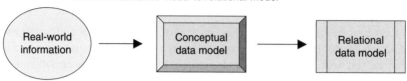

2. Traditional approach *(used for smaller, simpler databases)*:
    *   Create random two-dimensional table structures
    *   Normalize the data structures

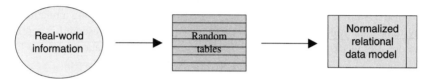

FIGURE 7-12   Relational data model: design approaches.

model, you may use the E-R data modeling technique. Some other modeling techniques would also produce conceptual data models.

Here are the general steps in this design approach:

*   Gather the information requirements of the organization.
*   Create a conceptual data model to truly represent the information requirements.
*   Review the overall conceptual data model for completeness.
*   Take each component of the conceptual data model at a time and examine it.
*   Transform each component of the conceptual data model into a corresponding component of the relational data model.
*   Pull together all the components of the relational data model resulting from the transformation from the conceptual data model.
*   Complete the relational data model.
*   Review the relational data model for completeness.

The next major section of this chapter elaborates on this approach to designing the relational data model. We will list the components of the conceptual model and the corresponding components of the relational model. We will determine how each component of the conceptual data model must be mapped to its corresponding component in the relational data model.

Traditional Method

Before the introduction and standardization of data modeling techniques, traditionally database practitioners had adopted a different method. A relational data model is, after all, a set of two-dimensional tables. Why not look at the information requirements and try to come up with the necessary tables to represent the data that would satisfy the information requirements? Why do you need an intermediary step of creating a conceptual data model? Does it not appear to be a practical design approach?

Although this approach is deceptively simple, as you will note in the next chapter, this method is subject to serious problems if the tables are not defined properly. You are likely to end up with a faulty set of tables in your relational data model with a high potential for data corruption and inconsistency.

Dr. Codd suggested an orderly methodology for making this design approach work. After an initial set of tables is put together intuitively, you must go through a step-by-step process of normalization of the initial tables. After completing the normalization steps, your relational data model will result in a set of tables that are free from redundancies and errors.

Here are the steps in this design approach:

- Gather the information requirements of the organization.
- Review the information requirements to determine the types of tables that would be needed.
- Come up with an initial set of tables.
- Ensure that your initial set of tables contains all the information requirements.
- Normalize the tables using a step-by-step methodology.
- Review the resulting set of tables, one by one, and ensure that none of the tables has potential redundancies or errors.
- Complete the relational data model.
- Review the relational data model for completeness.

Chapter 8 covers the data normalization method. In that chapter, we will have a detailed discussion of this approach to designing the relational data model. You will realize the need and motivation for the normalization process. We will list the normalization steps and show how to apply a single normalization principle at each step. You will note how, after each step, the set of tables gets closer to being the correct set of tables and being part of the final relational data model.

Evaluation of Design Methods

Naturally, when there are two ways for arriving at the same place, which path should you take? If both methods produce the same desired result, which method is more appropriate? The answers to these questions depend on the circumstances of the design process.

Note the following points about the two methods while making the choice between the two ways:

Same Result. If you carry out the transformation of the conceptual data model into a relational model or adopt the traditional method using normalization, you will arrive at the same relational data model. However, either method must be used carefully, making sure that every task is executed properly.

One Method Intuitive. In the traditional method, you are supposed to come up with an initial and complete set of tables. But, how do you come up with the initial set? Using what method? There is no standard method for arriving at an initial set of tables. You have to look at the information requirements and arrive at the initial set of tables mostly through intuition. You just start with the best possible set that is complete. Then you go and normalize the tables and complete the relational data model.

Other Method Systematic. The method of creating the conceptual data model first and then transforming it into the required relational data model is a systematic method with well-defined mapping algorithms. Creation of the conceptual data model is through clearly defined data modeling techniques. Then you take the components of the conceptual data model, one by one, and transform these in a disciplined manner.

Choosing Between the Two Methods. When can you adopt the traditional method? Only when you can come up with a good initial set of tables through intuition. If the information requirements are wide and complex, by looking at the information requirements it is not easy to discern the tables for the initial set. If you attempt the process, you are likely to miss portions of information requirements. Therefore, adopt the traditional approach only for smaller and simpler relational database systems. For larger and complex relational database systems, the transformation method is the prudent approach. As data modelers gain experience, they tend to get better at defining the initial set of tables and go with the normalization method.

MODEL TRANSFORMATION METHOD

This method is a straightforward procedure of examining the components of your conceptual data model and then transforming these components into components of the required relational data model. A conceptual model is a generic model. We have chosen to transform it into a relational model.

Let us study the transformation of a conceptual model created using E-R technique into relational data model. The discussions here may also be adapted to a conceptual model created using any other modeling technique. The transformation principles will be similar.

The Approach

Obviously, first you need to firm up your requirements definition before beginning any data modeling. We had discussed requirements gathering methods and contents of requirements definition in great detail. Requirements definition drives the design of the conceptual data model.

Requirements definition captures details of real-world information. After the requirements definition phase, you move to conceptual data modeling to create a replica of information requirements. From conceptual data modeling, you make the transition to a relational data model. This completes the logical design phase. Physical design and implementation follow; however, these are not completely within the purview of our study.

Merits. Why go through the process of creating a full-fledged conceptual model first and then transforming it into a relational data model? Does it not sound like a longer route to logical design? What are the merits and advantages of this approach? Although we have addressed these questions earlier in bits and pieces, let us summarize the merits and rationale for the model transformation approach.

Need for Conceptual Model. You must ensure that your final database system stores and manages all aspects of information requirements. Nothing must be missing from the database system. Everything should be correct. The proposed database system must be able to support all the relevant business processes and provide users with proper information. Therefore, any data model as a prelude to the proposed database system must be a true replica of information requirements.

A general data model captures the true and complete meaning of information requirements at a high level of abstraction understandable by user groups. The model is made up of a complete set of components such as entity types, attributes, relationships, and so is able to represent every aspect of information requirements. If there are variations in entity types or relationship types in the information requirements, a generic data model can correctly reflect such nuances.

Limitations of Implementation Models. Consider the conventional data models such as the hierarchical, network, or relational data models. These are models that are implemented in commercial database systems. You have hierarchical, network, and relational databases offered by vendors. The conventional or implementation models are the ones that stipulate how data is perceived, stored, and managed in a database system. For example, the relational data model lays down the structure and constraints on how data can be perceived as two-dimensional tables and how relationships may be established through logical links. As such, the implementation data models address data modeling from the point of view of storing and managing data in the database system.

However, the objectives of database development are to ensure that any data model used must truly replicate all aspects of information requirements. The conventional data models do not directly perceive data from the point of view of information requirements; they seem to come from the other side. Therefore, a conventional data model is not usually created directly from information requirements. Such an attempt may not produce a complete and correct data model.

Need for Generic Model. Imagine a process of creating a conventional data model from information requirements. First of all, what is the conventional data model that is being created? If it is a hierarchical data model, then you as a data modeler must know the components of the hierarchical data model thoroughly and also know how to relate real-world information to these model components. On the other hand, if your organization opts for a relational data model, again, you as a data modeler must know the components of the relational data model and also know how to relate real-world information to the relational model components.

However, data modeling must concentrate on correctly representing real-world information irrespective of whether the implementation is going to be hierarchical, network, or relational. As a data modeler, if you learn one set of components and gain expertise in mapping the real-world to this generic set of components, then your concentration will be on capturing the true meaning of real-world information and not on variations in modeling components.

Simple and Straightforward. The attraction for the model transformation method for creating a relational model comes from the simplicity of the method. Once the conceptual data model gets completed with due diligence, the rest of the process is straightforward. There are no complex, convoluted steps. You have to simply follow an orderly sequence of tasks.

Suppose your organization desires to implement a relational database system. Obviously, information requirements must be defined properly no matter which type of database system is being implemented. Information requirements define the set of real-world information that must be modeled. A data modeler who specializes in conceptual data modeling techniques creates a conceptual data model based on information requirements. At this stage, the data modeler need not have any knowledge of the relational data model. All the data modeler does is to represent information requirements in the form of a conceptual model. The next straightforward step for the data designer is to review the components of the conceptual data model and change each component to a component of the relational data model.

Easy Mapping of Components. A conceptual data model is composed of a small distinct set of components. It does not matter how large and expansive the entire data model is; the whole data model is still constructed with a few distinct components. You may be creating an E-R data model for a large multinational corporation or a small medical group practice. Yet, in both cases, you will be using a small set of components to put together the E-R data model.

What then is the implication here? Your conceptual data model, however large it may be, consists of only a few distinct components. This means you just need to know how to transform a few distinct components. From the other side, a relational data model also consists of a few distinct components. So, mapping and transforming the components becomes easy and very manageable.

When to Use this Method. When there is more than one method for creating a relational data model, a natural question arises as to how do you choose and adopt one method over the other? When do you use the model transformation method and not the normalization method? In a previous section, we had a few hints. The model transformation method applies when the normalization method is not feasible. Let us now list the conditions that would warrant the use of the model transformation method.

Large Database System. When a proposed database system is large and the data model is expected to contain numerous component pieces, the model transformation method is preferable.

Complex Information Requirements. Some set of information requirements may require modeling complex variations and many types of generalization and specialization. There may be several variations in the relationships, and the attributes themselves may be of different types. Under such conditions, modeling complex information requirements directly in the relational model bypassing the conceptual data model proves to be very difficult.

Large Project. A large project requires many data modelers to work in parallel to complete the data modeling activity within a reasonable time. Each data modeler will work on a portion of information requirements and produce a partial conceptual data model. When a project is large and the data model is expected to contain numerous partial models, the model transformation method is preferable. The partial conceptual data models are integrated and then transformed into a relational data model.

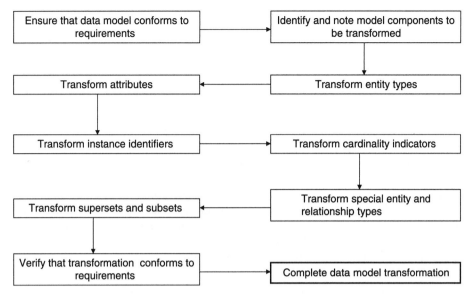

FIGURE 7-13 Model transformation: major steps.

Steps and Tasks. Figure 7-13 presents the major steps in the model transformation method. Study these major steps and note how each major step enables you to proceed toward the final transformation of the data model.

Mapping of Components

While creating an E-R data model, the data modeler uses the components or building blocks available in that technique to put together the data model. You have studied such components in sufficient detail. Similarly, in order to create a relational model, the building blocks are the ones available in the relational modeling technique. You reviewed these components also. Essentially, transforming an E-R data model involves finding matching components in the relational data model and transferring the representation of information requirements from one model to the other. Model transformation primarily consists of mapping of corresponding components from one data model to the other.

Let us recapitulate the components or building blocks for each of the two models—the E-R and the relational data models. The list of components makes it easier to begin the study of component mapping and model transformation.

Conceptual Data Model

ENTITY-RELATIONSHIP TECHNIQUE

Entity types
Attributes
Keys
Relationships
Cardinality indicators
Generalization/specialization

Relational Data Model

Relations or tables
Rows
Columns
Primary key
Foreign key
Generalization/specialization

Just by going through the list of components, it is easy to form the basic concepts for mapping and transformation. The conceptual data model deals with the things that are of interest to the organization, the characteristics of these things, and the relationships among these things. On the other hand, the relational model stipulates how data about the things of interest must be perceived and represented, how the characteristics must be symbolized, and how the links between related things must be established.

First, let us consider the mapping of things and their characteristics. Then we will move on to the discussion of relationships. As you know, a major strength of the relational model is the way it represents relationships through logical links. We will describe the mapping of relationships in detail and also take up special conditions. Mapping involves taking the components of the conceptual data model, one by one, and finding the corresponding component or components in the relational data model.

Entity Types to Relations

Let us begin with the most obvious component—entity type in the E-R data model. What is an entity type? If *employee* is a "thing" the organization is interested in storing information about, then *employee* is an entity represented in the conceptual data model. The set of all employees in the organization about whom data must be captured in the proposed relational database system is the entity type EMPLOYEE.

Figure 7-14 shows the mapping of entity type EMPLOYEE. The mapping shows the transformation of entity type represented in E-R modeling notation to a relation denoted in relational data model notation.

From the figure, note the following points about the transformation from E-R data model to relational data model:

- Entity type is transformed into a relation.
- Name of the entity type becomes the name of the relation.
- The entity instances perceived as present inside the entity type box transform into the rows of the relation.
- The complete set of entity instances becomes the total set of rows of the relation or table.
- In the transformation, nothing is expressed about the order of the rows in the transformed relation.

Attributes to Columns

Entities have intrinsic or inherent characteristics. So, naturally the next component to be considered is the set of attributes of an entity type. Figure 7-15 shows the transformation of attributes.

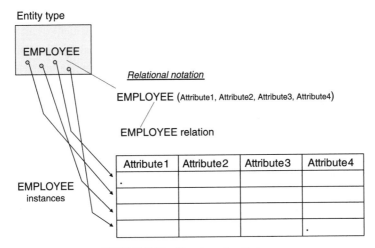

FIGURE 7-14   Mapping of entity type.

Make note of the following points with regard to the transformation of attributes:

- Attributes of an entity type are transformed into the columns of the corresponding relation.
- The names of the attributes become the names of the columns.
- Domain of values of each attribute translates into the domain of values for corresponding columns.
- In the transformation, nothing is expressed about the order of the columns in the transformed relation.
- A single-valued or a derived attribute becomes one column in the resulting relation.

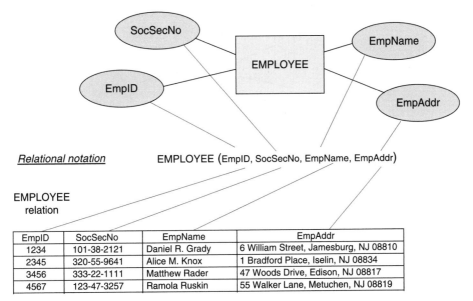

FIGURE 7-15   Mapping of attributes.

- If a multivalued attribute is present, then this is handled by forming a separate relation with this attribute as a column in the separate relation.
- For a composite attribute, as many columns are incorporated as the number of component attributes.

Identifiers to Keys

In the E-R data model, each instance of an entity type is uniquely identified by values in one or more attributes. These attributes together form the instance identifier. Figure 7-16 indicates the transformation of instance identifiers.

Note the following points on this transformation:

- The set of attributes forming the instance identifier becomes the primary key of the relation.
- If there is more than one attribute, all the corresponding columns are indicated as primary key columns.
- Because the primary key columns represent instance identifiers, the combined value in these columns for each row is unique.
- No two rows in the relation can have the same values in the primary key columns.
- Because instance identifiers cannot have null values, no part of the primary key columns can have null values.

Transformation of Relationships

Methods for conceptual data modeling have elegant ways for representing relationships between two entity types. Wherever you perceive direct associations between instances

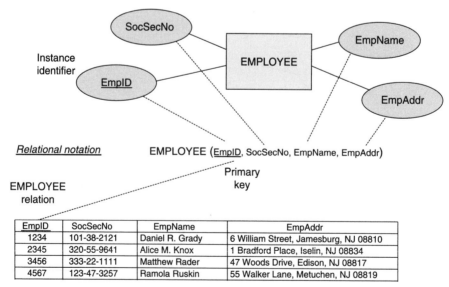

FIGURE 7-16   Mapping of instance identifiers.

of two entity types, the two entity types are connected by lines with a diamond in the middle containing the name of the relationship. How many instances of one entity type are associated with how many instances of the other? The indication about the numbers is given by cardinality indicators, especially the maximum cardinality indicator. The minimum cardinality indicator denotes whether a relationship is optional or mandatory.

You know that a relational data model establishes relationships between two relations through foreign keys. Therefore, transformation of relationships as represented in the conceptual model involves mapping of the connections and cardinality indicators into foreign keys. We will discuss how this is done for one-to-one, one-to-many, and many-to-many relationships. We will also go over the transformation of optional and mandatory conditions for relationships. While considering transformation of relationships, we need to review relationships between a superset and its subsets.

One-to-One Relationships. When one instance of an entity type is associated with a maximum of only one instance of another entity type, we call this relationship a one-to-one relationship. Figure 7-17 shows a one-to-one relationship between the two entity types CLIENT and CONTACT-PERSON.

If a client of an organization has designated a contact person, then the contact person is represented by CONTACT-PERSON entity type. Only one contact person exists for a client. But some clients may not have contact persons, in which case there is no corresponding instance in CONTACT-PERSON entity type. Now we can show the relationship by placing the foreign key column in CLIENT relation. Figure 7-18 illustrates this transformation.

Observe how the transformation gets done. How are the rows of CLIENT relation linked to corresponding rows of CONTACT-PERSON relation? The values in the foreign key columns and primary key columns provide the linkage. Do you note some foreign key columns in CLIENT relation with null values? What are these? For these clients, client contact persons do not exist. If the majority of clients do not have assigned contact persons, then many of the rows in CLIENT relation will contain null values in the foreign key column. This is not a good transformation. A better transformation would be to place the foreign key column in CONTACT-PERSON relation, not in CLIENT relation. Figure 7-19 presents this better transformation.

Foreign key links two relations. If so, you must be able to get answers to queries involving data from two related tables by using the values in foreign key columns. From Figure 7-19, examine how results for the following queries are obtained.

Who Is the Contact Person for Client Number 22222?. Read CONTACT-PERSON table by values in the foreign key column. Find the row having the value 22222 in the foreign key column.

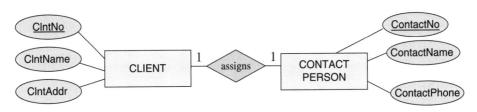

FIGURE 7-17 One-to-one relationship.

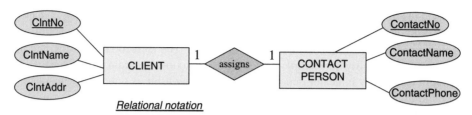

Relational notation

CLIENT (<u>ClntNo</u>, ClntName, ClntAddr, ContactNo)

    Foreign key:ContactNo REFERENCES CONTACT PERSON

    CONTACT PERSON (<u>ContactNo</u>, ContactName, ContactPhone)

CLIENT relation

ClntNo	ClntName	ClntAddr	ContactNo
11111	ABC industries	6 William Street, Jamesburg, NJ 08810	234
22222	Progressive systems	1 Bradford Place, Iselin, NJ 08834	123
33333	Rapid development	47 Woods Drive, Edison, NJ 08817	
44444	Richard associates	55 Walker Lane, Metuchen, NJ 08819	
55555	Quality consulting	35 Rues Ave., E. Brunswick, NJ 08821	345

CONTACT PERSON
relation

Contact No	ContactName	ContactPhone
123	Mary Williams	732-345-8100
234	Winston Poyser	732-555-4000
345	Lisa Moore	732-767-5300

FIGURE 7-18   Transformation of one-to-one relationship.

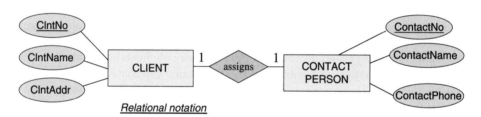

Relational notation

CLIENT (<u>ClntNo</u>, ClntName, ClntAddr)

    CONTACT PERSON (<u>ContactNo</u>, ContactName, ContactPhone, ClntNo)

    Foreign key:ClntNo REFERENCES CLIENT

CLIENT relation

ClntNo	ClntName	ClntAddr
11111	ABC industries	6 William Street, Jamesburg, NJ 08810
22222	Progressive systems	1 Bradford Place, Iselin, NJ 08834
33333	Rapid development	47 Woods Drive, Edison, NJ 08817
44444	Richard associates	55 Walker Lane, Metuchen, NJ 08819
55555	Quality consulting	35 Rues Ave., E. Brunswick, NJ 08821

CONTACT PERSON relation

ContactNo	ContactName	ContactPhone	ClntNo
123	Mary Williams	732-345-8100	22222
234	Winston Poyser	732-555-4000	11111
345	Lisa Moore	732-767-5300	55555

FIGURE 7-19   Better transformation of one-to-one relationship.

Who Is the Client for Contact Person Number 345?. Read CONTACT-PERSON table by values in the primary key column. Find the row having the value 345 in the primary key column. Get the foreign key value of this row, namely, 55555. Read CLIENT table by values in the primary key column. Find the row having the value 5555 for the primary key attribute.

Let us summarize the points about transformation of one-to-one relationships.

- When two relations are in one-to-one relationship, place a foreign key column in either one of the two relations. Values in the foreign key column for rows in this table matches with primary key values in corresponding rows of the related table.
- The foreign key attribute has the same data type, length, and domain values as the corresponding primary key attribute in the other table.
- It does not really matter whether you place the foreign key column in one table or the other. However, to avoid wasted space, it is better to place the foreign key column in the table that is likely to have the less number of rows.

One-to-Many Relationships. Let us begin our discussion of one-to-many relationship by reviewing Figure 7-20. This figure shows the one-to-many relationship between the two objects CUSTOMER and ORDER.

The figure also indicates how individual instances of these two entity types are associated with one another. You see a clear one-to-many relationship—one customer can have one or more orders. So how should you transform this relationship? As you know, the associations are established through the use of a foreign key column. But in which table do you place the foreign key column? For transforming one-to-one relationship, you noted that you might place the foreign key column in either relation. In the same way, let us try to place the foreign key in CUSTOMER relation. Figure 7-21 shows this transformation of one-to-many relationship.

What do you observe about the foreign keys in the transformed relations? In the CUSTOMER relation, the row for customer 1113 needs just one foreign key column to connect

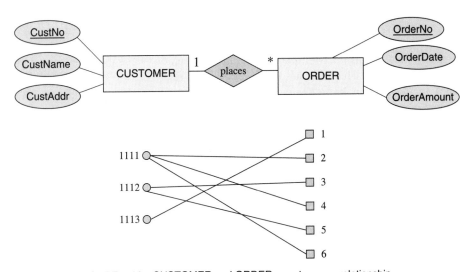

FIGURE 7-20 CUSTOMER and ORDER: one-to-many relationship.

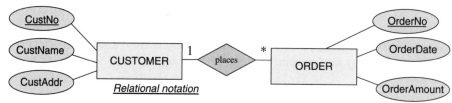

CUSTOMER (<u>CustNo</u>, CustName, CustAddr, OrderNo1, ...)
Foreign key:OrderNo1, OrderNo2, OrderNo3 REFERENCES ORDER

ORDER (<u>OrderNo</u>, OrderDate, OrderAmount)

CUSTOMER relation

CustNo	CustName	CustAddr	OrderNo1	OrderNo2	OrderNo3
1111	ABC industries	Jamesburg, NJ	2	4	6
1112	Progressive systems	Iselin, NJ	3	5	
1113	Rapid development	Edison, NJ	1		

ORDER relation

OrderNo	OrderDate	OrderAmount
1	10/1/2002	2,122.50
2	10/3/2002	3,025.00
3	10/6/02	4,111.25
4	10/17/2002	3,005.50
5	10/19/2002	7,000.00
6	10/25/02	6,540.00

FIGURE 7-21   Transformation of one-to-many relationship.

to order 1 in the ORDER relation. But the row for customer 1112 seems to need two foreign key columns, and the row for customer 1111 seems to require three foreign key columns. What if there is a customer with 50 orders? How many foreign key columns are sufficient in the CUSTOMER relation? How will you search for a particular ORDER from the several foreign key columns in the CUSTOMER relation? Obviously, this transformation is not right.

We can try another solution by placing the foreign key column in the ORDER relation instead of including the foreign key column in the other related table. Figure 7-22 illustrates the correct solution.

Examine this figure. First, you notice that there is no need for multiple foreign keys to represent one relationship. Multiple rows in ORDER relation have the same value in the foreign key column. This indicates the several orders related to the same customer. The values in the foreign key column link the associated rows. From the figure, let us examine how queries involving data from two related tables work.

Which Are the Orders Related to CUSTOMER Number 1112? Read ORDER table by values in the foreign key column. Find the rows having the value 1112 in the foreign key column.

What Is the Name of the Customer for Order Number 5? Read ORDER table by values in the primary key column. Find the row having the value 5 for the primary key attribute. Get foreign key value of this row, namely, 1112. Read CUSTOMER table by values in its primary key column. Find the row having the value 1112 in the primary key column.

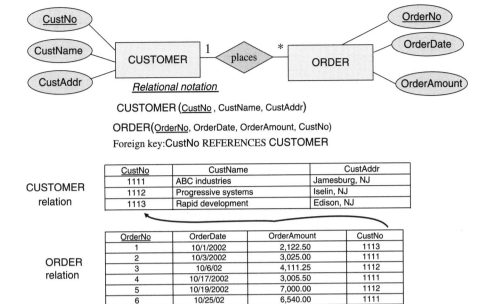

CUSTOMER (CustNo , CustName, CustAddr)

ORDER(OrderNo, OrderDate, OrderAmount, CustNo)

Foreign key:CustNo REFERENCES CUSTOMER

CUSTOMER
relation

CustNo	CustName	CustAddr
1111	ABC industries	Jamesburg, NJ
1112	Progressive systems	Iselin, NJ
1113	Rapid development	Edison, NJ

ORDER
relation

OrderNo	OrderDate	OrderAmount	CustNo
1	10/1/2002	2,122.50	1113
2	10/3/2002	3,025.00	1111
3	10/6/02	4,111.25	1112
4	10/17/2002	3,005.50	1111
5	10/19/2002	7,000.00	1112
6	10/25/02	6,540.00	1111

FIGURE 7-22   Correct transformation of one-to-many relationship.

Let us summarize the points about transformation of one-to-many relationships.

- When two relations are in one-to-many relationship, place the foreign key column in the relation that is on the "many" side of the relationship. Values in foreign key column for rows in this table match with primary key values in corresponding rows of the related table.
- The foreign key attribute has the same data type, length, and domain values as the corresponding primary key attribute in the other table.

Many-to-Many Relationships. As you know, in a many-to-many relationship, one instance of an entity type is related to one or more instances of a second entity type, and also one instance of the second entity type is related to one or more instances of the first entity type. Figure 7-23 presents an example of a many-to-many relationship.

One employee is assigned to one or more projects simultaneously or over time. Again, one project is related to one or more employees. Let us try to transform the E-R data model to a relational data model and establish the many-to-many relationship. For establishing the relationship, you have to create foreign key columns. While transforming a one-to-many relationship, we placed the foreign key column in the relation on the "many" side of the relationship; that is, we placed the foreign key column in the child relation.

In a many-to-many relationship, which of the two relations is the child relation? It is not clear. Both relations participate in the relationship in the same way. Look at the associations shown in Figure 7-23. Transform the entity types into relations and place the foreign key column in PROJECT relation. Figure 7-24 shows this transformation with the foreign key column placed in PROJECT relation.

Note the foreign keys in the transformed relations? In PROJECT relation, the rows for projects 1 and 4 need three foreign key columns, whereas the rows for projects 2, 3, and 4

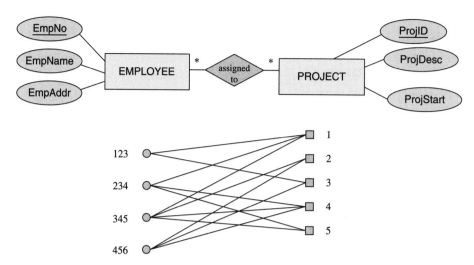

FIGURE 7-23 Example of many-to-many relationship.

need two foreign key columns each. You get the picture. If some projects are related to many employees, as many as 50 or so, how many foreign key columns must PROJECT relation have? So, it appears that this method of transformation is not correct.

Let us determine how queries involving data from two related tables work.

Which Are the Projects Related to Employee 456? Read PROJECT table by values in the foreign key columns But which foreign key columns? All of the foreign columns? Right away, you note that finding the result for this query is going to be extremely difficult.

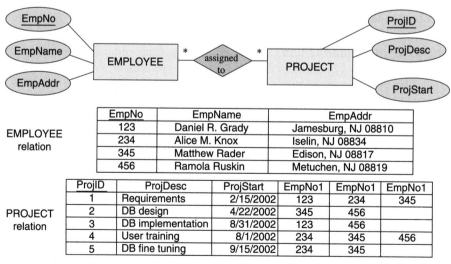

EMPLOYEE relation	EmpNo	EmpName	EmpAddr
	123	Daniel R. Grady	Jamesburg, NJ 08810
	234	Alice M. Knox	Iselin, NJ 08834
	345	Matthew Rader	Edison, NJ 08817
	456	Ramola Ruskin	Metuchen, NJ 08819

	ProjID	ProjDesc	ProjStart	EmpNo1	EmpNo1	EmpNo1
	1	Requirements	2/15/2002	123	234	345
PROJECT	2	DB design	4/22/2002	345	456	
relation	3	DB implementation	8/31/2002	123	456	
	4	User training	8/1/2002	234	345	456
	5	DB fine tuning	9/15/2002	234	345	

Related project-employee instance pairs: (1,123), (1,234), (1,345), (2,345), (2,456), (3,123), (3,456), (4,234), (4,345), (4,456), (5,234), (5,345)

FIGURE 7-24 Transformation of many-to-many relationship: first method.

What Are the Names of Employees Assigned to Project 1?. Read PROJECT table by values in the primary key column. Find the row having the value 1 for the primary key attribute. Get foreign key values of this row, namely, 123, 234, and 345. Read EMPLOYEE table by values in the primary key column. Find the rows having the values 123, 234, and 345 for its primary key attribute. Getting the result for this query seems to be workable.

Because the transformation from the first method does not work, let us try another solution by placing the foreign key columns in the EMPLOYEE relation instead of including the foreign key columns in the other related table. Figure 7-25 illustrates this method of transformation.

Where are the foreign keys in the transformed relations? In the EMPLOYEE relation, the row for employee 123 needs two foreign key columns, whereas the rows for employees 234 and 456 need three foreign key columns each and the rows for employee 345 needs four foreign key columns. By the reasoning similar to the one for the first method, if an employee is related to 25 projects over time, then you need to have that many foreign key columns in the EMPLOYEE relation.

Let us examine how queries involving data from two related tables work.

Which Are the Projects Related to Employee 456? Read EMPLOYEE table by values in the primary key column Find the row having the value 456 for the primary key attribute. Get foreign key values of this row, namely, 2, 3, and 4. Read PROJECT table by values in the primary key column. Find the rows having the values 2, 3, and 4 for its primary key attribute. Getting the result for this query seems to be workable.

What Are the Names of Employees Assigned to Project 1? Read EMPLOYEE table by values in the foreign key columns But which foreign columns? All of the foreign

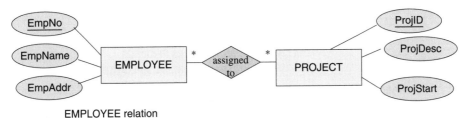

EMPLOYEE relation

EmpNo	EmpName	EmpAddr	ProjID1	ProjID2	ProjID3	ProjID4
123	Daniel R. Grady	Jamesburg, NJ 08810	1	3		
234	Alice M. Knox	Iselin, NJ 08834	1	4	5	
345	Matthew Rader	Edison, NJ 08817	4	2	1	5
456	Ramola Ruskin	Metuchen, NJ 08819	2	3	4	

PROJECT relation

ProjID	ProjDesc	ProjStart
1	Requirements	2/15/2002
2	DB design	4/22/2002
3	DB implementation	8/31/2002
4	User training	8/1/2002
5	DB fine tuning	9/15/2002

Related employee-project instance pairs: (123,1), (123,3), (234,1), (234,4), (234,5), (345, 4), (345, 2), (345,1), (345,5), (456,2), (456,3), (456,4)

FIGURE 7-25 Transformation of many-to-many relationship: second method.

columns? Right away, you note that finding the result for this query is going to be very difficult.

It is clear that the second method of transformation also does not work. We seem to be in a quandary. Where should you place the foreign key column—in which of the two related tables? Placing foreign key columns in either table does not seem to work. So, this second method of transformation is also not correct.

Note the pairs of related primary key values shown in Figures 7-24 and 7-25. Each pair represents a set of a project and a corresponding employee. Look at the pairs (1,123) and (1,234). Each pair indicates a set of related rows from the two tables. For example, the pair (1,123) indicates that the row for project 1 is related to employee 123, the pair (1,234) indicates that the row for project 1 is related to employee 234, and so on. In fact, you note that the complete set of pairs represents all the associations between rows in the two tables. In other words, the set of pairs establishes the many-to-many relationship. But, the values in the pairs are not present as foreign keys in either of the two tables. In our above two attempts at transformation, the real problem is that we do not know where to place the foreign keys—whether in the PROJECT relation or in the EMPLOYEE relation. What if you make a separate table out of these pairs of related values and use the values in the pairs as foreign key values? Then this new table can establish the many-to-many relationship. This elegant technique is the standard method for representing many-to-many relationships in the relational data model.

Figure 7-26 illustrates the correct method of transforming many-to-many relationship. The table containing the pairs of related values of primary keys is known as the intersection table.

Relational notation

EMPLOYEE (<u>EmpNo</u>, EmpName, EmpAddr)

PROJECT (<u>ProjID</u>, ProjDesc, ProjStart)

ASSIGNMENT (<u>ProjID</u>, <u>EmpNo</u>)
Foreign keys: ProjId REFERENCES PROJECT
EmpNo REFERENCES EMPLOYEE

EMPLOYEE relation

EmpNo	EmpName	EmpAddr
123	Daniel R. Grady	Jamesburg, NJ 08810
234	Alice M. Knox	Iselin, NJ 08834
345	Matthew Rader	Edison, NJ 08817
456	Ramola Ruskin	Metuchen, NJ 08819

PROJECT relation

ProjID	ProjDesc	ProjStart
1	Requirements	2/15/2002
2	DB design	4/22/2002
3	DB implementation	8/31/2002
4	User training	8/1/2002
5	DB fine tuning	9/15/2002

ASSIGNMENT relation

ProjID	EmpNo
1	123
1	234
1	345
2	345
2	456
3	123
3	456
4	234
4	345
4	456
5	234
5	345

FIGURE 7-26 Transformation of many-to-many relationship: correct method.

Note the primary key for the intersection table. The primary key consists of two parts: one part, the primary key of PROJECT table and the other part the primary key of EMPLOYEE table. The two parts act separately as the foreign keys to establish both sides of the many-to-many relationship. Also, observe that each of the two relations PROJECT and EMPLOYEE is in a one-to-many relation with the intersection relation ASSIGNMENT.

Now, let us review how queries involving data from the two related tables work.

Which Are the Projects Related to Employee 456? Read intersection table by values in one part of the primary key column, namely, EmpNo attribute showing values for employee key numbers. Find the rows having the value 456 for this part of the primary key. Read PROJECT table by values in its primary key column. Find the rows having the values 2, 3, and 4 for primary key attribute. Getting the result for this query seems to be workable.

What Are the Names of Employees Assigned to Project 1? Read intersection table by values in one part of the primary key column, namely, ProjID attribute showing values for project key numbers. Find the rows having the value 1 for this part of the primary key. Read EMPLOYEE table by values in its primary key column. Find the rows having the values 123, 234, and 345 for primary key attribute. Getting the result for this query is straightforward and easy.

To end our discussion of transformation of many-to-many relationships, let us summarize the main points.

- Create a separate relation, called the intersection table. Use both primary keys of the participating relations as the concatenated primary key column for the intersection table. The primary key column of the intersection table contains two attributes: one attribute establishing the relationship to one of the two relations and the other attribute linking the other relation.
- Each part of the primary key of the intersection table serves as a foreign key.
- Each foreign key attribute has the same data type, length, and domain values as the corresponding primary key attribute in the related table.
- The relationship of the first relation to the intersection relation is one-to-many; the relationship of the second relation to the intersection relation is also one-to-many. In effect, transformation of many-to-many relationship is reduced to creating two one-to-many relationships.

Mandatory and Optional Conditions. The conceptual model is able to represent whether a relationship is optional or mandatory. As you know, the minimum cardinality indicator denotes mandatory and optional conditions. Let us explore the implications of mandatory and optional conditions for relationships in a relational model. In our discussions so far, we have examined the relationships in terms of maximum cardinalities. If the maximum cardinalities are 1 and 1, then the relationship is implemented by placing the foreign key attribute in either of the participating relations. If the maximum cardinalities are 1 and *, then the relationship is established by placing the foreign key attribute in the relation on the "many" side of the relationship. Finally, if the maximum cardinalities are * and *, then the relationship is broken down into two one-to-many relationships by introducing an intersection relation. Let us consider a few examples with minimum cardinalities and determine the effect on the transformation.

Minimum Cardinality in One-to-Many Relationship. Figure 7-27 shows an example of one-to-many relationship between the two entity types PROJECT and EMPLOYEE.

Note the cardinality indicators (1,1) shown next to PROJECT entity type. Intentionally, the figure does not show the minimum cardinality indicator next to EMPLOYEE. We will discuss the reason very shortly. What is the meaning of the cardinality indicators next to PROJECT entity type? The indicators represent the following condition:

An employee can be assigned to a maximum of only one project.

Every employee must be assigned to a project. That is, an employee instance must be associated with a minimum of 1 project instance. In other words, every employee instance must participate in the relationship. The relationship as far as the employee instances are concerned is mandatory.

Now look at the foreign key column in the EMPLOYEE table. If every employee is assigned to a project, then every EMPLOYEE row must have a value in the foreign key column. You know that this value must be the value of the primary key of the related row in the PROJECT table. What does this tell you about the foreign key column? In a mandatory relationship, the foreign key column cannot contain nulls. Observe the Foreign Key statement under relational notation in the figure. It stipulates the constraints with the words "NOT NULL" expressing that nulls are not allowed in the foreign key attribute.

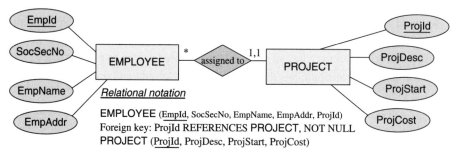

Relational notation

EMPLOYEE (EmpId, SocSecNo, EmpName, EmpAddr, ProjId)
Foreign key: ProjId REFERENCES PROJECT, NOT NULL
PROJECT (ProjId, ProjDesc, ProjStart, ProjCost)

EMPLOYEE relation

EmpId	SocSecNo	EmpName	EmpAddr	ProjId
1234	101-38-2121	Daniel R. Grady	6 William Street, Jamesburg, NJ 08810	DESN
2345	320-55-9641	Alice M. Knox	1 Bradford Place, Iselin, NJ 08834	IMPL
3456	333-22-1111	Matthew Rader	47 Woods Drive, Edison, NJ 08817	DESN
4567	123-47-3257	Ramola Ruskin	55 Walker Lane, Metuchen, NJ 08819	DESN

PROJECT relation

ProjId	ProjDesc	ProjStart	ProjCost
DESN	DB design	6/1/2000	200,000
IMPL	DB implementation	12/15/2000	100,000
USER	User training	10/22/2000	75,000
TUNE	DB fine tuning	3/1/2001	50,000

FIGURE 7-27 One-to-many relationship: mandatory and optional.

Next, consider the optional condition. Suppose the cardinality indicators (0,1) are shown next to PROJECT entity type. Then the indicators will represent the following condition:

An employee can be assigned to a maximum of only one project.

Not every employee need be assigned to a project. That is, some employee instances may not be associated with any project instance at all. At a minimum, an employee instance may be associated with no project instance or with zero project instances. In other words, not every employee instance needs to participate in the relationship. The relationship as far as the employee instances are concerned is optional.

It follows, therefore, that in an optional relationship of this sort, nulls may be allowed in the foreign key attribute. What do the rows with null foreign key attribute in the EMPLOYEE relation represent? These rows represent those employees who are not assigned to a project.

Minimum Cardinality in Many-to-Many Relationship. Figure 7-28 shows an example of many-to-many relationship between the two entity types PROJECT and EMPLOYEE.

Note the cardinality indicators (1,*) shown next to PROJECT entity type and (1,*) shown next to EMPLOYEE entity type. What do these cardinality indicators represent? The indicators represent the following condition:

An employee may be assigned to many projects.

A project may have many employees.

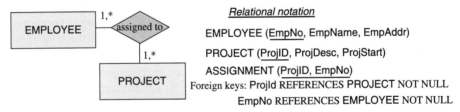

Relational notation

EMPLOYEE (EmpNo, EmpName, EmpAddr)

PROJECT (ProjID, ProjDesc, ProjStart)

ASSIGNMENT (ProjID, EmpNo)

Foreign keys: ProjId REFERENCES PROJECT NOT NULL

EmpNo REFERENCES EMPLOYEE NOT NULL

EMPLOYEE relation

EmpNo	EmpName	EmpAddr
123	Daniel R .Grady	Jamesburg, NJ 08810
234	Alice M. Knox	Iselin, NJ 08834
345	Matthew Rader	Edison, NJ 08817
456	Ramola Ruskin	Metuchen, NJ 08819

PROJECT relation

ProjID	ProjDesc	ProjStart
1	Requirements	2/15/2002
2	DB design	4/22/2002
3	DB implementation	8/31/2002
4	User training	8/1/2002
5	DB fine tuning	9/15/2002

ASSIGNMENT relation

ProjID	EmpNo
1	123
1	234
1	345
2	345
2	456
3	123
3	456
4	234
4	345
4	456
5	234
5	345

FIGURE 7-28 Many-to-many relationship: minimum cardinality.

Every employee must be assigned to at least one project. That is, an employee instance must be associated with a minimum of 1 project instance. In other words, every employee instance must participate in the relationship. The relationship as far as the employee instances are concerned is mandatory.

Every project must have at least one employee. That is, a project instance must be associated with a minimum of 1 employee instance. In other words, every project instance must participate in the relationship. The relationship as far as the project instances are concerned is mandatory.

Carefully observe the transformed relations described in the figure. Look at the intersection relation and the concatenated primary key of this relation. As you know, each part of the primary key forms the foreign key. Notice the two one-to-many relationships and the corresponding tables showing attribute values. As discussed in the previous subsection on one-to-many relationship, the foreign keys in the intersection table, that is, either of the two parts of the primary key table, cannot be nulls. You may stipulate the constraints with the words "NOT NULL" in the Foreign Key statement for the intersection table. However, the two foreign keys are part of the primary key and because the primary key attribute cannot have nulls, the explicit stipulation of "NOT NULL" may be omitted.

Next, let us take up optional conditions on both sides. Suppose the cardinality indicators (0,*) are shown next to PROJECT and EMPLOYEE entity types. Then the indicators will represent the following condition:

An employee may be assigned to many projects.

A project may have many employees.

Not every employee need be assigned to a project. That is, some employee instances may not be associated with any project instance at all. At a minimum, an employee instance may be associated with no project instance or with zero project instances. In other words, not every employee instance needs to participate in the relationship. The relationship as far as the employee instances are concerned is optional.

Not every project needs to have an employee. That is, some project instances may not be associated with any employee instance at all. At a minimum, a project instance may be associated with no employee instance or with zero employee instances. In other words, not every project instance needs to participate in the relationship. The relationship as far as the project instances are concerned is optional.

It follows, therefore, that in an optional relationship of this sort, nulls may be allowed in the foreign key columns. However, in the way the transformation is represented in Figure 7-28, allowing nulls in foreign key columns would present a problem. You have noted the foreign key attributes form the primary key of the intersection relation, and no part of a primary key in a relation can have nulls according to the integrity rule for the relational model. Therefore, in such cases, you may adopt an alternate transformation approach by assigning a separate primary key as shown in Figure 7-29.

What do the rows with null foreign key attributes in the ASSIGNMENT relation represent? These rows represent those employees who are not assigned to a project or those projects that have no employees. In practice, you may want to include such rows in the relations to indicate employees already eligible for assignment but not officially assigned and to denote projects that usually have employees assigned but not yet ready for assignment.

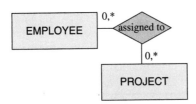

Relational notation

EMPLOYEE (EmpNo, EmpName, EmpAddr)

PROJECT (ProjID, ProjDesc, ProjStart)

ASSIGNMENT (AsmntNo, ProjID, EmpNo)
   Foreign keys: Projld REFERENCES PROJECT
      EmpNo REFERENCES EMPLOYEE

EMPLOYEE relation

EmpNo	EmpName	EmpAddr
123	Daniel R. Grady	Jamesburg, NJ 08810
234	Alice M. Knox	Iselin, NJ 08834
345	Matthew Rader	Edison, NJ 08817
456	Ramola Ruskin	Metuchen,NJ 08819

PROJECT relation

ProjID	ProjDesc	ProjStart
1	Requirements	2/15/2002
2	DB design	4/22/2002
3	DB implementation	8/31/2002
4	User training	8/1/2002
5	DB fine tuning	9/15/2002

ASSIGNMENT relation

AsmntNo	ProjID	EmpNo
10	1	123
11	1	234
12	1	345
13	2	345
14	3	123
15	4	234
16	4	345
17		456
18	5	

FIGURE 7-29   Many-to-many relationship: alternative approach.

Aggregate Objects as Relationships. Recall that in relationships, the participating entity types together form an aggregate entity type by virtue of the relationship itself. Let us discuss how such aggregate entity types are transformed into the components of a relational data model. Figure 7-30 illustrates such a transformation of an aggregate entity type ASSIGNMENT.

Notice the intersection relation and the attributes shown in this relation. These are the attributes of the aggregate entity type. You will note that the aggregate entity type becomes the intersection relation.

Identifying Relationship. While discussing conceptual data modeling, you studied identifying relationships. A weak entity type is one that depends on another entity type for its existence. A weak entity type is, in fact, identified by the other entity type. The relationship is, therefore, called an identifying relationship.

Figure 7-31 illustrates the transformation of an identifying relationship. Especially note the primary key attributes of the weak entity type.

Supersets and Subsets. While creating conceptual data models, you discover objects in the real world that are subsets of other objects. Some objects are specializations of other objects. On the other hand, you realize that individual entity types may be generalized in supertype entity types. Each subset of a superset forms a special relationship with its superset.

Figure 7-32 shows the transformation of a superset and its subsets. Notice how the primary key attribute and other attributes migrate from the superset relation to subset relations.

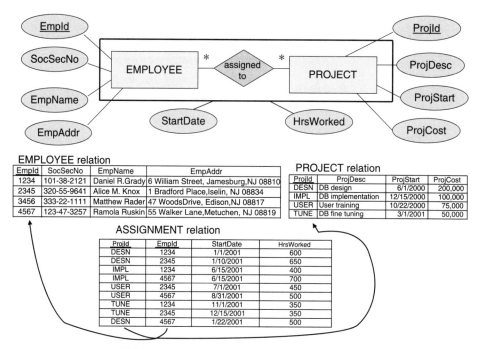

FIGURE 7-30 Transformation of aggregate entity type.

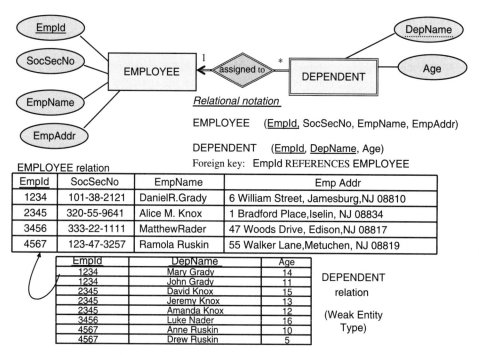

FIGURE 7-31 Transformation of identifying relationship.

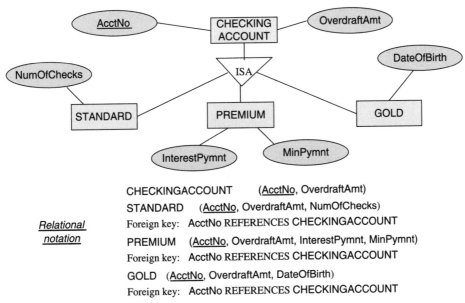

CHECKINGACCOUNT   (<u>AcctNo</u>, OverdraftAmt)

STANDARD   (<u>AcctNo</u>, OverdraftAmt, NumOfChecks)

Relational   Foreign key: AcctNo REFERENCES CHECKINGACCOUNT

notation   PREMIUM   (<u>AcctNo</u>, OverdraftAmt, InterestPymnt, MinPymnt)

Foreign key: AcctNo REFERENCES CHECKINGACCOUNT

GOLD   (<u>AcctNo</u>, OverdraftAmt, DateOfBirth)

Foreign key: AcctNo REFERENCES CHECKINGACCOUNT

FIGURE 7-32   Transformation of superset and subsets.

Transformation Summary

By now, you have a fairly good grasp of the principles of transformation of a conceptual data model into a relational data model. We took each component of the conceptual data model and reviewed how the component is transformed into a component in the relational model. Let us list the components of the conceptual data model and note how each component gets transformed.

Components of the conceptual data model and how they are transformed into relational data model:

Entity Type

STRONG

Transform into relation.

WEAK

Transform into relation. Include primary key of the identifying relation in the primary key of the relation representing the weak entity type.

Attribute

Transform into column.
Transform attribute name into column name.
Translate attribute domains into domains for corresponding columns.

SIMPLE, SINGLE-VALUED

Transform into a column of the corresponding relation.

COMPOSITE

COMPOSITE

Transform into columns of the corresponding relation with as many columns as the number of component attributes.

MULTIVALUED

Transform into a column of a separate relation.

DERIVED

Transform into a column of the corresponding relation.

Primary Key

SINGLE ATTRIBUTE

Transform into a single-column primary key.

COMPOSITE

Transform into a multicolumn primary key.

Relationship

ONE-TO-ONE

Establish relationship through a foreign key attribute in either of the two participating relations.

ONE-TO-MANY

Establish relationship through a foreign key attribute in the participating relation on the "many" side of the relationship.

MANY-TO-MANY

Transform by forming two one-to-many relationships with a new intersection relation in between the participating relations. Establish relationship through foreign key attributes in the intersection relation.

OPTIONAL AND MANDATORY CONDITIONS

Set constraint for the foreign key column. If nulls are not allowed in the foreign key column, it represents a mandatory relationship. Allowing nulls denotes an optional relationship. Mandatory and optional conditions apply only to the participation of the relation on the "many" side of a one-to-many relationship, that is, to the participation of rows in the relation that contains the foreign key column.

CHAPTER SUMMARY

- The relational model may be used as a logical data model. The relational model is a popular and widely used model that is superior to the earlier hierarchical and network models.
- The relational model rests on a solid mathematical foundation: it uses the concepts of matrix operations and set theory.
- The relation or two-dimensional table is the single modeling concept in the relational model.
- The columns of a relation or table denote the attributes and the rows represent the instances of an entity type.
- Relationships are established through foreign keys.
- Entity integrity, referential integrity, and functional dependency rules enforce data integrity in a relational model.
- There are two approaches to design from modeling: model transformation method and traditional normalization method.
- Model transformation method from conceptual to logical data model: entity types to relations, attributes to columns, identifiers to keys, relationships through foreign key columns.
- One-to-one and one-to-many relationships are transformed by introducing a foreign key column in the child relation.
- Many-to-many relationships are transformed by the introduction of another intersection relation.
- Optional and mandatory conditions in a relationship are indicated by allowing or disallowing nulls in foreign key columns of relations.

REVIEW QUESTIONS

1. Match the column entries:

   1. Relation tuples
   2. Foreign key
   3. Row uniqueness
   4. Entity integrity
   5. Model transformation
   6. Entity type
   7. Identifier
   8. Optional condition
   9. Multivalued attribute
   10. Relation columns

   A. Primary key
   B. Conceptual to logical
   C. Relation
   D. Column in separate relation
   E. Entity instances
   F. Primary key not null
   G. Order not important
   H. Establish logical link
   I. Nulls in foreign key
   J. No duplicate rows

2. Show an example to illustrate how mathematical set theory is used for data manipulation in the relational data model.

3. What is a mathematical relation? Explain how it is used in the relational model to represent an entity type.

4. Describe in detail how columns in a relation are used to represent attributes. Give examples.

5. Using an example, illustrate how foreign key columns are used to establish relationships in the relational data model.

6. Discuss the referential integrity rule in the relational model. Provide an example to explain the rule.

7. What are the two design approaches to create a logical data model? What are the circumstances under which you will prefer one to another?

8. Describe the features of the model transformation method.

9. Describe how many-to-many relationships are transformed into the relational model. Provide a comprehensive example.

10. Discuss the transformation of a one-to-one relationship. Indicate with an example where the foreign key column must be placed.

8

DATA NORMALIZATION

CHAPTER OBJECTIVES

- Study data normalization as an alternative approach to creating the relational model
- Scrutinize the approach for potential problems
- Learn how the methodology removes potential problems
- Establish the significance of step-by-step normalization tasks
- Provide in-depth coverage of the various systematic steps
- Note outcome at each systematic step
- Examine the fundamental normal forms in detail
- Review the higher normal forms

As you studied the model transformation method in the previous chapter, you might have wondered about the necessity of that method. You might have thought why you need to create a conceptual E-R data model first and then bother to transform that model into a relational data model. If you already know that your target database system is going to be a relational database system, why not create a relational data model directly from the information requirements? These are valid questions. Even though you learned the merits of the model transformation method, is it not a longer route for logical design?

In this chapter, we will pursue these thoughts. We will attempt to put together a relational data model from the information requirements. We will see what happens and whether the resultant model readily becomes a relational data model. If not, we will explore what should be done to make the initial outcome of this method become a good relational model.

Data Modeling Fundamentals. By Paulraj Ponniah
Copyright © 2007 John Wiley & Sons, Inc.

INFORMAL DESIGN

In a sense, this attempt of creating a relational model seems to be an informal design technique. Creating a conceptual data model first is a rigorous and systematic approach. On the other hand, if you want to create relational tables straight away, you seem to bypass standard and proven techniques. Therefore, first try to understand what exactly we mean by an informal design method.

Let us describe this method first. Then let us review the steps that can formalize this methodology. Although the attempt is to come up with relational tables in the initial attempt, you will note that the initial attempt does not always produce a good relational data model. Therefore, we need further specific steps to make the initial data model a true relational model.

As you know very well by now, a relational model consists of relations or two-dimensional tables with columns and rows. Because our desired outcome is a true relational data model, let us quickly review its fundamental properties:

- Relationships are established through foreign keys.
- Each row in a relation is unique.
- Each attribute value in each row is atomic or single-valued.
- The order of the columns in a relation is immaterial.
- The sequence of the rows in a relation is immaterial.
- Relations must conform to entity integrity and referential integrity rules.
- Each relation must conform to the functional dependency rule.

Forming Relations from Requirements

Thus, the attempt in this method is simply to come up with relations or tables from the information requirements. Figure 8-1 explains this seemingly informal approach in a simple manner.

Objectives:

- Create well-structured relations
- Avoid data redundancies
- Ensure that the data model conforms to relational rules
- Ensure data manipulation will not have problems or anomalies

Steps:

- Create random tables or relations
- Normalize the tables

FIGURE 8-1   Informal design of a relational data model.

Note the objectives of the method. When you create a relational data model using this method, you must come up with tables that conform to the relational rules and possess the right properties of a relational data model.

What are the steps to create a proper relational model? Create an initial data model by putting together a set of initial tables. Examine this initial set of tables and then apply procedures to make this initial set into a proper set of relational tables. As you will understand in the later sections, this application of procedures to rectify problems found in the initial set of tables is known as normalization.

Of course, an obvious question is why you should go through normalization procedures. Are you not able to produce a proper set of relational tables from information requirements in the initial attempt itself? Let us explore the reasons.

Potential Problems

Let us consider a very simple set of information requirements. Using these information requirements, we will attempt to create an initial relational data model and then examine the model. Creating an initial relational data model using this approach simply means coming up with an initial set of relational tables. Study the following statement of information requirements for which you need to create a relational data model:

Assignment of Employees to Projects

Employees work in departments. Information about the employees such as name, salary, position, and bonus amount must be represented in the data model. The model should include names of the departments and their managers. Project numbers and project descriptions are available. It is necessary to represent the start date, end date, and hours worked on a project for each employee. New employees are not assigned to a project before they finish training.

Examine the information requirements. Clearly, your data model must represent information about the employees and their project assignments. Also, some information about the departments must be included. Compared with other real-world information requirements, the information about employee–project assignments being modeled here is very simple. With this set of information requirements, you need to come up with two-dimensional tables. Let us say, you are able to put the data in the form of tables and also express the relationships within the tables. If you are able to do this, then you are proceeding toward creating the relational data model.

Looking at the simplicity of the information requirements, it appears that all the data can be put in just one table. Let us create that single table and inspect the data content. Figure 8-2 represents this single table showing sample data values.

Inspect the PROJECT-ASSIGNMENT table carefully. In order to uniquely identify each row, you have to assign EmpId and ProjNo together and designate the concatenation as the primary key. At first glance, you note that the table contains all the necessary data to completely represent the data content of the information requirements. The table contains columns and rows. Review each column. It represents an attribute, and the column name represents the name of the attribute. Now look at the rows. Each row represents one employee, a single instance of the entity represented by the table. So far, the table looks like it qualifies to be part the required relational data model.

PROJECT-ASSIGNMENT

EmpId	Name	Salary	Position	Bonus	DptNo	DeptName	Manager	ProjNo	ProjDesc	ChrgCD	Start	End	Hrs
100	Simpson	35000	Analyst	5000	3	Design	Ross	23	DB design	D100	Apr-02	Jul-02	200
140	Beeton	28000	Technician	3000	2	Operations	Martin	14	Network cabling	N140	Sep-02	Oct-02	120
160	Davis	30000	Technician	3000	4	Tech Suprt	Lucero	14	Network cabling	S160	Sep-02	Nov-02	150
								36	Network testing	S160	Nov-02	Dec-02	100
190	Berger	45000	DBA	6000	1	DB Suprt	Rawlins	45	Physical design	D190	Aug-02	Nov-02	300
								48	Space allocation	S190	Nov-02	Dec-02	80
100	Simpson	35000	Analyst	5000	3	Design	Ross	25	Reports	C100	Oct-02	Nov-02	100
110	Covino	34000	Analyst	5000	5	Analysis	Williams	31	Forms	D110	Mar-02	May-02	120
								25	Reports	D110	May-02	Jul-02	150
120	Brown	35000	Analyst	5000	5	Analysis	Williams	11	Order entry	D120	Jul-02	Sep-02	300
180	Smith	30000	Programmer	4000	6	Programming	Goldner	31	Forms	C180	Sep-02	Nov-02	250
								25	Reports	C180	Nov-02	Dec-02	200
200	Rogers	32000	Programmer	4000	6	Programming	Goldner	11	Order entry	D200	Sep-02	Oct-02	200
								12	Inventory Control	P200	Oct-02	Dec-02	200
								13	Invoicing	P200	Nov-02	Dec-02	100
100	Simpson	35000	Analyst	5000	3	Design	Ross	31	Forms	D100	Aug-02	Oct-02	150
130	Clemens	38000	Analyst	5000	3	Design	Ross	23	DB design	D130	Apr-02	Jun-02	200

FIGURE 8-2   Table created from information requirements.

Before proceeding further, let us have a brief explanation about the column named ChrgCD. When an employee is assigned to a project, a charge code is given for that assignment. The charge code depends on the type of work done by the employee in that assignment irrespective of his or her position or title. For example, when Simpson, an analyst, does design work in a project, a charge code of D100 is given for that assignment; when he does coding work in another project, a charge code of C100 is given for this assignment. Charge codes indicate the type of work done by an employee in the various projects.

Next, observe the projects for Davis, Berger, Covino, Smith, and Rogers. Each of the employees has been assigned to multiple projects. The resulting relational database must contain information about these multiple assignments. However, looking at the rows for these employees, these rows contain multiple values for some attributes. In other words, not all values in certain columns are atomic or single-valued. This is a violation of the attribute atomicity requirement in a relational data model. Therefore, the random PROJECT-ASSIGNMENT table we created quickly cannot be part of true relational data model.

Let us now examine the table further and see how it will hold up when we try to manipulate the data contents. As indicated in Figure 8-1, a proper relational data model must avoid data redundancies and also ensure that data manipulation will not cause problems. When we attempt to use the data model for data manipulation, you will find that we run into three types of problems or anomalies as noted below:

Update anomaly: occurs while updating values of attributes in the database.

Deletion anomaly: occurs while deleting rows from a relation.

Addition anomaly: occurs while adding (inserting) new rows in a relation.

We will discuss these anomalies in the next subsections. Try to understand the nature of these problems and how our PROJECT-ASSIGNMENT table has such problems and, therefore, cannot be correct. Unless we remove these anomalies, our table cannot be part of a true relational model.

Update Anomaly

If a relational two-dimensional table does not conform to relational rules, you find that problems arise when you try to do updates to data in a database based on such a table. Our data model at this point consists of the randomly created PROJECT-ASSIGNMENT table. Let us try to do an update to the data in the PROJECT-ASSIGNMENT table and see what happens.

After the database is populated, users find that the name "Simpson" is recorded incorrectly and that it should be changed to the correct name "Samson." How is the correction accomplished? The correction will have to be made wherever the name "Simpson" exists in the database. Now look at the example of data content shown in Figure 8-2.

Even in this extremely limited set of rows in the table, you have to make the correction in three rows. Imagine a database of 500 or 5000 employees. Even this is not a large database. It is not unusual to store data about many thousands of employees in a typical database. Now go back to the correction. In a large database covering a large number of rows for employees, the number of rows for PROJECT-ASSIGNMENT is expected to be many. Therefore, it is very likely that when you make the correction to the name, you will miss some rows that need to be changed. So, what is the effect of update anomaly in this case?

Update Anomaly

Results in data inconsistency because of possible partial update instead of the proper complete update.

Deletion Anomaly

Again, if the relational two-dimensional table does not conform to relational rules, you find that problems arise when you try to delete rows from a database based on such a table. Let us try to delete some data from the PROJECT-ASSIGNMENT table and see what happens.

Here is the situation. Employee Beeton leaves your organization. Therefore, it is no longer necessary to keep any information about Beeton in your database. You are authorized to delete all data about Beeton from the database. Now inspect the sample database contents shown in Figure 8-2.

How is the deletion of data about Beeton carried out? Luckily, you have to delete just one row, namely the second row in the PROJECT-ASSIGNMENT table, to get rid of all data about Beeton in the database. Now, consider another aspect of this operation. What happens when you delete this row? Data such as Beeton's EmpId, Name, Salary, Position, and his project assignment gets deleted. This is fine because this is what you intended to do.

Now examine the row as shown in the figure. When you delete this row, you not only remove data about Beeton, but you also delete data about Department 2. And by looking at the entire contents of the table, you notice that this is the only row that has information about Department 2. By deleting this row, you also delete data about Department 2 from the database. However, this is not your intention. Data about Department 2 has to be preserved in the database for possible future uses. But, if you delete the second row, unintentionally, data about Department 2 is also lost. Let us express the effect of deletion anomaly.

Deletion Anomaly

Results in unintended loss of data because of possible deletion of data other than what must be deleted.

Addition Anomaly

We have considered the effects of updates and deletions in a two-dimensional table that is put together in a random fashion from information requirements. You have noted that these operations cause anomalies or problems. Now, let us try to perform one more common data operation on this table. Try to add new data to the database.

This is the situation. A new employee Potter has joined your organization. As usual, the human resources department has already assigned a unique EmpId to Potter. So you need to add data about Potter to the database. However, Potter is still in training and, therefore, is not assigned to a project yet. You have data about Potter such as his salary, bonus, and the department in which he is hired. You can add all of this data to the database.

Begin to create a row for Potter in the database. You are ready to create a row in our PROJECT-ASSIGNMENT table for Potter. You can enter the name, department, and so on. But what about the unique primary key for this row? As you know, the primary key for this table consists of EmpId and ProjNo together. But you are unable to assign a value for ProjNo for this row because he is not assigned to a project yet. So, you can have null value for ProjNo until Potter is assigned to a project. But, can you really do this? If you place a null value in the ProjNo column, you will be violating the entity integrity rule that states no part of the primary key may be null. You are faced with a problem—an anomaly concerning added new data. Data about Potter cannot be added to the database until he is assigned to a project. Even though he is already an employee, data about Potter will be missing in the database until then. This is the effect of addition anomaly.

Addition Anomaly

Results in inability to add data to the database because of the absence of some data currently unavailable.

NORMALIZATION METHODOLOGY

Let us review our discussion so far. We inspected the information requirements about employees, departments, projects, and project assignments. Our intention was to create a relational data model directly from the study of the information requirements. This meant creating a data model consisting of two-dimensional tables or relations that normally make up a relational data model. Because of the simplicity of the information requirements, we were able to represent all the data in a single random table. So far, this is the relational data model for us. If it has to be a good relational model, it must conform to relational rules.

You have observed that the random table PROJECT-ASSIGNMENT violates some relational rules at the outset. More importantly, when you attempt to update data, delete data, or add data, our initial data model has serious problems. You have noted the problems of update, deletion, and addition anomalies. So, what is next step? Do you simply abandon the initial data model and look for other methods? Your goal is to create a good relational model even while you attempt to do this directly from information requirements.

It turns out that by adopting a systematic methodology you can, indeed, regularize the initial data model created in the first attempt. This methodology is based on Dr. Codd's approach to normalizing the initial tables created in a random manner directly from information requirements.

Strengths of the Method

Normalization methodology resolves the three types of anomalies encountered when data manipulation operations are performed on a database based on an improper relational data model. Therefore, after applying the principles of normalization to the initial data model, the three types of anomalies will get eliminated.

This method

- Creates well-structured relations
- Removes data redundancies
- Ensures that the initial data model is properly transformed into a relational data model conforming to relational rules
- Guarantees that data manipulation will not have anomalies or problems

Application of the Method

As mentioned, this normalization process is a step-by-step approach. It does not take place in one large activity. The process breaks down the problem and applies remedies by performing one task at a time. The initial data model is refined and standardized in a clear and systematic manner, one step at a time.

At each step, the methodology consists of examining the data model, removing one type of problem, and changing it to a better normal form. You take the initial data model created directly from information requirements in a random fashion. This initial model, at best, consists of two-dimensional tables representing the entire data content. Nothing more and nothing less. As we have seen, such an initial data model is subject to data manipulation problems.

You apply the principles of the first step. In this step, you are examining the initial data model for only one type of nonconformance and seek to remove one type of irregularity. Once this one type of irregularity is resolved, your data model becomes better and is rendered into a first normal form of table structures. Then you look for another type of irregularity in the second step and remove this type from the resulting data model from the previous step. After this next step, your data model becomes still better and becomes a data model in the second normal form. The process continues through a reasonable number of steps until the resulting data model becomes truly relational.

Normalization Steps

The first few steps of the normalization methodology transform the initial data model into a workable relational data model that is free from the common types of irregularities. These first steps produce the normal forms of relations that are fundamental to creating a good relational data model. After these initial steps, in some cases, further irregularities still exist. When you remove the additional irregularities, the resulting relations become higher normal form relations.

In practice, only a few initial data models need to go through all the above steps. Generally, a set of third normal form relations will form a good relational data model. You may want to go one step further to make it a set of Boyce–Codd normal form relations. Only very infrequently would you need to go to higher normal forms.

FUNDAMENTAL NORMAL FORMS

As explained earlier, normalization is a process of rectifying potential problems in two-dimensional tables created at random. This process is a step-by-step method, each step addressing one specific type of potential problem and remedying that type of problem. As we proceed with the normalization process, you will clearly understand how this step-by-step approach works so well. By taking a step-by-step approach, you will not over-look any type of anomaly. And, when the process is completed, you will have resolved every type of potential problem.

By the last subsection here, you will note that the first four steps that make up this portion of the normalization process transform the initial data model into the fundamental normal forms. After the third step, the initial data model becomes a third normal form rela-tional data model. As already mentioned, for most practical purposes, a third normal form data model is an adequate relational data model. You need not go further. Occasionally, you may have to proceed to the fourth step and refine the data model further and make it a Boyce–Codd normal form.

First Normal Form

Refer back to Figure 8-2 showing the PROJECT-ASSIGNMENT relation created as the initial data model. You had already observed that the rows for Davis, Berger, Covino, Smith, and Rogers contain multiple values for attributes in six different columns. You know that this violates the rule for a relational model that states each row must have atomic values for each of the attributes.

This step in the normalization process addresses the problem of repeating groups of attribute values for single rows. If a relation has such repeating groups, we say that the relation is not in the first normal form. The objective of this step is to transform the data model into a model in the first normal form.

Here is what must be done to make this transformation.

Transformation to First Normal Form (1NF)

Remove repeating groups of attributes and create rows without repeating groups.

Figure 8-3 shows the result of the transformation to first normal form.

Carefully inspect the PROJECT-ASSIGNMENT table shown in the figure. Each row has a set of single values in the columns. The composite primary key consisting of EmpId and ProjNo uniquely identifies each row. No single row has multiple values for any of its attributes. The result of this step has rectified the problem of multiple values for the same attribute in a single row.

Let us examine whether the transformation step has rectified the other types of update, deletion, and addition anomalies encountered before the model was transformed into first

PROJECT-ASSIGNMENT

EmpId	Name	Salary	Position	Bonus	DptNo	DeptName	Manager	ProjNo	ProjDesc	ChrgCD	Start	End	Hrs
100	Simpson	35000	Analyst	5000	3	Design	Ross	23	DB design	D100	Apr-02	Jul-02	200
140	Beeton	28000	Technician	3000	2	Operations	Martin	14	Network cabling	N140	Sep-02	Oct-02	120
160	Davis	30000	Technician	3000	4	Tech Suprt	Lucero	14	Network cabling	S160	Sep-02	Nov-02	150
160	Davis	30000	Technician	3000	4	Tech Suprt	Lucero	36	Network testing	S160	Nov-02	Dec-02	100
190	Berger	45000	DBA	6000	1	DB Suprt	Rawlins	45	Physical design	D190	Aug-02	Nov-02	300
190	Berger	45000	DBA	6000	1	DB Suprt	Rawlins	48	Space allocation	S190	Nov-02	Dec-02	80
100	Simpson	35000	Analyst	5000	3	Design	Ross	25	Reports	C100	Oct-02	Nov-02	100
110	Covino	34000	Analyst	5000	5	Analysis	Williams	31	Forms	D110	Mar-02	May-02	120
110	Covino	34000	Analyst	5000	5	Analysis	Williams	25	Reports	D110	May-02	Jul-02	150
120	Brown	35000	Analyst	5000	5	Analysis	Williams	11	Order entry	D120	Jul-02	Sep-02	300
180	Smith	30000	Programmer	4000	6	Programming	Goldner	31	Forms	C180	Sep-02	Nov-02	250
180	Smith	30000	Programmer	4000	6	Programming	Goldner	25	Reports	C180	Nov-02	Dec-02	200
200	Rogers	32000	Programmer	4000	6	Programming	Goldner	11	Order entry	D200	Sep-02	Oct-02	200
200	Rogers	32000	Programmer	4000	6	Programming	Goldner	12	Inventory Control	P200	Oct-02	Dec-02	200
200	Rogers	32000	Programmer	4000	6	Programming	Goldner	13	Invoicing	P200	Nov-02	Dec-02	100
100	Simpson	35000	Analyst	5000	3	Design	Ross	31	Forms	D100	Aug-02	Oct-02	150
130	Clemens	38000	Analyst	5000	3	Design	Ross	23	DB design	D130	Apr-02	Jun-02	200

FIGURE 8-3   Data model in first normal form.

normal form. Compare the PROJECT-ASSIGNMENT table shown in Figure 8-3 with the earlier version in Figure 8-2. Apply the tests to the transformed version of the relation contained in Figure 8-3.

Update: Correction of Name "Simpson" to "Samson"

The correction has to be made in multiple rows. Update anomaly still persists.

Deletion: Deletion of Data About Beeton

This deletion will unintentionally delete data about Department 2. Deletion anomaly still persists.

Addition: Addition of Data About New Employee Potter

Cannot add new employee Potter to the database until he is assigned to a project. Addition anomaly still persists.

So, you note that although this step has resolved the problem of multivalued attributes, still data manipulation problems remain. Nevertheless, this step has removed a major deficiency from the initial data model. We have to proceed to the next steps and examine the effect of data manipulation operations.

Second Normal Form

Recall the discussion on functional dependencies covering the properties and rules of the relational data model. If the value of one attribute determines the value of a second attribute in a relation, we say that the second attribute is functionally dependent on the first attribute. The discussion on functional dependencies in Chapter 7 concluded with a functional dependency rule.

Let us repeat the functional dependency rule:

Each data item in a tuple of a relation is uniquely and functionally determined by the primary key, by the whole primary key, and only by the primary key.

Examine the dependencies of data items in the PROJECT-ASSIGNMENT table in Figure 8-3. You know that this table is in the first normal form, having gone through the process of removing repeating groups of attributes. Let us inspect the dependency of each attribute on the whole primary consisting of EmpId and ProjNo. Only each of the following attributes depends on the whole primary key: ChrgCD, Start, End, and Hrs. The remaining non-key attributes do not appear to be functionally dependent on the whole primary key. They seem to be functionally dependent on one or the other part of the primary key.

This step in the normalization process specifically deals with this type of problem. Once this type of problem is resolved, the data model becomes transformed to a data model in the second normal form.

In other words, the condition for a second normal form data model is as follows:

If a data model is in the second normal form, no non-key attributes may be dependent on part of the primary key.

Therefore, if there are partial key dependencies in a data model, this step resolves this type of dependencies.

Here is what must be done to make this transformation.

Transformation to Second Normal Form (2NF)

Remove partial key dependencies.

If you look at the other attributes in the PROJECT-ASSIGNMENT table in Figure 8-3, you will note that the following attributes depend on just EmpId, a part of the primary key: Name, Salary, Position, Bonus, DptNo, DeptName, and Manager. The attribute ProjDesc depends on ProjNo, another part of the primary key. These are partial key dependencies. This step resolves partial key dependencies. Now look at Figure 8-4, which shows the resolution of partial key dependencies. The tables shown in this figure are in the second normal form.

Notice how the resolution is done. The original table has been decomposed into three separate tables. In each table, in order to make sure that each row is unique, duplicate rows are eliminated. For example, multiple duplicate rows for employee Simpson have been replaced by a single row in EMPLOYEE table.

Decomposition is an underlying technique for normalization. If you carefully go through each of the three tables, you will be satisfied that none of these have any partial key dependencies. Thus, this step has rectified the problem of partial key dependencies. But what about the types of anomalies encountered during data manipulation?

Let us examine whether the transformation step has rectified the types of update, deletion, and addition anomalies encountered before the model was transformed into second

PROJECT

ProjNo	ProjDesc
23	DB design
14	Network cabling
36	Network testing
45	Physical design
48	Space allocation
25	Reports
31	Forms
11	Order entry
12	Inventory Control
13	Invoicing

EMPLOYEE-PROJECT

EmpId	ProjNo	ChrgCD	Start	End	Hrs
100	23	D100	Apr-02	Jul-02	200
140	14	N140	Sep-02	Oct-02	120
160	14	S160	Sep-02	Nov-02	150
160	36	S160	Nov-02	Dec-02	100
190	45	D190	Aug-02	Nov-02	300
190	48	S190	Nov-02	Dec-02	80
100	25	C100	Oct-02	Nov-02	100
110	31	D110	Mar-02	May-02	120
110	25	D110	May-02	Jul-02	150
120	11	D120	Jul-02	Sep-02	300
180	31	C180	Sep-02	Nov-02	250
180	25	C180	Nov-02	Dec-02	200
200	11	D200	Sep-02	Oct-02	200
200	12	P200	Nov-02	Dec-02	200
200	13	P200	Nov-02	Dec-02	100
100	31	D100	Aug-02	Oct-02	150
130	23	D130	Apr-02	Jun-02	200

EMPLOYEE

EmpId	Name	Salary	Position	Bonus	DptN0	DeptName	Manager
100	Simpson	35000	Analyst	5000	3	Design	Ross
140	Beeton	28000	Technician	3000	2	Operations	Martin
160	Davis	30000	Technician	3000	4	Tech Suprt	Lucero
190	Berger	45000	DBA	6000	1	DB Suprt	Rawlins
110	Covino	34000	Analyst	5000	5	Analysis	Williams
120	Brown	35000	Analyst	5000	5	Analysis	Williams
180	Smith	30000	Programmer	4000	6	Programming	Goldner
200	Rogers	32000	Programmer	4000	6	Programming	Goldner
130	Clemens	38000	Analyst	5000	3	Design	Ross

FIGURE 8-4 Data model in second normal form.

normal form. Compare the relations shown in Figure 8-4 to the previous version in Figure 8-3. Apply the tests to the transformed version of the tables contained in Figure 8-4.

Update: Correction of Name "Simpson" to "Samson"

The correction has to be made only in one row in the EMPLOYEE table. The update anomaly has disappeared.

Deletion: Deletion of Data About Beeton

This deletion will unintentionally delete data about Department 2. The deletion anomaly still persists.

Addition: Addition of Data About New Employee Potter

You can now add new employee Potter to the database in the EMPLOYEE table. The addition anomaly has disappeared.

So, you note that although this step has resolved the problem of partial key dependencies, still some data manipulation problems remain. Nevertheless, this step has removed a major deficiency from the data model. We have to proceed to the next steps and examine the effect of data manipulation operations.

Third Normal Form

After transformation to the second normal form, you note that a particular type of functional dependency is removed from the preliminary data model and that the data model is closer to becoming a correct and true relational data model. In the previous step, we have removed partial key dependencies. Let us examine the resulting data model to see if any more irregular functional dependencies still exist. Remember the goal is to make each table in the data model in a form where each data item in a tuple is functionally dependent only on the full primary key and nothing but the full primary key.

Refer to the three tables shown in Figure 8-4. Let us inspect these tables, one by one. The attribute ProjDesc functionally depends on the primary key ProjNo. So, this table PROJECT is correct. Next, look at the table EMPLOYEE-PROJECT. In this table, each of the attributes ChrgCD, Start, End, and Hrs depends on full primary key EmpId, ProjNo.

Now examine the table EMPLOYEE carefully. What about the attributes Position and Bonus? Bonus depends on the position. Bonus for an Analyst is different from that for a Technician. Therefore, in that table, the attribute Bonus is functionally dependent on another attribute Position, not on the primary key. Look further. How about the attributes DeptName and Manager? Do they depend on the primary key EmpId? Not really. These two attributes functionally depend on another attribute in the table, namely, DptNo.

So, what is the conclusion from your observation? In the table EMPLOYEE, only the two attributes Name and Salary depend on the primary key EmpId. The other attributes do not depend on the primary key. Bonus depends on Position; DeptName and Manager depend on DptNo.

This step in the normalization process deals with this type of problem. Once this type of problem is resolved, the data model is transformed to a data model in the third normal form.

In other words, the condition for a third normal form data model is as follows:

If a data model is in the third normal form, no non–key attributes may be dependent on another non–key attribute.

In the table EMPLOYEE, dependency of the attribute DeptName on the primary key EmpId is not direct. The dependency is passed over to the primary key through another non–key attribute, DptNo. This passing over of the dependency means that the dependency on the primary key is a transitive dependency—passed over through another non–key attribute, DptNo. Therefore, this type of problematic dependency is also called a transitive dependency in a relation. If there are transitive dependencies in a data model, this step resolves this type of dependency.

Here is what must be done to make this transformation.

Transformation to Third Normal Form (3NF)

Remove transitive dependencies.

Figure 8-5 shows the resolution of transitive dependencies. The tables shown in the figure are all in the third normal form.

Notice how the resolution is done. EMPLOYEE table is further decomposed into two additional tables POSITION and DEPARTMENT. In each table, in order to ensure that each row is unique, duplicate rows are eliminated. For example, multiple duplicate rows for position Analyst in EMPLOYEE table have been replaced by a single row in POSITION table.

Again, you have already noted, decomposition is a basic technique for normalization. If you carefully go through each of the tables, you will be satisfied that none of these have

EMPLOYEE

Empld	Name	Salary	Posnld	DptNo
100	Simpson	35000	ANLY	3
140	Beeton	28000	TECH	2
160	Davis	30000	TECH	4
190	Berger	45000	DBAM	1
110	Covino	34000	ANLY	5
120	Brown	35000	ANLY	5
180	Smith	30000	PGMR	6
200	Rogers	32000	PGMR	6
130	Clemens	38000	ANLY	3

EMPLOYEE-PROJECT

Empld	ProjNo	ChrgCD	Start	End	Hrs
100	23	D100	Apr-02	Jul-02	200
140	14	N140	Sep-02	Oct-02	120
160	14	S160	Sep-02	Nov-02	150
160	36	S160	Nov-02	Dec-02	100
190	45	D190	Aug-02	Nov-02	300
190	48	S190	Nov-02	Dec-02	80
100	25	C100	Oct-02	Nov-02	100
110	31	D110	Mar-02	May-02	120
110	25	D110	May-02	Jul-02	150
120	11	D120	Jul-02	Sep-02	300
180	31	C180	Sep-02	Nov-02	250
180	25	C180	Nov-02	Dec-02	200
200	11	D200	Sep-02	Oct-02	200
200	12	P200	Nov-02	Dec-02	200
200	13	P200	Nov-02	Dec-02	100
100	31	D100	Aug-02	Oct-02	150
130	23	D130	Apr-02	Jun-02	200

PROJECT

ProjNo	ProjDesc
23	DB design
14	Network cabling
36	Network testing
45	Physical design
48	Space allocation
25	Reports
31	Forms
11	Order entry
12	Inventory Control
13	Invoicing

DEPARTMENT

DptNo	DeptName	Manager
3	Design	Ross
2	Operations	Martin
4	Tech Suprt	Lucero
1	DB Suprt	Rawlins
5	Analysis	Williams
6	Programming	Goldner

POSITION

Posnld	Position	Bonus
ANLY	Analyst	5000
TECH	Technician	3000
DBAM	DBA	6000
PGMR	Programmer	4000

FIGURE 8-5 Data model in third normal form.

any transitive dependencies—one non–key attribute depending on some other non–key attribute. So, this step has rectified the problem of transitive dependencies. But what about the types of anomalies encountered during data manipulation?

Let us examine whether the transformation step has rectified the other types of update, deletion, and addition anomalies encountered before the model was transformed into first normal form. Compare the tables shown in Figure 8-5 with the previous version in Figure 8-4. Apply the tests to the transformed version of the model contained in Figure 8-5.

Update: Correction of Name "Simpson" to "Samson"

The correction has to be made only in one row in the EMPLOYEE table. The update anomaly has disappeared.

Deletion: Deletion of Data About Beeton

Removal of Beeton and his assignments from the EMPLOYEE and EMPLOYEE-PROJECT tables does not affect the data about Department 2 in the DEPARTMENT table. The deletion anomaly has disappeared from the data model.

Addition: Addition of Data About New Employee Potter

You can now add new employee Potter to the database in the EMPLOYEE table. The addition anomaly has disappeared.

So, you note that this step has resolved the problem of transitive dependencies and the data manipulation problems, at least the ones we have considered. Before we declare that the resultant data model is free from all types of data dependency problems, let us examine the model one more time.

Boyce–Codd Normal Form

Consider the EMPLOYEE-PROJECT table in Figure 8-5. Think about the ChrgCD attribute. A particular charge code indicates the specific employee's role in an assignment. Also, each project may be associated with several charge codes depending on the employees and their roles in the project. The charge code is not for the project assignment. The attribute ChrgCD does not depend on the full primary key nor on a partial primary key. The dependency is the other way around.

In the EMPLOYEE-PROJECT table, EmpId depends on ChrgCD and not the other way around. Notice how this is different from partial key dependency. Here a partial key attribute is dependent on a non–key attribute. This kind of dependency also violates the functional dependency rule for the relational data model.

This step in the normalization process deals with this type of problem. Once this type of problem is resolved, the data model is transformed to a data model in the Boyce–Codd normal form (BCNF).

In other words, the condition for a Boyce–Codd normal form data model is as follows:

If a data model is in the Boyce–Codd normal form, no partial key attribute may be dependent on another non–key attribute.

Here is what must be done to make this transformation.

EMPLOYEE

EmpId	Name	Salary	PosnId	DptNo
100	Simpson	35000	ANLY	3
140	Beeton	28000	TECH	2
160	Davis	30000	TECH	4
190	Berger	45000	DBAM	1
110	Covino	34000	ANLY	5
120	Brown	35000	ANLY	5
180	Smith	30000	PGMR	6
200	Rogers	32000	PGMR	6
130	Clemens	38000	ANLY	3

PROJECT

ProjNo	ProjDesc
23	DB design
14	Network cabling
36	Network testing
45	Physical design
48	Space allocation
25	Reports
31	Forms
11	Order entry
12	Inventory Control
13	Invoicing

DEPARTMENT

DptNo	DeptName	Manager
3	Design	Ross
2	Operations	Martin
4	Tech Suprt	Lucero
1	DB Suprt	Rawlins
5	Analysis	Williams
6	Programming	Goldner

POSITION

PosnId	Position	Bonus
ANLY	Analyst	5000
TECH	Technician	3000
DBAM	DBA	6000
PGMR	Programmer	4000

FIGURE 8-6 Data model in Boyce–Codd normal form, part 1.

EMPLOYEE-PROJECT

EmpId	ProjNo	Start	End	Hrs
100	23	Apr-02	Jul-02	200
140	14	Sep-02	Oct-02	120
160	14	Sep-02	Nov-02	150
160	36	Nov-02	Dec-02	100
190	45	Aug-02	Nov-02	300
190	48	Nov-02	Dec-02	80
100	25	Oct-02	Nov-02	100
110	31	Mar-02	May-02	120
110	25	May-02	Jul-02	150
120	11	Jul-02	Sep-02	300
180	31	Sep-02	Nov-02	250
180	25	Nov-02	Dec-02	200
200	11	Sep-02	Oct-02	200
200	12	Nov-02	Dec-02	200
200	13	Nov-02	Dec-02	200
100	31	Aug-02	Oct-02	150
130	23	Apr-02	Jun-02	200

CHRG-EMP

ChrgCD	EmpId
C100	100
C180	180
D100	100
D110	110
D120	120
D130	130
D190	190
D200	200
N140	140
P200	200
S160	160
S190	190

PROJ-CHRG

ProjNo	ChrgCD
23	D100
14	N140
14	S160
36	S160
45	D190
48	S190
25	C100
31	D110
25	D110
11	D120
31	C180
25	C180
11	D200
12	P200
13	P200
31	D100
23	D130

FIGURE 8-7 Data model in Boyce–Codd normal form, part 2.

Transformation to Boyce-Codd Normal Form (BCNF)

Remove anomalies from dependencies of key components.

Figures 8-6 and 8-7 show the resolution of the remaining dependencies. The tables shown in both the figures together are all in the Boyce–Codd normal form.

Notice how the resolution is done. EMPLOYEE-PROJECT table is decomposed into two additional tables CHRG-EMP and PROJ-CHRG. Notice that duplicate rows are eliminated while forming the additional tables.

Again, notice decomposition as a basic technique for normalization. The final set of tables in Figures 8-6 and 8-7 is free from all types of problems resulting from invalid functional dependencies. The resulting model is a workable relational model. We may, therefore, refer to the tables in the final set as relations; that is, tables conforming to relational rules.

HIGHER NORMAL FORMS

Once you transform an initial data model into a data model conforming to the principles of the fundamental normal forms, most of the discrepancies get removed. For all practical purposes, your resultant data model is a good relational data model. It will satisfy all the primary constraints of a relational data model. The major problems with functional dependencies get resolved.

We want to examine the resultant data model further and check whether any other types of discrepancies are likely to be present. Occasionally, you may have to take additional steps and go to higher normal forms. Let us consider the nature of higher normal forms and study the remedies necessary to reach these higher normal forms.

Fourth Normal Form

Before we discuss the fourth normal form for a data model, we need to define the concept of multivalued dependencies. Consider the following assumptions about the responsibilities and participation of company executives:

- Each executive may have direct responsibility for several departments.
- Each executive may be a member of several management committees.
- The departments and committees related to a particular executive are independent of each other.

Figure 8-8 contains data in the form of an initial data model to illustrate these assumptions. The first part of the figure shows the basic table and the second part the transformed relation.

Note that for each value of Executive attribute, there are multiple values for Department attribute, and multiple values for Committee attribute. Note also that the values of Department attribute for an executive are independent of the values of Committee attribute. This type of dependency is known as multivalued dependency. A multivalued dependency exists in a relation consisting of at least three attributes A, B, and C, such that for each value of A, there is a defined set of values for B, and another defined set of values for C, and further, the set of values for B is independent of the set of values for C.

Now observe the relation shown in the second part of Figure 8-8. Because the relation indicating the relationship between the attributes just contains the primary key, the relation is even in the Boyce–Codd normal form. However, by going through the rows of this relation, you can easily see that the three types of anomalies—update, deletion, and addition—are present in the relation.

This step in the normalization process deals with this type of problem. Once this type of problem is resolved, the data model is transformed to a data model in the fourth normal form.

Initial table

Executive	Department	Committee
Jones	Administration	Planning
	Finance	Technology
	Info. Technology	
Cooper	Marketing	R & D
	Personnel	Recruitment
	Production	

Initial relation

Executive	Department	Committee
Jones	Administration	Planning
Jones	Finance	Planning
Jones	Info. Technology	Planning
Jones	Administration	Technology
Jones	Finance	Planning
Jones	Info. Technology	Planning
Cooper	Marketing	R & D
Cooper	Personnel	R & D
Cooper	Production	R & D
Cooper	Marketing	Recruitment
Cooper	Personnel	Recruitment
Cooper	Production	Recruitment

FIGURE 8-8   Multivalued dependencies.

RESPONSIBILITY

Executive	Department
Jones	Administration
Jones	Finance
Jones	Info. Technology
Cooper	Marketing
Cooper	Personnel
Cooper	Production

MEMBERSHIP

Executive	Committee
Jones	Planning
Jones	Technology
Cooper	R & D
Cooper	Recruitment

FIGURE 8-9   Data model in fourth normal form.

In other words, the condition for a fourth normal form data model is as follows:

If a data model is in the fourth normal form, no multivalued dependencies exist.

Here is what must be done to make this transformation.

Transformation to Fourth Normal Form (4NF)

Remove multivalued dependencies.

Figure 8-9 shows the resolution of the multivalued dependencies. The two relations are in the fourth normal form.

When you examine the two relations in Figure 8-9, you can easily establish that these relations are free from update, deletion, or addition anomalies.

Fifth Normal Form

When you transform a data model into second, third, and Boyce–Codd normal forms, you are able to remove anomalies resulting from functional dependencies. After going through the steps and arriving at a data model in the Boyce–Codd normal form, the data model is free from functional dependencies. When you proceed further and transform the data model into fourth normal form relations, you are able to remove anomalies resulting from multivalued dependencies.

A further step transforming the data model into fifth normal form removes anomalies arising from what are known as join dependencies. What is the definition of join dependency? Go back and look at the figures showing the steps for the earlier normal forms. In each transformation step, the original relation is decomposed into smaller relations. When you inspect the smaller relations, you note that the original relation may be reconstructed from the decomposed smaller relations. However, if a relation has join dependencies, even if we are able to decompose the relation into smaller relations, it will not be possible to put the decomposed relations together and re-create the original relation. The smaller relations cannot be joined together to come up with the original relation. The original relation is important because that relation was obtained directly from information requirements. Therefore, in whatever ways you may decompose the original relation to normalize it, you should be able to go back to the original relation from the decomposed ones.

Figure 8-10 shows a relation that has join dependency. Note the columns in the relation shown in the figure.

BUILDING-MATERIAL-SUPPLIER

BuildingID	Material	SupplierNo
B45	Sheet Rock	S67
B45	Ceiling Paint	S72
B51	Sheet Rock	S72
B51	Shower Stall	S67
B93	Ceiling Paint	S75

FIGURE 8-10   Relation with join dependency.

This relation describes the materials supplied by suppliers to various buildings that are being constructed. Building B45 gets sheet rock from supplier S67 and ceiling paint from supplier S72. Suppose you have a constraint that suppliers may supply only certain materials to specific buildings even though a supplier may be able to supply all materials. In this example, supplier S72 can supply sheet rock to building B45, but to this building B45, only supplier S67 is designated to supply sheet rock. This constraint imposes a join dependency on the relation. However, the way the relation is composed, it does impose the join dependency constraint. For example, there is no restriction to adding a row (B45, Sheet Rock, S72). Such a row would violate the join constraint and not be a true representation of the information requirements.

This step in the normalization process deals with this type of problem. Once this type of problem is resolved, the data model is transformed to a data model in fifth normal form.

In other words, the condition for a fifth normal form data model is as follows:

If a data model is in the fifth normal form, no join dependencies exist.

Here is what must be done to make this transformation.

Transformation to Fifth Normal Form (5NF)

Remove join dependencies.

Figure 8-11 shows the resolution of the join dependencies. The three relations are in the fifth normal form.

Notice something important in the relations shown in the figure. If you join any two of the three relations, the result will produce incorrect information, not the true real-world information with the join dependency. For arriving at the correct original real-world information with the join dependency constraint, you have to join all the three relations.

Domain-Key Normal Form

This normal form is the ultimate goal of good design of a proper relational data model. If a data model is in the domain-key normal form (DKNF), it satisfies the conditions of all the normal forms discussed so far. The objective of DKNF is to make one relation represent just one subject and to have all the business rules be expressed in terms of domain constraints and key relationships. In other words, all rules could be expressly defined by the relational rules themselves.

Domain constraints impose rules on the values for attributes—they indicate restrictions on the data values. In DKNF, every other rule must be expressed clearly in terms of keys

BUILDING-MATERIAL

BuildingID	Material
B45	Sheet Rock
B45	Ceiling Paint
B51	Sheet Rock
B51	Shower Stall
B93	Ceiling Paint

MATERIAL-SUPPLIER

Material	SupplierNo
Sheet Rock	S67
Ceiling Paint	S72
Sheet Rock	S72
Shower Stall	S67
Ceiling Paint	S75

BUILDING-SUPPLIER

BuildingID	SupplierNo
B45	S67
B45	S72
B51	S72
B51	S67
B93	S75

FIGURE 8-11 Data model in fifth normal form.

EMPLOYEE (EmpID, EmpName, SkillType, TrainerID)

TRAINER (TrainerID, TrainerName, Location, SubjectArea)

> Business rule:
>
> An employee can have many trainers, but only a specific trainer for each skill type. A trainer can train only in his or her subject area.

FIGURE 8-12 Relations not in domain-key normal form.

and relationships without any hidden relationships. Consider the relations shown in Figure 8-12 and also note the accompanying business rule.

How do you know if the relations are in DKNF? You cannot know this until you are aware of the business rule. From the business rule, you understand that an employee can have multiple skill types. Therefore, the primary key EmpId of the EMPLOYEE relation cannot be unique. Further, trainer is related to skill type, and this is a hidden relationship in the relation. There must also be an explicit relationship between skill type and subject area.

Figure 8-13 resolves these discrepancies and expresses the business rule and the relationships correctly. The resultant data model is in domain-key normal form.

EMPLOYEE (EmpID, EmpName)

TRAINING (EmpID, SkillType, TrainerID)
  Foreign KeyS: TrainerID REFERENCES INSTRUCTOR
          EmpID REFERENCES EMPLOYEE

INSTRUCTOR (TrainerID, TrainerName, Location, SubjectArea)
  Foreign Key: SubjectArea REFERENCES TRAINING

FIGURE 8-13 Data model in domain-key normal form.

NORMALIZATION SUMMARY

Let us go back and review the normalization approach covered so far. Compare this approach with the method of creating a conceptual data model first and then transforming the conceptual data model into a relational data model. Consider the merits and disadvantages of either method. Also, think about the circumstances and conditions under which one method is preferable to the other. You notice that either method finally produces a true and correct relational data model. In the final relational data model, every single relation or table represents just one object set or entity type. In each relation, every attribute is functionally dependent on the full primary key, and only on the full primary key.

As you know, the data model transformation method is a more straightforward approach. Systematically you create partial conceptual data models applying standard techniques. Then you integrate all the partial data models to produce the consolidated conceptual model. After this step, you transform the consolidated conceptual model into a final relational data model. Although straightforward, the data model transformation method might take longer to come up with the final relational data model.

On the other hand, the normalization approach starts out with an intuitive initial data model. If you cannot begin with an intuitive initial data model that reflects the real-world information requirements completely, then this method will not work. That is why this normalization approach is difficult when the real-world information requirements are large and complex. If you are able to start with a good initial data model, then it is a matter of rendering the initial data model into a successive series of normal forms. Each step brings you closer to the true relational data model. Observe, however, that each step in the normalization process is defined well. In each step, you know exactly the type of problem you have to look for and correct. For example, to refine the data model and make it a first normal form data model, you remove repeating groups of attributes. In order to refine the data model and make it a second normal form data model, you look for partial key dependencies and rectify this problem. This general technique continues in the normalization approach.

Review of the Steps

When we discussed the normalization steps, we grouped the steps into two major sets. The first set of steps deals with the refinement of the data model into the fundamental normal forms. The second set of steps relates to higher normal forms. As mentioned before, if you complete the first set of steps, then for a vast majority of cases, your resulting data model will be truly relational. You need not proceed to the second set of steps to produce higher normal forms.

What exactly do you accomplish in the first set of steps refining the data model into the fundamental normal forms? In the relational data model, for every relation, each attribute must functionally depend only on the full primary key. There should not be any other type of functional dependency. Update, deletion, and addition anomalies are caused by incorrect functional dependencies within a relation. Once you complete the first set of steps to produce the fundamental normal forms, all problems of invalid functional dependencies are removed.

The second set of normalization steps considers other types of dependencies. Such dependency problems are rare in practice. For that reason, the fundamental normal forms are more important.

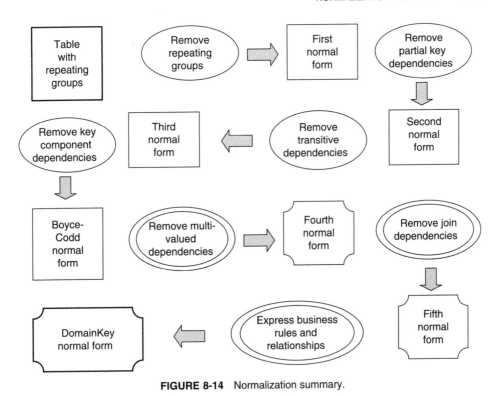

FIGURE 8-14 Normalization summary.

Figure 8-14 summarizes the normalization steps. Note the two sets of steps producing the two types of normal forms—fundamental normal forms and higher normal forms. In each step, you tackle one type of problem and only one. The result in each step is a progression toward the final true relational data model.

Normalization as Verification

In this whole chapter, we have considered the normalization approach as an alternative method for creating the relational data model. When implementing a relational database, the relational data model is the logical data model. Thus, normalization is used to produce the logical model for the design and deployment of a relational database supported by a relational DBMS.

Although normalization is presented as a method for creating a relational data model, the principles of normalization have valid uses even when you adopt the model transformation method detailed in Chapter 7. Let us explain what we mean.

Assume you are creating a large and complex relational database for a huge multinational business. The company has multiple locations in various countries with user groups spread far and wide. Obviously, the data modeling job will be the responsibility of multiple data modelers. Each data modeler will create partial conceptual models. These models will all be aggregated to form the complete conceptual data model. Let us say, the project team will be using the model transformation method. The complete and large conceptual model will have to be transformed into a relational model (logical model). This could turn out to be a monumental task. Anyway, assume that the final relational model is arrived at.

Considering the size and complexity of the resulting relational model, it will be prudent to adopt some proven technique to verify the correctness of each relation in the final relational model. This is where the principles of normalization could be very useful.

You can examine each relation and apply the principles of the normal forms. You can verify that each relation passes the tests for fundamental and higher normal forms. Therefore, the principles of the normalization approach may be applied to verify created relational models.

CHAPTER SUMMARY

- In the normalization approach, you adopt an informal methodology for creating a relational data model.
- In this methodology, intuitively you create an initial data model from information requirements and then normalize the initial model into a relational data model.
- An initial data model created through intuition contains potential anomalies relating to updates, deletions, and additions of data.
- The normalization methodology consists of systematically examining the initial data model, removing the causes for anomalies, and transforming the data model into a true relational data model. The approach consists of well-defined sequential steps.
- Each step removes one type of irregularity in the initial data model and transforms the model into a distinct normal form.
- The first four steps transform the initial data model into fundamental normal forms. Incorrect functional dependencies get removed. In practice, after the initial data model goes through the fundamental normal forms, the resultant relational model is good enough for completing the design process. No further normalization steps are usually necessary.
- The next three steps remove irregularities resulting from other types of incorrect dependencies in the original relations. These steps transform the model to higher normal forms.
- The principles of normalization may also be applied to verify the correctness of a relational data model created using the other method of data model transformation. This is especially relevant to a large and complex conceptual data model put together by several data modelers.

REVIEW QUESTIONS

1. True or false:
   A. Informal design of a relational data model begins with random tables created intuitively.
   B. Deletion anomaly prevents all deletion of data from a database.
   C. Each normalization step removes only one type of irregularity.
   D. When partial key dependencies are removed, a model is in the third normal form.

E. In most cases, the first four normalization steps for fundamental normal forms are sufficient to produce a truly relational model.

F. A table has transitive dependencies when every attribute is not functionally dependent on the full primary key.

G. A table in Boyce–Codd normal form is practically free from incorrect functional dependencies.

H. If a data model is in fourth normal form, no multivalued dependencies exist.

I. Join dependency in a relation is the same as multivalued dependency.

J. Decomposition of a table into multiple tables is the general technique for normalization.

2. Describe briefly the process of creating an initial data model from real-world information requirements. Why is this initial data model potentially incorrect?

3. What is addition anomaly in a database? Give an example.

4. "An update anomaly occurs when values of attributes are updated in a database." Explain with an example.

5. Normalization is a systematic step-by-step methodology. Describe how it is so with a small example.

6. When is a table not in the second normal form? Give an example. How do you transform it into second normal form tables?

7. What are transitive dependencies in a table? How do you remove transitive dependencies?

8. What is the Boyce–Codd normal form (BCNF)? Under what condition is a relation in BCNF?

9. What are multivalued dependencies? Explain with an example.

10. What is your understanding of the domain-key normal form? Why do you think this normal form is the ultimate goal of good design or a proper relational data model?

9

MODELING FOR DECISION-SUPPORT SYSTEMS

CHAPTER OBJECTIVES

- Introduce decision-support systems
- Explore data modeling methods for such systems
- Discuss data warehouse and its components
- Examine special aspects of modeling for data warehouse
- Study dimensional data modeling
- Learn about STAR and SNOWFLAKE schemas
- Review data modeling for OLAP systems
- Review modeling for data mining systems

Over the past decade, the role of computer and data systems has dramatically changed. Organizations need data systems not just to run the day-to-day business but also to help them in making strategic decisions. Decision-support systems have become commonplace in today's business environment. These systems enable the managers and executives to analyze buying and selling patterns, review past performances, and forecast trends. With the strategic information provided by decision-support systems, companies are able to survive and even excel in the marketplace.

Decision-support systems come in a few flavors—data warehousing, online analytical processing, and data mining. These systems and the databases supporting these systems differ from those supporting the regular operations of organizations. In these systems, the expectations are not support for routine operations such as taking an order, printing an invoice, or making an airline reservation. Here the emphasis lies on data systems suitable for interactive analysis and reporting. Therefore, data modeling for these

Data Modeling Fundamentals. By Paulraj Ponniah
Copyright © 2007 John Wiley & Sons, Inc.

decision-support systems requires techniques suitable for analysis. This chapter reviews such techniques.

Data warehousing is revolutionizing the manner in which businesses in a wide variety of industries perform analysis and make strategic decisions. Why are companies rushing into data warehousing? Why has there been a tremendous surge in interest? Data warehousing has become a mainstream phenomenon. In every industry across the board, from retail chains to financial institutions, from manufacturing enterprises to government departments, and from airline companies to utility businesses, data warehousing is transforming the way professionals perform business analysis and make strategic decisions. Many companies also make use of complex analytical methods falling within the purview of the discipline known as online analytical processing (OLAP). Several businesses also engage in data mining—a knowledge discovery paradigm. We will consider data modeling with regard to these decision-support systems.

DECISION-SUPPORT SYSTEMS

As an analyst, programmer, designer, data modeler, database administrator, or project manager, one would have been involved in the design and implementation of computer systems that support day-to-day business operations. Order processing, general ledger, inventory control, inpatient billing, checking accounts, insurance claims—all of these fall in the range of operational systems.

Operational systems run business operations. These process orders, maintain inventory, keep the accounting books, service the customers, receive payments, process claims, and so on. Without such computer systems, no modern enterprise could survive. Companies started using operational systems in the 1960s and have become completely dependent on these. Such systems gather, store, and process all the data needed to successfully perform the daily operations. So, the data modeling techniques and approaches we have considered so far relate to the data systems of operational applications.

In the 1990s, as businesses grew more complex, corporations spread globally, government deregulated industries, and competition became fiercer, business executives became desperate for information to stay competitive and improve the bottom line. However, the operational systems, although effective for routine operations, could not provide the types of information needed by executives for analysis and decision making. Executives needed different kinds of information that could be readily used for strategic decision making. Executives wanted to know where to build the next warehouse for storage and distribution, which product lines to expand, and which markets to strengthen. Operational systems, important as they are, could not provide strategic information. Business had to turn to new ways of getting strategic information. Data warehousing emerged as the vital, new paradigm specifically intended to provide strategic information.

Need for Strategic Information

Who needs strategic information in an enterprise? What exactly do we mean by strategic information? Executives and managers who are responsible for keeping the enterprise competitive need information for making proper decisions. They need information to formulate business strategies, establish goals, set objectives, and monitor results.

Here are a few examples of business objectives:

- Retain the current customer base.
- Increase customer base by 20% over the next 5 years.
- Gain market share by 10% in the next 3 years.
- Improve product quality levels in the top five product groups.
- Enhance customer service level in product shipments.
- Bring three new products to market in 2 years.
- Increase sales by 15% in the southwest division.

For making decisions about these objectives, executives and managers need information as follows: get in-depth knowledge of their company's operations; learn about the key business factors and how these affect one another; monitor how business factors change over time; measure the company's performance against the competition and industry benchmarks. Executives and managers have to focus on customer needs and preferences, emerging technologies, marketing results, and quality levels of products and services. The types of information needed to make decisions in the formulation and execution of business strategies and objectives are broad-based and encompass the entire organization. We may combine all these types of essential information into one group and refer to it as strategic information.

Strategic information is far more important than producing an invoice, making a shipment, settling a claim, or posting a withdrawal from a bank account. Strategic information concerns the very health and survival of a corporation. Critical business decisions depend on the availability of proper strategic information in an enterprise.

In summary, strategic information must possess the following characteristics:

Integrated. It must have a single, enterprise-wide view.

Data Integrity. Information must be accurate and conform to business rules.

Accessible. It must be easily accessible with intuitive access paths and be responsive for analysis.

Credible. Every business factor must have one and only one value.

Timely. Information must be available within the stipulated time frame.

History of Decision-Support Systems

For strategic decision-making, executives and managers must be able to review data from different business viewpoints. For example, they must be able to review sales quantities by product. You need to model and store data that will be suitable for such analysis and review.

For nearly two decades or more, attempts have been made to provide information to key personnel in companies for making strategic decisions. Sometimes a single computer application may produce ad hoc reports. However, in most cases, reports would need data from multiple systems requiring elaborate schemes to extract intermediary data that were required to be combined to produce useful reports. Most of these reports proved to be inadequate. The users could not clearly define what they wanted in the first instance. Once they saw the first set of reports, they wanted to see more data in different formats. The chain continued. This was mainly because of the very nature of the decision-making process. Information for strategic decision-making has to be available in an interactive manner.

In order to appreciate the reasons for failure of earlier decision-support systems to provide strategic information, we have to consider a brief history of the early systems. Depending on the size and nature of the business, most companies have gone through the following stages in their attempts at providing strategic information for decision making:

Ad Hoc Reports. This was the earlier stage. The IT department would write special programs to produce special reports whenever user departments, especially Marketing and Finance, sent requests.

Special Extract Programs. Somewhat anticipating the types of reports generally needed, the IT department would write a suite of programs and run the programs periodically to extract data from various applications and produce reports. Special additional programs would be written for out-of-the-ordinary requests.

Small Applications. The IT department would formalize the data extract process and create simple applications to produce reports based on extracted files.

Information Centers. Some major corporations created separate and distinct rooms where users could go and request ad hoc reports or see information on some special output screens. These were predetermined reports and screens. IT personnel would be present at information centers to assist the users.

Decision-Support Systems. In this stage, companies began to build more sophisticated systems intended to provide strategic information. But these systems were supported by data extract files as in earlier attempts.

Executive Information Systems. This was an attempt to bring strategic information to the executive desktop. However, only preprogrammed reports and screens were available. After seeing the total countrywide sales, if the executive wanted to see the breakdown by region, product, and sales office, it was not possible unless this level of breakdown was already programmed.

Every attempt in the past at providing strategic information to decision makers ended in failure and frustration. The information environment ideally suited for making strategic decisions has to be flexible and conducive for interactive analysis. The IT department had not been able to establish such an environment. Moreover, the fundamental reason for the failed past attempts is that all along, the IT department was trying to provide strategic information from operational systems. Operational systems are not designed or intended for strategic information. Only specifically designed informational systems can provide strategic information. What are the differences between the two types of systems?

Operational Versus Informational Systems

Operational systems and informational systems serve different purposes in an organization. They have different scope. Operational systems support the day-to-day running of the business—make the wheels of business turn. On the other hand, informational systems provide strategic information—enable professionals to watch the wheels of business turn.

It will, therefore, be worthless to dip into operational systems for strategic information as it has been done in the past. As companies face fiercer competition and businesses become more complex, continuing past practices leads to disaster.

Making the Wheels of Business Turn. Operational systems are online transaction processing (OLTP) systems running the routine core business operations. These are the so-called bread-and-butter systems in a company. These systems make the wheels of business turn. They support the basic business processes of the company. These systems typically get data into the database and use the data to process transactions. Each transaction processes data about a single entity such as a single order, a single invoice, or a single customer.

Generally, the emphasis is to *get the data in*. Making the wheels of business turn involves transactions such as

- Take an order
- Process a claim
- Make a shipment
- Generate an invoice
- Receive cash
- Reserve an airline seat

Watching the Wheels of Business Turn. On the other hand, specially designed and built decision-support systems are not meant to run the core business processes. These are used to watch how the business runs, how trends develop, and then make strategic decisions to improve the business.

Decision-support systems are developed to *get strategic information out*. Watching the wheels of business turn has features such as

- Show me the top-selling products
- Show me the problem regions
- Tell me why (drill down to districts and sales offices)
- Let me see other data (drill across to other regions)
- Display the highest margins
- Alert me when a district sells below target

System Types and Modeling Methods

You now realize that you need a new type of system environment with different features to obtain strategic information. Let us quickly examine the desirable features and processing requirements of this new type of environment.

A New Type of System Environment. Desired features of the new type of system environment include:

- Database designed for analytical tasks
- Data from multiple applications
- Easy to use and conducive for long interactive sessions by users
- Read-intensive data
- Direct interaction with the system by users without IT assistance
- Content stable with periodic updates only
- Content to include current and historical data
- Ability for users to run queries and get results online
- Ability for users to initiate reports

Most of the processing in the new environment has to be analytical. Four levels of analytical processing need to be available:

- Run simple queries and reports against current and historical data
- Perform "what if" analysis in several ways
- Query, step back, analyze, and then continue process to any desire length
- Spot historical trends and apply these for future results

Business Intelligence. The new environment encompasses informational systems such as data warehousing, OLAP, and data mining. These systems hold business intelligence for the enterprise to make strategic decisions. Of these systems, the most prevalent is data warehousing. Figure 9-1 shows the nature of business intelligence in the data warehouse.

At a high level of interpretation, the data warehouse contains critical measurements of business processes stored along business dimensions. For example, a data warehouse might contain units of sales, by product, day, customer group, sales district, sales region, and sales promotion.

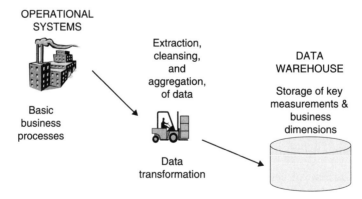

FIGURE 9-1   Business intelligence in the data warehouse.

From where does the data warehouse get its data? Data is derived from the operational systems that support the basic business processes of the organization. In between the operational systems and the data warehouse storage, there is a staging area. In this area, the operational data gets to be cleansed and transformed into a format suitable for placement in the data warehouse storage for easy retrieval and analysis.

Data Modeling for Decision Support. You know data modeling techniques for operational systems. We have looked at the E-R modeling technique in great detail. We have covered numerous examples of fragments of E-R data models. This technique served us well for creating data models for systems that run the routine operations. The conceptual data models for these systems may be transformed into logical data models and implemented as, perhaps, relational databases. These databases are designed for transaction processing.

However, the databases in data warehouses, data sets for OLAP, and data structures in data mining are primarily meant for analysis and not for transaction processing. How should the data be modeled for these applications? Will the same data modeling techniques be useful for decision-support systems as well?

As you will see shortly, the E-R technique as such is not adequate for modeling the information requirements of a data warehouse. We will consider another technique known as dimensional modeling for a data warehouse. You will appreciate how dimensional modeling is well suited in a data warehouse environment. Dimensional modeling portrays the data requirements in a data warehouse more appropriately. However, both E-R data models and dimensional data models may be implemented as relational databases.

DATA WAREHOUSE

In this section, let us focus on the most common of modern decision-support systems—the data warehouse. Let us look at its features; define what it is; study its components; and see how several technologies work together in a data warehouse environment. We will also consider some examples of data warehousing applications. Let us also introduce the reason for special requirements for doing a data model for the data warehouse.

Data Warehouse Defined

In the final analysis, data warehousing is a simple concept. It was born out of the need for strategic information and was the result of the search for a new way to provide such information. As we have seen, the methods of the past two decades using the operational computing environment were unsatisfactory. This new concept is not to generate fresh data, but to make use of the large volumes of existing data and to transform the data into formats suitable for providing strategic information.

The data warehouse exists to answer questions users have about the business, the performance of the various business operations, business trends, and about what could be done to improve the business. The data warehouse exists to provide business users with direct access to data, to provide a single unified version of performance indicators, to record the past accurately, and to provide the ability to view the data from many different perspectives. In short, the data warehouse is there to support decision-making processes.

This is the really simple concept behind data warehousing: take all the data you already have in the organization, clean and transform the data, and then provide strategic information.

An Environment, Not a Product. A data warehouse is not a single software or hardware product you purchase off the shelf to provide strategic information. It is rather a computing environment where users can find strategic information; an environment where users are put directly in touch with the data they need to make better decisions. It is a user-centric environment.

The defining characteristics of this new computing environment called the data warehouse include:

- An ideal environment for data analysis and decision making
- Fluid, flexible, and interactive
- Almost completely user-driven
- Responsive and conducive to the ask−answer−analyze−ask-again pattern of computing
- Ability to discover answers to complex, unpredictable questions

A Blend of Many Technologies. Let us reexamine the basic concept of data warehousing:

- Take all the data from operational systems
- Where necessary, include relevant data from outside
- Integrate all the data from various sources
- Remove inconsistencies and transform the data
- Store the data in formats suitable for easy access and analysis

Although a simple concept, data warehousing involves different functions: data extraction, data loading, data transformation, data storage, and provision of user interfaces. Therefore, in a data warehousing environment, several technologies are needed to support the various functions. Figure 9-2 shows how data warehousing is a blend of many technologies needed for the various functions.

Although many technologies are in use, they all work together in a data warehouse. The end result is the creation of a new computing environment for the purpose of providing the strategic information every enterprise needs desperately.

Major Components

We have quickly reviewed the basic definition and features of a data warehouse. We have established our position on what the term data warehouse means to us. We are now ready to examine its components.

Architecture is the proper arrangement of the components. You build a data warehouse with software and hardware components and arrange them in the most optimal manner. To suit the requirements of your organization, you arrange the building blocks in a certain way for maximum benefit. Figure 9-3 shows the basic components of a typical data warehouse.

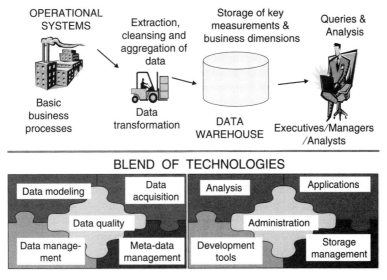

FIGURE 9-2   Data warehouse: blend of technologies.

You see the *Source Data* component shown on the left. The *Data Staging* component serves as the next building block. In the middle, you see the *Data Storage* component that holds and manages data warehouse data. This component not only stores and manages data, but it also keeps track of the data by means of a meta-data repository. The *Information Delivery* component shown on the right consists of all the different ways of making information from the data warehouse available to users.

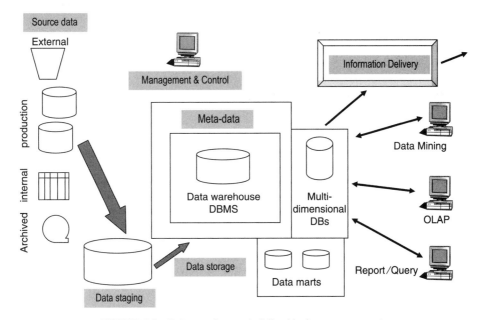

FIGURE 9-3   Data warehouse: building blocks or components.

Source Data Component. Source data coming into the data warehouse may be grouped into four broad categories:

Production Data. This comes from various operational systems of the enterprise. Depending upon the information requirements, segments of operational data get selected.

Internal Data. This is extracted from various private spreadsheets, documents, customer profiles, and sometimes departmental databases.

Archived Data. This is historical operational data stored away from production data bases.

External Data. This is data from external agencies such as competitors' market share, standard financial indicators for the industry, economic trends, and so on.

Data Staging Component. After extracting data from several disparate sources, the data needs to be changed, converted, and made ready in a format suitable to be stored for querying and analysis. The major functions that prepare the data take place in the data staging area. Data staging provides a place and an area with a set of functions to cleanse, change, combine, convert, deduplicate, and prepare source data for storage in the data warehouse data repository.

Three major functions that get performed in the staging area are as follows:

Data Extraction. A fairly complex function to extract data from varied data sources, from different source machines, and in diverse formats. Special data extraction software tools are generally used.

Data Transformation. As a necessary consequence of disparate sources of data, conversion and formatting becomes very important and elaborate. At the end of the transformation process, you have a collection of integrated data, cleansed, standardized, and summarized.

Data Loading. Consists of adding initial data to the data warehouse storage. Also, after the data warehouse is in operation, data loading takes place for daily additions and changes from operational systems.

Data Storage Component. Data storage for the data warehouse is a separate repository. Operational systems of your enterprise support day-to-day operations. These are online transaction processing applications. Data repositories for operational systems typically contain only current data. Also, the data repositories for operational systems contain data structured in highly normalized formats for fast and efficient processing. In contrast, for the data warehouse, you keep data in structures suitable for analysis, not for quick retrieval of individual pieces of information. Data storage for the data warehouse is, therefore, kept separately, not as part of the operational systems.

In your database supporting operational systems, updates to data happen in real time as transactions occur. Transactions hit the databases in a random fashion. How and when transactions change data in the database is not completely within your control. Data in operational databases may change from moment to moment. However, data in the data warehouse needs to be stable representing snapshots at specified periods. Analysts must be able to deal with stable data and produce consistent results from queries. Therefore, data warehouses are mostly "read-only" data repositories.

Periodically, data in the data warehouse repository gets changed. After the initial base loading of data, data in the data warehouse gets changed periodically. Depending on particular circumstances and requirements, parts of the data warehouse may be refreshed daily, weekly, monthly, and quarterly.

Information Delivery Component. Who are the users that need information from the data warehouse? The range is fairly comprehensive. The novice user comes to the data warehouse with no training and, therefore, needs prefabricated reports and preset queries. The casual user needs information once in a while, not regularly. This type of user also needs prepackaged information. The business analyst looks for ability to do complex analysis. The power user wants to be able to navigate through the data warehouse, pick up interesting information, format his or her own queries, drill through data layers, and create custom reports and ad hoc queries.

In order to provide information to the wide community of data warehouse users, the information delivery component includes several delivery methods. You have to include multiple information delivery mechanisms. Most commonly, you provide for online queries and reports. Users will enter their queries online and receive results online. Recently, provision of information over intranets using Web technology is becoming more and more prevalent.

Data Warehousing Applications

In the early stages, four significant factors drove companies to move into data warehousing: fierce competition, government deregulation, a need to revamp internal processes, and an imperative for customized marketing. Telecommunications, banking, and retail were the first industries to adopt data warehousing. That was largely because of government deregulation in telecommunications and banking. Fiercer competition pushed retail businesses into data warehousing. Utility companies joined the group as that sector became deregulated. In the next wave, companies in financial services, health care, insurance, manufacturing, pharmaceuticals, transportation, and distribution got into data warehousing.

At present, data warehouses exist in every conceivable industry. Now, companies have the ability to capture, cleanse, maintain, and use the vast amounts of data generated by their business transactions. Data warehouses storing several terabytes of data are not uncommon in retail and telecommunications.

Modeling: Special Requirements

In several ways, building a data warehouse is very different from designing and implementing an operational system. This difference also shows up in creating data models for the information requirements for a data warehouse. When we consider the information requirements, it will become clear why this is so.

Based on the data model we create for the data warehouse repository, we have to implement the database. The model must reflect data content of the data warehouse. So, let us explore the nature of information requirements so that we can come up with a modeling technique for the data warehouse.

Information Usage Unpredictable. Let us say you are building an operational system for order processing in your company. Based on the business functions that make up order processing and the data needed to support these functions, you can create a conceptual data model. You may use the E-R modeling technique. For an operational system such as order processing, users are able to give you precise details of the required functions, information content, and usage patterns.

In striking contrast, for a data warehousing system, users are generally unable to define their requirements precisely and clearly. They are unsure how exactly they will be using the data warehouse and cannot express how they would use the information or process it. Of course, they know that they will use the data warehouse for analysis, but they are not clear how exactly they would do that. The whole process of defining the information requirements for a data warehouse is nebulous. If so, how can you create a data model for something the users are unable to define clearly and precisely.

Dimensional Nature of Business Data. Fortunately, the situation is not as hopeless as it seems. Even though users cannot fully describe what they want in a data warehouse, they can provide you with some useful insights into how they think about the business. They can tell you what measurement units are important to them. Each department can let you know how they measure success in that department. Users can provide clues about how they combine the various pieces of information for strategic decision making.

Managers think of the business in terms of business dimensions. Let us understand what these business dimensions are by considering a few examples. Look at the following examples of the kinds of questions managers are likely to ask for decision making.

Marketing Vice President. How much did my new product generate *month by month, in the southern division, by user demographic, by sales office*, relative to the previous version and compared with plan?

Marketing Manager. Give me sales statistics *by products, summarized by product categories, daily, weekly, and monthly, by sales districts, by distribution channels.*

Financial Controller. Show me expenses, listing actual versus budget, *by months, quarters, and annual, by budget line items, by district, division, summarized for the whole company.*

The marketing vice president is interested in the revenue generated by her new product; but she is not interested in a single number. She is interested in the revenue numbers by month, in a certain division, by demographic, by sales office, relative to the previous product version, and compared with plan. So, the marketing vice president wants the revenue numbers broken down by month, division, customer demographic, sales office, product version, and plan. These are her business dimensions along which she wants to analyze her revenue numbers.

Similarly, for the marketing manager, his business dimensions are product, product category, time (day, week, month), sales district, and distribution channel. For the financial controller, the business dimensions are budget line, time (month, quarter, year), district, and division.

If users of a data warehouse think in terms of business dimensions for decision making, as a data modeler, you must also think of business dimensions for the modeling process.

Although the details of actual usage of the data warehouse could be unclear, the business dimensions used by managers are not ambiguous at all. So, as an early step in the data modeling process, determine the business dimensions.

Examples of Business Dimensions. The concept of business dimensions is fundamental to requirements definition and data modeling for the data warehouse. Therefore, let us look at a few examples. Figure 9-4 displays business dimensions for four different cases.

Let us quickly review the examples. For the supermarket chain, the measurements that are analyzed are the sales units. These are analyzed along four business dimensions: time, promotion, product, and store. For the insurance company, the business dimensions are different—more appropriate to that business. Here you want to analyze claim amounts by six business dimensions: time, agent, claim, insured party, policy, and status.

Observe the other two examples and note the business dimensions. These are different, more appropriate for the nature of the businesses. What we find from these examples is that the business dimensions are different and relevant to the industry and to the subject for analysis. We also note that generally the time dimension is a common dimension in all examples. Almost all business analyses are performed over time.

Information Package. Having understood the concept of business dimensions and how these enable us to move forward in data modeling, let us introduce the notion of an information package. Creation of an information package is a preliminary step for recording the requirements and preparing for the data modeling process.

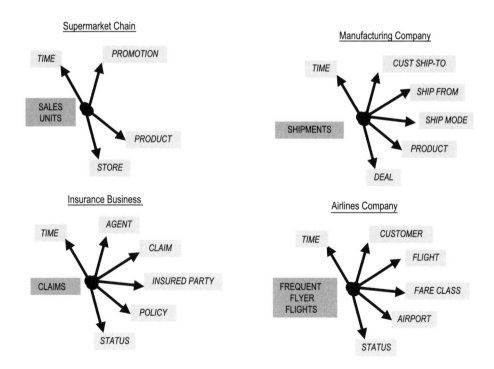

FIGURE 9-4 Examples of business dimensions.

Information subject: Automaker sales

Dimensions

Time	Product	Payment method	Customer demo-graphics	Dealer	
Year	Model name	Finance type	Age	Dealer name	
Quarter	Model year	Term (Months)	Gender	City	
Month	Package styling	Interest rate	Income range	State	
Date	Product line	Agent	Marital rtatus	Single brand flag	
Day of week	Product category		House-hold Size	Date first operation	
Day of month	Exterior color		Vehicles owned		
Season	Interior color		Home value		
Holiday flag	First Year		Own or rent		

Facts: Actual sale price, MSRP, Options price, Full price, Dealer add-ons, Dealer credits, Dealer invoice, Down payment, Proceeds, Finance

(left margin label: Hierarchies / Categories)

FIGURE 9-5   Information package: automaker sales.

An information package incorporates the basic measurements and the business dimensions along which the basic measurements may be analyzed. Each information package refers to one information subject. Figure 9-5 shows an information package for automaker sales.

Go through the figure carefully and note the following.

Business Dimensions. These are shown as column headings.

Key Business Metrics or Facts. These are the measurements that are analyzed along the business dimensions. These are shown at the bottom in the information package diagram. In this example, many different metrics are meant to be available for analysis.

Dimension Hierarchies/Categories. These are various levels of individual dimensions for drilling down or up. The hierarchy for the time dimension ranges from year to actual date. Note these hierarchy indicators in the dimension columns. These columns are also used to indicate categories within business dimensions. For example, Single Brand Flag is a category indicator. Here the intention is to analyze the metrics by dealers who sell only single brands.

DIMENSIONAL MODELING

You have reviewed information package diagrams. These diagrams reflect the ways in which managers and other professional tend to make use of the data warehouse for analysis and decision making. Information packages are information matrices showing the metrics, business dimensions, and the hierarchies and categories within individual business dimensions.

The information package diagrams form the basis for proceeding to the data modeling process. You can use the information contained in these packages to come up with a conceptual model and, thereafter, a logical model. As you know, the logical model may be a relational model if you are implementing your data warehouse using a relational DBMS. The modeling process results in what is known as a dimensional data model.

Dimensional Modeling Basics

Dimensional modeling gets its name from the business dimensions we need to incorporate into the model from the nature of business analysis. Dimensional modeling is a modeling technique to structure business dimensions and metrics that are analyzed along these dimensions. This modeling technique is intuitive for that purpose. In practice, a dimensional data model has proved to provide high performance for queries and analysis.

The multidimensional information package diagram is the foundation for the dimensional model. First, the dimensional model consists of specific data structures needed to represent the business dimensions. These data structures also contain the metrics or facts.

Figure 9-5 shows the information package diagram for automaker sales. Go back and review the figure. In the bottom section of the diagram, you observe the list of measurements or metrics that the automaker wants to use for analysis. Next, look at the columns headings. These are the business dimensions along which the automaker wants to analyze the metrics. Under each column heading, you notice the dimension hierarchies and categories within that business dimension. What you see under the column headings are the attributes relating to that business dimension.

Reviewing the information package diagram, we note three types of data elements: (1) measurements or metrics (called facts), (2) business dimensions, and (3) attributes for each business dimension. So, when we put together the dimensional model to represent the information contained in the information package, we need to come up with data structures to represent these three types of data elements. How to do this?

Fact Entity Type. First, let us work with the measurements or metrics seen at the bottom of the diagram. These are facts for analysis. In the automaker sales diagram, the facts are as follows: actual sale price, MSRP sale price, options price, full price, dealer add-ons, dealer credits, dealer invoice, amount of down payment, manufacturer proceeds, and amount financed.

Each of these items is a measurement or fact. Actual sale price is a fact about what the actual price is for the sale. Full price is a fact about what the full price is relating to the sale. As we review each of these factual items, we find that we can group all of these into a single data structure. Borrowing the terminology used in the examples of the previous chapters, we may call the data structure as a fact entity type. For the automaker sales analysis, this fact entity type would be the AUTOMAKER-SALES entity type. Therefore, each fact item or measurement would be an attribute for this entity type.

We have determined one of the data structures to be included in the dimensional model for automaker sales and derived the AUTOMAKER-SALES fact entity type with its attributes from the information package diagram. This is shown in Figure 9-6.

Dimension Entity Type. Let us move on to the other sections of the information package diagram, taking the business dimensions one by one. Look at the product business

Dimensions

	Time	Product	Payment method	Customer demo-graphics	Dealer	
	Year	Model name	Finance type	Age	Dealer name	
	Quater	Model year	Term (Months)	Gender	City	
	Month	Package styling	Interest rate	Income range	State	
	Date	Product line	Agent	Marital status	Single brand flag	
	Day of week	Product category		House-hold Size	Date first operation	
	Day of month	Exterior color		Vehicles owned		
	Season	Interior color		Home value		
	Holiday flag	First year		Own or rent		

Automaker Sales

Fact Entity Type

Actual sale price
MSRP
Options price
Full price
Dealer add-ons
Dealer credits
Dealer invoice
Down payment
Proceeds
Finance

Facts: Actual sale price, MSRP Sale price, Options price, Full price, Dealer add-ons, Dealer credits, Dealer invoice, Down payment, Proceeds, Finance

FIGURE 9-6 Formation of AUTOMAKER-SALES fact entity type.

dimension. This business dimension is used when we want to analyze by products. Sometimes our analysis could be a breakdown of sales by individual models. Another analysis could be at a higher level by product lines. Yet another analysis could be at even a higher level by product categories. The list of data items relating to the product dimension are as follows: model name, model year, package styling, product line, product category, exterior color, interior color, and first model year.

What can we do with all these data items in our dimensional model? All of these relate to the product in some way. We can, therefore, group all of these data items in one data structure and call it a dimension entity type. More specifically, this would be the PRODUCT dimension entity type. The data items listed above would all be attributes of the PRODUCT dimension entity type.

Look further into the information package diagram. You note the other business dimensions shown as column headings. In the case of automaker sales information package, these other business dimensions are dealer, customer demographics, payment method, and time. Just as we formed the PRODUCT dimension entity type, we can put together the remaining dimension entity types. The data items shown in each column would then be the attributes for each corresponding dimension entity type.

Figure 9-7 puts all of these together. It shows how the various dimensions tables are formed from the information package diagram. Study the figure carefully and note how each dimension entity type is formed.

Arrangement of Entity Types. Thus far, we have formed the fact and dimension entity types. How should these be arranged in a dimensional model? What are the relationships and how should the relationships be marked?

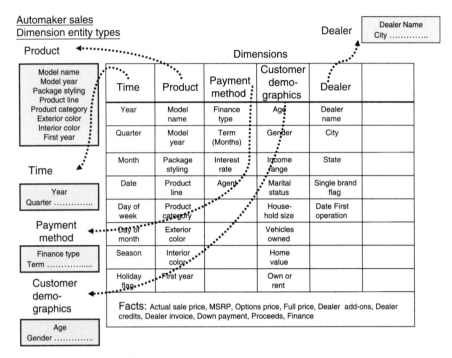

FIGURE 9-7 Formation of automaker dimension entity types.

Before we decide how to arrange the fact and dimension entity types in our dimensional model and mark the relationships, let us go over what the dimensional model needs to achieve and what its purposes are. Here are some criteria for combining the entity types into a dimensional model.

- The model should provide the best data access.
- The whole model must be query-centric.
- It must be optimized for queries and analyses.
- The model must express that the dimension entity types are related to the fact entity type.
- It must be structured in such a way that every dimension entity type can have an equal chance of interacting with the fact entity type.
- The model should allow drilling down or rolling up along dimension hierarchies.

With these requirements, we find that a dimensional model with the fact entity type in the middle and the dimension entity types arranged around the fact entity type appears to be the ideal arrangement. In such an arrangement, each dimension entity type will have a direct relationship with the fact entity type in the middle. This is necessary because every dimension entity type with its attributes must have an even chance of participating in a query to analyze the attributes in the fact entity type.

Such an arrangement in the dimensional model looks like a star formation. The fact entity type is at the core of the star and the dimensional entity types are along the spikes of the star. Figure 9-8 shows this star formation for automaker sales.

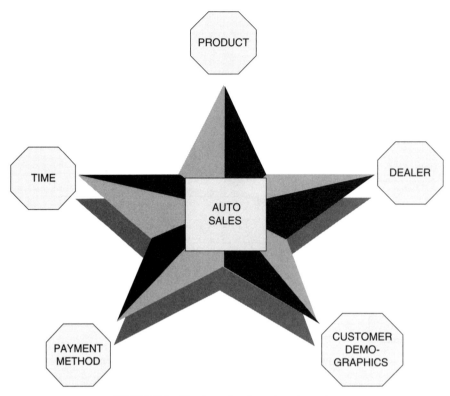

FIGURE 9-8 Star formation for automaker sales.

STAR Schema

The STAR formation introduced in the previous subsection is known as the STAR schema. Now that you have been introduced to the STAR schema, let us take a simple example and examine its characteristics. Creating the STAR schema is the fundamental data modeling task for the data warehouse storage. It is necessary to gain a good grip of this task.

Review of a Simple STAR Schema. Let us take a simple STAR schema designed for order analysis. Assume this to be a schema for a manufacturing company and that the marketing department is interested in determining how they are doing with the orders received by the company.

Figure 9-9 shows this simple STAR schema. It consists of ORDERS fact entity type shown in the middle of schema diagram. Surrounding the fact entity type are the four dimension entity types of CUSTOMER, SALESPERSON, ORDER-DATE, and PRODUCT.

Let us begin to examine this STAR schema. Look at the structure from the point of view of the marketing department. Users in this department will analyze the orders using dollar amounts of cost, profit margin, and sold quantity. This information is found in the fact entity type of the structure. Users will analyze these measurements by breaking down the numbers in combinations by customer, salesperson, date, and product. All these dimensions along which users will analyze are found in the structure. Thus, the STAR schema structure is a structure that can be easily understood by users and with which they can work

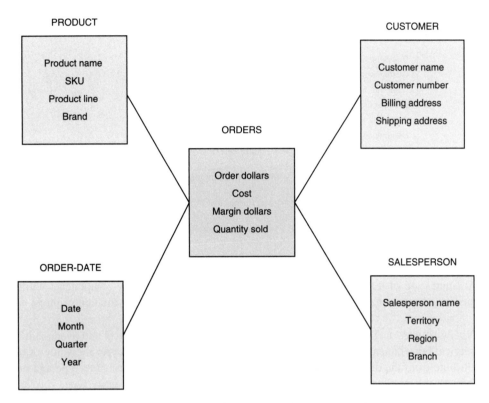

FIGURE 9-9 Simple STAR schema for order analysis.

comfortably. The structure mirrors how users normally view their critical measures along their business dimensions.

When you look at the order dollars, the STAR schema structure intuitively answers questions of what, when, by whom, and to whom. For example, users can easily visualize answers to questions such as: For a given set of customers for a certain month, what is the quantity sold of a specific product, enabled by salespersons in a given territory?

Inside a Dimension Entity Type. A significant component of the STAR schema is the set of dimension entity types. These represent the business dimensions along which the metrics are analyzed. Let us look inside a dimension entity type and study its characteristics. See Figure 9-10 showing the contents of one of the dimension entity types and also a set of characteristics.

Note the following comments about the dimension entity type and what is inside.

Dimension Entity Type Identifier. This is usually a surrogate identifier to uniquely identify each instance dimension entity. Sometimes, one or more attributes can be used as the identifier. However, a short surrogate identifier is preferred.

Entity Type Is Wide. Typically, a dimension entity type is wide in the sense it has many attributes. It is not uncommon for some dimension entity types to have even more than 50 attributes.

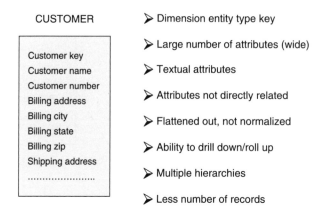

FIGURE 9-10   Inside a dimension entity type.

Textual Attributes. You will seldom find any numeric attributes used for calculations. Attributes are of textual format representing textual descriptions of components within business dimension. Users will compose their queries using these textual descriptors.

Not Normalized. The attributes in a dimension entity type are used over and over again in queries. For efficient query performance, it is best if the query picks up the value of an attribute from the dimension entity type and goes directly to the fact entity type and not through intermediary entity types. If you normalize the dimension entity type, you will be creating such intermediary entity types and that will reduce the efficiency in query processing.

Drilling Down, Rolling Up. The attributes in a dimension entity type provide the ability to get to the details from higher levels of aggregation to lower levels of details. For example, the three attributes zip, city, and state form a hierarchy. You may get the total sales by state, then drill down to total sales by city, and then by zip. Going the other way, you may first look at totals by zip and then roll up to totals by city and then state.

Multiple Hierarchies. In the example of the CUSTOMER dimension entity type, there is a single hierarchy going up from individual customer to zip, city, and state. But, dimension entity types often provide for multiple hierarchies. However, dimension entity types such as product may have dimension hierarchies such as marketing–product–category, marketing–product–department, finance–product–category, and finance–product–department so that different user groups may drill down or roll up differently.

Fewer Number of Occurrences. Usually, a dimension entity type has fewer instances than a fact entity type. A product dimension entity type for an automaker may just have 500 occurrences or less.

Inside the Fact Entity Type. Let us now get into a fact entity type and examine the components. Remember, this is the representation of where we keep the measurements. We may keep the details at the lowest possible level. In a department store's fact entity type for sales analysis, the level may be as units sold in each individual transaction at

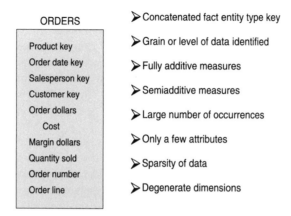

ORDERS
Product key
Order date key
Salesperson key
Customer key
Order dollars
Cost
Margin dollars
Quantity sold
Order number
Order line

➢ Concatenated fact entity type key

➢ Grain or level of data identified

➢ Fully additive measures

➢ Semiadditive measures

➢ Large number of occurrences

➢ Only a few attributes

➢ Sparsity of data

➢ Degenerate dimensions

FIGURE 9-11   Inside a fact entity type.

the cashier's checkout. Some fact entity types may represent storage of summary data. Such entity types are known as aggregate fact entity types.

Figure 9-11 shows the contents of a fact entity type and also a set of its characteristics. Note the following characteristics of the fact entity type.

Fact Entity Type Identifier. None of the attributes qualify to be an identifier for the fact entity type. These attributes are numeric units for measurements. We will discuss the identifier in a later subsection when studying the transition to logical model. It will be more meaningful at that point.

Data Grain. This is an important characteristic of the fact entity type. Data grain is the lowest level of detail for measurements or metrics. In the example of Figure 9-11, the metrics are at the detailed or lowest level. The quantity ordered relates to the quantity of a particular product on a certain day, for a specific customer, and procured by a specific sales representative. If we keep the quantity ordered as the quantity of a specific product for each month, then the data grain is different and it is at a higher level. So, when you model a fact entity type, be careful about the level of data grain it is supposed to represent through its attributes.

Fully Additive Measures. Let us look at the attributes OrderDollars, ExtendedCost, and QuantityOrdered. Each of these relates to a particular product on a certain date for a specific customer procured by an individual sales representative. In a certain query, let us say that the user wants the totals for the particular product, not for a specific customer, but for customers in a particular state. Then we need to find all the instances of the entity type relating to all the customers in that state and add OrderDollars, ExtendedCost, and QuantityOrdered to come with the totals. The values of these attributes may be summed up by simple addition. Such measures are known as fully additive measures. Aggregation of fully additive measures is done by simple addition. While designing a fact entity type, you must be cognizant of fully additive measures and note them in the model.

Semiadditive Measures. Consider the MarginDollars attribute in the fact entity type. For example, if OrderDollars has a value of 120 and ExtendedCost 100, then

MarginPercentage is 20. This is the calculated metric derived from OrderDollars and ExtendedCost. If you are aggregating the numbers from instances of the fact entity type relating to all customers in a particular state, you cannot add up MarginPercentage numbers from these instances and come up with the total. Derived attributes such as MarginPercentage are not additive. They are known as semiadditive measures. These are also common in fact entity types. Distinguish semiadditive measures from fully additive measures in your data model.

Entity Type Deep, Not Wide. Typically, a fact entity type contains fewer attributes than a dimension entity type. Usually, there are about 10 attributes or less. But the number of instances of a fact entity type is very large in comparison. Take a very simplistic example of 3 products, 5 customers, 30 days, and 10 sales representatives represented as instances of the corresponding dimension entity types. Even for this example, the number of fact entity type instances could be more than 5000, very large in comparison with the dimension entity type instances.

Sparse Data. We have said that a single instance of the fact entity type relates to a particular product, a specific calendar date, a specific customer, and an individual sales representative. In other words, for a particular product, calendar date, customer, and sales representative, there is a corresponding instance of the fact entity type. What happens when the date represents a holiday and no orders are received and processed? The fact entity type instances for such dates will not have values for the measures. Also, there could be other combinations of dimension entity type attributes, values for which fact entity type instances could be null measures. Do we need to keep such instances in our database of the data warehouse? No. Therefore, it is important to realize this type of sparse data and understand that the fact entity type instances could have gaps.

Degenerate Dimensions. Look close at the example of the fact entity type. You will find attributes such as OrderNumber and OrderLine. These are not measures or metrics or facts. Then why are these in the fact entity type? When you pick up attributes for the dimension and fact entity types from operational systems, you will be left with some data elements in operational systems that are neither facts nor strictly dimension attributes. Examples of such attributes are reference numbers like order numbers, invoice numbers, order line numbers, and so on. These attributes are useful in some types of analyses. For example, you may be looking for the average number of products per order. Then you have to group products by order number to calculate the average. Attributes such as OrderNumber and OrderLine in the example are called degenerate dimensions and get included as attributes of the fact entity type.

Factless Fact Entity Type. Apart from the identifier, a fact entity type contains facts or measures. There are no other attributes describing the entity type itself. Let us say, you are designing a fact entity type to track the attendance of students. For analyzing student attendance, the possible dimensions are student, course, date, room, and professor. The attendance may be related to any of these dimensions. When you want to mark the attendance relating to a particular course, date, room, and professor, what is the measurement you come up with for recording the event? In the fact entity type, the value relating to an instance is *one*. Every fact entity type instance means an attendance of *one*. If so, why bother to have an attribute in the fact entity type whose value will be *one* for

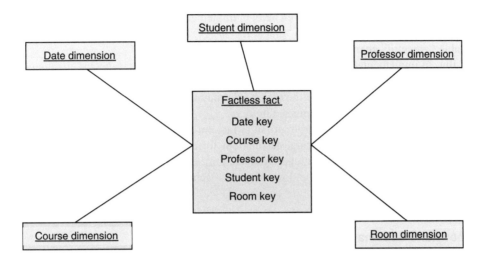

Tracks the attendance although no measured facts in the fact table

FIGURE 9-12   Factless fact entity type.

every instance? The very presence of a corresponding instance of the fact entity type will be sufficient to indicate the attendance. This type of situation arises when the fact entity type represents events. Such fact entity types really do not contain facts. They are a "factless" fact entity type. Figure 9-12 shows a typical factless fact entity type.

Data Granularity. By now, you know that granularity represents the level of detail in the fact entity type. If the fact entity type is at the lowest grain, then the facts or metrics are at the lowest possible level at which details could be captured from operational systems. What are the advantages of keeping fact entity type at the lowest grain? What is the trade-off?

When you keep the fact entity type at the lowest grain, users could drill down to the lowest level of detail from the data warehouse without the need to go the operational systems themselves. Base-level fact entity types must be at the natural lowest levels of all corresponding dimensions.

What are the natural lowest levels of the corresponding dimensions? In the example with the dimensions of product, date, customer, and sales representative, the natural lowest levels are an individual product, a specific individual date, an individual customer, and an individual sales representative, respectively. So, in this case, a single instance of the fact entity type should represent measurements at the lowest level for an individual product, order on a specific date, relating to an individual customer, and procured by an individual sales representative.

Let us say we want to add a new attribute of district in the sales representative dimension. When implemented, this change will not require any changes to the fact entity type because this is already at the lowest level by individual sales representative. This is a "graceful" change because all the old queries will continue to run without any changes. Similarly, assume we want to add a new dimension of promotion. Now, you will have to recast the fact entities to include promotion dimension. Still, the fact entity type grain will be at the lowest level. Even here, in implementation, the old queries will still run without any changes. This is also a "graceful" change. Fact entity types at the lowest grain enable "graceful" changes.

But, in implementation, we have to pay the price in terms of storage and maintenance for fact entity types at the lowest grain. Lowest grain necessarily means large numbers of fact entity instances. In practice, however, you may create aggregate fact entity types to support queries looking for summary numbers.

Two other advantages flow from granular fact entity types. Granular fact entity types, when implemented, serve as natural destinations for current operational data that may be extracted frequently from operational systems. Further, the recently popular data mining applications need details at the lowest grain. Data warehouses feed data into data mining applications.

Snowflake Schema

"Snowflaking" is a method of normalizing the dimension entity types in a STAR schema. Recall normalization discussed in Chapter 8. Although normalization was discussed as a method for creating a logical data model for implementation using relational technology, we can apply normalization principles for our discussion here.

When you completely normalize all the dimension entity types, the resultant structure resembles a snowflake with the fact entity type in the middle. First, let us begin with Figure 9-13, which shows a simple STAR schema for sales in a manufacturing company.

The sales fact entity type contains quantity, price, and other relevant metrics. Sales representative, customer, product, and time are the dimension entity types. This is a

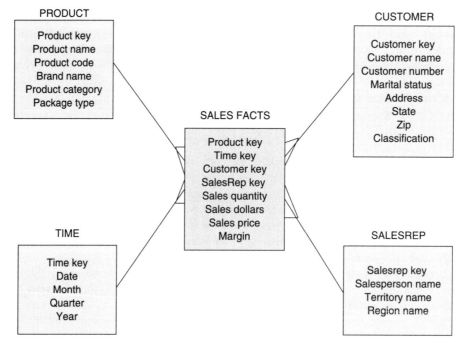

FIGURE 9-13   Sales: a simple STAR schema.

classic STAR schema, denormalized for optimal query access involving all or most of the dimensions. This model is not in the third normal form.

Options to Normalize. Assume there are 500,000 product dimension instances. These products fall under 500 product brands and these product brands fall under 10 product categories. Now suppose one of your users runs a query constraining just on product category. If the product dimension entity type is not indexed on product category, the query will have to search through 500,000 instances. On the other hand, even if the product dimension is partially normalized by separating out product brand and product category in separate entity types, the initial search for the query will have to go through only 10 instances in the product category entity type. Figure 9-14 illustrates this reduction in the search process.

In Figure 9-14, we have not completely normalized the product dimension. We can also move other attributes out of the product dimension table and form normalized structures. "Snowflaking" or normalization of the dimension entity types can be achieved in a few different ways. When you want to "snowflake," examine the contents and the normal usage of each dimension entity type.

The following options indicate the different ways you may want to consider for normalization of the dimension entity types.

- Partially normalize only a few dimension entity types, leaving the others intact
- Partially or fully normalize only a few dimension entity types, leaving the rest intact
- Partially normalize every dimension entity type
- Fully normalize every dimension entity type

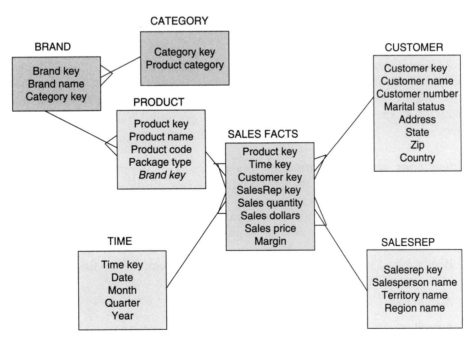

FIGURE 9-14   Product dimension: partially normalized.

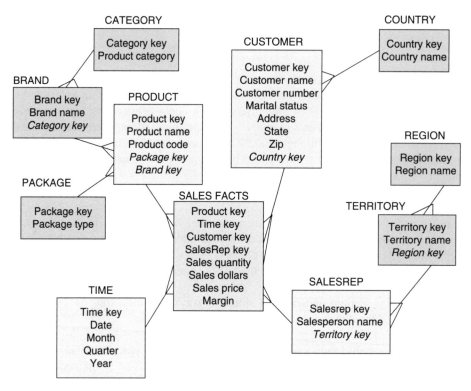

FIGURE 9-15 Sales: snowflake schema.

Figure 9-15 shows a version of the snowflake schema for sales in which every dimension entity type is partially or fully normalized.

The original STAR schema for sales as shown in Figure 9-13 contains only five entity types, whereas the normalized version now extends to 11 entity types. You will notice that in the snowflake schema, the attributes with low cardinality, that is, the ones with fewer distinct values, in each original dimension entity type are removed to form separate entity types. These new entity types are linked back to the original dimension entity types.

Advantages and Disadvantages. You may want to snowflake for one obvious reason. By eliminating from the dimension entity type all the textual attributes with long values, you may expect to save some space. For example, if you have "men's furnishings" as one of the category names, that text value will be repeated on every product instance in that category. But, usually removing such redundancies and "snowflaking" do not produce substantial space savings.

Here is a brief summary of the advantages and limitations of "snowflaking:"

Advantages

- Small savings in storage space
- Normalized structures, when implemented, are easier to update and maintain

Disadvantages

- Schema less intuitive and end-users put off by the complexity
- Difficult to browse through the contents
- Degraded query performance when too many entity types are involved

Families of STARS

When you look at a single STAR schema with its fact entity type and the surrounding dimension entity types, you can guess that it is not the extent of the data model for a data warehouse repository. Almost all data warehouses contain multiple STAR schema structures. Each STAR schema serves a specific purpose to track the measures stored in the fact entity type. When you have a collection of related STAR schemas, you may call that collection a family of STARS.

Families of STARS are formed for various reasons. You may form a family by just adding aggregate fact entity types with higher levels of grain. Derived dimension entity types will support aggregate fact entity types. Sometimes you may create a core fact entity type containing facts interesting to most users and customized fact entity types for specific user groups. Many factors lead to the existence of families of STARS. Look at the generic example provided in Figure 9-16.

The fact entity types of the STARS in a family share dimension entity types. Usually, the time dimension is shared by most of the fact entity types in the group. In the above example, all the three fact entity types are likely to share the time dimension. Going the other way, dimension entity types from multiple STARS may also share the fact entity type of one STAR.

If you are in a business like banking or telephone services, it makes sense to capture individual transactions as well as snapshots at specific time intervals. You may then use families of STARS consisting of transaction and snapshot schemas. If you are in

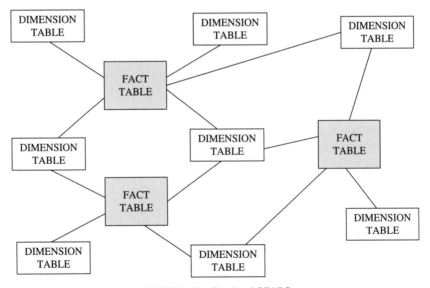

FIGURE 9-16 Family of STARS.

manufacturing, your company needs to monitor the metrics along the value chain. Some other institutions like a medical center do not add value in a chain but add value at different stations or units of the institution. For these institutions, a family of STARS may support the value chain or the value circle.

Transition to Logical Model

We have covered the various aspects of the dimensional model. You have looked at fact and dimension entity types in detail. You have walked through the types of attributes normally included in these two types of entities. We have also discussed some variations of the STAR schema.

Now we want to proceed with the logical design. The dimensional data model must be transformed into a logical model. Let us assume that we want to implement our data warehouse using a relational DBMS. In such a case, the relational model will be our logical model. Therefore, the dimensional model will have to be transformed into a relational data model. We covered the features of the relational model in elaborate detail in Chapter 7. There is no need to repeat them here. You are already very familiar with them. So, let us take an example of a dimensional model and transform it into a relational data model.

Dimensional to Relational. Refer back to Figure 9-9, which shows a dimensional model for orders analysis. We will consider this dimensional model and transform it into a relational model. Remember, a relational model consists of relations or two-dimensional tables with columns and rows. You know that each row in a relational table represents a single entity.

Entity Types. The figure presents a fact entity type ORDERS. You see four dimension entity types, namely, PRODUCT, CUSTOMER, ORDER-DATE, and SALESPERSON. There are five entity types in all.

Each entity type transforms into a relational table with rows and columns. ORDERS entity type converts into a table with the same name. The four dimension entity types PRODUCT, CUSTOMER, ORDER-DATE, and SALESPERSON transform into four relational tables, each with the same name as the entity type in the dimensional model. These five tables have rows and columns.

Attributes. Consider the attributes in the fact entity type. These are measures or metrics we want to use in analysis. These are not real characteristics of an entity type called ORDERS; these are merely a list of metrics. That is how a fact entity type is designed.

Each attribute transforms into a column of the fact relational table. The column headings or names are meaningful texts, not shortened abbreviations. Users need to understand the meanings while performing analysis.

Review the attributes in each dimension entity type. These are generally characteristics of the entity types. However, as you know, some attributes, although not characteristics, are present in the dimension hierarchy. This is especially true of the attributes in ORDER-DATE dimension entity type. All dimension attributes transform into columns in dimension relational tables. The column headings are full texts to indicate the elements used for analysis.

Figure 9-17 shows these fact and dimensional tables with rows and columns. Notice the table names and column names. Also, review the sample data in the tables.

PRODUCT

ProdName	SKU	ProdLine	Brand
Coffee Maker	98162287	Small Appliances	Mr. Coffee
Blender	98164391	Small Appliances	Cuisinart
Refrigerator	45113784	Large Appliances	GE
Washer	45125377	Large Appliances	Whirlpool
Television	37159133	Electronics	Sony

CUSTOMER

CustName	CustNo	BillCity	ShipCity
SuperClub	987287	Milltown	Brunswick
ServiceMart	346901	Baldwin	Monroe
Marcus	454813	Holbrook	Oceanside
PCR	551398	Manville	Somerset
Circuit Town	321876	Hillside	Watershed

ORDERS

OrdDollar	Cost	Margin	Qty	OrdNo
10000	2000	7000	20	21-859
9000	2500	6000	15	21-547
8000	2000	5000	100	21-135
20000	4000	14000	50	21-765
10000	3000	5000	200	21-698

ORDER-DATE

Dte	Mth	Qtr	Year
10	Jan	Q1	2006
6	Apr	Q2	2006
24	May	Q2	2006
16	Aug	Q3	2006
23	Dec	Q4	2006

SALESPERSON

SalPerName	Territory	Region	Branch	SocSecNo
Michael	North	Zone 1	Chicago	101553291
Amanda	East	Zone 2	Boston	534579898
Samuel	South	Zone 4	Georgia	236806353
Kaitlin	West	Zone 3	Austin	111578796
Andrew	East	Zone 1	Trenton	432876543

FIGURE 9-17   Fact and dimensional tables.

Identifiers. Let us begin with the consideration of identifiers for dimension entity types. The identifiers transform into primary keys. First, let us look at possible candidate keys that may be derived from the corresponding operational systems. The following are candidate keys:

PRODUCT	SKU
CUSTOMER	CustNo
ORDER-DATE	Date (YYYYMMDD)
SALESPERSON	SocSecNo

If we choose these as the primary keys, there could be some problems. Consider the implications. Assume that the product code in the operational system is an 8-position code, two positions of the code indicating the code of the warehouse where the product is normally stored, and two other positions denoting the product category. Consider what happens when we use the operational system product code as the primary key for the product dimension table.

The data warehouse contains historical data. Assume that the product code gets changed in the middle of a year because the product is moved to a different warehouse. So, we have to change the product code in the data warehouse. If the product code is the primary key for the dimension table, then the newer data for the same product will now be stored with a different product code. This could cause problems if we need to aggregate the data with numbers before and after the change.

Now consider the primary key for customer dimension table. In some companies, when customers leave the company and are dormant for a while, the companies tend to reuse customer numbers. So, when you look at the historical data in the data warehouse, metrics for two different customers—old and dormant as opposed to new—may be stored with the same customer numbers.

Because of such problems encountered while using operational system keys as primary keys for dimension tables, the practice in a data warehouse is to use surrogate keys or system-generated sequence numbers. While extracting data from operational systems, you can match up the surrogate keys with the operational system keys.

Relationships. Each dimension entity type and the fact entity type are in a one-to-many relationship. Thus, after transformation, in the relational data model, each dimension table is in a one-to-many relationship with the central fact table. As you know, each dimensional table must be linked to the fact table by means of a foreign key present in the fact table.

In our example, there are four dimension tables. Therefore, you must have the primary key of each of these four dimension tables as a foreign key in the fact table to establish the one-to-many relationships. There will be four foreign keys in the fact table.

Let us examine the options for the primary key for the ORDERS fact table. There are three choices:

1. *A single compound primary key whose length is the total length of the keys of the individual dimension tables.* With this option, in addition to the large compound primary key, the four foreign keys must also be kept in the fact table as additional attributes in the fact table. This option increases the size of the fact table.

2. *A concatenated primary key that is the concatenation of all the primary keys of the dimension tables.* Here, you need not keep the primary keys of the dimension tables as additional attributes to serve as foreign keys. The individual parts of the concatenated primary key themselves will serve as foreign keys.

3. *A system-generated primary key independent of the keys in the dimension tables.* In addition to the generated primary key, you must keep the foreign keys as additional attributes. This option also increases the size of the fact table.

In practice, option (2) is used in most fact tables. This option enables you to relate the fact table rows with the dimension table rows easily.

Figure 9-18 shows all the five relational tables with attributes, primary, and foreign keys, with some sample date. Carefully observe all the components of these

PRODUCT

ProdKey	Prod Name	SKU	Prod Line	Brand
1	Coffee Maker	98162287	Small Appliances	Mr. Coffee
2	Blender	98164391	Small Appliances	Cuisinart
3	Refrigerator	45113784	Large Appliances	GE
4	Washer	45125377	Large Appliances	Whirlpool
5	Television	37159133	Electronics	Sony

CUSTOMER

CustKey	CustName	CustNo	BillCity	ShipCity
1	SuperClub	987287	Milltown	Brunswick
2	ServiceMart	346901	Baldwin	Monroe
3	Marcus	454813	Holbrook	Oceanside
4	PCR	551398	Manville	Somerset
5	Circuit Town	321876	Hillside	Watershed

ORDERS

ProdKey	CustKey	DteKey	SlprKey	OrdDollar	Cost	Margin	Qty	OrdNo
3	4	357	5	10000	2000	7000	20	21-859
5	5	097	3	9000	2500	6000	15	21-547
2	1	010	1	8000	2000	5000	100	21-135
4	3	227	4	20000	4000	14000	50	21-765
1	2	145	2	10000	3000	5000	200	21-698

ORDER-DATE

DteKey	Dte	Mth	Qtr	Year
010	10	Jan	Q1	2006
097	6	Apr	Q2	2006
145	24	May	Q2	2006
227	16	Aug	Q3	2006
357	23	Dec	Q4	2006

SALESPERSON

SlprKey	SalPerName	Territory	Region	Branch	SocSecNo
1	Michael	North	Zone 1	Chicago	101553291
2	Amanda	East	Zone 2	Boston	534579898
3	Samuel	South	Zone 4	Georgia	236806353
4	Kaitlin	West	Zone 3	Austin	111578796
5	Andrew	East	Zone 1	Trenton	432876543

FIGURE 9-18 Data warehouse relational model.

tables and note the rows in the dimension rows and how they relate to the rows in the fact table.

OLAP SYSTEMS

We have mentioned online analytical processing (OLAP) in passing. You have some idea that OLAP is used for complex and advanced analysis. The data warehouse provides the best opportunity for analysis, and OLAP is the vehicle to do complex analysis. In today's data warehousing environment, with such tremendous progress in analysis tools from various vendors, you cannot have a data warehouse without OLAP.

We will explore the nature of OLAP and why it is essential. There are two major methods of implementing OLAP. Each method is supported by specific data repositories. We will look at the structure of the data repositories and discuss data modeling in that context. Many of the data repositories supporting OLAP are proprietary databases from vendors. These specific data structures determine how data modeling has to be done for OLAP. You may be able to adapt general data modeling principles to suit the requirements of OLAP data structures.

Features and Functions of OLAP

A data warehouse stores data and provides simpler access and analysis of data. However, OLAP complements the data warehouse facilities: OLAP provides complex analysis along multiple dimensions and the ability to perform intricate calculations.

Figure 9-19 summarizes the general features of OLAP. Note the distinction between basic and advanced features. The list includes most of the features you observe in practice in most OLAP environments.

BASIC FEATURES		
Multidimensional analysis	Consistent performance	Fast response times for interactive queries
Drill-down and roll-up	Navigation in and out of details	Slice-and-dice or rotation
Multiple view modes	Easy scalability	Time intelligence (year-to-date, fiscal period)

ADVANCED FEATURES		
Powerful calculations	Cross-dimensional calculations	Precalculation or preconsolidation
Drill-through across dimensions or details	Sophisticated presentation & displays	Collaborative decision making
Derived data values through formulas	Application of alert technology	Report generation with agent technology

FIGURE 9-19 General features of OLAP.

Dimensional Analysis

Dimensional analysis is a strong suit in the arsenal of OLAP. Any OLAP system devoid of multidimensional analysis is useless. Thus, let us describe the facility in OLAP systems for dimensional analysis.

Take an example of a STAR schema with three business dimensions, namely, product, time, and store. The fact entity type contains sales as the metrics. Figure 9-20 shows the schema and a three-dimensional representation of the model as a cube, with products on the X-axis, time on the Y-axis, and stores on the Z-axis. What are the values represented along each axis? For example, in the STAR schema, time is one of the dimensions and month is an attribute of the time dimension. Values of this attribute are represented on the Y-axis. Similarly, values of the attributes product name and store name are represented on the other two axes.

From the attributes of the dimension tables, pick the attribute product name from product dimension, month from time dimension, and store name from store dimension. Now look at the cube representing the values of these three attributes along the primary edges of the physical cube. Go further and visualize sales for coats in the month of January at the New York store to be at the intersection of the three lines representing the product, coats; month, January; and store, New York.

If you are displaying the data for sales along these three dimensions on a spreadsheet, the columns may display product names, the rows may display months, and the pages may display sales data along the third dimension of store names. See Figure 9-21 showing a screen display of a page of this three-dimensional data.

The page displayed on the screen shows a slice of the cube. Now look at the cube and move the slice or plane passing through the point on the Z-axis representing Store: New York. The intersection points on this slice or plane relate to sales along product

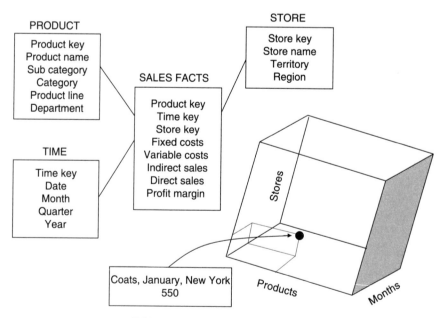

FIGURE 9-20 Simple STAR schema.

Store: New York

PAGES: STORE dimension

COLUMNS: PRODUCT dimension

ROWS: TIME dimension

	Hats	Coats	Jackets	Dresses	Shirts	Slacks
Jan	200	550	350	500	520	490
Feb	210	480	390	510	530	500
Mar	190	480	380	480	500	470
Apr	190	430	350	490	510	480
May	160	530	320	530	550	520
Jun	150	450	310	540	560	330
Jul	130	480	270	550	570	250
Aug	140	570	250	650	670	230
Sep	160	470	240	630	650	210
Oct	170	480	260	610	630	250
Nov	180	520	280	680	700	260
Dec	200	560	320	750	770	310

FIGURE 9-21   A three-dimensional display.

and time business dimensions for Store: New York. Try to relate these sale numbers to the slice of the cube representing Store: New York.

Now we have a way of depicting three business dimensions and a single fact on a two-dimensional page and also on a three-dimensional cube. The numbers in each cell on the page are sale numbers. You could run a number of queries to get sale numbers and perform various types of three-dimensional analysis. The results of each query will be represented in columns, rows, and pages.

In a typical multidimensional analysis session, users may issue the following sequence of queries:

1. Display the total sales of all products for past 5 years in all stores.
2. Compare total sales for all stores, product by product, between years 2006 and 2005.
3. Show comparison of total sales for all stores, product by product, between years 2006 and 2005 only for those products with reduced sales.
4. Show comparison of sales by individual stores, product by product, between years 2006 and 2005 only for those products with reduced sales.
5. Show results of the previous query, but rotating and switching columns with rows.
6. Show results of the previous query, but rotating and switching pages with rows.

This multidimensional analysis can continue until the analyst determines how many products showed reduced sales and which stores suffered the most.

In the above example, we had only three business dimensions and each of the dimensions could, therefore, be represented along the edges of a cube or the results displayed as columns, rows, and pages. Now add another business dimension, namely, promotion, bringing the number of dimensions to four. When you have three business dimensions, you are able to represent these as a physical cube with each edge of the cube denoting one dimension. You are also able to display the data on a spreadsheet with two dimensions showing as columns and rows and the third as pages. But, when you have four or more dimensions, how can you represent the data? Obviously, a three-dimensional cube will not work. Also, you will have a problem displaying the data as columns, rows, and pages. Therefore, how do we deal with multidimensional analysis when there are more than three dimensions?

Hypercubes

The necessity to perform multidimensional analysis with more than four dimensions leads us to the discussion of hypercubes. Let us begin with the two business dimensions of product and time. Usually, business users wish to analyze not just sales but other metrics as well. Assume that the metrics to be analyzed are fixed cost, variable cost, indirect sales, direct sales, and profit margin. These are five common metrics.

The data described here may be displayed on a spreadsheet showing metrics as columns, time as rows, and products as pages. See Figure 9-22 showing a sample page of the spreadsheet display. In the figure, please also note the three vertical lines, two of which represent the two business dimensions and the third the metrics. You can independently move up or down along the straight lines. This representation of vertical lines is known as a multidimensional domain structure (MDS). The figure also shows a three-dimensional cube representing data points along the edges. With three groups of data— two groups of business dimensions and one group of metrics—we can easily visualize the data as being along the edges of a cube.

Now add another business dimension to the model. Let us add the store dimension. That results in three business dimensions plus the metrics data—four data groups in all. How can you represent these four groups of data as edges of a three-dimensional physical cube? This is where an MDS comes in handy. You need not try to perceive four-dimensional data as along the edges of a three-dimensional cube. All you have to do is draw four vertical lines to represent the data as an MDS. This intuitive representation is

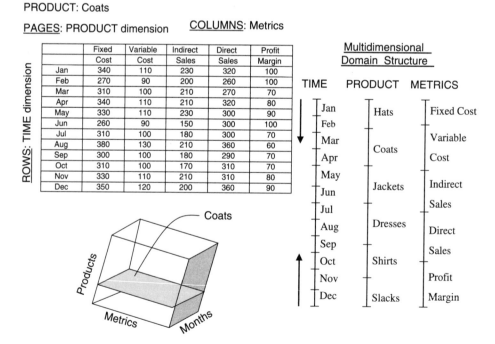

FIGURE 9-22 An MDS with three data groups.

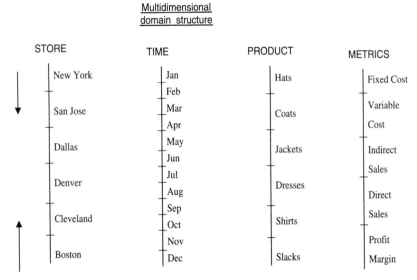

FIGURE 9-23   An MDS with four data groups.

a hypercube—a "cube" with any number of edges. A hypercube is a general metaphor for representing multidimensional data. Figure 9-23 shows an MDS with four data groups.

The next question relates to display of four-dimensional data on the screen. How can you possibly display four data groups with just rows, columns, and pages. Observe Figure 9-24 to note how this is usually done. By combining multiple logical dimensions within the same

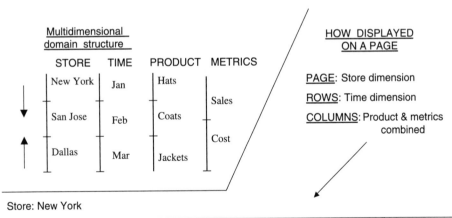

Store: New York

	Hats:Sales	Hats:Cost	Coats:Sales	Costs:Cost	Jackets:Sales	Jackets:Cost
Jan	450	350	550	450	500	400
Feb	380	280	460	360	400	320
Mar	400	310	480	410	450	400

FIGURE 9-24   Page display for four data groups.

display group, you can resolve this issue. Notice how product and metrics are combined to display as columns. The displayed page represents sales for Store: New York.

OLAP Implementation Approaches

Before we get into the discussion of data modeling for OLAP, let us look at two major approaches for implementing OLAP. The primary difference between the two approaches is how you store data for OLAP. After our review of multidimensional analysis, you must already get the notion that different types of data structures would be appropriate for OLAP. The traditional way of perceiving data as relational tables may not be the right approach.

In the first approach, data is stored in multidimensional databases (MDDB). It is, therefore, called MOLAP, or multidimensional OLAP. Typically, proprietary DBMSs by specific vendors run these MDDBs.

In the second approach, data is stored in relational databases but used as multidimensional data by the OLAP applications. This approach is known as ROLAP, or relational OLAP. Regular, powerful relational DBMSs administer the data repository in this method.

MOLAP. In the MOLAP model, data for analysis is stored in specialized multidimensional databases. Large multidimensional arrays form the storage structures. For example, to store sales number of 500 units for product ProductA, in the month number 2006/11, in store StoreS1, under distribution channel Channel07, the sales number of 500 is stored in an array represented bv values (ProductA, 2006/11, StoreS1, Channel07).

The array values indicate the location of the cells. These cells are the intersections of the values of the dimensional attributes. If you note how cells are formed, you will realize that not all cells have values for the metrics. If a particular store is closed on Sundays, the corresponding cells will contain nulls.

Figure 9-25 presents the architecture for the MOLAP model. Precalculated and prefabricated multidimensional hypercubes are stored in the MDDB. The MOLAP engine in the application layer pushes a multidimensional view of the data from the MDDB to the users.

Multidimensional database systems are proprietary software systems. These systems provide capabilities to create hypercubes and to consolidate them where necessary during the process that loads data into the MDDB from the main data warehouse. Users who can use summarized data enjoy fast response times from the consolidated data.

ROLAP. In this model, data is store in relational databases. Data is perceived as relational tables with rows and columns. However, the model presents data to users in the form of multidimensional hypercubes. In order to hide the storage structure to the user and present data multidimensionally, a semantic layer of meta-data is created. The meta-data layer supports the mapping of dimensions to the relational tables. Additional metadata supports summarizations and aggregations. You may store meta-data in relational tables.

Figure 9-26 shows the architecture of the ROLAP model. You are looking at a three-tier architecture. The analytical server in the middle-tier application layer creates multidimensional views on the fly. The multidimensional system at the presentation layer provides a multidimensional view of data to the users.

When users issue complex queries based on this multidimensional view, the queries are transformed into complex SQL directed to the relational database. Unlike the MOLAP model, static multidimensional hypercubes are not precreated and stored.

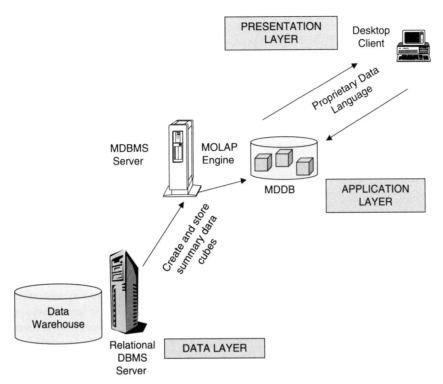

FIGURE 9-25   The MOLAP model.

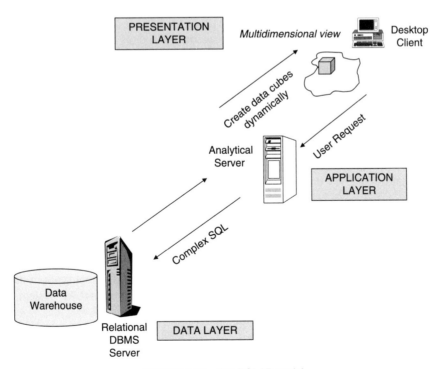

FIGURE 9-26   The ROLAP model.

Data Modeling for OLAP

In order to perform data modeling for OLAP, let us first examine some significant characteristics of data in such a system. Review the following list highlighting differences between OLAP and warehouse data:

- An OLAP system stores and uses much less data compared with a data warehouse.
- Data in an OLAP system is summarized. The lowest level of detail as in the data warehouse is very infrequent.
- OLAP data is more flexible for processing and analysis partly because there is much less data to work with.
- Every instance of the OLAP system is customized for the purpose that instance serves. In other words, OLAP tends to be more departmentalized, whereas data in the data warehouse serves corporate-wide needs.

Implementation Considerations. Before we specifically focus on modeling for OLAP, let us go over a few implementation issues. An overriding principle is that OLAP data is generally customized. When you build an OLAP system with system instances serving different user groups, this is an important point. For example, one instance or specific set of summarizations would be meant for one group of users, say the marketing department.

The following techniques apply to the preparation of OLAP data for a specific group of users or a particular department such as marketing.

Define Subset. Select the subset of detailed data the marketing department is interested in.

Summarize. Summarize and prepare aggregate data structures in the way the marketing department needs for combining. For example, summarize products along product categories as defined by marketing. Sometimes, marketing and accounting departments may categorize products in different ways.

Denormalize. Combine relational tables in exactly the same way the marketing department needs denormalized data.

Calculate and Derive. If some calculations and derivations of the metrics are department-specific, use the ones for marketing.

OLAP Data Types and Levels. The OLAP data structure contains several levels of summarization and a few kinds of detailed data. You need to model these levels of summarization and details. Figure 9-27 indicates the types and levels of data in an OLAP system.

The types and levels shown in the figure must be taken into consideration while performing data modeling for OLAP systems. Pay attention to the different types of data in an OLAP system. When you model the data structures for your OLAP system, you need to provide for these types of data.

Data Modeling for MOLAP. As a prerequisite to creation and storage of hypercubes in proprietary MDDBs, data must be in the form of multidimensional representations. You need to consider special requirements of the selected MDDBMS for data input for creation

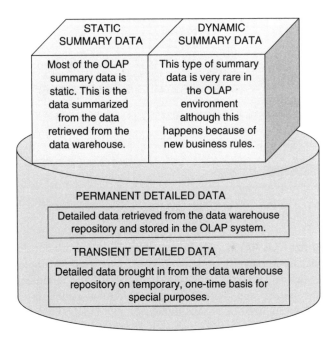

FIGURE 9-27 OLAP data types and levels.

of hypercubes. Essentially, data in MOLAP systems is stored in multidimensional arrays, not relational tables. Again, the specifications of the particular MDDBMS determine how input for the arrays must be prepared.

You are now quite familiar with multidimensional domain structures (MDSs) and how they are able to present multidimensional representations of data. MDSs are essential tools for the process of data modeling for MOLAP. Based on the requirements, determine the various levels of summarizations needed. Construct the MDSs and use them to proceed to implementation.

Figure 9-28 presents the steps in the modeling, design, and implementation for MOLAP. Note each step carefully as shown in the figure. Remember, proper summarizations is a key to better MOLAP performance.

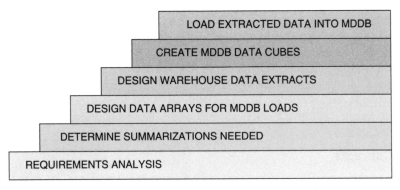

FIGURE 9-28 MOLAP data design and implementation.

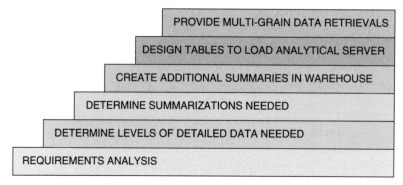

FIGURE 9-29 ROLAP data design and implementation.

Data Modeling for ROLAP. As you know, ROLAP systems do not store prefabricated hypercubes in MDDBs; generally, relational DBMSs are used for implementation. Data storage implementations in data warehouses also generally use relational DBMSs.

However, there is one significant difference: relational tables in a data warehouse environment are denormalized. A typical dimension table in a STAR schema is a denormalized structure. Duplicate values of dimension attributes are stored to facilitate selection during queries. In the ROLAP environment, fast access times are of paramount importance. Therefore, normalized structures are preferred.

Just as in the case of MOLAP, several high levels of summarizations are established during the modeling and design process. Although data is not stored in multidimensional arrays, multidimensional representation of data is essential in the design process. MDSs play a key role in multidimensional representation.

Figure 9-29 illustrates data modeling, design, and implementation for ROLAP. Note each step carefully as shown in the figure. Remember, proper summarizations and normalization are factors for better ROLAP performance.

DATA MINING SYSTEMS

Most of you know that data mining has something to do with discovering knowledge. Some of you possibly have come across data mining applications in marketing, sales, credit analysis, and fraud detection. All of you know vaguely that data mining is somehow connected to data warehousing. Data mining is used in just about every area of business from sales and marketing to new product development, inventory management, and human resources.

There are perhaps as many variations in the definition of data mining as there are vendors and proponents. Some experts include a whole range of tools and techniques from simple query mechanisms to statistical analysis in the definition. Others restrict the definition to just knowledge discovery methods. A workable data warehouse, although not a prerequisite, will give a practical boost to the data mining process.

Basic Concepts

Before providing some formal definitions of data mining, let us put it in the context of decision-support systems. Like all decision-support systems, data mining delivers information, not for running the day-to-day operations, but for strategic decision making. So let's place data mining in this context.

In the evolution of decision-support systems, data mining is of recent origin. Over the years, organizations have accumulated a huge collection of computer data. But, any application however sophisticated needed direct human involvement for analysis and use. The task, however, has become overwhelming for users. Is there a suite of techniques that could automatically dig or mine through the mountains of data and discover knowledge? Data mining is a response to this need.

Evolution to Data Mining. The earliest approach to decision-support systems was quite primitive, Next came database systems providing more useful decision-support information. In the 1990s, data warehouses with query and analysis tools began to appear as primary and valuable sources of decision-support information. For more sophisticated and complex analysis, OLAP tools became available. Up to this point, the approach for obtaining information was driven by users.

But the sheer volume of data renders it impossible for anyone to use analysis and query tools personally and discern useful information. For example, in marketing analysis, it is almost impossible to think through all the probable associations and gain insights by querying and drilling down into the data warehouse. You need a technology that can learn from past associations and transactions and predict customer behavior. You need a tool that by itself will discover knowledge with minimum human intervention. You want a data-driven approach, not a user-driven one. Data mining, at this point, takes over from the users.

Figure 9-30 displays the progress of decision-support systems. Note the stages and the evolution to data mining.

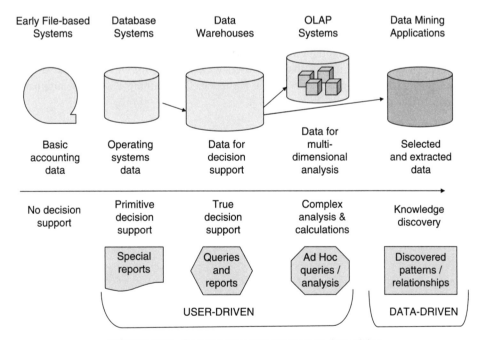

FIGURE 9-30 Decision-support progresses to data mining.

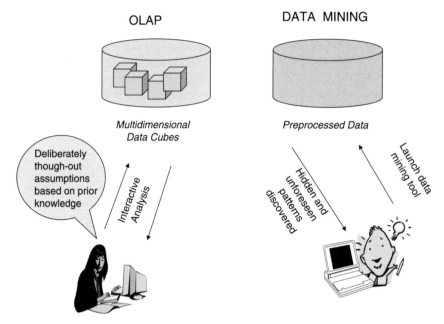

FIGURE 9-31   OLAP and data mining.

OLAP Versus Data Mining. From our earlier discussion on OLAP, you have a clear idea about the features of OLAP. With OLAP queries and analysis, users are able to obtain results and derive interesting patterns from the data.

Data mining also enables users to uncover interesting patterns, but there is an essential difference in the way the results are obtained. Figure 9-31 points out the essential difference between the two approaches.

Although both OLAP and data mining are complex information delivery systems, the basic difference lies in the interaction of the users with the systems. OLAP is a user-driven methodology; data mining is a data-driven approach. Data mining is a fairly automatic knowledge discovery process.

Data Mining: Knowledge Discovery. The knowledge discovery in data mining technology may be broken down into the following basic steps:

- Define business objectives
- Prepare data
- Launch data mining tools
- Evaluate results
- Present knowledge discoveries
- Incorporate usage of discoveries

Figure 9-32 amplifies the knowledge discovery process and shows the relevant data repositories.

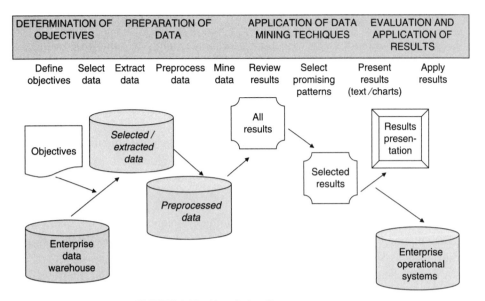

FIGURE 9-32 Knowledge discovery process.

Data Mining/Data Warehousing. How and where does data mining fit in a data warehousing environment? The data warehouse is a valuable and easily available data source for data mining operations. Data in the data warehouse is already cleansed and consolidated. Data for data mining may be extracted from the data warehouse.

Figure 9-33 illustrates data mining in the data warehouse environment. Observe the movement of data for data mining operations.

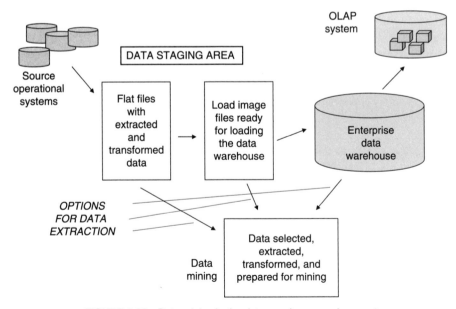

FIGURE 9-33 Data mining in the data warehouse environment.

Data Mining Techniques

Although a discussion of major data mining techniques might be somewhat useful, our primary concentration is on the data and how to model the data for data mining applications. Detailed study of data mining techniques and algorithms is, therefore, outside the scope of our study. These techniques and algorithms are complex and highly technical. However, we will just touch on major functions, application areas, and techniques.

Functions and Techniques. Refer to Figure 9-34 showing data mining functions and techniques.

Look at the four columns in the figure and try to understand the connections. Review the following statements.

- Data mining algorithms are part of data mining techniques.
- Data mining techniques are used to carry out data mining functions. While performing specific data mining functions, you are applying data mining processes.
- A certain data mining function is generally suitable to a given application area.
- Each application area is a major area in business where data mining is actively used.

Applications. In order to appreciate the tremendous usefulness of data mining, let us list a few major applications of data mining in the business area.

Customer Segmentation. This is one of the most widespread applications. Businesses use data mining to understand their customers. Cluster detection algorithms discover clusters of customers sharing same buying characteristics.

Application Area	Examples of Mining Functions	Mining Processes	Mining Techniques
Fraud detection	Credit card frauds Internal audits Warehouse pilferage	Determination of variations from norms	Data visualization memory-based reasoning
Risk assessment	Credit card upgrades Mortgage loans Customer retention Credit ratings	Detection and analysis of links	Decision trees Memory-based reasoning
Market analysis	Market basket analysis Target marketing Cross selling Customer relationship marketing	Predictive modeling Database segmentation	Cluster detection Decision trees Link analysis Genetic algorithms

FIGURE 9-34 Data mining functions and techniques.

Market Basket Analysis. This is a very useful application for retail. Link analysis algorithms uncover affinities between products that are bought together. Other businesses such as upscale auction houses use these algorithms to find customers to whom they can sell higher-value items.

Risk Management. Insurance companies and mortgage businesses use data mining to discover risks associated with potential customers.

Delinquency Tracking. Loan companies use the technology to track customers who are likely to be delinquent on loan repayments.

Demand Prediction. Retail and other distribution businesses use data mining to match demand and supply trends to forecast demand for specific products.

Data Preparation and Modeling

Data for your mining operations depend on the business objectives—what you expect to get out of the data mining technique being adopted to work on the data. You will be able to come up with a set of data elements whose values are required as input into the data mining tool. For getting the values, you need to determine the data sources.

Go back and revisit Figure 9-33, which shows data preparation from the enterprise data warehouse. You know the sources that feed the data warehouse. It is assumed that the data warehouse contains data that has been integrated and combined from several sources. The data warehouse is also expected to have clean data with all the impurities removed in the data staging area. If data mining algorithms are allowed to work on inconsistent data, the results could be totally useless.

In this subsection, we will concentrate on a box that indicates data selected, extracted, transformed, and prepared for data mining. We will discuss how the data selection and preparation are done. Once the data is prepared, you need to store the prepared data suitably for feeding the data mining applications. What are good methods for this data storage? How do you prepare the data model for this data repository?

Data Preprocessing

Depending on the particular data mining application, you may find that the needed data elements are not present in your data warehouse. Be prepared to look to other outside and internal sources for additional data. Further, incomplete, noisy, and inconsistent data is not infrequent in corporate databases and large data warehouses. Do not simply assume the correctness of available data and just extract data from these sources and feed the data mining application.

Data preprocessing generally consists of the following processes:

- Selection of data
- Preparation of data
- Transformation of data

Let us discuss these briefly. That would give us an idea of the data content that should be reflected in the data model for the preprocessed source data for data mining.

Data Selection. Of course, what data is needed depends on the business objectives and the nature of the data mining application. Remember, data mining algorithms work on data at the lowest grain or level of detail. Based on a list of data elements, you need to identify the sources. Maybe most of the data can be extracted from the data warehouse. Otherwise, determine the secondary sources.

Data mining algorithms work on data variables. Values of selected active variables are fed into the data mining system to perform the required operations. Active variables would be data attributes that may be found within the fact and dimension tables of the data warehouse repository.

Suppose your data mining application wants to perform market basket analysis, that is, to determine what a typical customer is likely to put in a market basket and go to the checkout counter of a supermarket. The active variables in this case would possibly be number of visits and variables to describe each basket such as household identification (from supermarket card), date of purchase, items purchased, basket value, quantities purchased, and promotion code.

Active variables generally fall into following categories:

Nominal Variable. This has a limited number of values with no significance attached to the values in terms of ranking. Example: gender (male or female).

Ordinal Variable. This has a limited number of values with values signifying ranking. Example: customer education (high school or college or graduate school).

Continuous Measure Variable. Difference in values of the variable measurable. Continuous variations. Examples: purchase price, number of items. Values for this variable are real numbers.

Discrete Measure Variable. Difference in values of the variable measurable. Discrete variations. Example: number of market basket items. Values for this variable are integers.

Data Preparation. This step basically entails cleansing the selected data. First, this step begins with a general review of the structure of the data in question and choosing a method to measure quality. Usually, measuring data quality gets done by a combination of statistical methods and data visualization techniques.

Most common data problems appear to be the following:

Missing Values. No recorded values for many instances. Need to fill in the missing values before using the variable. Several techniques are available to estimate and fill in the missing values.

Noisy Data. A few instances have values completely out of line. Example: daily wages exceeding a million dollars. Several smoothing techniques are available to deal with noisy data.

Inconsistent Data. Synonyms and homonyms in various source systems may produce incorrect and inconsistent data. Sources must be reviewed and inconsistencies removed.

Removal of data problems signals the end of the data preparation step. Once the selected data is cleansed, it is ready for transformation.

Data Transformation. The prepared data is getting ready to be used as input to the data mining algorithm. The data transformation step converts the prepared data into a format suitable for data mining. You may say that data transformation changes the prepared data into a type of analytical model. The analytical model is simply an information structure representing integrated and time-dependent formatting of prepared data.

For example, if a supermarket wants to analyze customer purchases, it must first be decided if the analysis will be done at the store level or at the level of individual purchases. The analytical model includes the variables and the levels of detail.

Following the identification of the analytical model, detailed data transformation takes place. The objective is to transform the data to fit the exact requirements stipulated by the data mining algorithm. Data transformation may include a number of substeps such as:

- Data recoding
- Data format conversion
- Householding (linking of data of customers in the same household)
- Data reduction (by combining correlated variables)
- Scaling of parameter values to a range acceptable by data mining algorithms
- Discretization (conversion of quantitive variables into categorical variable groups)
- Conversion of categoric variable into a numeric representation.

Data Modeling

Data modeling for data mining applications involve representations of the pertinent data repositories. In our discussions of data mining so far, we have been referring to the data requirements for data mining applications. We pointed out certain advantages of data extraction from the data warehouse. However, data warehouse is not a required source; you may directly extract data from operational systems and other sources.

Figure 9-35 shows the data movements, the data preprocessing phase, and the data repositories.

Study the figure carefully and note the following data repositories for which we need to create data models as suggested below:

DM Source Repository. This is a general data store for all possible data mining applications. Periodically, data is extracted from the data warehouse and stored in this repository.

> *Data Model.* Normalized relational data model to represent low-level data content for all possible active variables available from the data warehouse.

Application Analytical Repository. This is a data store for a specific data mining application. Data is extracted from the above DM Source Repository and other sources and stored in this repository. Only the required active variables are selected.

> *Data Model.* Normalized relational data model is recommended to represent data content at the desired data level for only those active variables relevant to the specific data mining application.

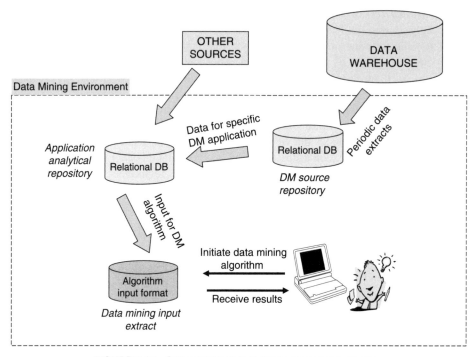

FIGURE 9-35 Data mining: data movements and repositories.

Data Mining Input Extract. This data store is meant to be used as input to the data mining algorithm. Data in the Application Analytical Repository is transformed and moved into this data store. This data store contains transformed values for only the required active variables.

> *Data Model.* Flat file or normalized relational data model with two or three tables to represent data content to be used as direct input to the data mining algorithm.

CHAPTER SUMMARY

- Data modeling for decision-support systems is not the same as modeling for operational systems.
- Decision-support systems provide information for making strategic decisions. These are informational systems as opposed to operational systems needed to run day-to-day operations of an organization.
- Data warehousing is the most common of the decision-support systems widely used today. It is a blend of several technologies. Major components of a data warehouse are source data, data staging, data storage, and information delivery.
- Decision makers view business in terms of business dimensions for analysis. Therefore, data modeling for a data warehouse must take into account business dimensions and the business metrics. Dimensional modeling technique is used.
- A dimensional data model, known as a STAR schema, consists of several dimension entity types and a fact entity type in the middle. Each of the dimension entity types

is in a one-to-many relationship with the common fact entity type. The STAR schema is not normalized. A snowflake schema, sometimes useful, is a normalized version. The data model for a given data warehouse usually consists of families of STARS.

- The conceptual data model in the form of a STAR schema is transformed into a logical model. If the data warehouse is implemented using a relational DBMS, the logical model in this case is a relational model.
- OLAP systems provide complex dimensional analysis. Data modeling for MOLAP: representation of multidimensional arrays suitable for the particular MDDBMS selected. Data modeling for ROLAP: E-R model of summarized data as required.
- Data mining is a fairly automatic knowledge discovery system. Data modeling for data mining systems consists of modeling for the data repositories: DM source repository, application analytical repository, and DM input extract.

REVIEW QUESTIONS

1. Match the column entries:

1. Informational systems	A. Uses MDDBMS
2. Data staging area	B. Semiadditive
3. Dimension hierarchies	C. Normalized
4. Fact entity type	D. Knowledge discovery
5. Dimension table	E. Decision support
6. Profit margin percentage	F. For drill-down analysis
7. Snowflake schema	G. Data cleansed and transformed
8. Hypercube	H. Generally wide
9. MOLAP	I. Metrics as attributes
10. Data mining	J. Represents multiple dimensions

2. A data warehouse is a decision-support environment, not a product. Discuss.
3. What data does an information package contain? Give a simple example.
4. Explain why the E-R modeling technique is not completely suitable for the data warehouse? How is dimensional modeling different?
5. Describe the composition of the primary keys for the dimension and fact tables. Give simple examples.
6. Describe the nature of the columns in a dimension table transformed from the corresponding conceptual STAR schema. Give typical examples.
7. What is your understanding of a value chain and a value circle in terms of families of STARS? What are the implications for data modeling?
8. Describe the main features of a ROLAP system. Explain how data modeling is done for this.
9. Distinguish between OLAP and data mining with regard to data modeling.
10. Discuss data preprocessing for data mining. What data repositories are involved and how do you model these?

IV

PRACTICAL APPROACH TO DATA MODELING

10

ENSURING QUALITY IN THE DATA MODEL

CHAPTER OBJECTIVES

- Establish the significance of quality in a data model
- Explore approaches to good data modeling
- Study instituting quality in model definitions
- Introduce quality dimensions in a data model
- Examine dimensions of accuracy, completeness, and clarity
- Highlight features and benefits of a high-quality model
- Discuss quality assurance process and the results
- Understand data model review and assessment

We are at a crucial point in our discussions of data modeling. We have traveled quite far covering much ground. You have a strong grip on data modeling by now. You are an expert on the components of a data model. You know how to translate the information requirements of an organization into a suitable data model using model components. You have studied a number of examples of data models. In short, you now possess a thorough knowledge of what data modeling is all about. What more is left to be covered?

In this chapter, we are now ready to turn our attention to an important aspect of data modeling—ensuring quality of the model. Having gone through the multifarious facets of data modeling, it is just fitting to bring all that to a logical conclusion by stressing data model quality.

In recent decades, organizational user groups and information technology professionals have realized the overwhelming significance of data modeling. A data modeling effort precedes every database implementation. However, what we see in practice is a number of

Data Modeling Fundamentals. By Paulraj Ponniah
Copyright © 2007 John Wiley & Sons, Inc.

bad or inadequate models out there. Many models are totally incorrect representations of the information requirements. It is not that a bad model lacks a few attributes here and there or portrays a small number of relationships incorrectly. Many bad models lead to disastrous database implementations. Some bad data models are abandoned midstream and shelved because of improper quality control. The efforts of many weeks and months are down the drain.

This chapter addresses the critical issues of data model quality. First, you will get to appreciate the significance of data model quality. Next, we will move to a discussion of quality in the definitions of various components. We will then explore the dimensions and characteristics of high-quality models and learn how to apply the fundamental principles of model quality. Quality assurance is a distinct process in the modeling effort; you will cover quality assurance in sufficient detail.

SIGNIFICANCE OF QUALITY

It is obvious that high quality in anything we create is essential. That goes without having to mention it specifically. Then is not that maxim true for data modeling as well? Why emphasize quality in data modeling separately? There are some special reasons.

The concepts of data modeling are not that easy to comprehend. Data modeling is a specialized effort needing special skills. A data modeler must be a business analyst, draftsman, documentation expert, and a database specialist—all rolled into one. It takes skill and experience to gain a high degree of proficiency in data modeling. It is easy to overlook the essentials and produce bad data models. In a large organization, piecing together the various components into a good data model requires enormous discipline and skill. It is not difficult to slip on model quality. We need to pay a high degree of special attention to quality.

Why Emphasize Quality?

Recall the fundamental purposes of a data model. Go back to the reasons for creating a data model in the first place. What is the role a data model plays in the development process of the data system for an organization?

First, a data model is meant as a communication tool for confirming the information requirements with the user groups. Next, a data model serves as a blueprint for the design and implementation of the data system for the organization. We have covered these two themes in elaborate detail. Figure 10-1 summarizes these two essential purposes of a data model.

Good Communication Tool. Quality in a data model is essential because the model has to be a good and effective means of communication with the user groups. As a data modeler, you delve into the information requirements; you want the data content of the ultimate database system to reflect the information requirements exactly. How do you ensure this?

You create a data model as a true replica of the information requirements. Then you use the data model as a tool for communication with the user groups. You have to show them that you have captured all the information requirements properly. You need to point out the various components of the data model to the user groups and get their confirmation. You can do this correctly and effectively only if your data model is good and of high quality.

Good Database Blueprint. The database of an organization is built and implemented from the data model. Every component of the data model gets transformed into one or

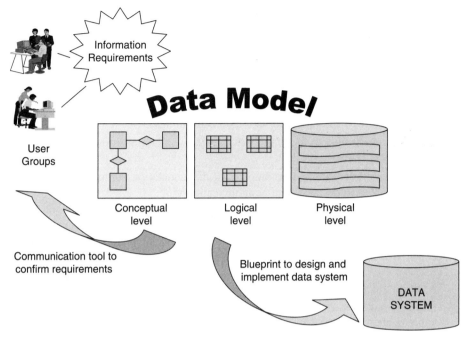

FIGURE 10-1 Purposes of a data model.

more parts of the database. If the entity types in a data model are erroneous or incomplete, the resulting database will be incorrect. If the data model does not establish the relationships correctly, the database will link the data structures incorrectly.

For building and implementing the database of an organization accurately and completely, the data model should be of good quality. A good data model is a good blueprint; a good blueprint ensures a good database—the end product.

Good and Bad Models

You have again noted the two primary purposes of a data model. Figure 10-1 presents the two purposes again. Now, the question arises: If our goal is to produce a good data model, can we recognize good and bad models?

In order to examine and find out if a model is good or bad, let us get back to the two primary purposes of a data model. We will examine a data model from the view of these purposes and note the characteristics of good and bad models. The first purpose is the use of a data model as a communication tool for working with the user groups and stakeholders, that is, people outside the IT community. The second purpose of a data model is its use as a blueprint for database design and implementation.

Communication Tool. A good data model has distinct characteristics including:

- Symbols used in the model have specific and unambiguous meanings.
- Users can intuitively understand the data model diagram.
- The model diagram conveys correct semantics.
- The layout of the model diagram is clear, uncluttered, and appealing.

- Users are able to understand the representations noted in the data model.
- Users can easily relate model components to their information requirements.
- The data model reflects the business rules correctly.
- Users are able to notice problems of representations, if any, easily.
- Users are able to note any missing representations without difficulty.
- Users are able to suggest additions, deletions, and modifications easily.
- The model is free from hidden or ambiguous meanings.
- The data model is able to facilitate back-and-forth communication with user groups effectively.
- The data model diagram and accompanying documentation complement each other and work well together as a joint communication tool.

A bad data model does not possess the above characteristics. Further, a data model may be dismissed as bad if, in addition to the absence of the above characteristics, the model has specific negative features including the following:

- The data model diagram is confusing and convoluted.
- The data model is incomplete and does not represent the complete information requirements.
- There are several components in the data model that are vague and ambiguous.
- The symbols lack clarity; meanings are not distinct and clear.
- The layout of the data model diagram is horrific.
- Users find numerous representation errors in the data model.

Blueprint for Database. A good data model from the point of view of its use as a detailed plan for the database has distinct characteristics including:

- Component-to-component mapping between the conceptual data model and the logical data model is easy.
- Each component in the conceptual data model has equivalent part or parts in the logical model.
- All symbols are clear for making the transition.
- All meanings are easily transferable between the conceptual and logical data models.
- The data model is a complete blueprint.
- The data model can be broken down in cohesive parts for possible partial implementations.
- The connections or links between model components are easily defined.
- The business rules may easily be transposed from the conceptual data model to the logical data model.

A bad data model does not possess the above characteristics. Moreover, a data model may be considered bad if, in addition to the absence of the above characteristics, the model has specific negative features including the following:

- The data model contains insufficient information for all the transitions to the logical data model to be rendered possible.

- The links or connections between components are ambiguous.
- The data model diagram is too intricate and unnecessarily complex.

Approach to Good Modeling

Let us now turn our attention to the various aspects of quality in data models. We will look at various factors that contribute to high-quality data models. You will learn about data model quality dimensions and their implications. However, at the outset let us mention a few guiding principles for creating good data models. What is the best approach for good data modeling?

We highlight in the following a few fundamentals of good data modeling practice.

Proper Mindset. Everyone on the project team must recognize the importance of high quality in the output of the data modeling process. The data modelers have full responsibility to bear this in mind throughout the entire modeling process—from collection of information requirements to creating the final data model.

Practice of Agile Modeling. Recently, organizations have come to realize that agile software development principles and practice prove to be effective. Use and application of agile data modeling principles produce good data models. We will discuss agile modeling further in Chapter 11.

Continuous Ensuring of Quality. Quality assurance is not to be considered as an ornamental add-on to the data modeling process. From beginning to end, continuous quality assurance is essential.

Periodic Control and Assurance. In addition to the employment of quality assurance principles by the data modelers themselves, periodic review and control by qualified professionals takes quality assurance of data models to a higher level.

QUALITY OF DEFINITIONS

When you create a data model and draw the data model diagram, your model diagram must be supported by an accompanying model document that contains information and clarifications about the data model. Among other contents, the data model document has a set of definitions. These relate to each individual component in the data model.

If there are 15 entity types represented in your data model, the model document must contain definitions of these entity types. If TRANSFER is an entity type in your model, what does transfer mean and represent? You must have a clear definition of "transfer." In the same way, the attributes must be defined, the relationships must be defined, and so on. The definitions are some kind of meta-data—data about data. These definitions must themselves be of high quality.

What is quality in a definition? Let us say, you have an attribute CustomerName. You can indicate that customer names must be textual data with a maximum length of 60 characters. You can also describe and define what you mean by CustomerName. How is this attribute understood by the user groups? Are customers also known as clients in some departments of the organization? If you definition of the attribute is of a high quality, all of these will be clearly and succinctly answered. We will explore the aspects of quality in definitions.

Importance of Definitions

Before we get into the aspects of high-quality definitions, we need to clearly understand what we mean by definitions. What roles do definitions play in data modeling? What happens if the definitions are bad? What benefits accrue if the definitions are really good?

Meaning of a Definition. A definition, in simplest terms, may be thought of as a description, in textual form, about the thing that is being defined, providing an effective meaning of the thing. If you are defining an entity type, then the definition tells the readers exactly what that entity type means.

A definition must

- be a word, phrase, or sentences providing the meaning of the object being defined,
- make the meaning of the object clear,
- convey the basic or fundamental character of the object, and
- provide insight into what the object stands for.

Role of Definitions. Let us say you come across an entity type called ASSOCIATE in the data model for a retail operation. What does this entity type represent? All employees? Only some specific type of employees? Does this connote a level in the hierarchical structure? A clear definition of the term would clarify these issues and describe what exactly is being represented by the entity type.

It is very important that everyone involved in creating, designing, discussing, confirming, and implementing the data model must clearly understand what that entity type actually represents. What are the individual entities? The user groups must clearly know what the data model means when it includes an entity type ASSOCIATE. The designer and database developer must clearly understand what they are implementing.

Definitions are crucial because they provide a clear basis for understanding the data model. Definitions allow meaningful and useful discussions about the components in the data model. As noted earlier, frequently you come across homonyms and synonyms while gathering information requirements and creating a data model. Definitions help resolve issues about homonyms and synonyms.

Bad and Good Definitions. The quality of definitions indicates the quality of the data model itself. Unfortunately, not too much attention is paid to the quality of definitions in a data modeling project. Definitions are quickly added to the model document, sometimes, toward the end of the project. Even more troublesome is that many of the components in a data model are not even defined anywhere. Lack of definitions is a major problem.

We have all run into bad definitions of terms. For example, some definitions are just a rephrasing of the name of the object itself. The definition of CustomerNumber may just be "number of customer." Some other definitions may be quite vague and incomprehensible. The definition for PROPERTY-TRANSFER may be given as "transfer of property from one place to another, provided the movement is sequential."

When you review a number of definitions, you will develop a gut feel for whether a particular definition is good or bad. A good definition makes you understand what exactly the term means, what it stands for, and what its characteristics are. A bad definition leaves you in a state of confusion.

We will look into the aspects that make a definition good or bad. Why would some definitions be considered good and others bad? We will get deeper into individual aspects of quality in definitions.

Aspects of Quality Definitions

So far, we have been somewhat vague about quality of definitions. We explored how definitions may be considered bad or good. We mentioned the significance of quality in definitions. Now, let us make things more concrete and definitive. Are there specific aspects of definitions that make them good or bad? What determines whether a definition is good?

These are four major factors that contribute to high quality in definitions.

Correctness. If the definition is not accurate, the definition is completely flawed. It the definition conveys the wrong meaning, then serious consequences follow. The definition must be consistent with how the object is truly known in the organization. The definition must also be thoroughly reviewed and confirmed by the appropriate authorities in the user groups.

Completeness. The definition must have everything needed to make it complete and to stand alone. A balance must be struck; the definition must not be too narrow and specific on the one hand and not too broad and generic on the other. The definition, wherever necessary, must include examples.

Clearness. Clarity is of paramount importance. The definition must not be a restatement of what appears to be obvious. Obscure technical jargon must be avoided. There should be only limited use of abbreviations and, that too, only widely accepted ones. Ambiguity and dual meanings must be carefully avoided.

Format. Appropriate length is necessary for a good definition—not too long, not too short. Poor grammar and misspellings degrade the quality of a definition.

We will now proceed to explore each of these factors of quality definitions in some detail.

Correctness

This factor is concerned with the accuracy of the definition. A definition must convey the correct meaning of the object it defines. The definition must match exactly what the object means in the organization and be consistent with the overall purpose and functions of the organization. Remember, when we are discussing the definition of an attribute such as EmployeeService, we are not validating the values that attribute might take; we are only referring to the definition of the term "EmployeeService."

Let us consider some aspects of ensuring correctness of a definition.

Reviewed and Confirmed. To ensure correctness of a definition, the definition must be thoroughly reviewed and confirmed by the appropriate authority in the user groups. If there is a data quality steward in the organization, the responsibility lies with this person.

The first step is to ascertain whether a particular definition has been reviewed and approved. This may be done through the use of a checklist. If it is not yet done, then you have to locate the proper authority qualified to do the review and authorized to give the approval. Once the proper authority is identified, the next step is to get the actual review under way. The review effort should be intense and thorough. The approval of the data quality steward should meet the standards set up in the organization.

Consistent with Organizational Understanding. Once a definition is reviewed and approved by an individual authority, you have to broaden the scope to ensure that the definition fits into the general understanding of the object in the wider organization. This activity will ensure that the definition does not conflict with any other objects and their definitions in the organization.

When you tried to match the object and its definition with others in the organization, you will conclude with one of the following results. The following also indicates the appropriate actions.

Unique. The object and its definition are unique—no match with any other in the organization. Your definition for the object will become the definition for it in the entire organization.

Identical. There are one or more objects with the same name and almost similar definitions. This means that this object in the data model is the same as the others. Make sure the definition becomes a closer match with the other definitions.

Homonym. You have found another object in the organization with the same name, but the definitions are different. In this case, probably you have used the name of an already existing object for the object in your data model. So, change the name of your object, and then restart the matching process.

Synonym. You have found another object with the same definition, but with a different name. You will have to change the name for the object in your data model to the name already in use in the organization.

Completeness

The completeness factor includes making sure that the definition is sufficiently detailed with examples and any information about how the object could be derived. If the definition is too generic and broad, it will not be of much use when you want to explain the specifics to user groups or when you want to consider every part of the data model for implementation. On the other hand, if the definition is too specific and confined, the definition may not be relevant to a wider circle of users and database practitioners. A complete definition is self-contained.

Let us discuss some requirements to make a definition complete.

Not Too Broad. A broad or generic definition is usually made up so that the definition may gain wider acceptance. We want our definition agreeable to all user groups. Because of this intention, the definition is generally kept short and, therefore, incomplete. Broad definitions usually have the following features.

Dictionary Meanings. Tend to contain dictionary meanings of the names of the objects. If the name of the object consists of compound words, for example, CustomerAddress, then the definition consists of dictionary meanings of the individual words *Customer* and *Address*. Very few can argue with exact dictionary meanings. Therefore, the definition expects to be generally accepted.

Ambiguity. Broad definitions seek to avoid conflicts; therefore, intentionally they use ambiguous words that can confuse everyone. Each group will try to interpret the definition in their own terms and agree with the definition.

Excessive Abstraction. Broad definitions tend to use abstract words such as person to mean employee in one case and again person to mean customer in another case.

Measures. Many data elements refer to measurements of quantity or currency. For example, ProductQuantity needs to be identified whether the quantity is defined in terms of units, pounds, or kilograms. Similarly, UnitPrice has to be stipulated in terms of the currency such as U.S. dollars, pounds sterling, euro, and so on. Broad definitions are likely to omit the units of measurements.

Tracking down generic definitions is not an easy task. You have to examine the definition with identifying features of generic definitions in mind. Are there merely dictionary meanings in the definition? Is the definition intentionally kept ambiguous? Is the definition filled with abstract terms? Does the object indicate something that involves units of measurements?

In order to fix a broad definition, begin with the assumption that the definition is too generic. Read and reread the definition to look for traces of ambiguity. If the definition is ambiguous, replace it with words that can mean the same to all user groups. Continue and look for abstract terms such as person, account, and price. Replace these with more specific words. If there are any units of measurements to be mentioned, state them explicitly in the definition.

Not Too Narrow. Definitions that are too specific may mean that the definition is correct and valid only with a limited scope. Narrow definitions reveal the following traits.

Specific to Certain Departments Only. Narrow definitions tend to limit the meaning and reference to only certain departments—not to the entire organization.

Specific to Particular Applications Only. Again, narrow definitions refer to only certain business applications in the organization.

Business Purpose Only. Without stating the meaning of the object, a narrow definition mentions only the purpose of the object.

Derivations Only. Without stating the meaning of the object, a narrow definition mentions only how the value for the object is derived, for example, a narrow definition for ProfitMargin.

Current Meaning Only. Narrow definitions specifically state only the meanings as applicable today and not those that are generally applicable.

Examples Only. Although examples are important, narrow definitions tend to define an object only with examples and do not include meanings.

For fixing narrow definitions, look for the traits listed above and then take appropriate actions. If all the above characteristics are present in a definition, then the definition is too narrow. It requires a lot of work to make it complete. If there are references only to some departments or only to some applications, then widen the definition and amplify its scope. Narrow definitions stating just the business purpose usually stand out. Add the meanings of the objects to such definitions.

If an object is being defined with examples only, then add the meaning to the definition. Broaden the scope of the definition, if it includes only point-in-time meaning. If a definition just tells you how to derive the value of the object, then use the definition as a starting point and then add more intrinsic meaning.

Self-Contained. When you look at a data model diagram, you see the various components and the underlying structure of how these components fit in. Sometimes, definitions are composed in such a way that you cannot understand the meaning of the object defined unless you view the object in its place in the structure. In other words, the definition is not complete in the sense it is not self-contained. You need to know the structure and perhaps the definitions of the other objects in proximity.

Dependencies of definitions that do not stand alone may be classified in two ways.

Structure Dependency. In this case, you need to know the structure of the data model and the place of the object in the structure to understand the definition.

Relationship Dependency. For understanding a definition of this kind, you need to know the relationship of this object with other objects in the data model.

To cure a definition that is not self-contained, first read the definition and check if you have to refer to the data model for understanding the definition. Then, it obviously means that the definition cannot stand alone. Examine the definition and the names of the related objects in the definition to make it complete.

Shows Derivation. Many attributes in a data model may be derived attributes. The values for these attributes may be derived or calculated from the values of other attributes of the same entity type or other entity types. When you define derived attributes, the definitions may be incomplete because of the following reasons.

Incomplete Derivation. The derivation contained in the definition is not enough for the definition to be complete.

Missing Derivation. The definition is totally devoid of derivation where such details are absolutely essential to complete the definition.

The first step in fixing this problem is to identify derived attributes. Examining the attributes in a data model would easily reveal such attributes with problematic definitions. Then review the definition of each derived attribute. Are there any details about the derivation at all? If not, provide the missing derivation details to the definition. On the other hand, if there are insufficient details about derivation, then expand the definition by adding more derivation details.

Supplemented with Examples. Examples always enhance the value of a definition. After including the meaning of an object in the definition, if you add some examples of the object, then you provide additional insight into the meaning. Supplementing a definition with examples adds more value to any definition, more so in the following cases:

Abstract Objects. When you define abstract objects such as Student, Employee, Client, Shipper, and so on, add examples to your definitions.

Organizational Codes. Codes with specific values are frequently used in an organization. State codes, marital status codes, gender codes, and credit codes are a few of the kinds of codes used. Whenever you define a code, include some examples and possible values in the definition.

Clearness

A clear definition leaves no room for ambiguity. As soon as you begin reading the definition, you are able to understand the meaning of the object. Every word in the definition makes apparent sense.

We will examine a few characteristics of definitions that lack clarity. We will also consider ways to look for such definitions and methods for remedying them.

Repeating the Obvious. Such definitions just restate what was already mentioned in an earlier part or is easily available elsewhere. No new information is given in the definitions. Definitions of this kind are both annoying and even dangerous.

Fortunately, several indications are available for tracking down such a definition. The text of the definition may just repeat the name of the object. Sometimes, the definition may contain one or two words in addition to words in the name of the object itself. In other cases, the definitions may just contain synonyms of the name of the object.

Some other cases involve misplacement of the definitions. The definition may define the parent of the object instead of the object itself. Also, the definition may define the child of the object instead of the object.

If the repetition in the definition is the name of the object and if the definition contains additional new details, it may be all right to leave the repetition. If there is no new information in the definition or it only contains a restatement of the obvious, then you need to make the definition clearer by adding the meaning of the object. If the repetition refers to a parent or child, remove this part from the definition.

Containing Obscure Terminology. Most industries and organizations have specific terminology that is understood only within limited circles. When you create a model to be used and understood only within the confines of the industry or organization, some specific terminology may be acceptable. However, make sure the terminology is understood well by all concerned. If there are any reservations about the meaning of a particular technical term or word used in the definition, then, by all means, replace such term with a more common term.

Sometimes, the same object name in different industries may refer to different things. For example, LotNumber in an auction company refers to the sequential number assigned to property lots sold in an auction. But LotNumber in a manufacturing organization is associated with the time and location stamp for a particular product and, therefore, has different purposes. If you come across any such objects, add proper clarification to the terminology.

Using Relatively Unknown Abbreviations. Abbreviations used in organizations are somewhat similar to industry-specific terminology. Abbreviations in definitions may not be completely avoided. In fact, sometimes abbreviations are more commonly used than the complete versions of the phrases indicated by the abbreviations.

Use abbreviations sparingly in definitions. Then, too, use only standard and well-understood abbreviations.

Format

Length of a definition gives a good clue as to the robustness of a definition. A very long definition usually includes irrelevant details, contains repetitions, and obscures the meanings. On the other hand, a very brief definition lacks sufficient details and fails to describe the meaning of the object clearly and fully.

In practice, if you notice a definition running into more than two or three paragraphs, then you should immediately examine the need for such length. Check if each word or phrase in the definition refers only to the object being defined and nothing else. If they reference objects or other data elements outside the scope of the definition, remove the extraneous details. Carefully look for repetitions of words and phrases and remove anything that does not add to the effectiveness of the definition. Retain only the verbiage directly related to the object being defined.

Right away, misspelled words in a definition, though fairly harmless, produce a negative impression in the minds of those that read and use the definition. Correct all the misspelled words in every definition. There is no excuse for misspellings with modern-day spell checks. Similarly, poor grammar in a definition raises a red flag while reading the definition. Use correct grammatical constructions. Get your definitions edited by a competent person before releasing the definitions for general use.

Checklists

We explored the various aspects of quality of definitions in sufficient detail. Each factor is essential for a good definition. You have also noted how to examine a definition and detect the deficiencies. You also reviewed some of the methods for fixing poor definitions.

A Definition Checklist is a valuable tool for the review of a definition to ensure that the definition possesses all the characteristics of a good definition. The checklist is in the form of a two-dimensional table or spreadsheet. The rows contain the criteria for evaluating a definition. The column headings are usually the names of the objects for which the definitions are being evaluated. This is the general idea. You can have an amended format of the checklist to suit your specific purposes. You may firm up your criteria and mark them in the rows. In one sheet of the checklist, you may opt for a certain number of objects. Also, you may decide on the components of the data model that would need definition checklists—entity types, attributes, identifiers, relationships.

Initially, when you review a definition, you will record the findings on your checklist by indicating whether the definition passed a certain criterion or not. This is the initial pass. Based on the initial review, the definitions will be amended suitably to meet all the criteria. A second pass would indicate any residual problems. This iterative process

Entity   Types

Quality Criteria	Consignor	Transfer	Shipper	Dealer
Correctness				
Reviewed and confirmed	●	●	●	
Conforms to general usage	●	●		●
Completeness				
Not too broad	●	●	●	
Not too narrow	●			●
Self-contained	●		●	
Shows derivation				●
Has examples	●	●	●	●
Clearness				
Does not repeat the obvious	●	●	●	
No obscure terminology	●		●	●
Abbreviations okay			●	●
Format				
Not too short	●	●	●	
Not too long		●	●	●

FIGURE 10-2   Definition checklist for entity types.

may continue until the definitions satisfy all the criteria. Now, you will have a set of GOOD definitions.

Figures 10-2 and 10-3 illustrate the use of checklists. You may add such checklists for other data model components.

Attributes

Quality Criteria	BuyerType	TopBid	HammerPrice	ReservePrice	ItemProvenance
Correctness					
Reviewed and confirmed	●	●	●	●	●
Conforms to general usage	●	●		●	
Completeness					
Not too broad	●	●	●		●
Not too narrow		●		●	
Self-contained	●	●	●		
Shows derivation	●		●	●	
Has examples	●	●	●	●	●
Clearness					
Does not repeat the obvious	●	●	●	●	●
No obscure terminology	●	●	●	●	
Abbreviations okay	●		●	●	●
Format					
Not too short	●	●	●		●
Not too long	●	●	●	●	

FIGURE 10-3   Definition checklist for attributes.

Entity Types

Refer to Figure 10-2.

Attributes

Refer to Figure 10-3.

HIGH-QUALITY DATA MODEL

Having reviewed the need for high quality in model definitions, we now turn our attention to the data model itself. We looked at methods to recognize good and bad definitions; we also covered remedial measures for fixing and transforming a bad definition into a good definition.

We will cover quality in a data model in a similar fashion. First, you need to understand the meaning of quality as it applies to a data model. You need to explore the dimensions of data model quality. How to recognize a high-quality data model? What are its characteristics? What benefits accrue to the user groups, the data modelers, and other database practitioners from a good data model?

Meaning of Data Model Quality

As you know, a data model is a representation or a replica. A representation of what? In a data model, you attempt to represent precisely and correctly the information required by an organization to run its business. A model does not contain the actual information; it is not the data content. But it is a replica of the data content. In a data model, you capture all the pertinent aspects of the information requirements in a form that is readily understandable and at the same time useful for ultimately designing and implementing the database.

You know that for creating a data model, you need building blocks or components that can represent individual aspects of the information requirements. Symbols are used for this purpose. Each symbol connotes a specific meaning; connections between symbols indicate relationships. At this stage, you are well-versed with the symbols, use of symbols, meanings of symbols, and the way symbols represent real-world information requirements. You are also familiar with several modeling techniques, their specific symbols, and the usage of the symbols. The proper use and arrangement of the symbols to represent real-world information constitutes data modeling. A data model is such a representative arrangement.

Combining the appropriate symbols to convey the correct meanings can be difficult. If you do not have the right combination of the modeling symbols, your data model cannot be used effectively to communicate with the users and to construct the ultimate database. In other words, if your data model is of a poor quality, it cannot serve its two major purposes.

When is a data model useless? It is so if its quality is poor. What do we mean by this? We mean to say that the data model does not possess the necessary basic characteristics to be useful. Thus, quality in a data model is the presence or absence of certain characteristics that make the data model good or bad.

When we consider a data model to be of good quality, we refer to the following characteristics:

Accurate. The data model is a correct representation of the information requirements. Every component, every linkage, every arrangement—the entire representation is totally right.

Useful. The model is completely suitable for its intended uses: as a communication tool with the users and as a database blueprint for the database.

Meets Expectations. The data model meets and even surpasses expectations by user groups and database practitioners.

Comprehensive. User groups and all others concerned can understand the data model very easily.

Elegant. The model diagram looks elegant, free from convoluted or haphazard arrangements of symbols.

Thus, mainly, when we talk about the high quality of a data model, we refer to correctness and completeness. The data model truly and correctly represents the selected real-world information requirements. It is also a complete representation.

Quality Dimensions

We want to dig deeper and explore the concept of quality in a data model in greater detail. The reason for this exercise is simple. Once you have a full understanding of data model quality, you can then apply your comprehension to creating high-quality data models. In order to get a handle on data model quality, let us tear a data model apart and get a glimpse on the inside.

You have a set of symbols arranged in a certain way. The arrangement itself must conform to accepted standards. When we mention the proper arrangement of the symbols, we are really referring to the syntax of modeling technique. For a data model to be of high quality, the arrangement must be correct and it must also be complete. That is, the data model must be syntactically correct and complete.

In a data model, the symbols may be right and the arrangement may also be correct. But, what is the purpose of the arrangement in the first place? Is it not the proper representation of the business requirements? The purpose of the arrangement—the concept behind the arrangement—must be right. The concept behind the arrangement is the right representation of real-world information requirements. That is, the data model must be conceptually correct and complete.

The correctness and completeness of a data model are to be evaluated in a broader context of the entire organization. You do not just look only at the set of components in the data model and the arrangement. You need to place the data model in the context of the overall organization and verify its correctness and completeness. Does the data model represent the information requirements of the real-world domain of the entire organization? Or, does it represent some part of the domain? If so, is it correct and complete in relation to other parts of the domain? There is a contextual factor in the mix for assessing the quality of a data model.

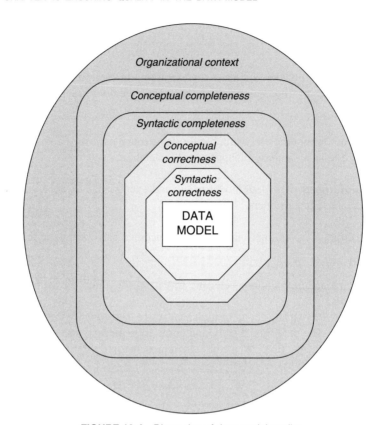

FIGURE 10-4 Dimension of data model quality.

We can, therefore, arrive at the dimensions of quality in a data model by interleaving the two primary aspects of correctness and completeness with the two qualifications of syntactical and conceptual representation. The contextual factor of a data model is the enveloping dimension of data model quality.

Figure 10-4 shows these five dimensions of data model quality. Notice how these quality dimensions mesh together in order for a data model to be of a high quality.

Correctness. Accuracy in a data model is of great importance. If the data model does not represent the information requirements correctly, the resultant database will be flawed. Users will not be able to perform their functions. A data model must use the symbols and arrangement correctly; the model must correctly represent the real-world information.

Syntactic Correctness. The correct set of symbols is used in the data model. The symbols are used in the data model for exactly their intended purposes. The arrangement of the symbols does not violate any rules of the modeling technique. The linkages between model components are expressed correctly.

Conceptual Correctness. Each symbol in the data model correctly represents the part of real-world information it is intended to represent. The linkages between components correctly and truly represent the actual relationships that exist in the real world. The overall arrangement of symbols in the data model is a true replica of the broad information requirements.

Completeness. Unlike correctness, completeness does not focus on individual components of a data model. Here, the entire data model is in view. You look at the whole model and ascertain if the representation for any part of information requirements is missing in the model. However, correctness and completeness are like two sides of the coin of quality in a data model.

Syntactic Completeness. This refers to the data modeling process rather than to the data model itself. However, if the modeling process in not complete, then the model itself will be incomplete. Depending on the selected modeling technique, the process consists of distinct steps in putting together the components. The first step may be to identify and represent the entity types. The second step may be representation of relationships among the entity types. Next, perhaps, is the representation of attributes, and so on. Review and refinement of the steps would also come in-between. Syntactic completeness implies that the modeling process has been carried out completely and thoroughly to produce a good data model.

Conceptual Completeness. When a model is conceptually complete, it represents every aspect of the information domain it set out to do. Every business object gets represented. No known attributes of the objects are missing in the data model. All relationships are expressed completely. Within each relationship, relationship cardinalities are completely shown. The data model is a complete representation of the information requirements.

Organizational Context. If correctness and completeness are like the two sides of the coin of data model quality, then organizational context is like the rim of the coin. It envelops the other quality dimensions.

Mostly, every data model is a representation of part of the information requirements of an organization. Sometimes, the whole information domain is taken to be modeled. Usually, modeling and implementation of a database, as an initial effort, covers a high-return and high-visibility area of the information domain. Next, the scope is expanded to other areas. Therefore, whenever you create a data model, you need to consider the scope of the model in terms of the whole information domain of the organization.

If your data model is the first one in the organization for implementation of the initial database, you need to keep it open and flexible enough for future models to be integrated with yours. If your data model is a subsequent model, then your model must be designed in such a way to incorporate it into the earlier models. Keeping the organizational context in view while modeling information domains is crucial for your model to be a high-quality model.

What Is a High-Quality Model?

So, a data model must be correct syntactically and conceptually; it must be complete syntactically and conceptually. A data model must be created within the context of the organization's information domain.

Apart from these, are there any general characteristics of a good data model? Can we examine a particular model, look at its features, and declare that it is a high-quality data model. A high-quality data model possesses the following general characteristics.

Built by Expert Modelers. Who created a data model has a direct bearing on the quality of the model. Data modeling requires training and developed skills.

Built with Proven Technique. For building a good data model, you need to employ a proven technique such as the E-R modeling technique. The rules of the technique will prevent errors from creeping in.

Follows Accepted Standards. In addition to the modeling technique itself, use of accepted standards of the organization is important. This includes naming standards, general documentation standards, and so on.

Involves Right User Groups. If the right domain experts and stakeholders get involved in the entire data modeling process, the chances of the model being of a high quality are good.

Incorporates All Business Rules. A data model is good if it embodies all the pertinent business rules so that these may be properly implemented in the database.

Supported by Documentation. The quality of the accompanying model documentation is an indication of the quality of the data model itself. An important feature of a good data model is its good supporting documentation.

Benefits of High-Quality Models

In a data system development project, a high-quality data model produces several benefits. Without a data model, it is almost impossible to develop a good database system unless the database is extremely small and simple. Even then, a somewhat crude data model would be necessary. For developing and implementing a substantial database, a good data model is an essential prerequisite.

We want to highlight and reiterate the usefulness and benefits of a good data model for two purposes.

High-Quality Design. For implementing a successful database, you need to start with a high-quality design, both logical and physical. If your conceptual data model is of high quality, it could readily be transformed into a good logical model to complete the logical design process.

Proper Requirements Definition. A high-quality data model, reviewed and confirmed by the relevant user groups, serves as the best definition of information requirements. Proper requirements definition is absolutely essential for successful design and implementation phases.

QUALITY ASSURANCE PROCESS

We had introduced the notion that quality assurance in data modeling is a continuous process. No product may be allowed to be fully developed before subjecting it to review and correction. This is true of data modeling as in any other creative and productive effort. Too many errors might creep in along the way, and finally the output might just be worthless. Just like other production efforts, data modeling is also a human enterprise; humans are not infallible.

You must be familiar with quality assurance (QA) programs in connection with other activities. You must be aware of peer reviews and code walkthroughs in software development projects. You yourself must have experienced the outcome of such reviews where a number of errors were uncovered to be fixed later. This would avoid rushing to finish a half-baked product without pausing to check periodically.

Of course, as a data modeler you would pursue your task with utmost diligence. You would attempt to follow the best practices. You know the dimensions of quality in data modeling. You would conform to the proper norms and apply the most effective principles. This is being mindful of quality during the modeling process by the modelers themselves. But, it works out to be always better when someone else with appropriate expertise looks at the model and verifies its correctness and completeness. This review must be methodical and at the right intervals. A need arises for an established quality assurance program if a data modeling project is to be successful.

Aspects of Quality Assurance

So, what is a good quality assurance program for data modeling? What is it made up of? Let us go over some of the major aspects of a quality assurance program.

Generally, the following must be in place for a good quality assurance program.

Quality Assurance Plan. A plan for the quality assurance program must be formulated up front. The plan emphasizes quality assurance to be an integral part of the data modeling effort. Usually, the plan is laid out by a team consisting of the project manager, senior data modeler, user representative, and some senior IT executive.

The plan specifies the frequency of quality assurance reviews, sets up guidelines, and assigns responsibilities to the reviewers. A time line is sometimes suggested. Most importantly, the plan expresses how actions must follow the review process for rectifying any errors.

Quality Assurance Coordinator. Quality assurance involves a number of administrative tasks. Scheduling the reviews and making them happen in a timely fashion itself is a major responsibility. If there are more than a few reviewers, managing their schedules and assigning them optimally takes time and effort. Settling issues that come up in the reviews is another major activity.

A good quality assurance coordinator is a major asset in the data modeling project. If there is already a quality assurance group in your IT department, then someone from that group is an ideal candidate for this responsibility. If not, the organization must look for any available senior professional either from within or outside.

Data Model Reviewers. Of course, a quality assurance program cannot get off the ground without good reviewers. Depending on the size and scope of the data modeling project, you may need more than one reviewer. If a few data modeling projects are running concurrently in the organization, a team of reviewers may rotate among the various projects.

The qualification and skills of the reviewers are important. They must know data modeling well enough to be able to look deeply for quality problems in a data model. Good reviewers come out of the ranks of good, experienced data modelers.

Standards. The data modelers and the reviewers must have very definitive guidelines and rules about how a data model must be created in your organization. Standards must be developed with utmost care. The standards must encompass all aspects of data modeling.

Standards lay down the confines within which the modeling effort must be made. They set the boundaries. They define the tolerance limits for deviations. Both data modelers and data model reviewers need to use the standards manual in carrying out their responsibilities. A good standards document serves as a good training tool for data modelers and analysts on the project.

Review and Action Document. As soon as the initial review of a data model takes place, the reviewer prepares a review and action document in cooperation with the data modeler. The document incorporates information on the review process. In subsequent reviews of the data model, this document will get updated continually. This document will be part of the overall data model documentation.

The review and action document provides a general description of how the review was conducted. It lists the findings of the reviewer. It includes suggested actions to rectify any quality problems cited. It maintains a diary for follow-up.

Stages of Quality Assurance Process

The quality assurance process is based on a systematic approach of planning and execution. Based on the quality assurance plan, every quality assurance process has definite stages of activities. The plan would indicate the frequency of the quality assurance reviews. In a typical data modeling project of reasonable size, at least two reviews are necessary: One at the midway point, and one when the modeling effort is nearing completion. But many organizations, depending on the availability of resources, opt for three review sessions: One when the project has proceeded one-third of the way, another when two-thirds of the model is done, and the final review when the modelers have nearly completed their work.

Whatever may be the frequency of the quality assurance reviews in your organizations, each review goes through the three stages. Each review session gets initiated with a planned document discussed at an initiation meeting. Then the expert reviewers perform the actual review. Finally, the review effort is deemed to be complete when action takes place on the findings and issues raised in the review. We will quickly go through each of these three stages.

Review Initiation. The reviewers sit down in a meeting with the data modeling team. Appropriate user liaison persons should also be encouraged to attend the meeting. The meeting must have a definite agenda of topics and issues to be discussed and agreed to

Review Item	Syntactical Review	Conceptual Review
Data Model		
Data Model Diagram	●	●
Complete List of Definitions	●	
Supplemental Documentation	●	●
Data Modeler's Notes	●	
Business Rules and Concepts		
Operational Plans	●	●
Business Plans (Summaries)	●	●
Policies and Procedures	●	●
Industry Norms and Guidelines		
Business Processes		
Organization's Overall Operations	●	●
Departments, Locations, and Functions	●	●
Information Requirements Definition	●	
Other Relevant Studies		
CASE Tool Outputs		
Analysis Reports	●	●
Validation Reports	●	●
Issues and Concerns		
General Issues	●	
Data Modeling Concerns		●
Standards and Methods		
Industry Standards		●
Organizational Standards	●	
IT Standards		
Data Modeling Standards	●	●
Validation Methods and Principles		●

FIGURE 10-5   Model review checklist.

at the meeting. A model review checklist is a useful tool in the entire review process. Figure 10-5 is a sample model review checklist. You may alter the checklist to suit the requirements of your organization and the specific data model to be reviewed.

Review initiation meeting marks the beginning of the quality assurance review session. If quality assurance in your particular situation consists of three reviews, then each review gets initiated with a separate initiation meeting. Of course, the review initiation for the very first review would be more elaborate. By the second and third reviews, the reviewers and the modeling team would have learned to work and collaborate together. The preparation for these subsequent reviews would be less and takes less time.

The following are the main tasks of review initiation:

Model Review Checklist. The reviewers and the modeling team go over the items listed in the checklist. Generally, the list indicates all the materials and resources necessary for the review. The checklist is used to collect the materials through the modeling team and the user liaison person.

Model Building Standards. The reviewers and the modeling team go over the standards and parameters in the organization for creating data models. The modeling team informs the reviewers how these standards have been applied in the efforts. This is especially important if the reviewers are recruited from outside to conduct the reviews.

Model Status. The reviewers ascertain from the modeling team the extent of completion of the data model. The reviewers get a sense of the general state of the data model. If this is a second or third review, the modeling team indicates to the reviewers what new modeling components have been added or modified subsequent to the previous review.

Specific Issues. The data modeling team informs the reviewers of any specific issues of concern. If some areas of the model are sensitive to specific user groups, the reviewers get to know about these. Also, the user groups relevant to important areas of the data model are highlighted.

Next Phases. The modeling team also brings the reviewers up-to-date on the immediate next phases of the modeling effort.

Data Model Review. This is the important phase of the reviewing process consuming most of the time. This has to be done thoroughly. The model review checklist will be used continually during this stage to check off review items completed. At the same time, during the review process, the reviewers will prepare a separate document to record their findings. Figure 10-6 is an example of a format for recording the findings and issues.

The next subsection deals with data model review in more detail.

Review Topics	Findings and Issues	Action Items	Responsible Department/Person
Policies and Procedures			
Business Processes			
Standards and Methods			
Documentation Study			
Data Modeling Team			
Data Model Review			
.			

FIGURE 10-6 Model review: findings and issues.

Actions on Findings. The record of findings and issues indicates who would be responsible for the resolutions of the items. Sometimes, user representatives may be named as those for taking particular actions. A report of actions taken on the findings will be added as a supporting document to the findings document.

The completion of all actions for the resolution of issues and findings marks the end of the model review at this point. If this is the first review of a data model, the reviewers have an opportunity to give specific pointers and guidance to the project team.

Data Model Review

This subsection describes the actual data model review stage in sufficient detail. It lists the major activities of the stage. The list given orders the activities in their logical sequence of how these should take place.

As indicated earlier, the model review checklist is used extensively and continually in this stage. The goal is to complete all the items listed in that checklist. However, the handling of the items on the list happens in a systematic manner.

Preliminary Model Review. This is just a quick glimpse of the data model—nothing detailed at this point. The reviewers perform a quick walk-through of the data model diagram with the modeling team. They also scan through the contents of accompanying data model document.

Again, this is not an elaborate step. If the data model is quite small or moderate, this step may also be done during the model review initiation.

Assessment of Modeling Team. During the model review initiation, the reviewers get a chance to get acquainted with the modeling team and other user representatives. The reviewers need to build up lasting relationships with the team in order to complete their work.

The reviewers get to understand the level of the skills and experience of the members of the modeling team. This will help the reviewers to match up the team's background with the particular data model and help them to concentrate more on specific parts of the modeling effort. If the team members are not sufficiently strong on identifying relationships among categories of relationships, then this is an area for particular attention by the model reviewers.

Review of Model Standards and Management. The data modeling team has to follow approved standards in the organization and manage its data modeling effort accordingly. Data model reviewers have a responsibility to ensure that this had happened.

The data model reviewers study the standards and procedures of the organization carefully. If there is a pool of approved standard entity types and attributes, then the data modeling team must draw their components from this pool as far as feasible. If the current data model is an add-on to existing data models that had been implemented, then the model reviewers need to know the standards for integrating data models.

Documentation Study. This is an important prerequisite for performing the data model assessment effectively. Before launching a very detailed assessment of the data model, the model reviewers study various documents and materials in great detail.

The following indicate the materials and documents to be studied:

- Other data models already completed and in use
- The place of the organization in the industry
- Organization's core business
- Organization's overall business operations
- Business plans
- Relevant policy documents
- Applicable business rules
- Notes from interviews and group sessions held by the modeling team

Data Model Assessment

So far, we have covered the preliminary activities that lead to the detailed review and assessment of the data model itself. The outcome of the assessment would be a series of findings of the data model reviewers. Proper actions to resolve the issues and rectify errors pointed out as findings measure the success of the entire review and assessment process.

Data model assessment consists of several tasks. If you have transformed your conceptual data model into a logical data model in the form of a relational system or any other prevalent types, then data model assessment becomes more intricate and involved. However, if the model to be assessed is a conceptual data model at a higher level, then model assessment becomes comparatively easier.

In order to discuss model assessment in a more intricate form, we will take up the assessment of a logical data model. Once you understand the principles for a logical data model, then applying the principles of model assessment to a generic conceptual model would be simpler.

For a relational database system, remember the logical model is the relational data model. Data is represented as two-dimensional tables. The following gives an indication how data model assessment proceeds and which tasks are normally performed.

Data Model Subdivision. The first task is to make the model assessment task manageable. Subdivide the data model into logical subsets. Then the assessment of each subset could become easier. A few methods are available for subdividing a data model. If the parts of the model can be clearly connected with the responsibilities of particular user groups, then each such subset may be handled separately.

The data model reviewers will work with the modeling team in determining the proper method for subdividing the model. Once the model is subdivided using the best approach, then the reviewers can arrive at a sequence for assessing individual submodels.

Component Clusters. If the data model does not subject itself to subdivision by user groups, another popular method is to subdivide the model into component clusters. You check for clusters of entity types that are linked together by entity dependencies.

Here, we need to assume that all many-to-many relationships have been resolved into one-to-many relationships. The structures are in the Boyce–Codd normal form. Optional attributes have been pushed down to the subtype entities in generalization and specialization.

While adopting the entity-dependency method for identifying component clusters, use the following steps:

- Review the entire data model and identify the entity types that have no children. These will be seen as end points in the data model diagram.
- From each of the end points, trace back to the parent entity types, one step at a time. Stop when you reach entity types that have no parents. These would typically be independent entity types. While you trace back, all the entity types that were touched along the way would form a family or cluster of components.
- Name each cluster of entity types and note for model assessment. Later on, in the assessment and documentation, these names may be used for reference.
- Note and mark the attributes, identifiers, and relationships in each cluster as a complete unit for assessment.
- Determine the ideal sequence for assessing the clusters, one at a time.

Figure 10-7 shows a partial data model diagram and notes how a cluster is identified.

Data Model Evaluation. As soon as the clusters are identified, the actual evaluation activity ensues. The reviewer takes each cluster, object by object, and begins the evaluation. All the supporting documents provide the necessary information for performing the evaluation.

The following tasks make up data model evaluation.

Syntax Verification. Begin by reviewing and evaluating independent entity types. Evaluate the attributes of each of these independent entity types. Check the relationships that emanate from these entity types. Next, do the same tasks for dependent entity types.

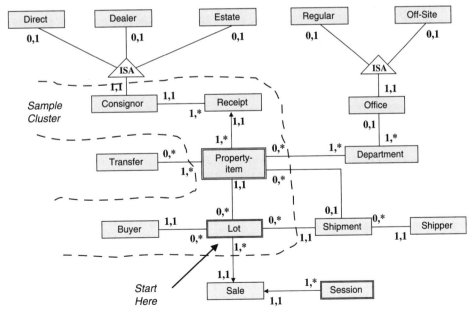

FIGURE 10-7 Model assessment: identification of clusters.

Reverification. In order to confirm the verification, perform a backward pass. Trace back the same paths starting from the end points. Evaluate the entity types that were not evaluated in the forward pass.

Business Rules Representation. Go through documentation of business rules governing relationships among entity types. Evaluate the data model to ensure that these are properly represented.

Conceptual Review. Use the same set of component clusters to perform this task. Here, the task ensures that every business concept and statement found in the requirements definition finds an expression in the data model.

Findings and Actions. The cluster references may be used to record the findings of the quality assurance process. The following tasks comprise the documentation of findings, actions on findings, and termination of the quality assurance process.

Recording Findings and Issues. Reference each cluster evaluated and record full details of results of the evaluation. If any CASE tool is available in the organization for performing this task, take advantage of the availability.

Keeping Track of Evaluations. Use the findings documentation to keep track of all reviews, findings, and actions.

Resolution of Issues. Arrange to provide assistance to the modeling team for resolving issues and errors that surfaced during the evaluation process. Also, provide methods for documenting how each issue gets resolved.

DATA MODEL QUALITY ASSURANCE Findings and Required Actions	Reference Rules/Standards	RESPONSIBLE DEPARTMENT/PERSO
1 Business Process: Dealers may be local and international dealers. Data Model does not represent this distinction. To determine how this must be handled.	If necessary, include in *Consignor* generalization hierarchy.	Consignor Accounts department/data modeler
2 Primary Key: SSN is a better candidate for primary key in STUDENT entity type. Change primary key to SSN from Srudentld. Data Modeling Team	Choice of primary key.	Data modeler
3 Foreign Key: The foreign key Employeeld is missing in PROJECT entity type. Include foreign key.	Relationship through foreign keys.	Data modeler
4 Dependent Entity Type: PROPERTY-ITEM entities seem to depend on RECEIPT entities for existence Confirm with responsible departments and change relationship in the data model.	Identifying relationship.	Reception department/ data modeler

....
....
....
....

FIGURE 10-8 QA: findings and actions.

Termination Meeting. Reviewers conduct a final meeting for each review with the project team and any user liaison persons. They go through the findings document and all settle on how follow-up will be done.

Figure 10-8 shows a sample findings document and notes how findings and actions are documented.

CHAPTER SUMMARY

- Quality is important in the data model as well as in the definitions of individual components.
- A data model must be of high quality for it to serve as an effective tool for communicating with the users and to be an efficient blueprint for database construction.
- Good definitions of data model components have the following characteristics: correctness, completeness, clearness, and right format.
- Correct definitions imply the following: reviewed and confirmed, and consistent with organizational understanding. Complete definitions are not too broad, not too narrow, are self-contained, and are supplemented with examples. Clear definitions do not repeat the obvious, contain obscure terminology, or use unknown abbreviations.
- Data model quality dimensions: correctness (syntactic and conceptual), completeness (syntactic and conceptual), and proper organizational context.
- Stages of quality assurance process: review initiation; data model review and assessment; action on findings.
- Phases of data model review: preliminary review; assessment of modeling team; study of standards; and documentation study. Phases of data model assessment: data model subdivision; ascertaining component clusters; data model evaluation; findings and actions.

REVIEW QUESTIONS

1. True or false:
   A. Users can understand a good data model diagram intuitively.
   B. A definition of a model object may be considered good if it conveys a general overall idea about the object.
   C. It is not necessary for all definitions to be reviewed and confirmed by domain experts.
   D. Good definitions must not be too broad or too narrow.
   E. Data model quality implies correctness and completeness.
   F. If the correct symbols are used in a data model, the model is said to be conceptually correct.
   G. Responsibility of a quality assurance coordinator is mostly administrative.
   H. Every data modeling project must have three data model review cycles.
   I. Preliminary model review is usually a detailed examination of a data model by the reviewers.
   J. Broad definitions intentionally use ambiguous words in order to avoid conflicts.

2. Do you agree that quality of a data model is of paramount importance? Give your reasons and explain.

3. Describe the meaning and role of definitions of data model components. What are the aspects of quality definitions?

4. When can you say a definition is correct and complete? List the factors.

5. Name any three characteristics of a good data model. Give examples of each.

6. Discuss the quality dimensions of a data model. Differentiate between correctness and completeness.

7. Describe the role of the quality assurance coordinator for a data modeling project.

8. Data model quality control and assurance is a mindset. Discuss.

9. List the quality assurance phases of data model review and data model assessment. Describe the detailed activities in any two of the phases.

10. The success of quality assurance completely depends on the data model reviewers. Discuss this statement giving your reasons.

11

AGILE DATA MODELING IN PRACTICE

CHAPTER OBJECTIVES

- Introduce the agile movement
- Review the principles of agile software development
- Understand agile data modeling
- Explore basic and auxiliary principles of agile modeling
- Examine primary and additional practices of agile modeling
- Discuss agile documentation
- Learn to recognize agile data models
- Study evolutionary data modeling in detail

The adoption of agile software development methodology is a recent phenomenon. The benefits derived from the practice of this method have propelled this new set of principles and practices to wider acceptance. More and more organizations have begun using the new methodology. It has now permeated every aspect of software development—analysis, design, data modeling, generating code, and even project management.

Lately, several books have appeared on the scene, notably by Scott W. Ambler and Sanjiv Augustine. I am indebted to these authors for the material in this chapter. Note the reference to these publications and others in the bibliography at the end of the book.

As this methodology is likely to be unfamiliar to many readers, we will begin with an introduction to the *agile movement* itself. As you will see, the methodology is not a set of "how-to's." It actually consists of overarching guidelines for the practice of some fundamental principles. Practicing agile principles requires a certain mindset; a certain willingness to be flexible and nimble in software development. Change is real and change must

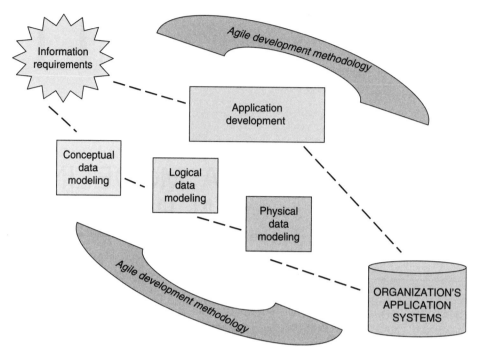

FIGURE 11-1 Agile software development.

even be welcome—this is an underlying theme. When you develop software or create a data model in an incremental manner, you are really adopting agile principles.

Figure 11-1 illustrates how the agile software development methodology envelopes the development effort.

You will get a good feel for agile development by exploring its core and supplementary principles. You will learn how agile development takes shape in practice. We will then examine how agile development principles and practices apply to data modeling. We will conclude with a close look at evolutionary data modeling—a direct outcome of adopting agile development principles.

THE AGILE MOVEMENT

Although principles of agile development cover the wider aspects of software development, our primary focus is on the data-oriented issues, and particularly on data modeling. Software development like most human activities requires people to work together to achieve common goals. A data modeler cannot create a data model in isolation but has to cooperate and work with other members of the data and application groups as well as with the users and stakeholders. The environment must be set up as shared with joint ownerships and joint responsibilities.

However, in a development project, cooperation and collaboration appears to be difficult. Specialists tend to have a narrow focus, just concentrating on fragments of the whole effort. Priorities and expectations of different groups are not synchronized. Poor communication poses serious problems. Inadequate documentation—too little or too much—defeats its very purpose. Guidelines on application and data system development are mostly absent.

Organizations suffer far-reaching consequences. Development efforts take too long and become too expensive. Users and stakeholders get frustrated. Finger-pointing is a common feature of such environments. Ongoing feuds among groups in the development team result in rampant political maneuvers. Important issues slip through the cracks.

How It Got Started

The agile movement was initiated to address the problems of traditional development efforts. The challenges faced by developers had to be recognized and solutions found. Organizations were not prepared to tolerate budget overruns and inordinate delays in development projects. A radically new way of approaching development efforts was called for.

Answering the clarion call for reformation, an initial group of 17 methodologists met in February 2001 in the city of Snowbird, Utah, and formed the Agile Software Development Alliance (commonly known as the Agile Alliance). This group did not consist of professionals of exactly the same skills and background; the group spanned a panel of professionals with different backgrounds and experience levels. They met with one primary goal: dramatically improve the software development process.

The initial members of the Agile Alliance agreed on a bold manifesto for bringing about a change in the software development effort. And based on the manifesto, the group compiled a list of core and supplementary principles to guide better software development.

Agile Alliance Manifesto. Four simple value statements defined the manifesto. It is a way of highlighting four core values in software development and emphasizing these over others. The manifesto enumerates preferential and underlying themes for successful software development. These are fairly obvious values; nevertheless, grossly neglected up till then.

The following describes these fundamental and significant values.

People and Interactions. People on a project and how they react with one another make or break a project. People create success, not the tools and processes. Tools, techniques, and distinct processes are important; but, more significant are the people working together and performing the processes using the tools and techniques.

Usable Software. The goal of a software development project is usable, working software. If you produce a wonderful piece of documentation detailing how the software will perform without the actual working software itself, the project has failed. Documentation has its place; but, more than documentation, the focus should be more on producing working software.

User Collaboration. Free and open participation of the various user groups becomes extremely essential for successful software development. They are the ones who can tell you what they need. For participation, a set of roles and responsibilities may be devised. More than a contract-type arrangement for user participation, a willing collaboration is a lot more effective.

Acceptance of Change. Everyone knows that changes are inevitable in all projects. However, people working on software development projects make little provision to handle changes while the development effort is in progress. Focus more on accommodating changes than rigidly following the original plans and losing the game at the end.

Principles of Agile Development

Based on the core values expressed in the Agile Alliance manifesto, the group defined a set of 12 fundamental principles for guiding software development including agile data system development. Again, many of these principles appear to be commonsense notions, nevertheless neglected in development projects until then. The principles condition the way agile development must take place. You can derive the agile development practices for these principles.

Listed below are the basic principles:

1. Top priority is satisfaction of the user groups by providing valuable, working software.
2. Simplicity—doing the essential and avoiding the complex—is a key to success.
3. Welcome and embrace changes even at late stages; provide mechanisms to accommodate changes.
4. Deliver working software at frequent intervals; early deliverables instill confidence.
5. Business professionals and developers must work in collaboration on a daily basis throughout the project.
6. Encourage motivated individuals with proper support and conducive environment so that projects may be successful.
7. Face-to-face interaction among team members and with user personnel is the best form of communication.
8. Measure progress only through working software, not by size of the documentation.
9. Promote sustainable, steady pace among developers and user groups.
10. Pay continuous attention to technical excellence and good design.
11. Self-organizing teams produce the best architectures, requirement definitions, and designs.
12. At regular intervals, the entire team must get together for status assessment, reflection on effectiveness, in-flight corrections, and fine-tuning adjustments.

Philosophies

The agile data (AD) method applies to all activities relating to data modeling and design of the database system. The agile principles stated above act as guidelines for the agile data method. The principles are rooted in certain underlying philosophic considerations.

Agile data philosophies include the following.

Significance of Data. An organization's data is the centerpiece of all applications. Mostly, applications are just concerned with the manipulation of data—storage, retrieval, modification, and deletion of data.

Uniqueness of Every Project. Each and every project is unique with its own specific challenges and opportunities. Data considerations are directly connected to the particular project issues.

Crucial Nature of Teamwork. Working together cannot be overemphasized. All barriers to cooperation must be removed.

Need for Optimal Solutions. Without going to extremes on either side, the project team must create solutions that work optimally and are best suited for the conditions of the project.

Striving for Overall Fit. The project must be executed within the overall architecture and software goals of the organization. The project must be totally enterprise-aware.

Generalizing Specialists

Development projects of modern days tend to be large and complex. A variety of skills are called for to make the project a success. You need business analysts, systems analysts, programmers at various levels, data modelers, data administrators, database administrators, documentation specialists, and so on. All these professionals must be well coordinated for producing the desired results. Each person on the project becomes highly specialized with a limited set of skills.

The problem with specialists is that their focus is usually narrow. They fail to see the big picture and do not greatly appreciate how all efforts in a project fit together. Specialists find it hard to work together because they fail to see clearly how the others need to function in the project.

Agile development practitioners seek to remedy the situation by introducing the concept of *generalizing specialists*. Generalizing specialists have begun to support agile development projects. A generalizing specialist starts with one or two types of skills and then moves on to acquire more and more different types. They seek to fulfill different roles in a development project. A person with data modeling skills become adept at database implementation and administration. A programmer acquires analysis skills. A generalizing specialist understands how everything fits together in a development project. The basic expectation is that a project composed of generalizing specialists will be more effective than one made up of specialists alone.

AGILE MODELING

So far, we have considered agile development in broad terms. We dealt with the reasons for the emergence of agile development and noted how the agile alliance got started. We will now turn to our main focus in this book, namely, data modeling and how agile development principles would apply to data modeling. Let us begin our discussions of agile modeling.

Agile development has a wider connotation. The term may be applied to a collection of values, philosophies, and practices for requirements, analysis, architecture, and design. We will narrow these down to the data modeling effort in a development project.

Agile development practitioners say that the secret of agile modeling is not the data modeling techniques themselves but how the techniques are applied and used. Agile modeling is not prescriptive—it does not define procedures on how to put together a particular type of model. Instead, it concentrates on how to become a good modeler by applying the agile development principles. Perhaps, agile modeling must be thought of as an *art* rather than as a *science*.

What Is Agile Modeling?

Agile modeling (AM) recognizes the primary values promoted by the Agile Alliance as key to success for creating effective data models. Very quickly, these values are summarized as follows:

- Individuals and interactions *over* processes and tools
- Working software *over* elaborate documentation
- User collaboration *over* contract negotiation
- Response to change *over* strictly adhering to plan

Two important objectives drive agile modeling:

Effective, Lightweight Modeling. Put into practice agile development principles and values to ease the modeling effort.

Agile Approach in Technique Application. Apply modeling techniques always in the context of agile development principles.

Again, the general values of agile development apply to agile modeling with full force.

Simplicity. Strive for the simplest data model that truly and optimally represents the information requirements.

Communication. Promote effective communication among data modelers and within the overall project team.

Feedback. Receive early and frequent feedback on the modeling effort from users and other stakeholders.

Steadfastness. Stick to your steady pace and objectives.

Humility. Have eagerness and humility to recognize shortcomings and admit input from others.

Basic Principles

Agile development practitioners enumerate several core principles to guide agile modeling. These principles expand the values and philosophy of agile modeling.

Let us highlight the important principles applicable to agile modeling.

Keep It Simple. Assume that the simplest data model is the best model. Avoid complexities and intricate representations.

Embrace Change. Learn to accommodate changes as the data model evolves. Incorporate changes in small increments.

Secondary Goal. After this phase of the modeling effort is complete, the model must be flexible enough to get integrated with the next data modeling effort.

Model with a Purpose. Constantly step back and review the purpose of the model. Keep the purpose of the model in view at all times.

Maximize User Investment. A data model must provide maximum return to the users for their investment of time and resources to the project.

Open Communication. Provide for free and honest communication among data modelers and the rest of the project team.

Quality Output. Be mindful of the quality of the data model that is being created.

Rapid Feedback. Place high premium on feedback from the users and other members on the data model at various stages.

Keep It Light. Do just enough modeling and create just enough documentation.

Auxiliary Principles

Agile development practitioners also specify a few supplementary principles for agile modeling.

Know Your Tools. Have sufficient knowledge to choose the right techniques and use them appropriately.

Listen to Instincts. Experienced data modelers and software developers in general learn to pay attention to "gut feel" and input through instincts.

Local Adaptation. Adapt your methodologies and techniques to your particular environment in the organization.

Project-Wide Learning. Encourage team members to learn from one another. This will promote team cooperation. Everyone can learn from everyone else.

Content More Important. The content of the data model in terms of its components is more important that how the contents are laid out.

PRACTICING AGILE MODELING

We have covered the values and principles of agile modeling. These cannot remain just as principles. Without application, principles are of little value. You may understand the principles. But to produce results, the principles must be put into practice.

In this subsection, we will enumerate the primary and additional practices in agile modeling. Again, these are not methods or techniques. These indicate the way overall modeling is carried out when you adopt agile modeling. These practices are underlying guidelines for agile modeling.

Primary Practices

Primary agile modeling practices include the following.

Use Simple Tools. CASE modeling tools are useful, but sometimes for certain situations a paper-and-pencil technique itself may be sufficient. Do not go for complex tools.

Show Model Components Simply. Keep the arrangement of model components in a model diagram as simple and straightforward as possible.

Emphasize Simple Components. Use the simplest modeling components for the purpose at hand.

Adopt Incremental Modeling. Create partial data models in small increments.

Share Ownership. Allow all data modelers collective ownership of the models.

Promote Collaborative Modeling. Ensure that data modelers can work together and cooperate.

Apply the Right Modeling Artifact. Use the proper component for the specific requirement.

Iterate to More Suitable Artifact. If a particular component does not serve the purpose for correct representation, shift to a more suitable component. For example, use an entity type instead of an attribute.

Strongly Encourage Active User Participation. Projects usually fail because of lack of active user participation.

Additional Practices

A few additional practices of agile modeling also apply.

Create Model to Understand. A good model helps all concerned understand the information requirements.

Create Model to Communicate. A good model is also an excellent means for communication with user groups and among data modelers and application developers.

Adhere to Modeling Standards. Formulate standards for model development and follow the standards rigorously.

Create and Discard Temporary Models. In the course of iterative data modeling, intermediary and temporary models will be created. Make the best use of such temporary models and discard them after they serve their purposes.

Formalize Contract Models Cautiously. When outside teams require the data model that is being created for further implementation, firm up and formalize the contract models carefully.

Use and Reuse Resources. Standard models for industries and model templates are available for use to create the particular model. Use such resources.

Role of Agile DBA

In a traditional development project, the database administrator (DBA) creates a physical data model from the logical model and implements the model as a database using the selected database management system (DBMS). The DBA's role begins late in the development project. It tends to concentrate more on the administration and maintenance functions for a database.

However, as agile development promotes generalizing specialists, an agile DBA has an expanded role. Perhaps, an agile DBA in an organization could have acquired additional data modeling skills to create the conceptual and logical data models as well. This arrangement may work well in a smaller environment where the DBA's responsibilities may be enlarged to include several types of activities.

An agile DBA's functions may include the following:

- Accommodate changes and keep database schemas synchronized with changing models.
- Develop data models in an iterative, incremental manner.
- Enforce data modeling standards and procedures.
- Mentor other project team members in data modeling methodologies.

Agile Documentation

Documentation is usually the bane of a development project. Developers have a symptomatic dislike for creating documentation. Nevertheless, documentation is an integral part of every development effort.

Documentation itself may be made agile when certain principles are applied. It may even be made palpable to developers. The following principles apply to agile documentation.

Documents Are Just Sufficient. Avoid unnecessary details and be free from repetitions.

Documents Are Properly Indexed. Provide indexes to find information in the documents easily and quickly.

Documents Are Accurate and Consistent. Various parts of the documents are consistent with one another, and the documents provide correct information.

Documents Contain Critical Information. Only highly important information gets documented.

Documents Describe Fairly Firmed Up Details. Documents do not contain fluid information that is constantly changing.

Documents Fulfill a Purpose. Documents fulfill a defined purpose in a cohesive manner.

Documents Maximize User Investment. Documents provide maximum benefits to user groups by providing essential information.

Documents Are Meant for Specific Groups. Each set of documents is compiled and written for specific development groups such as programmers, analysts, users, and so on.

Recognizing an Agile Model

Having reviewed the principles and practices of agile modeling, we can now ask the question: Given a data model, can you recognize that the model is agile? What are the features of an agile data model?

Let us just summarize the hallmarks of an agile model. A data model may be said to be agile if it is

- as simple as possible,
- clearly understandable,
- fulfilling its purpose,
- sufficiently accurate,
- sufficiently consistent,
- sufficiently detailed, and
- provides desired value.

Feasibility

Can all organizations adopt agile development? Are there any restrictions? If your organization is committed and geared toward prescriptive processes, then agile development may not be encouraged. Government agencies and large, established financial institutions are not likely candidates for agile development. Also, agile development may not be conducive to large development teams with teams geographically dispersed. Close collaboration among team members enables agile development.

Agile modeling is likely to be successful under the following circumstances.

Stakeholder and Management Support. AM, by its very nature, cannot succeed without total management support and active involvement of the stakeholders.

Free Hand for Development Team. The project team must be given ample freedom and proper mandate to practice AM although this may be new to your organization.

Motivated Team Members. If the project team is not completely sold on AM, it is not likely to succeed.

Availability of Sufficient Resources. Apart from other things, AM needs people to work together and collaborate. Resources are needed to facilitate close collaboration, such as contiguous work spaces, meeting rooms, suitable CASE tools and other tools, and so on.

Commitment to Incremental Development. Communication, feedback, action based on feedback—essential practices of AM can thrive only when the modeling process is performed incrementally and iteratively.

Suitability of Agile Approach. The specific modeling process must be amenable for using agile principles and practices.

Changing and Uncertain Requirements. When volatile requirements are a norm, agile modeling provides practices to accommodate changes and revisions.

Strong Support of AM Enthusiast. You need the complete support of an AM champion at a sufficiently high executive level, especially if agile development is new to your organization.

EVOLUTIONARY DATA MODELING

Evolutionary data modeling is a key for the adoption of agile modeling principles and practices. Evolutionary modeling allows for the creation of the data model in small increments with suitable reiterations.

We will begin our discussion by reviewing the traditional approach to data modeling and the types of problems it poses. We will reason out why flexibility is critical in the modeling process. We will then examine some features of evolutionary modeling and derive the benefits possible from this methodology.

Traditional Approach

Many organizations adopt an "up-front firm design" approach to software development and, in particular, to modeling. The data models, once created, are frozen before proceeding to the remaining phases of the overall development efforts.

This traditional approach is perpetuated in several organizations. Some key reasons for the continuance of the approach seem to be the following:

- Lack of experience with iterative and incremental development
- Entrenched organizational culture opposing change
- Traditional mindset of developers
- Commitment to prescriptive processes
- Dearth of enabling tools

Here are a few problems resulting from the data-oriented, up-front firm design approach:

- The approach does not promote close interpersonal collaboration.
- The approach tends to encourage too much specialization.
- Data and data models are important; but, implementation issues are equally important. Data models need to be kept flexible.
- It is impossible to think through and envision at the beginning. Things evolve.
- Changes are anathema to this approach.
- Every project is different, so a "one size fits all" approach does not work.

Need for Flexibility

In incremental and iterative development, the need for flexibility pervades the entire process. You have to keep your models flexible enough to adapt to possible changes in the requirements even in late stages. The revisions in requirements filter down to the data models and then on to the subsequent outputs in the development effort. Flexibility is the key in every phase.

Figure 11-2 illustrates the significance of flexibility in agile modeling and agile development.

The need for flexibility extends to the choice of tools and techniques as well. A few reasons for this are as follows:

- Modeling tasks vary in extent and complexity.
- External constraints may be different.
- Team strengths, skills, and experience levels vary.
- Every individual working on the project is unique.
- Different techniques are suitable for different technologies.

Nature of Evolutionary Modeling

When you perform data modeling in an evolutionary manner, a key element in the whole process is the accommodation of feedback and change. You do modeling in small increments. You pause and look for feedback. You incorporate changes based on feedback and reiterate. The cycle continues until the data model is right up till then.

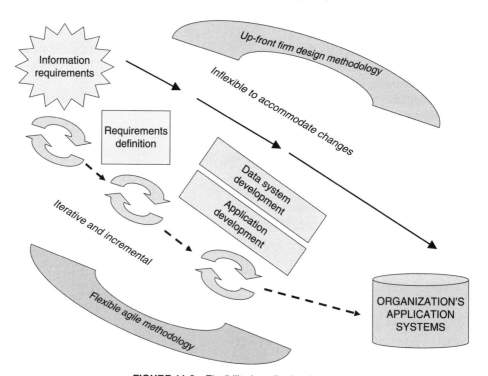

FIGURE 11-2   Flexibility in agile development.

In an evolutionary model, the evolution takes place based on stimuli from either side of the model creation effort. What do we mean by this? Let us examine the evolution.

A data model, as you know, is the abstract representation of information requirements. All aspects of information requirements get incorporated in the data model. As you collect information requirements and create the data model, the model evolves in a "creation–feedback–revision" cycle.

After the initial set of iterations, the data model is nearly complete. However, as the data model is taken down further into the remaining development phases, feedback is sent backward for certain revisions to the data model. Issues further down the line reveal the necessity for certain revisions in the data model itself. The model evolves further in "creation–feedback–revision" cycle.

Figure 11-3 shows these two aspects of data model evolution. Notice the reiteration cycles. The data model is deemed to be complete when all action on the final feedback is done.

Benefits

Evolutionary data modeling produces a correct and complete model. Let us summarize the important benefits derived from evolutionary data modeling.

- As modeling is performed in small, manageable increments, the modeling task is simplified.
- Iterative modeling fine-tunes the model at each iteration.
- It promotes review and feedback by users at frequent and regular intervals.
- It enables changes to requirements to be incorporated in the model as the iterations continue.

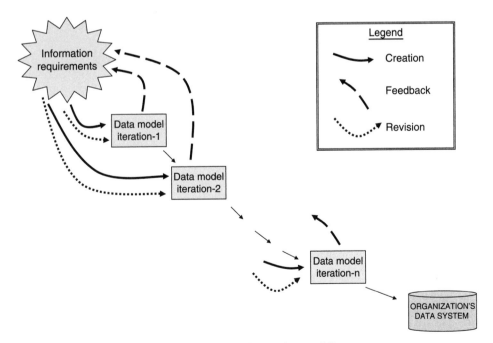

FIGURE 11-3 Evolutionary data modeling.

- It allows for changes resulting from design and implementation issues to be back-pedaled and accommodated.
- Iterations and fine-tuning promotes correctness of the model.
- Incorporation of feedback from both sides even in late stages promotes completeness of the model.

CHAPTER SUMMARY

- Agile software development methodology, a fairly recent phenomenon, is bringing about a dramatic improvement in software development.
- Agile development principles and practices are extended to data modeling.
- The Agile Alliance manifesto establishes fundamental and significant values on people interactions, usable software, user collaboration, and acceptance of change.
- Agile development rests on a number of underlying principles. It is not exactly a set of techniques, a collection of "how-to's," but a new creative way of software development.
- Agile modeling emphasizes a set of core principles and practices to keep the modeling process simple, light, and flexible. It encompasses all aspects of data modeling.
- Features of an agile model: as simple as possible, clearly understandable, fulfilling its purpose, sufficiently accurate, sufficiently consistent, sufficiently detailed, and providing desired value.
- Evolutionary data modeling is a key for the adoption of agile modeling principles and practices. This is different from the traditional approach of up-front firm design. Evolutionary modeling produces a number of benefits.

REVIEW QUESTIONS

1. Match the column entries:

   1. Agile methodology   A. Measurement of progress
   2. Changes   B. Discard after use
   3. Users and Developers   C. Provides desired value
   4. Working software   D. Too much specialization
   5. Optional solution   E. Just sufficient, concise
   6. Temporary models   F. Inevitable in software development
   7. Agile documentation   G. Incremental and iterative
   8. Agile model   H. Collaboration essential
   9. Traditional modeling   I. Set of principles and practices
   10. Evolutionary modeling   J. No extremes, moderate

2. Agile development is a new approach to development. It is not a set of specific techniques. Discuss.
3. What problems in software development did the agile movement seek to resolve? Why do you think it is succeeding?
4. List any six basic principles of agile development. Describe any one of these.

5. Agile development promotes optimal solutions. Explain the principle of not going to extremes on either side.

6. Who are the generalizing specialists? How is this concept necessary and applicable to today's software development environment?

7. State any six principles of agile modeling. Pick out any two of these principles and explain how these two improve the data modeling process.

8. Describe how the data modeling process will change when you adopt agile modeling. Give a simple example.

9. How is evolutionary data modeling different from the traditional approach? Describe briefly.

10. List the benefits of evolutionary data modeling.

12

DATA MODELING: PRACTICAL TIPS

CHAPTER OBJECTIVES

- Specify the nature and usefulness of practical tips
- Cover tips for conceptual modeling and prior phases
- Provide tips for exploring and defining requirements
- Highlight tips on obtaining effective stakeholder participation
- List tips on iterative modeling
- Consider tips for special cases in modeling
- Enumerate tips for conceptual model layout
- Expand practical suggestions to logical modeling

As we reach the end of our study of data modeling, we would like to provide some practical suggestions and tips. As you gain more and more experience in data modeling, you come across special situations and out-of-the-ordinary cases. You may have to adapt your techniques to suit the conditions. As you run into variations, you learn to use your modeling skills more and more effectively.

In this chapter, we will consider practical tips on conceptual data modeling and requirements definition, its prerequisite. At the end of the chapter, we will expand the suggestions to logical data modeling. Remember, these suggestions and tips may not apply exactly to your particular circumstances. Nevertheless, they will provide insights into how you can best adapt them and use them.

Data Modeling Fundamentals. By Paulraj Ponniah
Copyright © 2007 John Wiley & Sons, Inc.

TIPS AND SUGGESTIONS

Although several of the tips and suggestions provided have been distilled out of long experiences and expert skills of data modeling practitioners, these are not silver bullets. These suggestions have practical significance in that they have worked before and are likely to work again in similar circumstances. In every data modeling project, there will be special cases and unusual situations. When you are faced with such circumstances, these tips will help you to address the special issues and find effective solutions.

Some of the suggestions are general tips that will be useful in most projects. Certain others focus on single types of issues or situations. Both categories of suggestions are provided here, perhaps intermingled and connected.

Nature of Tips

The suggestions given in this chapter mostly relate to important phases of the development effort—conceptual and logical data modeling. Even so, suggestions on physical data modeling and subsequent phases of the development effort are not included here. As these are, in a strict sense, outside the scope of our discussions, you will have to look elsewhere at other literature for these phases.

Here are some characteristics of the suggestions provided here. These tips

- deal with application of modeling techniques in special cases,
- relate to people interactions,
- are about modeling procedures,
- touch upon documentation,
- provide insights for geographically dispersed user groups,
- focus on stakeholder involvement,
- advise on iterative modeling, and
- cover streamlining and enhancing model layouts.

How Specified

Sometimes when you are given practical suggestions, you are also provided detailed information on the actual instances where the suggestions were applied. First you are given a history and description of the actual circumstances. Then you are exposed to the practical suggestions that applied to the actual cases. This approach may have some merit.

However, such an approach will lengthen the overall narration. No two situations in different modeling projects are exactly same. Therefore, the solutions also are likely to differ. Therefore, we have taken the approach of just stating the suggestions as they apply to different circumstances without detailing the history and narratives of the circumstances themselves.

The subheadings inform you of the circumstances and the special cases. Then, within each subsection, you will find the suggestion. This is a shorter method, a simpler approach.

How to Use Them

Not every suggestion may be applicable to each individual reader or each individual project. The conditions vary; the situations differ. Nevertheless, each suggestion may point to a way of dealing with a similar situation even though remotely similar.

Quickly go through the broad array of suggestions in this chapter. If some are of particular interest to you, revisit them. However, keep a general inventory of the range of tips. Whenever you are faced with special situations, then go back and look up suggestions on similar circumstances.

There are some general guidelines on specific phases in the development life cycle. These could be of use for every data modeler irrespective of the particular modeling projects. Review such general guidelines carefully and adopt them in practice.

REQUIREMENTS DEFINITION

We begin with some suggestions on the requirements definition phase. Although requirements definition is an iterative effort, the final definition of requirements drives the data modeling effort. Bad requirements definition invariably results in bad data model.

Requirements definition consists of several tasks. There are many aspects to the requirements definition phase. We have selected a few significant aspects of the phase and provide a few practical tips.

Interviews

Interviewing user groups to determine requirements—a traditional method—is still one of the useful methods for requirements gathering. You organize interviews with users, document the results of the interviews, try to understand the requirements, and then use the results of the interviews along with other information to start your data modeling process.

Here are few tips on user interviews:

- Always prepare for each interview. Do not conduct any interview without adequate preparation.
- Every interview must have a published list of topics to be covered.
- Ensure that the user is also prepared and ready to discuss.
- Users have their own day-to-day responsibilities. Make sure they block the time for the interviews without any interruptions.
- If possible, use a neutral and convenient venue.
- Interviews are generally one-on-one. Keep the size of the group of users to be interviewed together to three or less. Otherwise, the interviews turn into large group sessions.
- Although called interviews, requirement gathering sessions are interactive sessions—not just you asking the questions, and they providing the answers.
- Make sure you understand the information received from the users clearly. Users cannot always articulate their requirements clearly. When you get each piece of information, play it back, and then get your understanding confirmed.
- Make sure you interview users at every level—executive, managerial, and operational. There is a tendency to bypass managerial and executive staff.
- Document the proceedings of every interview and get the document reviewed and confirmed by the particular user.

Group Sessions

Apart from one-on-one interviews, group sessions become necessary for information gathering. Group sessions happen for several reasons. After interviews with individuals in a department, you may want a joint group session with the entire department. Sometimes you can get the whole group together to confirm the requirements gathered piecemeal earlier in individual interviews. Some issues may be thrashed out quickly in large group session—individual interviews take time.

Whatever may be the reason for a group session, group sessions have specific nuances. Here are some suggestions on group sessions:

- Treat a group session as a more formal meeting.
- Always have a published agenda distributed well in advance.
- Include action items in the agenda under each topic.
- Set a time limit for each group session.
- Ensure that the key players among the users are able to be present.
- It is difficult to organize too many group sessions; therefore, plan each of the few possible ones very carefully.
- Choose a convenient location with amenities for presentations.
- Two popular methods for group sessions: roundtable discussion or classroom type presentation. Choose the appropriate type according to what is desired to be achieved in the group session.
- Establish methods for getting a consensus from the group.
- Assign responsibilities and time limits for action items.
- Nominate user representatives for follow-up.
- Document proceedings in a summary of discussion format and distribute.

Geographically Dispersed Groups

If you are data modeling for a worldwide organization, the chances are that your user groups will be located at geographically dispersed sites in different countries. Even in most domestic organizations, the users are dispersed at various sites within the country. This phenomenon has become quite common in modern times. Here are a few specific suggestions on requirements definition where user groups are geographically dispersed:

- First and foremost, be conscious of the local languages and cultures. If you are not careful enough, you are likely to offend prevailing practices.
- If you dealing with multinational groups, the differences are all the more striking. A requirements gathering effort in Germany is substantially different from the same effort in France. One group would be more methodical and give undue consideration for details; the other group may attend more to qualitative than quantitative considerations.
- The methods for interviews and group sessions are the same even if the user groups are dispersed. However, coordinating and organizing them would be difficult.
- Before face-to-face meetings, do all the preliminary work over the phone, conference calls, and video-conferencing.

- Conducting group sessions tends to be difficult, especially if you do not speak the local language. Try to use an associate who is fluent in the local language.
- In group sessions, the participants will tend to break out into minigroups conversing in the local language and frustrating the overall meeting. Be aware of this problem and set acceptable rules and guidelines before the start of each session.

Documentation

Documentation of the requirements is essential. It is a means for confirming your initial understanding of the requirements. It also forms the basis to get the modeling effort started.

Here are some tips on requirements definition documentation:

- Remember, documentation must be just sufficient—not too much, not too meager. Based on your particular data modeling effort, find the golden mean.
- A well-organized document is a useful document. Subdivide the document according to departments, functions, geographical locations, or some other way suitable to your particular project.
- Do not wait until the end of the requirements definition phase to start on the document. Prepare it in increments.
- The supplementary document that accompanies the data model diagram finds information from the requirements definition document. Keep this in mind while defining requirements.
- Requirements definition documentation evolves as the definition phase continues. Make provision for accepting changes and revisions as the documentation evolves.
- For some period of time, requirements gathering and data modeling efforts are likely to overlap. Allow for changes to the definition document even at this stage.
- In traditional development projects, requirements definition used to be frozen at a given point and changes were completely barred after that. This was not always feasible. In an agile development effort, changes are meant to be accommodated as long as possible without extending the project indefinitely.

Change Management

In an iterative development approach, accommodation of changes as you go along in the development effort is a necessary factor. This is somewhat a departure from traditional development approaches. So, accept the notion of providing for changes right from the beginning of the project.

Here are a few suggestions on change management:

- First of all, establish a definitive change management procedure.
- Inform your users about change management and impress upon them the need to use it judiciously.
- Discuss with users clearly how they will request for changes and how changes will be incorporated in the model during work-in-progress.
- Document all changes—initiation, reason, incorporation of the changes, and so on.

- Making change management as formal as possible depends on your organizational culture. Do not make it too rigid and turn your users off. On the other hand, making it too informal encourages users to pay little attention at the beginning. This will render your initial cut of the data model completely worthless.
- Set up an acceptable approval process to filter the changes.
- As you do incremental modeling, relate each version of the model to the changes incorporated. Document the version status.
- Changes cannot go on forever. There must be cutoff points. This may be done in several ways. You may set cutoff points for each partial model and then when all the partial models are integrated. You may set cutoff points by iterations.
- The desire to accommodate changes can lead to making change management a project by itself. Avoid undue effort just on change management. Change management is important, but that is not the whole project.

Notes for Modeling

Notes for modeling—what, another piece of documentation? We looked at the requirements definition document, how it evolves and gets finalized. Can we not use that document as notes for modeling? There are several reasons why separate notes are useful. First of all, although the requirements definition document may be used for reference all the time, the set of notes of modeling is kept by the data modelers for their specific use. The requirements definition is a common document meant for many groups participating in the development project.

Notes for modeling are prepared by data modelers, primarily for their private use. Here are a few tips:

- Tailor-make the notes to suit your particular preferences. There are no standards.
- The medium on which you keep your notes is also up to you.
- Make sure your notes are kept synchronized with the requirements definition document as it evolves. Note down all the changes to the data model as and when they are requested.
- Separate sections for entity types, attributes/identifiers, and relationships may be a good method for dividing up the notes.
- Note down special cases in a separate section.
- Have a separate section for issues you need to get clarified by the users. Make a note of the resolutions.
- If you are modeling for a global organization, contact information with phone numbers proves to be very useful.
- Index your notes.
- As in every type of document, strive for an optimal level of documentation.

STAKEHOLDER PARTICIPATION

Participation and involvement of stakeholders and user groups are of such enormous importance that we should separately consider some suggestions on this aspect of the software development effort. In this section, we will review a few different facets of the participation and go over a few tips on how to make the participation effective.

When we mention stakeholders, we include a variety of people and groups. Anyone outside of the information technology group who has a direct interest in the outcome of the software development effort is necessarily included in this broad category. These people are experts in the subject areas in which context the development takes place. These are the ones who will be using the resulting database regularly. These are the ones who can continually provide input on what the information requirements are.

Let us consider four distinct factors of participation: how to organize participation, how to establish user liaison persons, how to promote continuous interaction, and what to do when stakeholders are at multiple distant sites.

Organizing Participation

Organizing stakeholder participation includes promotion of the concept, methods for promoting participation, setting up participation parameters, making participation really happen on a day-to-day basis, and so on. Participation may be left to happen on an ad hoc basis; the stakeholders probably would like this informal, laid-back approach. However, unless stakeholder participation is put down as a definitive objective and emphasized enough, you will not see enough participation. Not that the stakeholders are irresponsible, but software development is not their main job as it is for you in the information technology department.

Here are a few tips on how to organize stakeholder participation:

- At the very beginning of the project during project initiation itself, stress the importance of their participation to the stakeholders. Emphasize that their involvement is indispensable for the success of the project. Do this orally at initial meetings and also through written memos.
- Describe the scope of stakeholder participation to them clearly.
- From the beginning, foster a sense of joint ownership of the project with the stakeholders.
- Go to great lengths to describe the benefits of participation and illustrate with examples.
- Also, present the dangers of project failure if the participation falls below required levels.
- Make each stakeholder understand his or her role in the cooperative effort.
- Endeavor to make it easy for each stakeholder to participate so that he or she will still be able to perform his or her normal duties. As far as possible, try to work around their routine responsibilities.
- Set up and publish timetables for the participation showing who will be involved in what roles.
- Think of ways to encourage stakeholders with rewards for participation.

User Liaison

User liaison persons play a special role in software development. These persons are selected from the pool of stakeholders. In most organizations, for the duration of the development project, user liaison persons are relieved of most of their daily routine work. They need to spend most of their time on the project itself. Those stakeholders who could be on the project almost full-time are known as user representatives on the project.

As the term *liaison* implies, user liaison persons act as catalysts for collaboration between the information technology team and the stakeholders at various levels. They keep the interactions alive and smooth.

The following suggestions apply to user liaison persons:

- User liaison persons must have excellent interpersonal skills. They must be able to work well with people at various levels. Recommend only such persons for this role.
- User liaison persons need not be subject area experts, but they must know the workings of the departments and the overall structure and functions of the organization.
- Depending on the availability and qualifications of user liaison persons, nominate a few to be continually on the project as user representatives.
- Attempt to have at least one user liaison person for each department.
- Spell out the responsibilities of each user liaison person clearly.
- The user liaison person will act as the conduit to the respective department or set up other means of communication with the department.
- All important issues concerning a department will go through the user liaison person.
- Use the liaison person to coordinate interviews and group discussions.
- Let the user liaison person get the requirements definition confirmed.
- Channel all changes and feedback through the user liaison persons.

Continuous Interaction

We discussed stakeholder participation and also user liaison persons who facilitate such participation in a development project. One aspect has to be clear about the participation of the stakeholders. The cooperation and collaboration of the stakeholders with the information technology team cannot be sporadic. The interaction must be continuous and ongoing.

Let us list a few suggestions on continuous interaction between the two groups.

- Dispel wrong ideas about continuous interaction from the minds of the stakeholders. Even today, many user departments assume that initially they spell out a few requirements of theirs to the information technology department, whose members then go and do the software development all by themselves.
- Explain the necessity to consult with them throughout the project.
- Describe the iterative nature of software development, especially data modeling.
- Specify each iteration and indicate what is expected of the stakeholders at each iteration.
- Explain to the stakeholders the interaction at each phase from beginning to end of the project. Set a continuous timetable for interaction.
- Share responsibilities with users from the beginning.
- Choose suitable users for interaction at different stages.
- User groups may share the collaborative efforts so that no one group is overburdened.
- Develop long-term personal relationships with the stakeholders. Both groups are there together for the long haul.
- In order to sustain the interaction, stipulate how completion of documents becomes a joint responsibility.

Multiple Sites

In a global organization, stakeholder participation has to be extended to multiple sites. You will have user groups residing in various countries. Whenever a project spans stakeholders in multiple sites, the joint effort needs special consideration.

Here are a few tips on stakeholder participation from multiple sites:

- Keep top management at each site involved in the project.
- Find a primary promoter of the project at each site.
- Appoint at least one liaison person from each site.
- Each contiguous or logical group of sites may have one user representative to be part of the project effort on a continual basis.
- Encourage participation through group meetings. As necessary, invite users from contiguous sites for group meetings at a site more or less central for that set of sites.
- From time to time, invite key personnel from the dispersed sites to meet with members of the project team at the headquarters for the project team.
- Choose and send appropriate project team members to visit sites periodically to keep the two-way communication going.
- Keep progress at all sites coordinated and balanced.
- Keep all sites continually informed of the overall progress.
- Encourage ownership of specific parts of the data models by individual sites if this is feasible.

ITERATIVE MODELING

Iterative modeling and incremental modeling go hand-in-hand. You break up the modeling effort into manageable chunks and work incrementally on one fragment at a time. As you proceed from one fragment to the next, you integrate the previous fragment to the current fragment being worked on.

Even when working on a single fragment, you go through an iterative process. You create an initial cut of the model for that fragment, present the initial version to the users, get their feedback, and refine and produce the next version. A few iterations of the creation–feedback–refinement take place.

In this section, we will cover cycles of iteration, logical increments for modeling, interaction between requirements definition and modeling, and integration of all the completed fragments. Each of these aspects is significant for iterative modeling.

Establishing Cycles

Iterative modeling consists of cycles of iterations. Each cycle contains a creation phase, a review and feedback phase, and a phase in which the model is refined. These iterations take place for each fragment of the data model.

The following are a few suggestions for establishing and managing iteration cycles:

- Do not overdo the iterations. Just two or three iterations are practical.
- Define the purpose of each cycle precisely.

- Define each phase of the iteration cycle clearly: creation/refinement–review–feedback.
- Prepare and use a checklist of tasks for each phase.
- Establish responsibilities in each phase.
- Determine phase duration for each model fragment.
- Avoid long phases. Redo fragment sizes if necessary.
- Establish a schedule for each iteration and stick to the schedule.
- The same number of iterations may not be necessary for every model fragment.
- Define user participation clearly in each phase.

Determining Increments

Each increment of the data model builds on the previous increment. What is the ideal increment size? What are the best practices for integrating each increment with the data model version from the previous? We need to know how to break up the modeling effort into manageable increments.

The following tips apply to the determination of the increments for iterative modeling:

- Smaller model fragments for iterative development are more manageable.
- Choose the size of model fragments according to experience of modelers and users.
- Choose the best approach to incremental modeling that suits your circumstances—component by component or fragment by fragment. In the first approach, you create all components of one type, then move on to the next type of component, and so on. In the second approach, you create all components for each fragment, then move on to the next fragment, and so on.
- Fragmentation of the model by functions or user groups works well.
- Every model fragment need not be of the same size.
- If you are implementing a pilot system, choose fragments for the model necessary for the pilot.
- If you have planned a staged delivery of the overall system, the stages determine the nature and size of the model fragments.
- As you complete iterations for one fragment, finish integrating the fragment into the earlier version of the data model. Then proceed to the next model fragment.
- As you progress through the model fragments, one by one, maintain continuity of integration.
- Consider iterating the whole model if the model is sufficiently small—containing less than 20 entity types.

Requirements: Model Interface

The data model is expected to be the true representation of the information requirements of an organization. Therefore, while iterations takes place for refining the data model, there must be constant interaction between requirements definition and the evolving data model.

Here are some suggestions on how this interaction needs to happen:

- At each iteration of the model fragment, check back with the corresponding part of the requirements definition.
- Allow for reworking of the requirements definition. Until the modeling phase is complete, the requirements definition could accommodate revisions.
- Constantly ensure that each iteration of the data model is kept synchronized with the requirements definition.
- In small projects, requirements definition and modeling can be taken together for iterative development.
- In global projects, interaction between requirements and data model may be kept at the individual site level.
- When the overall model is nearly complete, review the model in the light of the complete requirements definition.

Integration of Partial Models

As newer fragments of the data model are created and refined, they must be integrated with the previous versions of the data model. This is a continual task—by no means simple.
The following are a few suggestions on the integration.

- If you are fragmenting the data model component type by component type, integrate the entire model only when all component types are completed.
- If you are fragmenting the data model function by function, integrate when you complete the iteration cycles for each function.
- Each integration must be complete before you proceed to the next model fragment.
- Only when the overall model is small, postpone integration until all fragments are completed separately.
- For global projects, integration, site by site, proves to be successful.
- Sometimes, integration may be performed at different levels—integrate many partial models into a smaller set of partial models, then into still smaller set of partial models, and so on, until you arrive at the final model.
- If you have a pilot system, integrate the partial models for the pilot first.
- If your system has staged deliverables, integrate partials for each stage.
- Use a checklist for integration tasks.
- When the final integration is done, perform one final review, get feedback, and incorporate final revisions.

SPECIAL CASES

Now we turn our attention to some special cases of data modeling. During our discussions in the previous chapters, we had considered a few special cases from time to time. Here we want to add a few more special cases and provide suggestions to deal with these.

Each special case is described with an example. You will note why suggestions are useful in these special cases.

Legal Entities

Consider examples of legal entities such as CLIENT, CUSTOMER, or SHAREHOLDER. In each of these, the entity may represent a single person or an institution. A client may be a single person or an organization. Similarly, a customer may be an individual or a company. In the same way, a shareholder may be a single person or an institution.

In each case, information must be represented for two types of entities while preserving the similarities and still maintaining their uniqueness. Let us specifically take the entity type CLIENT. Clients consign property items to an auction company to be sold at auction. Therefore, CLIENT must be shown as an entity type in the data model for the auction company. You can have individuals as clients or art dealer companies as clients. The data modeler faces the problem of representing CLIENT data type. Of course, the business rules would guide the representation.

We can show the representation in three different ways. Let us look at the three ways and note the comments of the three representations.

Figure 12-1 shows the method of representing CLIENT as a supertype of INDIVIDUAL and DEALER.

This representation, although it may be in line with the business rules, could be cumbersome if we have to represent complex relationships between INDIVIDUAL and DEALER. An individual may be the contact person for a dealer company.

Another method for representation is to make CLIENT as a subtype of both INDIVIDUAL and DEALER. See Figure 12-2.

This is perhaps a common method of representation. Although this representation preserves the independence of INDIVIDUAL and DEALER, it introduces much redundancy. Further, this representation does not clearly connote the meaning of the entity type CLIENT.

Now look at the representation indicated by Figure 12-3 where clients are represented by relationships.

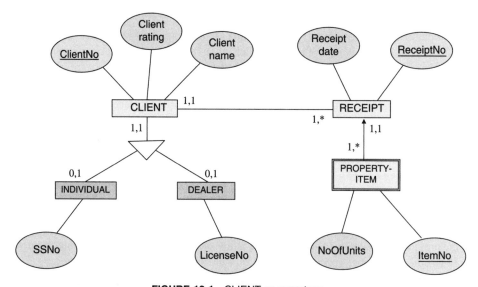

FIGURE 12-1 CLIENT as supertype.

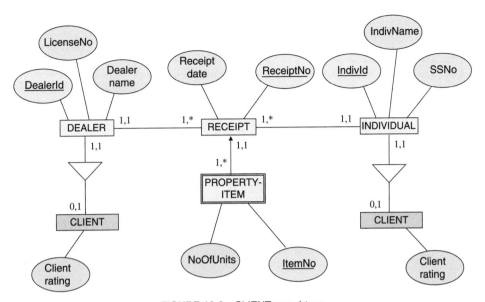

FIGURE 12-2   CLIENT as subtype.

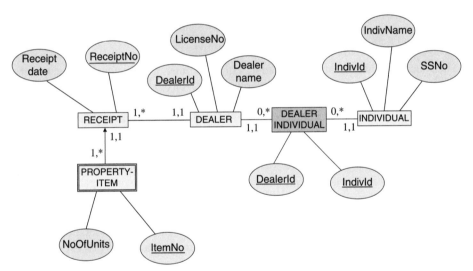

FIGURE 12-3   CLIENT as relationships.

However, this representation makes it difficult for addition of client-specific attributes.

Figure 12-4 illustrates the ideal representation. This representation preserves the independence of INDIVIDUAL and DEALER. Also notice the lack of duplication of entity types and attributes.

Locations and Places

Many kinds of business objects would fall under the category of location or place. A location may be identified by three coordinates x, y, and z. In a medical center, a room

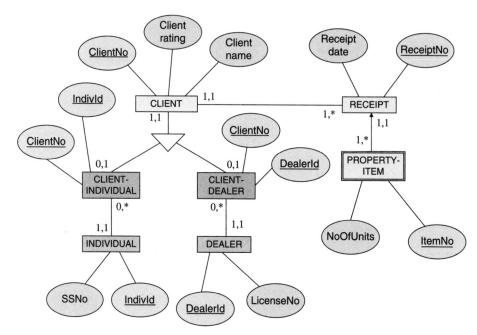

FIGURE 12-4   CLIENT: ideal representation.

and bed number would constitute a location. For a customer, a street address would refer to a location. Apartment number, PO box number, state, city, zip code, postal code—all of these relate to locations.

How to represent locations in a data model? There seems to be a very large number of business objects that could be included in the category of locations or places. Also, you can combine a few of these together to signify a location.

We will examine a few standard methods for representing locations. You may adapt these to suit your information requirements and the practices in your organization.

Simplistic Method. In this method, a location is simply described as an object with an artificial identifier and other attributes. Apart from the selected attributes, all other possible attributes for the location are ignored. This simplistic method assumes that every location entity possesses only the selected attributes and no other.

Figure 12-5 illustrates this simple and straightforward method.

Locations as Subtypes. This method uses a generalization–specialization structure. As you come across newer kinds of locations, you add each new kind to the model as a subtype. This method is more flexible and wider in scope than the previous simplistic method.

Figure 12-6 shows locations as subtypes. Also note how this structure may be used to find specific locations for individual persons.

Abstraction of Location. This method presents a method for abstracting location as a coordination object. In this case, the location entity type has no other attributes except an identifier. Use this method only if you have several types of locations in your organizations

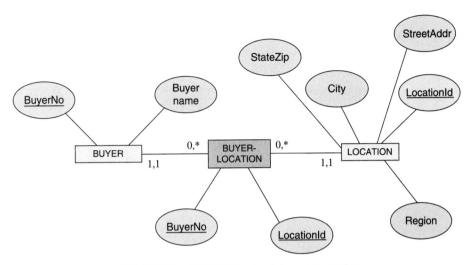

FIGURE 12-5 LOCATION: simplistic representation.

that need to be modeled. This high level of abstraction is also less amenable for the data model to be used as a communication tool with the users.

Figure 12-7 presents the abstraction method for representing locations. Review the figure carefully.

Time Periods

In the business world, time periods such as a calendar year, fiscal year, fiscal quarter, evening shift, second semester, and so on are important. These must be included in the data model for proper representation of the business.

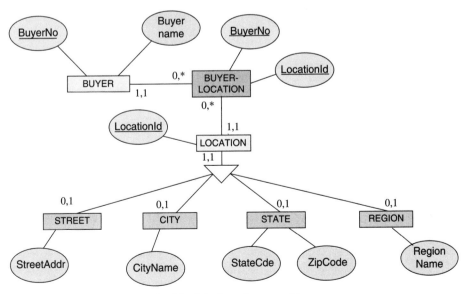

FIGURE 12-6 Locations as subtypes.

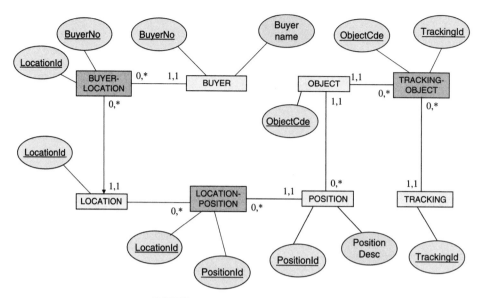

FIGURE 12-7 Abstraction of location.

Before attempting to define time periods in your data model, find out the specifics. What are the requirements? Does a specific time period have start and end dates? Should start/end times be included in addition to start/end dates? Are there any requirements to aggregate units such as sale units or revenue units over periods of time? Depending upon the answers to such questions, determine whether you need a separate time period object in your data model.

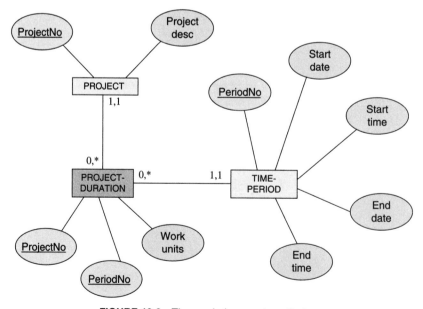

FIGURE 12-8 Time period: separate entity type.

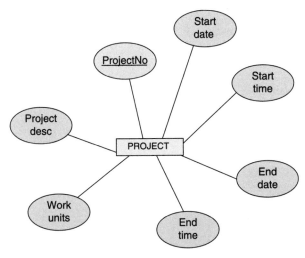

FIGURE 12-9 Time data as attributes.

Figure 12-8 shows a partial data model with time period as a separate entity type. Note the other entity types in the figure and see how they are related to the time period entity type.

However, in most data models, time periods are not shown as separate entity types. You will adopt the method of showing time period as a separate entity type only if you need to show the capture of time-dependent information.

See Figure 12-9 where data about time are included as attributes of other entity types.

Persons

Essentially, data modelers adopt two approaches for modeling persons and their attributes. The adopted approach depends on whether you want the data model to represent just the

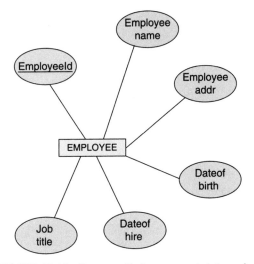

FIGURE 12-10 Person entity type: current status only.

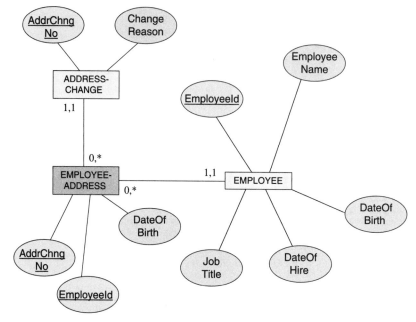

FIGURE 12-11   Person entity type: all revisions.

current state of the person's attributes or whether you need the model to keep track of the changes.

Figure 12-10 represents the simpler approach to allow representation of only the current values of the attributes of persons.

Notice how Figure 12-11 is an improvement over the first approach. This method allows the representation of all revisions in the attributes of persons.

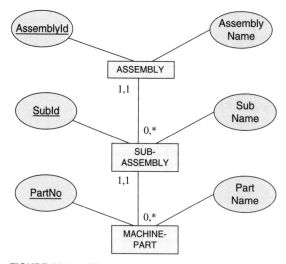

FIGURE 12-12   Bill-of-materials: top-down representation.

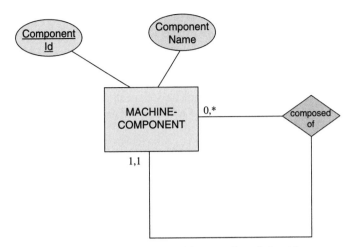

FIGURE 12-13 Bill-of-materials: recursive relationships.

Bill-of-Materials

As you know, in manufacturing, a product is made up of components, a component made up of subcomponents, a subcomponent composed of parts. This hierarchy from product to component to part may extend to several levels depending on the manufacturing environment. The hierarchical structure is known as a bill-of materials structure.

Frequently, you will be faced with the task of modeling bill-of-materials structures. Your model must preserve the hierarchical nature of the relationships. We now show two methods of modeling bill-of-materials structures. The first is a straightforward top-down representation. The second method uses recursive relationships.

Figure 12-12 shows the top-down representation. Note the hierarchical arrangement of the data model components.

Figure 12-13 illustrates the use of recursive relationships. Note the cardinality indicators of the relationships.

CONCEPTUAL MODEL LAYOUT

We now want to consider the actual layout of the data model itself in the form of a diagram. Data models primarily consist of data model diagrams and accompanying supplementary documentation. Data models integrate graphics and textual matter. These can be fairly complex and not understood readily. We need to take special effort to make data models readable and comprehensible.

In this subsection, let us examine the laying out of the model components in a data model diagram. Let us look at a few tips on improving the model layout.

Readability and Usability

After you have designed the entity types and the relationships and even after you have established all other components of the data model, your data modeling task does not really end. Recall one of the primary purposes of a data model. You need to make it as best a communication tool as possible. You must ensure that the data model is readable by user groups for whom the cryptic notations and semantics of model elements are not part of their daily routine. They must be able to use the model continuously for review and confirmation of information requirements.

There are several ways by which you can enhance the data model diagram and its layout. You can make the data model not only appealing but also as a readily usable deliverable of the project. Suggestions to enhance a data model fall into the following categories of tasks.

Component Arrangement. A data model consists of several model components, and these are shown in a model diagram to represent the information requirements. If the components are arranged in an orderly and logical manner, then the model becomes easy to review and follow along from component to component.

Enhancement with Texts. Titles, captions, legends, version numbers, and so on greatly add to the ease of understanding of a data model.

Visual Improvements. A data model can be perked up with the use of special graphics, color, and font variations. Such improvements tend to lead the reviewer to the important parts of the data model quickly and easily.

We will discuss each of these techniques for adding to the value of a data model. We will take up each technique, one by one.

Component Arrangement

Component arrangement in a data model includes placing the various components or parts of the data model in a logical manner so that the model is intelligible to the user groups and stakeholders. When they review the model, they must be able to anticipate which component would follow which other.

From the point of view of programmers and database implementers, the arrangement of entity types that makes the most sense would be the order in which data ought to be created and loaded in the database. However, this may not be the ideal arrangement for user groups and stakeholders. You may find that there would be a marked difference in the two arrangements—those for database practitioners and user groups. If so, consider arranging the entity types in one way for the user groups in the conceptual data model. Use another arrangement for the logical data model. The logical model is closer to the database practitioners than it is for the user groups.

In this section, we will concentrate on the practical tips for the layout of the conceptual model. We will extend these principles to the logical data model in the next section.

Layout of Entity Types. Layout of the entity types in a data model influences the appearance of the model diagram to a great extent. Proper placement of entity types improves readability of the data model. Also, when you arrange the entity types in an orderly manner, you are more likely to detect any errors in the data model. Principles of proper layout enforce a standard that can be applied to partial data models created by several data modelers in a large project.

The model diagram usually runs into multiple pages whether you use a specialized CASE tool or use standard diagramming and presentation software. First of all, organize

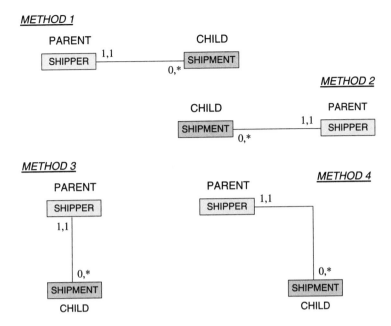

FIGURE 12-14 Layout of parent and child entity types.

these pages. Keep the natural combination of entity types on a single page. Do not crowd each page with too many entity types.

A few other general suggestions are indicated below.

Parent and Child Entity Types. As far as it is feasible, place the child entity types below the corresponding parent entity type. If this is not always feasible, position the child entity types toward the center of the page. See Figure 12-14 showing these methods of arrangement.

Supertype and Subtype Entities. Here again, place the subtypes below the supertype or position the subtypes toward the center of the page. Figure 12-15 illustrates how this method organizes the positioning compared with a chaotic representation also shown in the figure.

Hierarchical Structures. Generally, a hierarchical structure is placed in a top-down fashion vertically or in left-to-right arrangement of entity types. See Figure 12-16 showing these two methods of arranging a hierarchical structure.

Multiple, Connected One-to-Many Relationships. Depending on the space availability, adopt one of the two methods shown in Figure 12-17. One is a top-down placement; the other a toward-the-center placement.

Intersection Entity Types. Placing intersection entity types properly would show their purpose clearly in a data model. See Figure 12-18 for suggested methods for placement of intersection entity types.

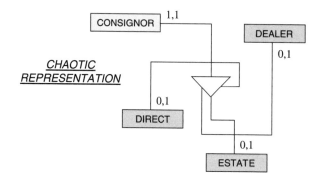

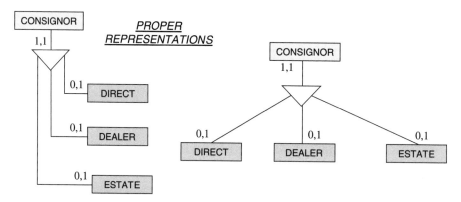

FIGURE 12-15   Placement of supertypes and subtypes.

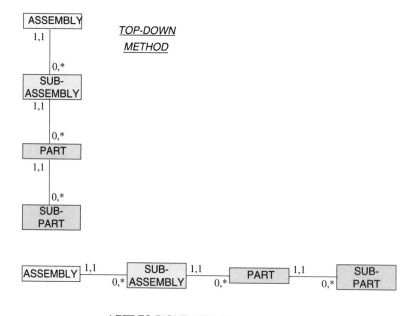

FIGURE 12-16   Placement of hierarchical structure.

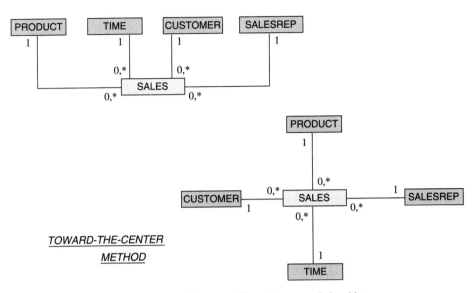

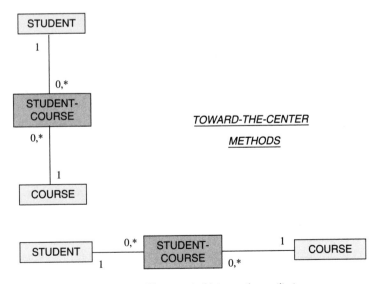

FIGURE 12-17 Placement of one-to-many relationships.

Layout of Relationships. Laying out the relationships in a data model depends on how the related entity types are placed in a data model. Therefore, while positioning entity types, be cognizant that the positioning will affect the drawing of the relationship lines.

We provide just three general suggestions for showing relationships in a data model. Note the following.

FIGURE 12-18 Placement of intersection entity type.

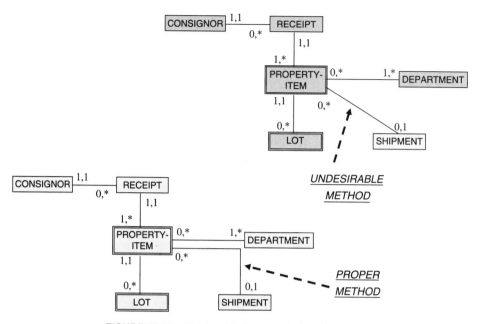

FIGURE 12-19 Relationship lines: vertical and horizontal.

Vertical and Horizontal Relationship Lines. It is a well-accepted practice to keep the relationships lines either vertical or horizontal—never sloping. If you cannot reach the two related entity types with a single vertical or horizontal line, use combinations of vertical and horizontal lines connected to each other. Figure 12-19 illustrates this principle.

Minimum Crossing of Relationship Lines. It is not always possible to avoid crossing of one relationship line with another. However, review your data model, and, wherever possible, remove the crossing of relationship lines. Figure 12-20 shows how the clumsiness of too many crossing lines is corrected.

Relationships Line Cutting Through Entity Types. A data model appears awkward when it shows relationship lines running through entity type boxes. Avoid such running of relationship lines. Correct this by rearranging the entity type boxes in the data model. Figure 12-21 illustrates this problem and shows how this may be rectified.

Ordering of Attributes. As a data modeler, when you collect attributes for each entity type, generally you tend to list them in the order in which each attribute has been made known to you. Data modelers are more concerned about the completeness of the set of attributes within an entity type than with sequencing and listing them appropriately.

After making a list of the attributes for an entity type, rearrange them in a logical sequence. Based on the conditions for each entity type, there must be a certain order of the attributes that will be easier for you as a modeler to complete your modeling task and for the user groups to confirm that the information requirements have been correctly captured. Try to arrange the attributes in a sequence that makes business sense. For a conceptual data model, the most important criterion for the order of the attributes is whether the order conforms to the understanding of the entity type by the user groups.

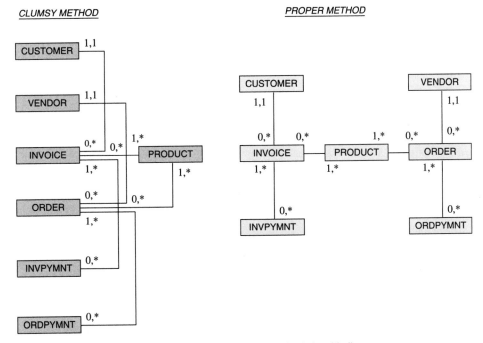

FIGURE 12-20 Minimal crossing of relationship lines.

The following order is usually recommended for the attributes within an entity type:

- Primary identifier—list as the first attributes.
- Other attributes that may be used as the primary identifier but not chosen to be so—list next to the primary identifier.

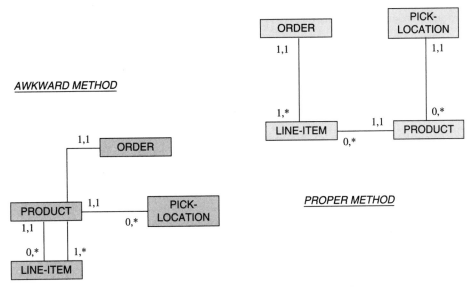

FIGURE 12-21 Relationship lines through entity type boxes.

Entity Type: PROPERTY-ITEM

Attributes arranged randomly

Attributes ordered according to
sequence of business concepts

ItemDescription	Primary { ReceiptNo
HighEstimate	identifier { ItemNo
CurrencyCode	ItemDescription
RestorationCost	Receipting { ItemSpecialMarking
ItemProvenance	ItemCondition
ItemSpecialMarking	HighEstimate
ReceiptNo	LowEstimate
RevisedHighEstimate	Initial ReservePrice
RevisedLowEstimate	inspection CurrencyCode
LowEstimate	NSVNote
ReservePrice	RestorationCost
ItemAuthenticity	Restoration { RestorationSeverityLevel
ItemCondition	ItemRestoredCondition
NSVNote	Authenticity { ItemAuthenticity
ItemNo	verification { ItemProvenance
RestorationSeverityLevel	RevisedHighEstimate
RevisedReservePrice	RevisedLowEstimate
ItemAdditionalRemarks	Cataloguing { RevisedReservePrice
ItemRestoredCondition	ItemCatalogueText
ItemStatus	ItemAdditionalRemarks
ItemCatalogueText	Status [ItemStatus
	tracking

FIGURE 12-22 Ordering of attributes within entity type.

- System-generated attributes and other attributes not having business significance—list them at the end placing the attribute that has the least business significance at the very end.
- Group remaining attributes by business concepts—place attributes relating to the business concept most relevant to the entity type to follow the alternative identifiers, attributes relating to the business concept slightly less relevant next, and so on.

Figure 12-22 illustrates the principles for ordering attributes. Note the various groups of attributes and their placement within the entity type.

Adding Texts

If a data model is not enhanced with appropriate texts, the model would look bald and incomplete. Textual data that is not generally part of standard model conventions can improve readability of the data model a great deal. This textual information, if applied in proper measure, will enable the user groups to understand the data model even more easily. For you, the data modeler, textual data will serve as handles to pick up different parts of the data model and present them to the user groups and communicate with them.

The following types of textual data applied to a data model are found to be useful.

Headings. Provide headings for each page containing the data model. Subheadings may be used whenever you want to identify parts of a data model.

Titles. Titles serve as overall cryptic descriptions. Use them extensively.

Legends. These are used to translate abbreviations. Legends and meanings may be shaded for added emphasis.

Notes. Wherever appropriate, add short notes and comments.

Version Data. Include complete data about the version of the data model.

Visual Highlights

After laying out the entity types in the best possible way, ensuring that relationships are properly presented, ordering attributes in each entity type correctly, and adding textual data, what more can you do to improve your data model further? You can definitely add some visual enhancements.

Use your imagination and add visual highlights. The following visual enhancements spruce up the data model.

Icons, Images, and Graphics. If used judiciously, these can add emphasis and meanings to entity type names and attribute names. Consider using appropriate icons.

Color. If you are printing the data model using a color printer or doing computer or projector presentation of your data model, the usage of color is a great aid to visual highlights. Consider using appropriate colors for entity type boxes, relationships, and attribute names.

Shading. In addition to highlighting with color, you may also apply different shading for model components to enhance their appearance.

Size. Variations in size could also provide visual highlights. You may vary the size of the entity boxes for added emphasis. You can also vary the size of the fonts to show highlights for attribute and entity names.

Style. Variations in font styles for entity names, attribute names, and relationship names can provide additional highlights wherever appropriate.

LOGICAL DATA MODEL

Our considerations for enhancement of a conceptual data model focused on making the model readable and comprehensible. As you know, this was because the primary purpose of a conceptual data model is to be used as a communication tool. We want to dress up the conceptual data model with visual highlights so that it will become all the more presentable.

However, a logical model serves more as a database blueprint than as a means for communication with the user groups. The logical model is closer to the IT personnel on the project team. They are already familiar with the significance of the model. Therefore, for a logical model, the suggestions for enhancement relate more to implementation issues. How do you make the logical model a better blueprint for database implementation?

Enhancement Motivation

The motivation for enhancement to the logical model is different from that for a conceptual model. As your modeling tasks get closer to database implementation, your concerns for enhancement of the model shift more toward actual implementation. You want to conserve space; you want your database to perform well; you want to make implementation easy.

Let us briefly address these important considerations of database implementation.

Easier Database Implementation

Any enhancement you make to the logical data model that eases the implementation is welcome. After completing the logical data model, the remaining steps include transition to a physical model, space allocation for the various data structures, defining of the structures to the data dictionary, populating the database with initial data, deployment of the database to user groups, maintenance, and so on. For a relational database system, you know that the logical model is the relational model consisting of two-dimensional tables. Thus, suggestions for enhancement would apply to the relational model.

For enhancing your relational model for smoother database implementation, consider the following suggestions.

Arrangement of Entity Types.
Arrange the tables in the logical model in the order in which they have to be populated while loading the database with initial data. You have to populate a parent table before you can populate its child tables.

Annotations for DD Entries.
Provide annotations for tables and attributes that will help in the coding of structure definitions for recording in the data dictionary (DD). Annotations would include range values for attributes, allowing nulls as attribute values, default values for attributes, and so on. You can be quite creative in providing annotations.

Estimates for Space Allocation.
Show space allocation estimates in the data model, such as number of initial occurrences of entities and growth percentage. Also, indicate allocation of tables to physical files.

Notes for User Authorizations.
General notes as to access authorizations and restrictions of entity types for user groups could be useful.

Performance Improvement

Performance improvement in a database environment implies faster retrieval of data from the database. Although performance issues are said to fall within the scope of physical modeling, database implementation, and subsequent fine-tuning, the logical model itself can be made conducive to performance improvement. You can achieve this by the arrangement of attributes within entity types.

Here are a few suggestions.

Primary Key.
For parent tables, this is the most used attribute for retrieval. Place the primary key as the first attribute. For a composite primary key, as the initial attribute,

place the part of the key that is most used, then place the part of the key next in the level of usage, and so on.

Foreign Keys. Place foreign keys next to the primary key. Order the foreign keys in the order of their usage—most used first, slightly less used next, and so on.

Indexed Attributes. If there are multiple indexed attributes in a table, place the attribute that is mostly used for retrieval before the one that is slightly less used, and so on.

Clustering. Clustering is a method for performance improvement. For example, if you have ORDER and ORDER-DETAIL tables in your data model, retrieval of data usually takes place by retrieving an order entity along with the order detail entities for that order. It would, therefore, make sense to cluster the order entity with its order detail entities and store them close by on storage. In your logical data model, mark those entity types that must be clustered for performance improvement.

Storage Management

Storage allocation and management rank high in importance for database implementation. As far as possible, storage must be conserved. Wastage of storage space must be avoided.

Storage management would also include facilities to shut down certain parts of the database for backup, restoration, or recovery. This means that relational tables may be fragmented by rows or by columns so that individual fragments may be properly assigned separate storage spaces.

The following suggestions apply to the logical data model for helping in subsequent storage management.

Attributes Where Nulls Are Not Allowed. For attributes defined as containing text data (character strings) of variable length, in the table arrange the shortest attribute before the slightly longer, then place the slightly longer attribute to be followed by the attribute a little longer than the previous, and so on.

Attributes Where Nulls Are Allowed. In the table, place these attributes after those where nulls are not allowed. Also, place the shortest first, followed by other attributes in the order of increasing lengths.

Fragmentation of Relational Tables. In the logical data model, indicate the large tables that may be fragmented so that fragments may be stored separately for ease of maintenance. Also, indicate the type of fragmentation—horizontally by rows or vertically by columns.

Enhanced Representation

Let us now look at an example and note how to apply the principles of enhancement of a logical data model. Figure 12-23 shows a partial data model where the tables are arranged randomly and the attributes are placed haphazardly within the tables.

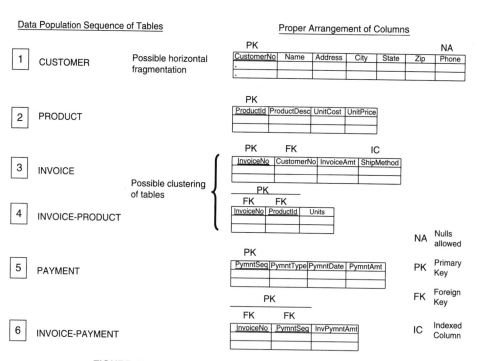

Random Sequence of Tables

1 INVOICE

2 PRODUCT

3 CUSTOMER

4 INVOICE-PAYMENT

5 INVOICE-PRODUCT

6 PAYMENT

Random Arrangement of Columns

InvoiceNo	ShipMethod	InvoiceAmt	CustomerNo

ProductDesc	UnitCost	ProductId	UnitPrice

Name	Zip	CustomerNo	Address	City	Phone	State

InvPymntAmt	PymntSeq	InvoiceNo

ProductId	Units	InvoiceNo

PymntAmt	PymntDate	PymntSeq	PymntType

FIGURE 12-23 Logical data model: random representation.

Data Population Sequence of Tables

1 CUSTOMER — Possible horizontal fragmentation

2 PRODUCT

3 INVOICE

Possible clustering of tables

4 INVOICE-PRODUCT

5 PAYMENT

6 INVOICE-PAYMENT

Proper Arrangement of Columns

PK						NA
CustomerNo	Name	Address	City	State	Zip	Phone

PK			
ProductId	ProductDesc	UnitCost	UnitPrice

PK	FK		IC
InvoiceNo	CustomerNo	InvoiceAmt	ShipMethod

PK		
FK	FK	
InvoiceNo	ProductId	Units

PK		
PymntSeq	PymntType	PymntDate	PymntAmt

PK		
FK	FK	
InvoiceNo	PymntSeq	InvPymntAmt

NA — Nulls allowed

PK — Primary Key

FK — Foreign Key

IC — Indexed Column

FIGURE 12-24 Logical data model: enhanced representation.

Apply the suggestions and enhance the logical model. Rearrange the tables and reorder the attributes so that the logical model may aid in the subsequent database implementation. Examine Figure 12-24 and observe how this figure shows an enhanced logical data model.

CHAPTER SUMMARY

- Practical suggestions for requirements definition cover user interviews, group sessions, geographically dispersed user groups, requirements documentation, and change management.
- During requirements definition, data modelers find it useful to compile specific notes for their private use. You can have separate sections in your notes for different components such as entity types, relationships, attributes, and so on.
- Stakeholder participation is crucial for the success of a modeling project. Practical tips cover organizing participation, user liaison, continuous interaction, and multiple sites.
- Useful suggestions on iterative modeling relate to establishing iteration cycles, determining increments for modeling, and integration of partial models.
- Review and adapt practical suggestions on special cases of data modeling: legal entities, locations, time periods, persons, and bill-of-materials.
- A conceptual data model must be readable and usable. In order to achieve these goals, pay attention to arrangement of components, orders of attributes within entity types, adding text, and visual highlights.
- Logical model improvements focus on storage management and performance. Adapt and use the suggestions on logical model representation.

REVIEW QUESTIONS

1. True or false:
    A. Conducting interviews is no longer useful for gathering information requirements.
    B. While dealing with multinational user groups, pay attention to local cultures and practices.
    C. Iterative development approach does not allow for changes in requirements.
    D. In good data modeling projects, stakeholder participation is optional.
    E. In a multisite environment, keep progress at all sites coordinated and balanced.
    F. Iterative modeling consists of cycles of iteration.
    G. For iterative modeling, fragmentation of the model by functions or user groups works well.
    H. If your system has staged deliverables, integrate partial models at each stage.
    I. Visual highlights of a data model enhance the model greatly.
    J. Practical suggestions on data modeling are meant to be adapted and used.
2. List any six suggestions on conducting interviews with users for requirements definition. Explain how these make sense.

3. How do you deal with geographically dispersed groups while defining requirements? List some practical suggestions.

4. Consider the major aspects of stakeholder participation in a data model project. List any eight practical suggestions.

5. Give a few practical suggestions for managing changes to requirements in a data modeling project. Explain why they are likely to work.

6. Describe iterative modeling. What are the major activities to make modeling iterative?

7. In iterative modeling, what do we mean by an iteration cycle? Make some suggestions for establishing cycles.

8. Discuss how you can divide up a modeling effort into fragments. How does model fragmentation make the modeling effort more efficient?

9. Do you have suggestions how to keep the data model true to the information requirements during the entire data modeling phases? List the suggestions and briefly describe each.

10. What is integration of partial models? Give some practical suggestions for performing the integration tasks.

BIBLIOGRAPHY

Allen, Sharon, *Data Modeling for Everyone*, Birmingham, UK: Curlingston, 2002.

Ambler, Scott W., *Agile Modeling*, Hoboken, NJ: Wiley, 2002.

Ambler, Scott W., *Agile Database Techniques*, Hoboken, NJ: Wiley, 2003.

Augustine, Sanjiv, *Managing Agile Projects*, Upper Saddle River, NJ: Prentice-Hall, 2005.

Barker, Richard, *Case Method Entity Relationship Modeling*, Boston, MA: Addison-Wesley, 1990.

Batini, Carlo, et al., *Conceptual Database Design: An Entity Relational Approach*, Boston, MA: Addison-Wesley, 1991.

Bekke, J.H. ter, *Semantic Data Modeling*, Upper Saddle River, NJ: Prentice-Hall, 1992.

Carlis, John, and Joseph Maguire, *Mastering Data Modeling*, Boston, MA: Addison-Wesley, 2000.

Connolly, Thomas M., et al., *Database Systems: A Practical Approach to Design, Implementation, and Management*, Boston, MA: Addison-Wesley, 1998.

Elmasri, Ramez, and Shamkant B. Navathe, *Fundamentals of Database Systems*, Boston, MA: Addison-Wesley, 2000.

Fowler, Martin, and Scott Kendall, *UML Distilled: A Brief Guide to Standard Object Modeling Language*, Boston, MA: Addison-Wesley, 2000.

Halpin, Terry, *Information Modeling and Database Design: From Conceptual Analysis to Logical Design*, San Francisco, CA: Morgan Kaufman, 2001.

Hoberman, Steve, *Data Modeler's Workbench*, Hoboken, NJ: Wiley, 2002.

Quatrani, Terry, *Visual Modeling with Rational Rose and UML*, Boston, MA: Addison-Wesley, 1998.

Ramakrishnan, Raghu, and Johannes Gehrke, *Database Management Systems*, New York: McGraw-Hill, 2000.

Reingruber, Michael C., and William W. Gregory, *The Data Modeling Handbook: A Best-Practice Approach to Building Quality Data Models*, Hoboken, NJ: Wiley, 1994.

Schmidt, Bob, *Data Modeling for Information Professionals*, Upper Saddle River, NJ: Prentice-Hall, 1999.

Silberschatz, Abraham, et al., *Database System Concepts*, New York: McGraw-Hill, 1999.

Data Modeling Fundamentals. By Paulraj Ponniah
Copyright © 2007 John Wiley & Sons, Inc.

Silverston, Len, *The Data Model Resource Book: A Library of Universal Data Models for All Enterprises*, Hoboken, NJ: Wiley, 2001.

Simsion, Graeme, and Graham Witt, *Data Modeling Essentials*, San Francisco, CA: Morgan Kaufman, 2005.

Tsichritzis, Dionysios C., and Frederick H. Lochovsky, *Data Models*, Upper Saddle River, NJ: Prentice-Hall, 1982.

GLOSSARY

Aggregation Entity Type. Represents a three-way, four-way, or a higher degree relationship.

Agile Modeling. Data Modeling using agile software development principles.

Agile Movement. A movement initiated in early 2001 to address the problems of traditional software development and find a radically new methodology.

Anomalies. Inconsistencies or errors resulting from manipulating data in random tables containing redundant data. Three types of anomalies are encountered: update, deletion, and addition.

Attribute. An intrinsic or inherent characteristic of an entity that is of interest to an organization.

Binary Relationship. Relationship in which two entity types participate. This is the most common form of relationship between entity types.

Boyce-Codd Normal Form (BCNF). A relation or table is in BCNF if it is already in the third normal form and no key attribute is functionally dependent on any non-key attribute.

Business Intelligence. A term used to refer to information available in an enterprise for making strategic decisions.

Business Object. A thing or an object of interest to an organization. Data about business objects are stored in the organization's database.

Business Rules. Specifications based on business practices of an organization that need to be incorporated in the logical data model.

Candidate Key. A single attribute or a set of attributes that uniquely identifies an instance of an object set or entity type and can be a candidate to be chosen as the primary key.

Cardinality. Cardinality of the relationship between two entity types indicates how many instances of the first entity type may be related to how many of the second.

CASE. Computer-Aided Software Engineering. CASE tools or programs that help to develop software applications. A set of CASE tools many include code generators,

Data Modeling Fundamentals. By Paulraj Ponniah
Copyright © 2007 John Wiley & Sons, Inc.

data modeling tools, analysis and design tools, and tools for documenting and testing applications.

Circular Structure. A data structure consisting of three or more entity types forming cyclical relationships where the first is related to the second, the second to the third, and so on, and finally the last related back to the first. In a good data model, circular structures are resolved.

Composite Key. Primary key made up of more than one attribute.

Concatenated Key. *Same as* **Composite Key**.

Conceptual Completeness. Conceptual completeness of a data model implies that it is a complete representation of the information requirements of the organization.

Conceptual Correctness. Conceptual correctness of a data model implies that it is a true replica of the information requirements of the organization.

Conceptual Data Model. A generic data model capturing the true meaning of the information requirements of an organization. Does not conform to the conventions of any class of database systems such as hierarchical, network, relational, and so on.

Conceptual Entity Type. Set representing the type of the objects, not the physical objects themselves.

Data Dictionary. Repository holding the definitions of the data structures in a database. In a relational database, the data dictionary contains the definitions of all the tables, columns, and so on.

Data Integrity. Accuracy and consistency of the data stored in the organization's database system.

Data Manipulation. Operations for altering data in the database. Data manipulation includes retrieval, addition, update, and deletion of data.

Data Mining. Knowledge discovery process. Data mining algorithms uncover hidden relationships and patterns from a given set of data on which they operate. Knowledge discovery is automatic, not through deliberate search and analysis by analysts.

Data Model. Representation of the real-world information requirements that gets implemented in a computer system. A data model provides a method and means for describing real-world information by using specific notations and conventions.

Data Repository. Storage of the organization's data in databases. Stores all data values that are part of the databases.

Data View. *See* **User View**.

Data Warehouse. A specialized database having a collection of transformed and integrated data, stored for the purpose of providing strategic information to the organization.

Database. Repository where an ordered, integrated, and related collection of the organization's data is stored for the purpose of computer applications and information sharing.

Database Administration. Responsibility for the technical aspects of the organization's database. Includes the physical design and handling of the technical details such as database security, performance, day-to-day maintenance, backup, and recovery. Database administration is more technical than managerial.

Database Administrator (DBA). Specially trained technical person performing the database administration functions in an organization.

Database Practitioners. Includes the set of IT professionals such as analysts, data modelers, designers, programmers, and database administrators who design, build, deploy, and maintain database systems.

DBMS. Database Management System. Software system to store, access, maintain, manage, and safeguard the data in databases.

DDLC. Database Development Life Cycle. A complete process from beginning to end, with distinct phases for defining information requirements, creating the data model, designing the database, implementing the database, and maintaining it thereafter.

Decomposition of Relations. Splitting of relations or tables into smaller relations for the purpose of normalizing them.

Degree. The number of entity types or object sets that participate in a relationship. For a binary relationship the degree is 2.

Dimension Entity Type. In a STAR schema, a dimension entity type represents a business dimension such as customer or product along which metrics like sales are analyzed.

DKNF. Domain Key Normal Form. This is the ultimate goal in transforming a relation into the highest normal form. A relation is in DKNF if it represents one topic and all of its business rules, being able to be expressed through domain constraints and key relationships.

Domain. The set of all permissible data values and data types for an attribute of an entity type.

DSS. Decision Support System. Application that enables users to make strategic decisions. Decision support systems are driven by specialized databases.

End-Users. *See* **Users.**

Entity. A real-world "thing" of interest to an organization.

Entity Instance. A single occurrence of an entity type. For example, a single invoice is an instance of the entity type called INVOICE.

Entity Integrity. A rule or constraint to ensure the correctness of an entity type or relational table.

ERD. Entity-Relationship Diagram. A graphical representation of entities and their relationships in the Entity-Relationship data modeling technique.

Entity Set. The collection of all entity instances of a particular type of entity.

Entity Type. Refers to the type of entity occurrences in an entity set. For example, all customers of an organization form the CUSTOMER entity type.

E-R Data Modeling. Design technique for creating an entity-relationship diagram from the information requirements.

Evolutionary Modeling. Data modeling as promoted by the Agile Software Development movement. This is a type of iterative modeling methodology where the model evolves in "creation—feedback—revision" cycles.

External Data Model. Definition of the data structures in a database that are of interest to various user groups in an organization. It is the way users view the database from outside.

Fact Entity Type. In a STAR schema, a fact entity type represents the metrics such as sales that are analyzed along business dimensions such as customer or product.

Feasibility Study. One of the earlier phases in DDLC conducting a study of the readiness of an organization and the technological, economic, and operational feasibility of a database system for the organization.

Fifth Normal Form (5NF). A relation that is already in the fourth normal form and without any join dependencies.

First Normal Form (1NF). A relation that has no repeating groups of values for a set of attributes in a single row.

Foreign Key. An attribute in a relational table used for establishing a direct relationship with another table, known as the parent table. The values of the foreign key attribute are drawn from the primary key values of the parent table.

Fourth Normal Form (4NF). A relation that is already in the third normal and without any multivalued dependencies.

Functional Dependency. The value of an attribute B in a relation depending on the value of another attribute A. For every instance of attribute A, its value uniquely determines the value of attribute B in the relation.

Generalization. The concept that some entity types are general cases of other entity types. The entity types in the general cases are known as super-types.

Generalizing Specialists. A trend in software developers, as promoted by the agile software development movement, where specialists acquire more and more diverse skills and expand their horizons. Accordingly, data modelers are no longer specialists with just data modeling skills.

Gerund. Representation of a relationship between two entity types as an entity type itself.

Homonyms. Two or more data elements having the same name but containing different data.

Identifier. One or more attributes whose values can uniquely identify the instances of an entity type.

Identifying Relationship. A relationship between two entity types where one entity type depends on another entity type for its existence. For example, the entity type ORDER-DETAIL cannot exist without the entity type ORDER.

Inheritance. The property that sub-sets inherit the attributes and relationships of their super-set.

Intrinsic Characteristics. Basic or inherent properties of an object or entity.

IT. Information Technology. Covers all computing and data communications in an organization. Typically, the CIO is responsible for IT operations in an organization.

Iterative Modeling. This implies that the modeling process is not strictly carried out in a sequential manner such as modeling all entity types, modeling all relationships, modeling all attributes, and so on. Iterative modeling allows the data modeler to constantly go back, verify, readjust, and ensure cohesion and completeness.

Key. One or more attributes whose values can uniquely identify the rows of a relational table.

Logical Data Model. Also sometimes referred to as a conventional data model, consists of the logical data structure representing the information requirements of an organization. This data model conforms to the conventions of a class of database systems such as hierarchical, network, relational, and so on. The logical data model for a relational database system consists of tables or relations.

Logical Design. Process of designing and creating a logical data model.

Matrix. Consists of members or elements arranged in rows and columns. In the relational data model, a table or relation may be compared to a matrix thereby making it possible to apply matrix algebra functions to the data represented in the table.

MDDMBS. Multi-dimensional database management system. Used to create and manage multi-dimensional databases for OLAP.

Meta-data. Data about the data of an organization.

Model Transformation. Process of mapping and transforming the components of a conceptual data model to those of a logical or conventional data model.

MOLAP. Multidimensional Online Analytical Processing. An analytical processing technique in which multidimensional data cubes are created and stored in separate proprietary databases.

Normal Form. A state of a relation or table, free from incorrect dependencies among the attributes. *See also* **Boyce-Codd Normal Form, First Normal Form, Second Normal Form, and Third Normal Form**.

Normalization. The step-by-step method of transforming a random table into a set of normalized relations free from incorrect dependencies and conforming to the rules of the relational data model.

Null Value. A value of an attribute, different from zero or blank to indicate a missing, non-applicable or unknown value.

OLAP. Online Analytical Processing. Powerful software systems providing extensive multidimensional analysis, complex calculations, and fast response times. Usually present in data warehousing systems.

Physical Data Model. Data model representing the information requirements of an organization at a physical level of hardware and system software, consisting of the actual components such as data files, blocks, records, storage allocations, indexes, and so on.

Physical Design. Process of designing the physical data model.

Practitioners. *See* **Database Practitioners**.

Primary Key. A single attribute or a set of attributes that uniquely identifies an instance of an object set or entity type and chosen as the primary key.

RDBMS. Relational Database Management System.

Referential Integrity. Refers to two relational tables that are directly related. Referential integrity between related tables is established if non-null values in the foreign key attribute of the child table are primary key values in the parent table.

Relation. In relational database systems, a relation is a two dimensional table with columns and rows, conforming to relational rules.

Relational Data Model. A conventional or logical data model where data is perceived as two-dimensional tables with rows and columns. Each table represents a business object; each column represents an attribute of the object; each row represents an instance of the object.

Relational Database. A database system built based on the relational data model.

Relationship. A relationship between two object sets or entity types represents the associations of the instances of one object set with the instances of the other object set. Unary, binary, or ternary relationships are the common ones depending on the number of object sets participating in the relationship. A unary relationship is recursive—instances of an object set associated with instances of the same object set. Relationships may be mandatory or optional based on whether some instances may or may not participate in the relationship.

Repeating Group. A group of attributes in a relation that has multiple sets of values for the attributes.

ROLAP. Relational Online Analytical Processing. An online analytical processing technique in which multidimensional data cubes are created on the fly by the relational database engine.

Second Normal Form (2NF). A relation that is already in the first normal form and without partial key dependencies.

Set Theory. Mathematical concept where individual members form a set. Set operations can be used to combine or select members from sets in several ways. In a relational data model, the rows or tuples of a table or relation may be considered as forming a set. As such, set operations may be applied to manipulation of data represented as tables.

Specialization. The concept that some entity types are special cases of other entity types. The entity types in the special cases are known as sub-types.

SQL. Structured Query Language. Has become the standard language interface for relational databases.

Stakeholders. All people in the organization who have a stake in the success of the data system.

STAR Schema. The arrangement of the collection of fact and dimension entity types in the dimensional data model, resembling a star formation, with the fact entity type placed in the middle and surrounded by the dimension entity types. Each dimension entity type is in a one-to-many relationship with the fact entity type.

Strategic Information. May refer to information in an organization used for making strategic decisions.

Strong Entity. An entity on which a weak entity depends for its existence. *See also* **Weak Entity**.

Sub-types. *See* **Specialization**.

Subset. An entity type that is a special case of another entity type known as the superset.

Super-types. *See* **Generalization.**

Superset. An entity type that is a general case of another entity type known as the subset.

Surrogate Key. A unique value generated by the computer system used as a key for a relation. A surrogate key has no business meaning apart from the computer system.

Synonyms. Two or more data elements containing the same data but having different names.

Syntactic Completeness. Syntactic completeness of a data model implies that the modeling process has been carried out completely to produce a good data model for the organization.

Syntactic Correctness. Syntactic correctness of a data model implies that the representation using the appropriate symbols does not violate any rules of the modeling technique.

Third Normal Formn (3NF). A relation that is already in the second normal form and without any transitive dependencies—that is, the dependencies of non-key attributes on the primary key through other non-key attributes, not directly.

Transitive Dependency. In a relation, the dependency of a non-key attribute on the primary key through another non-key attribute, not directly.

Triad. A set of three related entity types where one of the relationships is redundant. Triads must be resolved in a refined data model.

Tuple. A row in a relational table.

UML. Unified Modeling Language. Its forerunners constitute the wave of object-oriented analysis and design methods of the 1980s and 1990s. UML is a unified language because it directly unifies the leading methods of Booch, Rumbaugh, and Jacobson. OMG (Object Management Group) has adopted UML as a standard.

User View. View of the database by a single user group. Therefore, a data view of a particular user group includes only those parts of the database that group is concerned with. The collection of all data views of all the user groups constitutes the total data model.

Users. In connection with data modeling, the term users includes all people who use the data system that is built based on the particular data model.

Weak Entity. An entity that depends for its existence on another entity known as a strong entity. For example, the entity type ORDER DETAIL cannot exist without the entity type ORDER. *See also* **Strong Entity**.

XML. eXtensible Markup Language. Introduced to overcome the limitations of HTML. XML is extensible, portable, structured, and descriptive. In a very limited way, it may be used in data modeling.

INDEX

Data Modeling Fundamentals. By Paulraj Ponniah
Copyright © 2007 John Wiley & Sons, Inc.